THE NEW NATURALI

A SURVEY OF BRITISH NATUR

DRAGONFLIES

THE NEW NATURALIST LIBRARY

DRAGONFLIES

PHILIP S. CORBET &
STEPHEN J. BROOKS

With many colour photographs by
Robert Thompson

Collins

Dedicated with affection and gratitude to
Sarah Jewell and Ann Brooks

This edition published in 2008 by Collins,
an imprint of HarperCollins Publishers

HarperCollins Publishers
77–85 Fulham Palace Road
London w6 8jb
www.collins.co.uk

First published 2008

A cip catalogue record for this book is available
from the British Library.

Set in ff Nexus by
Rowland Phototypesetting Ltd
Bury St Edmunds, Suffolk

Printed in Hong Kong by Printing Express
Reprographics by Saxon Photolitho, Norwich

Hardback
isbn: 978-0-00-715168-4

Paperback
isbn: 978-0-00-715169-1

Contents

FRONTISPIECE. Sequential digital still photography is a wonderful tool for tracking this male *Orthetrum cancellatum* as he flies by. The technique can be used to reveal the natural attitude of the wings, abdomen, head and legs while a dragonfly is in flight (Steve Cham).

Editors' Preface

DRAGONFLIES ARE OF particular interest to naturalists because they are lively, beautiful and interesting, and amenable to study without expensive equipment or laboratory facilities. Furthermore, well illustrated field guides make it relatively easy to recognise the British species. An earlier New Naturalist, published in 1960, did much to bring the interest of dragonfly biology to the attention of naturalists, and to stimulate further research. Since then, dragonflies have become popular among both amateur naturalists and research workers; they have been transformed from an enigmatic group of minority interest to a focus of enthusiastic amateur study and exciting research on diverse aspects of ecology, behaviour and physiology. We now understand much more about what they do, and how and why they do it; so they deserve this completely new New Naturalist. Both of the authors have made major contributions to the study of British dragonflies, and have done much to encourage naturalists to appreciate them. Their book, illustrated with Robert Thompson's magnificent photographs, will enrich the study of dragonflies by the many naturalists who are already committed to this group, and will surely encourage new recruits to take up that interest.

In Memory of Philip S. Corbet 1929–2008

PHILIP CORBET WAS without doubt the world's foremost odonatologist and one who has had the greatest influence in the burgeoning interest in dragonflies for the past 50 years. With his Reading B.Sc dissertation and Cambridge Ph.D thesis he made the first strides in a monumental research career involving dragonflies.

His varied and distinguished appointments included research positions with the East African High Commission in Uganda; Director to the Research Institute, Canada Department of Agriculture; Professorships with the Universities of Waterloo (Canada) and Canterbury (NZ); Commonwealth Visiting Professor (University of Cambridge); and Professor, University of Dundee from which he retired in 1990 as Professor Emeritus.

Corbet's research interests emphasised periodicity, rhythmic behaviour and development in dragonflies and mosquitoes. These have been the co-ordinating strands in studies relating to taxonomy, morphology, life histories, arthropod-borne virus diseases, reproductive physiology, ecology of fishes and crocodiles, and arctic microclimates.

After retirement in 1990 he concentrated on the production of two major books: *Dragonflies: Behaviour and Ecology of Odonata*, published in 1999 is a definitive synthesis for which he was awarded the Neill Medal for Natural History by the Royal Society of Edinburgh. This masterly volume appeared in Japanese translation in 2006. This fine current *New Naturalist* with Steve Brooks is a fitting closure to an extraordinary career.

Philip Corbet's numerous awards include four higher doctorates: the Gold Medal for Outstanding Achievement from the Entomological Society of Canada, election to Fellowships of three prestigious societies, Honorary memberships to three national dragonfly societies; and he was elected to the Presidency of the Worldwide Dragonfly Association 2001-2003.

Michael J. Parr
Inaugural President,
Worldwide Dragonfly Association.
1998–2001

Preface by Former Keeper of Entomology, The Natural History Museum, London

EW INSECT GROUPS command more awe or are more immediately recognisable to so many people as the dragonflies. They are a source of beauty and inspiration to all who take time to watch them. Their aerial skills and finely honed hunting abilities on the wing are second to none, yet these creatures retain many attributes that first evolved in recognisable ancestors more than 300 million years ago. Dragonflies tell us a great deal about what insects were like before the origin of flexing wings or complete metamorphosis, characters that foreshadowed the vast number of 'higher' insect species. Dragonflies are superb animals for the study of countless aspects of biology. Their aquatic larvae are important components of freshwater ecosystems and are indicators of water quality. Their territoriality and hunting skills make them excellent subjects for learning about animal behaviour. Their large size permits a much broader range of observations in the field than is possible for most other kinds of insects. Making these spectacular animals accessible to a wider audience is a worthy goal, and one fulfilled admirably by this volume.

There are no contemporary natural historians whom I admire more than Philip Corbet and Steve Brooks, nor any who are in a better position to have prepared this book. We are truly fortunate that they have combined their unmatched knowledge, experience and observational and writing skills to pull together such a wealth of material on British odonates. The book provides a wonderful foundation for anyone discovering the study of odonates for the first time or seeking to expand their knowledge by better understanding the breadth of dragonfly biology. The range of subject matter in this book is impressive, covering such diverse topics as habitats, populations, life history, parasitoids, feeding behaviour, seasonality, flight, sexual behaviour and maturation. This provides a firm foundation for in-depth studies of dragonflies in general and the British fauna in particular.

With this background and the authors' sound advice on how to locate, collect, photograph and identify British dragonflies, a spectacular world is opened to the interested observer. This constitutes one of the best introductions to odonatology available and will, I predict, contribute to the widening interest in dragonflies in Britain and the education of a new generation of both professional and amateur odonatologists who delight in the study of these most fascinating of creatures. As our environments continue to change rapidly in the decades ahead, a growing awareness and understanding of our dragonflies will prove essential to science and biological conservation. No one who would truly understand either insect evolution or the function of ecosystems associated with fresh waters can do so by ignoring the Odonata. The growth of expertise on any taxon depends heavily on access to reliable and inspiring literature; the dragonflies will profit immensely from just such a contribution from Corbet and Brooks.

Quentin D. Wheeler
Former Keeper of Entomology
The Natural History Museum
London

Authors' Foreword and Acknowledgements

D RAGONFLIES ARE THE largest, most conspicuous, flying insects one is liable to encounter in Britain in sunny weather. Because during their growth stages dragonflies live in water, the adults are usually encountered near ponds, lakes, streams or rivers, where they can often be seen engaging in elaborate aerobatics. Their vivid colours and aerial agility command, and hold, the attention of any observer. Except in highly specific situations, dragonflies are of no economic importance. Being generalised predators, both as larvae and as adults, they are unlikely ever to suppress the numbers of 'pest' organisms down to levels that meet human demands for health, profit or comfort: when one prey organism becomes too scarce to encounter readily, a dragonfly will simply switch its attention to another.

So why are so many people fascinated by dragonflies?

Perhaps the most convincing way to answer this question is to list some of the reasons why we, the authors, have become interested in these insects. An important reason, for any field naturalist, is that dragonflies are sufficiently large and conspicuous that one can often understand what they are doing; and, thanks to the great amount of research conducted by scientists on the behaviour of dragonflies, one can often interpret their actions in terms of their main adaptive needs, such as foraging (i.e. seeking prey) and reproducing. Moreover, for almost all the actions they perform, as larvae as well as adults, one can usually infer the significance of their behaviour in the context of their life history, which is steadily becoming better understood.

In Britain, compared with the continent of Europe, we have a marginal, impoverished fauna and flora. For example, Britain contains (as residents) only about 34 per cent (39/114) of the dragonfly species inhabiting the Continent. Having relatively few species can be an incentive to know them, to record them and to understand what influences their distribution in Britain. And there is the dragonfly life history, in which the larval and adult stages alternate between water and land in an impressive and hazardous transition: at the time of egg laying and then again at emergence (i.e. transformation from larva to adult). These are some of the objective reasons for our interest. Others, equally compelling though thoroughly subjective, lie in the excitement, admiration and awe that we experience whenever we encounter a dragonfly or learn of a newly discovered fact about the life history. We are not alone in our enthusiasm and affection for dragonflies. In addition to the British Dragonfly Society, with its 1,600 or so members, two well-subscribed international societies are devoted to the study of dragonflies, each producing a periodical containing scientific reports about dragonfly biology. Odonatology (the study of dragonflies) receives special mention in Chapter 1, and the history of odonatology in Britain is reviewed in Chapter 10.

This book is not a textbook on dragonflies; nor is it an identification manual. Useful literature of that kind is listed in Chapter 1. This book is about the natural history of dragonflies in Britain. (Our use of the terms 'Britain' and 'British Isles' is chosen for convenience only, and has no political connotation. We use these designations to denote the archipelago that comprises Britain and Ireland and associated islands.) Because our emphasis is on natural history, we have devoted little attention to the morphology or physiology of dragonflies, sources for which are listed in Chapter 1.

We hope that the information presented in this book will enhance the pleasure and inspiration that people derive from watching and studying dragonflies. We find dragonflies to be limitless sources of wonder and delight, and we regard it as a singular privilege to be able to share these sentiments with others by writing about dragonfly natural history.

This book is intended for the informed enthusiast with a leaning towards natural history. In presenting it, we have four principal aims:

- to show or remind the reader what beautiful, elegant and superbly adapted animals dragonflies are, and to make the case for conservation of their species and their habitats;
- to enable the observer to understand better the biological significance of dragonfly behaviour;
- to help the reader place the ecology and behaviour of British species in the context of what is known about dragonfly biology worldwide, hoping that this broader perspective will illuminate understanding of the species in Britain; and
- to expose opportunities for further investigation that can be pursued without specialised equipment or facilities.

We have adopted certain conventions in the text. Specialised terms are italicised on first mention, thus indicating that they have been defined in the Glossary on pages 373–381. Sources of information are cited in the text by superscript numbers. These correspond to abbreviated references, assembled under chapters in the section Endnotes on pages 382–394, and these in turn correspond to citations given in full in the Bibliography on pages 395–442. There are two indexes at the end of the book: one to authors cited in the text, and one to species, topics and people.

It is a pleasure for us to acknowledge help we have received during preparation of this book.

Our primary debt is to the many odonatologists whose careful (sometimes inspired!) observations, ideas and experiments have yielded the information from which our text is drawn. For the most part they are authors of publications, dating from the eighteenth century to recent times;[1] but a few are contemporaries who have devoted their time and expertise to constructive criticism of parts of the text. In this regard we make special mention of our colleagues Mike Parr (Chapters 1 and 7 and Appendix 2), Mike Siva-Jothy (Chapter 9) and Hansruedi Wildermuth (Chapters 3 and 5). We thank the compilers of *Odonatological Abstracts* (Bastiaan Kiauta) and the Odonatological Abstract Service (Martin Lindeboom and Martin Schorr) for the immensely valuable service they perform in enabling odonatologists to keep track of the many publications that appear annually. We are very grateful to Ann Brooks, Sally Corbet and Sarah Jewell for their valued comments on successive drafts of the text. We thank Robert Thompson for his generosity in allowing us to use a large number of his beautiful colour photographs, the inclusion of which greatly enhances the book's appearance. We are indebted also to Ann Brooks, Kevin Caley, Steve Cham, Zoë Greenwell, Ruary Mackenzie Dodds, Jürgen Ott and Hansruedi Wildermuth for allowing us to include photographs, the source of which is acknowledged in the captions.

We thank Faber and Faber for permission to reproduce the poem 'Dragonfly' by the former Poet Laureate, Ted Hughes.

For permission to reproduce black-and-white illustrations (the figure numbers being recorded in parentheses) we thank the following publishers and copyright holders: American Society of Limnology and Oceanography (55); Blackwell Publishing (44, 69, 73, 85, 86, 88, 89, 120); The British Dragonfly Society (74); K. Caley (128); E.W. Classey (102); S. Eda (for *Tombo*) (97); Elsevier (45, 117); Finnish Zoological and Botanical Publishing Board (114); Gem Publishing Co. (53, 54); Harley Books (45); HarperCollins (44 by S. Beaufoy); C. Inden-Lohmar (96), B. Kiauta (for Societas Internationalis Odonatologica) (92, 97); The Natural History Museum (57 by A.E. Gardner, 126 (a–d), 127(a–d)); Naturforschenden

Gesellschaft in Zürich (101); Royal Entomological Society (59); Springer Verlag (116); F. Weihrauch (for *Libellula*) (51, 70, 71).

We are indebted to several members of the editorial staff of HarperCollins with whom it has been a pleasure to work. In particular, we thank Helen Brocklehurst, Julia Koppitz and Isobel Smales for their encouragement, forbearance and valued advice.

S.B. is grateful to the Trustees of The Natural History Museum for enabling him to work on this book in official time, and we both thank Professor Quentin Wheeler, former Keeper of Entomology at The Museum, for contributing a Preface.

During our pursuit of odonatology, and during the preparation of this book, we have enjoyed unfailing support from Ann Brooks and Sarah Jewell.

P.S.C.
S.B.
Crean Mill, St Buryan,
Cornwall
and
The Natural History Museum,
Cromwell Road, London.
February 2007

DRAGONFLY

Now let's have another try
To love the giant dragonfly.
Stand beside the peaceful water.
Next thing – a whispy, dry clatter
And he whizzes to a dead stop
In mid-air, and his eyes pop.
Snakey stripes, a snakey fright!
Does he sting? Does he bite?
Suddenly he's gone. Suddenly back. A
Scarey jumping cracker –
Here! Right here!
An inch from your ear!
Sizzling in the air
And giving you a stare
Out of the huge cockpit of his eyes – !
Now say: 'What a lovely surprise!'

Ted Hughes

CHAPTER 1

Introduction

DRAGONFLIES

A S AERIAL PREDATORS, adult dragonflies have few peers. Their extraordinary agility is unequalled among animals, except perhaps some of the smaller birds of prey, bats and bee-eaters; and they have an outstanding ability to detect the movement of small flying objects.

Dragonflies are robust insects comprising the order Odonata ('toothed ones'). Almost all species are aquatic in the larval (growth) stage and aerial as adults. In all but the first larval stage they are *obligate* predators, using powerful mandibles to masticate their prey. All odonate larvae catch their prey by explosive extension of a specialised lower lip (*labium*) (Fig. 60, p.115) derived from the fusion of the second maxillae. Among the senses used for prey detection, the *compound eyes* steadily acquire primacy during larval development. Concealment, immobility and occasionally rapid movement are among the attributes that make larvae effective predators of other, usually smaller, animals. Adults catch prey while on the wing and likewise masticate it using the mandibles. The compound eyes are well developed, especially in the adult.

In common with other morphologically generalised insects, dragonflies lack a pupal stage between larva and adult; the larva, though possessing rudimentary wings, otherwise broadly resembles the adult.

Odonata derive, with little structural change, from the Protodonata, an extinct order that flourished in the Upper Carboniferous, more than 300 million years ago. Those early dragonflies broadly resembled extant species but were much larger, having a wingspan of about 70 centimetres.[1] Some authorities attribute this gigantism to the higher concentrations of oxygen in the atmosphere at the time.[2] Together with their 'sister' group, the mayflies, or Ephemeroptera, Odonata, by direct lineage, are among the most ancient of flying insects surviving to the present day. Mayflies and dragonflies (together comprising the Palaeoptera) are believed to have shared a common ancestor that separated from the progenitors of all other winged insects (the Neoptera) early in the *evolution* of insect flight. Larvae of the extant Palaeoptera are almost all aquatic. Unfortunately, no fossil larvae of the early Palaeoptera have been found, so it is not known when larvae of Odonata became aquatic, although this may well have taken place during the Lower Permian.[3]

Today Odonata are to be found in every continent except Antarctica. In the northern hemisphere they occur from the equator to latitudinal tree line. About 6,000 species have been described, although the world fauna probably exceeds this number by several hundred. New species are being described at a steady rate, especially from tropical rainforest, where the diversity of species and suitable *habitats* is greatest. Because this *ecosystem* is being rapidly lost due to human impact, odonate taxonomists are aware that they are working against time to describe many species before they become extinct. The extent to which species and families of Odonata are endangered on a global scale is better known than for most other insect orders.[4]

We subscribe to the view that there are two extant suborders of Odonata: Zygoptera and Anisoptera. Some odonatologists recognise a third suborder, Anisozygoptera, but we share the opinion[5] that members of this third suborder occurred only during the Triassic, Jurassic and Cretaceous periods and so have been long extinct.[6] Extant Zygoptera and Anisoptera are each represented by about 3,000 described species.

Adult Zygoptera ('similar wings') (Fig. 8, p.25), known as damselflies, are typically small and slender; the fore and hind wings are similar in shape and (except in Calopterygidae) are stalked (petiolate) at the base; the wing-loading and flight speed are low, the Zygoptera being 'forward-thrust' fliers.[7] The larvae are slender and usually bear three conspicuous leaflike or sac-like appendages at the tip of the abdomen (Fig. 20, p.35). Inside the abdomen they lack recognisable gills and a muscular diaphragm. They swim by lateral movements of the abdomen, wriggling like a fish.

Adult Anisoptera ('dissimilar wings') (Fig. 30, p.50) are typically large and robust. Their wing-loading is high[7] and they can fly rapidly and powerfully. In some, the base of the hind wing is much expanded, facilitating gliding and soaring, a modification found especially in species that habitually migrate. The larvae (Fig. 28, p.46) are robust and within the abdomen possess gills and a muscular diaphragm. The diaphragm plays a triple role: it controls pumping movements that generate inhalant and exhalant currents that ventilate the gills lining the rectum; it applies this capability in a more vigorous mode to enable a larva to swim by jet propulsion, as a means of escape; and it regulates the increase in blood pressure that enables the labium to project forwards suddenly when prey is being captured (Fig. 60, p.115). Larvae of Zygoptera can also project the labium abruptly, but do not employ a muscular diaphragm to do so.

The Zygoptera comprises 18 extant families and the Anisoptera comprises 12, one of which, the Epiophlebiidae, is assigned by some odonatologists to the suborder Anisozygoptera (see above).

ODONATOLOGY

Odonatology is the study of dragonflies with the explicit aim of learning about their biology and making the information so acquired generally available, in a formal way, through recognised channels. Practised for at least 250 years, odonatology has yielded a treasure house of fascinating information, many items of which have been acquired, serendipitously, by skilled observers. Such disparate facts, together with the products of observations and field experiments, provide the tesserae of a rich mosaic that await assembly and interpretation. Present and future odonatologists face the challenge of arranging and interpreting these tesserae so as to construct a coherent picture of dragonfly biology, and preferably one that will throw light on the paths along which evolution by *natural selection* has moulded the patterns of behaviour and ecology found in the order today. We hope that our treatment of this legacy of information constitutes a modest step towards this goal, especially as regards the British species.

The odonatologists, past and present, to whom we owe this legacy of facts (and hypotheses) have come from many walks of life (Chapter 10). Despite their varied backgrounds, they share certain attributes that have enabled them to contribute importantly to odonatology: enthusiasm and affection for Odonata; willingness to apply scientific rigour to their methods of study; and willingness to undergo the self-imposed discipline of communicating their findings to other odonatologists. We, their beneficiaries, are much in their debt, and are under obligation to maintain the rigour that is a feature of their work.

All odonatologists share a common, implicit, overriding objective: to increase the likelihood of the long-term survival of vigorous populations of dragonflies. Virtually all that is known about dragonflies, including the contents of this book, derives from the science of odonatology, practised with the rigour that underpins all branches of biology. We have recently detected trends in human behaviour that may threaten the integrity and reputation of odonatology as a respected branch of science. Some involve the perceived propriety of collecting specimens for scientific study, a stance that can sometimes give rise to conflict. Odonatologists today have a responsibility to ensure that they prove worthy custodians of the legacy they have inherited from those practitioners who, by their dedication and skill, have made this science a respected and influential branch of biology. As practising odonatologists, we see ourselves as under obligation to try to improve the prospects for odonatology in Britain. Here we address two aspects of odonatology that could benefit from attention and reform. They relate, respectively, to nomenclature and collecting specimens.

NAMING DRAGONFLIES

Every species of dragonfly known to science has been assigned a scientific name according to the rules laid down by the International Commission for Zoological Nomenclature (Box 1). The official, required name of any dragonfly consists of four elements: genus, species, name of author of first published description and date of that description. To comply with the rules, the first (definitive) description should designate a type specimen (i.e. the specimen on which the description was based) and say where it has been deposited. The latter provision is mandatory and necessary because comparison with the type specimen is often the only way in which a future taxonomist can verify that a specimen of a species suspected of being undescribed is indeed new to science.

Following Carolus Linnaeus, who devised and established this binomial system of nomenclature for animals in 1758,[8] all names of species follow a Latinate form which is used by zoologists internationally when referring to species.

In Britain, naturalists have long shown a tendency to assign English names to some of the more conspicuous and handsome insects (such as butterflies, moths and dragonflies). Unlike butterflies and moths, dragonflies have been given English names relatively recently, so some of the names appear contrived. Cynthia Longfield, in the first (1937) edition of her book,[9] and in a successful attempt to make dragonflies more accessible to the non-specialist, gave each species of British dragonfly an English name. She was apparently unaware of the English names that had already been assigned to British dragonflies and which were revealed by Richard Gabb's examination of a collection in the Grosvenor Museum in Poynton, Cheshire.[10] Her approach was to retain the scientific

BOX 1

SYSTEMATIC POSITION OF *ANAX IMPERATOR* LEACH, 1815, THE EMPEROR DRAGONFLY

Taxon	Name	Distinguishing attributes
Phylum	Arthropoda	Jointed, chitinous exoskeleton; jointed limbs.
Class	Insecta	Tripartite, segmented body; *thorax* bearing a pair of legs on each of its three segments.
Subclass	Exopterygota	Incomplete *metamorphosis* (i.e. no pupal stage).
Order	Odonata	Two pairs of long, membranous wings; larva typically aquatic; biting mouthparts in larva and adult; larva with specialised, protractible labium.
Suborder	Anisoptera	Fore and hind wings differ in shape; larva has muscular diaphragm and gills inside abdomen.
Family	Aeshnidae	Diagnostic features of wing venation and shape.
Genus	*Anax*	Diagnostic features of body, especially colour pattern, and shape of abdominal appendages and *genitalia*.
Species	*imperator*	Diagnostic features of body, especially colour pattern, and shape of abdominal appendages and genitalia.
Authority	Leach	The authority who first described and named the species and designated the type specimen.
Date	1815	The year in which Leach's description of the species was first published, giving the location of the type specimen (which in this case has been lost).

generic name, so leaving no doubt about the genus to which the English name applied. Thus *Aeshna juncea* became the Common Aeshna, and *Sympetrum striolatum* became the Common Sympetrum. Since then the nomenclature has undergone several changes. In 1977 Cyril Hammond gave all generic names English equivalents.[11] As a result, *Aeshna juncea* became the Common Hawker and *Sympetrum striolatum* became the Common Darter. When some writers began to show originality in their use of English names, it became desirable to standardise the nomenclature and, beginning in 1991, the British Dragonfly Society (BDS) has listed in each issue of its journal the scientific name and its approved English equivalent for all species found in Britain. All these names, except that for *Gomphus vulgatissimus*, conform to those in Hammond's book and are accepted as definitive in English usage today, at least in Great Britain.

There have recently been two significant developments.

First, in their book on the dragonflies of Ireland, Brian Nelson and Robert Thompson introduced English names different from those in the BDS list for eight genera and 20 species, retaining the same names for only 14 species.[12] In the Irish list, *Calopteryx* becomes Jewelwing (instead of Demoiselle) and *Lestes* becomes Spreadwing (instead of Emerald Damselfly). These two generic names (and some others in the Irish list) conform with those approved for North American dragonflies in 1996 by the Dragonfly Society of the Americas (DSA),[13] although the English names used for four genera (*Anax, Ischnura, Leucorrhinia* and *Sympetrum*) do not.

Second, in response to a perceived need, coupled with range expansions of European dragonflies into Britain (see Chapter 10), English names have been generated for Odonata of continental Europe for 29 species not on the British list.[14] The names chosen have in general conformed with the system already in use by the BDS.

Two long-term goals among naturalists and odonatologists who wish to use English names must be to achieve quick recognition and to avoid ambiguity. As long as naturalists adhere to the names in the BDS list, it does not matter whether the English name or the scientific name is used, at least among odonatologists in Britain. However, it makes life much easier for non-British readers if odonatologists use the scientific names in their published work. Indeed it was to remove ambiguity deriving from the use of vernacular names that Linnaeus developed his system of nomenclature in the first place! We hope that before long unanimity can be reached so that a list of vernacular equivalents can be agreed upon that applies to both Britain and Ireland. Such a list could with benefit conform closely to North American usage. In this book we use only scientific names throughout the text for the species of British dragonflies. In

Appendix 1 we list the scientific names of all species found in Britain, together with their vernacular equivalents in Britain (excluding Ireland).

The position is less straightforward regarding the names of the suborders of Odonata. At some time, probably early in the nineteenth century, the English term 'damselfly' was adopted to denote a member of the suborder Zygoptera. This was unfortunate, because a corresponding English term for the suborder Anisoptera was not introduced at the same time. The precedent for the word 'damselfly' was probably the French 'demoiselle' which, according to Réaumur,[15] was the vernacular name applied throughout France to *all* Odonata, not merely Zygoptera. By restricting this term to Zygoptera, English-speaking odonatologists laid the foundation for the ambiguity we now address. After Réaumur, Fabricius (1745–1808), a pupil of Linnaeus, separated dragonflies from the Neuroptera (of Linnaeus), assigning them to the order Odonata in 1793.[16] Much later, in 1853, Selys recognised and defined the suborders Zygoptera and Anisoptera.[17] Because the term 'dragon fly' or 'dragonfly' had already been pre-empted to mean a member of the order Odonata, some English-speaking authors decided subsequently that an English term for Anisoptera was needed, but unfortunately a valuable opportunity was missed. Having decided to call Zygoptera 'damselflies', authors in North America[18] and Britain[9] chose to meet this need in several ways: by calling Anisoptera 'dragonflies proper'; by hyphenating the word 'dragon-flies';[19] or by using a lower-case initial letter (for 'dragonfly') to denote the suborder, and a capital initial letter to denote the order.[20, 21] Such suggestions have proved unworkable, partly because the initiators themselves sometimes failed to conform with the remedies they suggested! So the existing situation perpetuates an absurdity and stands in urgent need of reform.

German-speaking odonatologists have tackled this difficulty by calling Zygoptera 'Kleinlibellen' and Anisoptera 'Grosslibellen'. But for English-speaking odonatologists no such solution has been sought. Until a corresponding English name is adopted to denote Anisoptera, English-speaking odonatologists will continue to experience embarrassment, either by having repeatedly to explain in which sense they are using the term 'dragonfly' or by tolerating an ambiguity; and poor Linnaeus (one may suppose) will continue to turn in his grave. We believe that correction of this anomaly is long overdue and accordingly take this opportunity to recommend the following terminology for those who feel compelled to use an English name for Anisoptera. Thus we would have:

Odonata: dragonflies
Zygoptera: damselflies
Anisoptera: warriorflies.

We use this terminology in Appendix 1 but have no need to do so elsewhere in the text, where the terms 'Zygoptera' and 'Anisoptera' suffice.

COLLECTING DRAGONFLIES

There is a second respect in which the conduct of odonatology needs urgent attention.

As odonatology (or at least dragonfly watching) has grown in popularity for field naturalists and photographers, the ranks of dragonfly watchers have been enlarged (and enriched) by new enthusiasts, many of whom have come to dragonflies after seeing them while out watching birds. Birdwatchers typically claim that they do not need to capture a specimen to identify it reliably. Such an option is often unavailable to entomologists, including odonatologists, despite the fact that dragonflies have been nicknamed 'the birdwatcher's insect'.[22] It is clearly understood among odonatologists that, to pursue their science with rigour, they sometimes need to capture and preserve a specimen and that, when this need arises, they *alone* (as odonatologists) should decide whether or not a specimen needs to be collected. The conduct of odonatology can be severely compromised if non-odonatologists try to prevent odonatologists from collecting specimens. It has happened recently that an odonatologist trying to collect a specimen for deposition in The Natural History Museum was obstructed, and subsequently abused, by self-appointed vigilantes who had chosen to intervene in the field.[23] We cannot emphasise strongly enough that such behaviour constitutes a severe threat to the future viability of odonatology – as a science – and so should be promptly and unequivocally denounced.[24]

Odonatology is a science. Much of the information in this book would not exist had specimens of dragonflies not been collected and preserved for study. In the first place, as explained above, a species cannot be validly described and named unless represented by a designated type specimen. Furthermore, *voucher specimens* preserved for later study are essential for the pursuit of several branches of biology as well as for some aspects of conservation management and habitat protection. Appendix 2 explains further why voucher specimens are sometimes needed for the pursuit of odonatology.

No one, especially an odonatologist, likes to deprive a dragonfly of life. On the contrary, many odonatologists are deeply committed to conserving habitats on which the survival of dragonfly populations depends. Aware of their responsibility for the conduct of odonatology, and for its image, some odonatological societies have drawn up codes of conduct that apply to collecting. The most balanced, useful and comprehensive code known to us is included in Appendix 2.

THIS BOOK

The first book on dragonflies in the New Naturalist series, by Philip Corbet, Cynthia Longfield and Norman Moore, was published in 1960.[25] It was reprinted in 1985, in a paperback edition, but is now very difficult to obtain. It broke new ground in focusing on behaviour and ecology, but the information it contains has long been superseded. Since 1960 there have been massive advances in our knowledge and understanding of dragonfly biology. These have been reviewed, from a global perspective, in 1962, 1980 and 1999.[26]

By far the most significant of these advances has been the discovery of *sperm displacement*.[27] This entails the dual function of the penis of the male dragonfly during copulation – as an organ for transferring sperm to the female and also as a device for removing or repositioning the sperm of rival males already in the female's body. Sperm displacement has pervasive implications for almost every facet of dragonfly biology, and its discovery has revolutionised our perception of the evolutionary implications of reproductive behaviour of both sexes.[28] Almost every action associated with reproduction can now be understood better, and interpreted, in terms of the struggle between males and males, and between males and females, to secure parentage of offspring that themselves will compete successfully to leave vigorous descendants. An important part of this increased understanding is our interpretation of intramale contests during territorial activity. Noteworthy advances have been made in other fields of dragonfly biology, especially in larval ecology and behaviour; and we now have a much clearer understanding of the ways in which life cycles are regulated and are adapted to seasonal changes in the environment.

This book is about the natural history of dragonflies that inhabit Britain. Readers interested in the natural history of British species should be aware of several excellent books on western European dragonflies in French[29] and German.[30]

After briefly describing dragonflies, as animals and insects, in this chapter, we introduce the British species in Chapter 2; and in Chapters 3 to 9 we explore each stage of the life history in detail, giving weight to behaviour and ecology. Although a great deal is known about the biology of dragonflies, many questions remain to be tackled, and we conclude each of Chapters 3 to 9 with suggestions for investigations that enthusiasts may wish to undertake. We recommend that, to save time and effort, would-be investigators consult the relevant literature before embarking on a project. To facilitate this we provide a Bibliography on pages 395–442 listing details of the literature sources cited under each topic in the text. In Chapter 10 we trace the development of odonatology in Britain, including the history and status of conservation – of dragonflies and their habitats – and the relevant, anticipated effects of prospective climate change. We do not provide scale bars on any of the photographs that appear in this book. Readers are referred to the books by Hammond[31] and Brooks[32] where measurements are given for adults and larvae of all British species. Certain terms italicised in the text are used in a specialised sense and are defined in the Glossary on pages 373–381.

Appendices comprise:
1) a checklist of species occurring in Britain, giving scientific names and their English (largely BDS) equivalents;
2) an introduction to the practice and philosophy of collecting specimens and advice for photographing dragonflies in the field;
3) the odonatological criteria according to which a site can qualify for designation as a Site of Special Scientific Interest (SSSI) in Britain; and
4) maps showing the distribution in Britain of British dragonflies, categorised according to date.

LITERATURE

Until 1960, when the predecessor of this volume appeared,[25] books and monographs on British dragonflies were concerned primarily with identification – of adults, by Lucas[33] and Longfield[34] and of larvae by Lucas[35] and Gardner[36]. The identification of larvae was placed on a firmer footing by Eric Gardner who reared and described many British species from egg to adult. The keys he produced[36] were reprinted in the New Naturalist book *Dragonflies*, published in 1960,[25] and in the book by Hammond in 1977 and 1983.[31]

Useful manuals exist for the identification of adults and larvae, for the Odonata of Britain (by Hammond, McGeeney, Miller and Brooks)[37] and Europe (by Askew),[38] and all except the book by Miller contain information about distribution. Miller's book also contains quality information about biology, especially behaviour. A publication focusing on distribution and conservation status and including summary information about the biology of each British species is the Atlas by Merritt, Moore and Eversham.[39]

The lay reader interested in dragonflies on a global scale will be well served by recent books by Silsby[40] and Brooks.[41] Both titles are liberally furnished with colour images and the former is unique in illustrating an example of an adult representing each of the 73 subfamilies of Odonata. Specialised information about the behaviour and ecology of Odonata as an order can be found in two books and an article by Corbet.[26] The classic book *The Biology of Dragonflies*, by R.J. Tillyard, one of the giants of odonatology,[42] was published in 1917.[43] It emphasised morphology and systematics; it is now long out of print and has become a collector's item. It is packed with information not easily found in modern publications. Fortunately, thanks to the initiative and industry of Richard Rowe, it is now available on the worldwide web.[44]

The BDS, established in 1983, collates information about British Odonata, maintains a vigorous education programme and publishes the *Journal of the British Dragonfly Society*, featuring research reports about British species, as well as a bulletin, *Dragonfly News*, which gives details of field and indoor meetings. The BDS supports a standing committee, the Dragonfly Conservation Group, which *inter alia* advises statutory bodies on the conservation needs of dragonflies. There are now several books describing the dragonflies of different regions or counties in Britain (Box 2, p.14).

Two bodies serve odonatologists internationally: the Foundation Societas Internationalis Odonatologica publishes *Odonatologica* and *Notulae Odonatologicae*, and The Worldwide Dragonfly Association publishes *The International Journal of Odonatology* and the newsletter *Agrion*.

CHAPTER 2

The British Species

IDENTIFICATION OF SPECIES

D RAGONFLIES ARE A rewarding group to study because, unlike most insect groups, there are relatively few species to get to know; they are large and easy to find and, after some practice, many species can be identified in flight and from photographs. One of the most obvious features of a dragonfly is its large eyes. The dragonfly's world is a visual world. They recognise each other by sight, either by their striking colours or by their mode of flight and behaviour. And we too can hone our observational skills and soon learn to identify many species of dragonflies in the same way. Most species can be identified from their unique combination of markings, especially those on the abdomen. Many species are sexually dimorphic, that is the females and males of the same species have a different appearance (Figs 16 & 17, p.32). This means that twice as many types must be learnt, but also that it is often quite easy to tell the difference between males and females. For those species that are not sexually dimorphic, males can usually be recognised by the swelling under the base of the abdomen produced by the secondary genitalia, and females usually by the swelling or spike towards the tip of the abdomen formed by the *ovipositor*. Some species are very easy to recognise by their unique appearance. *Aeshna grandis* is the only British species of anisopteran to have amber-coloured wings. Others may require more detailed examination. For example, males of the *Coenagrion* species are identified by the shape of the small black marking on the top of the second abdominal segment. When viewed through binoculars, this marking is often visible, even on specimens several metres away. Some species can be identified reliably in the hand only by close examination of the anal appendages (e.g. *Lestes*, Corduliidae), or leg coloration and genitalia (e.g. *Sympetrum*) but, with experience, even species in these groups can often be identified without the need to net them. That said, it may be necessary to secure a voucher specimen (see Appendix 2). Sometimes visual, or even photographic, records are insufficient to permit secure identification, especially in species which differ in small subtleties of morphology.

Dragonfly larvae are much more difficult to identify than adults, especially in the early *stadia*. A few species have a characteristic appearance and can be identified in the field from the markings on the *caudal appendages* (*Pyrrhosoma nymphula*), the shape of the head (*Anax imperator*) or distinctive thoracic markings (*Cordulia aenea*). The number and shape of the abdominal spines can be a useful character for distinguishing species of Libellulidae, but these may be difficult to see if they are obscured by debris. Also, the extent of the development of these spines may depend on the presence of insectivorous fish. Other species can be distinguished only by close examination under a hand lens or low-powered microscope. For example, most species of Aeshnidae differ in the shape and relative lengths of the caudal appendages (*epiprocts* and *paraprocts*) but these are too small to see clearly with the naked eye. The shape of the labium and arrangement of labial *setae* also provide important characters in many groups, but the setation may only be visible in dead or anaesthetised larvae. There are no known characters that will reliably distinguish the larvae of *Coenagrion puella* and *C. pulchellum* or *Sympetrum striolatum* and *S. sanguineum*. The F-0 *exuviae*, the shed skins of larvae left on emergent plants after adults have emerged, of Anisoptera and Zygoptera are usually identifiable to species and provide the most reliable way of establishing which species are completing their life cycles at a particular site. However, the problems of identifying larvae should not be underestimated. The shape and appearance of the *caudal lamellae* of Zygoptera change greatly during development (Fig. 60, p.115), the number of labial setae can be highly variable and is not always diagnostic, and abdominal spines can be variably developed. There is still much work to be done to establish reliable characters for larval identification.

This book is not intended to be an identification guide. For this purpose, we refer you to other books which serve this function (Box 2). Instead, in this chapter, we review the broad distribution of dragonflies in Britain, and the factors thought to influence this, before describing the characteristics of each family that occurs in Britain.

....

BOX 2

SOME IDENTIFICATION GUIDES TO THE
BRITISH SPECIES

Brooks, S.J. (Ed.) (1997) (4th revised edition, 2004). *Field guide to the dragonflies and damselflies of Great Britain and Ireland.* British Wildlife Publishing: Hook.
Cham, S. (2007). *Field guide to the larvae and exuviae of British dragonflies.* Volume 1: Dragonflies (Anisoptera). British Dragonfly Society.
Cham, S. (2008). *Field guide to the larvae and exuviae of British dragonflies.* Volume 2: Damselflies (Zygoptera). British Dragonfly Society.
Hill, P. & Twist, C. (1996). *Butterflies and dragonflies: a site guide.* Arlequin Press: Chelmsford.
McGeeney, A. (1986). *A complete guide to British Dragonflies.* Jonathan Cape: London.
Miller, P.L. (1995). *Dragonflies.* The Richmond Publishing Co. Ltd: Slough.
Nelson, B. & Thompson, R. (2004). *The natural history of Ireland's dragonflies.* The National Museums and Galleries of Northern Ireland: Belfast.
Powell, D. (1999). *Guide to the dragonflies of Great Britain.* Arlequin Press: Chelmsford.
Hammond, C.O. (1977) (1983, 2nd edition revised by R. Merritt). *The dragonflies of Great Britain and Ireland.* Harley Books: Colchester.
Smallshire, D. & Swash, A. (2004). *Britain's dragonflies.* WildGuides: Old Basing.

....

....

BOX 3

REGIONAL GUIDES TO BRITISH DRAGONFLIES

Averill, M. (1996). *The dragonflies of Worcestershire.* Mike Averill: Kidderminster.
Belden, T.A. (2004). *Dragonflies of Sussex.* Sussex Wildlife Trust: Chichester.
Benton, E. (1988). *The dragonflies of Essex.* Essex Field Club: London.
Brook, J. & Brook, G. (2001). *Dragonflies of Kent. An account of their biology, history and distribution.* Transactions of the Kent Field Club **16**: 1–115.

Brownett, A. (1996). *The dragonflies of Oxfordshire.* Brookside Books: Banbury.

Cham, S. (2004). *Dragonflies of Bedfordshire.* Bedfordshire Natural History Society: Bedford.

Coker, S. & Fox, T. (1985). *West Wales Dragonflies.* Mountain Books: Mountain.

Collingwood, N. (1997). *The dragonflies of Staffordshire.* Stoke-on-Trent City Museum and Art Gallery: Stoke-on-Trent.

Dunn, R. & Budworth, D. (2005). *Dragonflies in Derbyshire: status and distribution 1977–2000.* Derbyshire & Nottinghamshire Entomological Society: Derby.

Follet, P. (1996). *Dragonflies of Surrey.* Surrey Wildlife Atlas Series 2. Surrey Wildlife Trust: Woking.

Gabb, R. & Kitching, D. (1992). *The dragonflies and damselflies of Cheshire.* National Museums & Galleries on Merseyside: Liverpool.

Garner, P. (2005). *The dragonflies of Herefordshire.* Herefordshire Biological Records Centre: Hereford.

Grover, S. & Ikin, H. (1994). *Leicestershire dragonflies.* Leicestershire Museums: Leicester.

Holland, S. (1991). *Distribution of dragonflies in Gloucestershire.* Mrs Twissell: Cheltenham.

Lockton, A.J. (Ed.) (1996). *The dragonflies of Shropshire.* Wildscan Ecological Consultants on behalf of BIOS: Shrewsbury.

Mendell, H. (1993). *Suffolk dragonflies.* Suffolk Naturalists' Society: Ipswich.

Prendergast, E.D.V. (1991). *The dragonflies of Dorset.* Dorset Natural History and Archaeological Society: Dorchester.

Randolph, S. (1992). *Dragonflies of the Bristol region.* Bristol/Avon Regional Environmental Records Centre: Bristol.

Saunders, J.W. (1986). *Dragonflies of Pembrokeshire.* Pembrokeshire Coast National Park Authority: Pembrokeshire.

Saville, B. (Ed.) (1997). *Dragonflies of the Lothians.* Scottish Wildlife Trust: Edinburgh.

Smout, A.-M. & Kinnear, P. (1993). *Dragonflies of Fife: a provisional atlas.* Fife Nature: Glenrothes.

Taverner, J., Cham, S. & Hold, A. (2004). *The dragonflies of Hampshire.* Pisces Publications: Newbury.

Taylor, P. (2003). *Dragonflies of Norfolk.* Norfolk and Norwich Naturalists' Society: Norwich.

Tyrell, M. (2006). *The dragonflies of Northamptonshire.* Northants Dragonfly Group: Northampton.

DISTRIBUTION OF DRAGONFLIES IN BRITAIN

The distribution maps shown in this book (Appendix 4) are based on records plotted at a resolution of 10 km². The records have been built up over a period of about 160 years. The latest maps which appear in Appendix 4 have been updated to the year 2006 and are based on 363,959 records from 48,881 sites. They represent a massive effort from the amateur Odonata recording community. While these maps provide a good idea of the broad distribution of the British species, areas of Scotland[1] and Ireland[2] remain less well covered than England and Wales. The maps may also provide a rather optimistic view of the status of the British species. The records are largely based on sightings of adults and no account is taken of numbers seen, whether or not the species were breeding at the places in which they were seen, whether these were one-off sightings or if the species has been recorded over a period of many years at the same site. It is also unclear from the maps how many sites are present within each 10-km square. A species may be recorded consistently from a particular 10-km square over several decades but may actually be declining if it is being lost from a series of sites within that square. An actual range contraction will become visible on the map only when the species disappears from the last site in that square. For this reason, county maps, plotted at 1-km² or 2-km² resolution and based on breeding records, are much more useful as a conservation tool.[3]

Thirty-nine species of dragonflies are known to breed in Britain and Ireland today. These resident species are supplemented by another twelve or so migrant species which appear more or less regularly, often in small numbers, but sometimes in their thousands. Most of the migrant species are encountered in southwest England if they originate in western Europe, whereas migrants that have set off from central Europe are most likely to be seen in southeast England and East Anglia. Migrant species usually make landfall during late summer, but they can turn up at almost any time of year and in any part of Britain. Dragonflies seen at unusual times of the year and in unusual places should be looked at closely to confirm their identity because they could well be migrant species. Judging from past experience, a strong case exists for securing a voucher specimen of any such migrant encountered in Britain, and depositing it in a museum (Appendix 2). Records of migrants are compiled annually by the BDS (Chapter 10). Many of the species resident in Britain, especially Aeshnidae and Libellulidae, disperse after emerging from breeding sites and this can sometimes take solitary adults far outside their normal distributional range and habitat.

The local-scale distribution of dragonflies in Britain is governed by habitat preferences of individual species (Chapter 3). However, regional-scale distribution is controlled by climate. The British Odonata exhibit five principal patterns of distribution that are likely to be influenced by climate.

Widespread

Some species, for example *Lestes sponsa, Pyrrhosoma nymphula, Enallagma cyathigerum, Libellula quadrimaculata* and *Sympetrum striolatum* (Fig. 1), occur throughout Britain and Ireland and do not appear to be climatically constrained in Britain. Nevertheless, *Sympetrum striolatum* is less common in the northeast of Britain, suggesting that this region is too cold for it, because otherwise the species has broad habitat requirements.

Southern

Some species are restricted to the south of Britain, suggesting that the summers (or winters) are not warm enough for them to complete their life cycle elsewhere. Species having a southern distribution include *Calopteryx splendens, Ceriagrion tenellum, Ischnura pumilio, Aeshna cyanea* (Fig. 2), *Anax imperator, Orthetrum cancellatum* and *Libellula depressa*. These species are likely to respond to global

FIG 1. *Sympetrum striolatum* is widespread throughout Britain (Robert Thompson).

FIG 2. *Aeshna cyanea* is common in southern England, but becomes scarce in the north and Scotland (Robert Thompson).

warming by expanding their distributional range northwards. Indeed, some of them are already doing so (pp.295–6).

Northern

Species restricted to Scotland or having a predominantly northern distribution include *Coenagrion hastulatum* (Fig. 3), *Aeshna caerulea*, *Somatochlora arctica* and *Leucorrhinia dubia*. These species are likely to lose ground if current trends in global warming continue (see p.296).

FIG 3. *Coenagrion hastulatum* is one of the few British species with a northern distribution (Robert Thompson).

Continental

A continental climate is typified by hot summers, cold winters and low rainfall. As far as this can be expected in an island in the northwest of Europe, these conditions are found in southeast England. Species that appear to have a continental distribution in Britain include *Erythromma najas* (Fig. 4), *Aeshna mixta*, *Libellula fulva* and *Sympetrum sanguineum*.

Oceanic

Cordulegaster boltonii and *Orthetrum coerulescens* (Fig. 5) occur in the west of Britain, suggesting that they prefer the wetter summers and milder winters provided by the Gulf Stream. The absence of *C. boltonii* from Ireland may be an indication that the species did not arrive in England until after the land bridge between Ireland and Great Britain was inundated by the Irish Sea shortly after the end of the last ice age.

FIG 4. *Erythromma najas* is largely confined to central and eastern England (Robert Thompson).

FIG 5. *Orthetrum coerulescens* is most abundant in western Britain and southern England (Robert Thompson).

DRAGONFLY HABITATS IN BRITAIN

Within the broad-scale, predominately climate-driven distribution patterns of British dragonflies, the local distribution and abundance of species is strongly influenced by habitat availability. Whereas the restriction to southeast England of *Libellula fulva* probably reflects the influence of a continental climate, its patchy distribution within this region is tied to the availability of the slow-flowing rivers in which it breeds. *Sympetrum danae* has a predominantly northern distribution, but also occurs in parts of southwest and southern England. The virtual absence of this species from much of the English Midlands, East Anglia and southeast England probably reflects the paucity in this region of heathland and moorland, and bogs with acidic, nutrient-poor pools. Certain critical environmental variables such as nutrients and dissolved oxygen also influence the distribution of dragonflies. An oxygen-poor lake or sluggish, *eutrophicated*, lowland river may support a large population of the pollution-tolerant *Ischnura elegans*, while other Odonata species are absent. Similarly, physical factors have an impact on species distribution. *Platycnemis pennipes* is restricted to southern England by a requirement for a relatively warm climate. Locally it is found only on unpolluted, slow-flowing rivers and canals, although along the course of a river it may be absent from stretches that have undergone extensive bankside clearance of vegetation. In a study at Epping Forest, to the northeast of London,[4] a population of *Cordulia aenea* was found to be centred on the largest pond within a large block of woodland, which functioned as a *stem habitat* (Box 6, p.76). Small populations were present at other ponds within that block of woodland which served as *secondary habitats* (Box 6). However, some other ponds within the forest had not been colonised by this species, even though they appeared to be suitable. These ponds were in separate woodland blocks divided from the population centre by housing and expanses of grassland. Evidently, adult *Cordulia aenea* did not disperse far from the emergence site and were reluctant to leave the woodland canopy.

In Britain, there are five key wetland types that support different assemblages of dragonflies. Relatively few species are confined to flowing water, and fast-flowing streams are species poor. Slow-flowing rivers may support a few specialist species, but many species that breed in ponds and lakes also breed in sluggish rivers. Most British species breed in standing waters, but sites that combine a mosaic of different wetland types have the greatest potential for high species diversity.

Ponds and lakes

Acid-water pools on bogs, heaths and moorland support their own specialist dragonfly fauna that will be considered separately. In addition, the ditches and dykes that support a rich diversity of aquatic plants and are typical of lowland levels and fens have several specialist dragonflies which are likewise discussed below. Ponds (Fig. 6) and lakes, farm and garden ponds, woodland ponds, gravel pits, reservoirs and shallow temporary pools support many generalist species that also breed in most of the other wetland types considered here, but also a few specialists that are not found elsewhere.

As interest grows in wildlife gardening, many people are now creating garden ponds (Box 23, p.281). If these ponds are kept fish-free, they will soon support many different dragonfly species, even in the heart of the largest conurbations. Species that may arrive in the first few years after creation of a pond, before the aquatic plants have occupied much of it, include *Libellula depressa, Sympetrum striolatum, Aeshna mixta* and *Anax imperator*. As the pond matures, these species may become less abundant, and others, such as *Pyrrhosoma nymphula, Aeshna cyanea* and *Coenagrion puella*, that prefer luxuriant plant growth and plenty of plant debris at the bottom, come to dominate the dragonfly fauna. Large lakes

FIG 6. This shallow pond on Hatchet Moor, in the New Forest, Hampshire, is ideal for dragonflies, having a profuse growth of aquatic vegetation and the sheltering, but not overshadowing, belt of trees (Robert Thompson).

will also attract these species but, in addition, other species that favour open expanses of water (e.g. *Enallagma cyathigerum, Aeshna grandis*), floating-leaved plants (e.g. *Erythromma najas, E. viridulum*) and patches of bare ground on the banks (e.g. *Orthetrum cancellatum*) may become established. Woodland ponds, large enough to let plenty of light into the water, and those with profuse growth of emergent vegetation, are likely to support *Cordulia aenea, Somatochlora metallica* (Fig. 7), *Lestes sponsa* and *Sympetrum sanguineum*. In Scotland, small, well-vegetated ponds may also support *Coenagrion hastulatum. Coenagrion lunulatum* occurs in small, *mesotrophic*, well-vegetated, clear-water lakes in Ireland.

Lowland rivers and canals
The slow-flowing lowland rivers of England are home to two of our least common species: *Gomphus vulgatissimus* and *Libellula fulva*. These rivers also support two other more widespread river specialists, *Calopteryx splendens* (Fig. 8) and *Platycnemis pennipes*. Other species which commonly breed in lakes and ponds frequently breed in sluggish rivers as well. Among these are *Erythromma najas, Coenagrion puella, Enallagma cyathigerum, Ischnura elegans,*

FIG 7. Some dragonflies, like this *Somatochlora metallica*, prefer shaded woodland ponds in which to breed (Robert Thompson).

Aeshna grandis and *Anax imperator*. All these species require rivers that have clear water with luxuriant growth of submerged, floating-leafed and emergent plants. In addition, a scattering of overhanging trees and plenty of tall herbs and grasses along the banks is usually beneficial (but see Chapter 3) (Fig. 9).

FIG 8. *Calopteryx splendens* is restricted to slow-flowing lowland rivers (Robert Thompson).

FIG 9. The River Rother at Stopham Bridge in Hampshire where both *Libellula fulva* and *Platycnemis pennipes* breed (Robert Thompson).

Streams and upland rivers

Fast-flowing streams and rivers support a less diverse dragonfly fauna than do their slow-flowing counterparts. Few of the species that breed in standing or slow-flowing rivers occur in fast-flowing waters. It is likely that the high current speed, lack of submerged vegetation and cold, unproductive waters make such habitats unsuitable for these species. *Calopteryx virgo* can be expected on the fast-flowing sections of streams and rivers that have overhanging trees and luxuriant growth of bankside vegetation. *Cordulegaster boltonii* (Fig. 10) is common on small, unshaded streams cutting through heathland and moorland, especially in the western uplands of Britain. Shallow, unshaded, trickling streams with a gravel bed (Fig. 11) support populations of the rare *Coenagrion mercuriale*.

FIG 10. A male *Cordulegaster boltonii*. This species is common on shallow moorland streams in southern and western Britain (Robert Thompson).

FIG 11. The warm, shallow, trickling waters of this calcareous flush at Latchmoor, in the New Forest, Hampshire, provide an ideal breeding site for *Coenagrion mercuriale* and *Cordulegaster boltonii* (Robert Thompson).

Bogs, moorland and heathland

Many of the widespread pond species shun acid waters, where they are replaced by a distinctive dragonfly fauna not found elsewhere. In waters that lack fish or are too acidic for them, anisopteran larvae are usually the top predators. As a result, large populations of dragonflies can be supported even in water that is relatively nutrient poor. At large bog pools the air may be filled with whirling male *Aeshna juncea* (Fig. 12), *Libellula quadrimaculata*, *Orthetrum coerulescens* and *Sympetrum danae*. In northern Britain these species may be joined by *Aeshna caerulea* and *Somatochlora arctica*, particularly where patches of woodland are present, and by *Leucorrhinia dubia* on more open bogs. On the heaths of southern England and Wales even the smallest bog pool may be attended by *Ceriagrion tenellum*, and shallow seepages are frequented by *Ischnura pumilio*. Both these species require warm, shallow water to complete development, but are not

FIG 12. *Aeshna juncea* is abundant on bogs, moorland and heathland (Robert Thompson).

FIG 13. Lough Beg in Killarney National Park, Co. Kerry, Ireland, supports a wide variety of acid bog specialists (Robert Thompson).

restricted to acidic habitats and also occur in suitable base-rich sites such as clay pits and fens. In Ireland, populations of *Coenagrion lunulatum* occur on cut-over bogs (Fig. 13).

Levels, fens and marshes

The flat, low-lying levels of Somerset, the river flood plains and coastal marshes of north Kent, south Essex, Pevensey and the Arun Valley in Sussex, and the fens and Broads of East Anglia (Fig. 14) typify grazing marshes and flood meadows that provide rich dragonfly habitat. Wet grasslands crisscrossed by ditches, some of which dry out during the summer, but which are rich in aquatic plants and dense stands of reeds and rushes, provide ideal conditions for some dragonflies. These are the haunts of many of our common and widespread pond and lake species but also of some less common species that specialise in these plant-choked waters, including *Lestes dryas*, *Coenagrion pulchellum* (Fig. 15), *Brachytron pratense* and *Aeshna isosceles*. The turloughs of western Ireland, those mysterious pools that fill from time to time, are favoured breeding sites for odonate species that are vulnerable to fish predation but whose life cycle allows them to tolerate

FIG 14. Bough Common, Norfolk, is a breeding site for *Aeshna isosceles* (Robert Thompson).

FIG 15. *Coenagrion pulchellum* can be abundant on marshes, levels and fens, but elsewhere is uncommon (Robert Thompson).

periods of drought. Foremost among them is *Lestes dryas*, which maintains large colonies at some of these sites.

SPECIES ACCOUNTS

There have been relatively few detailed studies of the larval duration (*voltinism*) of the British Odonata. In the following accounts, if no precise, published study exists on voltinism of a British population we have provided an inference (prefaced by 'probably') derived from a general impression stated in an authoritative source.

We have listed the families in systematic order, starting with the most primitive, least derived, families in each suborder. Genera and species are listed alphabetically within each family.

ZYGOPTERA – DAMSELFLIES

Calopterygidae – Demoiselles
The Calopterygidae includes two British species: *Calopteryx splendens* and *C. virgo*. Both are widespread throughout Europe. They are large, conspicuous, and characterised by their metallic green or blue bodies and, in males, by dark blue wing patches (Fig. 16). Females lack the dark blue wing pigmentation (Fig. 17). Both species are largely restricted to running waters. The extent of the wing pigmentation serves to distinguish the species. Males are strongly territorial, but territories are relatively small, so males may be present in large numbers at some sites, amongst emergent vegetation, often in dappled shade. Males vigorously defend their territories against rivals, and a single male may remain in the same *territory* for up to ten days. There the individual displays his own suitability and that of his territory to females in an elaborate *courtship* ritual involving wing fluttering and intermittently throwing himself onto the water surface. Copulation is brief, lasting less than five minutes. Males guard females during *oviposition*, although they do not remain in *tandem*. Females lay eggs *endophytically* into a wide variety of emergent vegetation. Eggs are ready to hatch after about 14 days. The larvae are large. They have long antennae and long legs and superficially resemble stick insects (Fig. 18). The caudal appendages are long, narrow, triangular in cross section and banded. The larvae live amongst plant debris at the bottom of the river and development of both British species usually takes two years.[5]

FIG 16. The wings of male *Calopteryx virgo* are deep indigo (Robert Thompson).

FIG 17. The wings of female *Calopteryx virgo* are suffused with the colour of amber. The white *pseudopterostigma* is present only in female calopterygids (Robert Thompson).

FIG 18. Larva of *Calopteryx virgo* in stadium F-o. Its long antennae are typical of Calopterygidae (Robert Thompson).

Calopteryx splendens (Banded Demoiselle) (Fig. 8, p.25) has a graceful, butterfly-like flight; the wing beat is slow. The males are especially conspicuous as they flit between sunlit patches under overhanging trees, the sunlight reflecting off the inky-blue patches on their wings and metallic blue bodies. The species is common in slow-flowing lowland rivers with a muddy bottom, and in lakes adjacent to rivers, in most of England and Ireland. It is absent from Scotland and the very north of England. Adults are on the wing between the middle of May and early September. *Calopteryx splendens* requires stands of emergent plants which are used as perches and oviposition sites. Its occurrence appears to be positively correlated with the height of riverside vegetation and to be negatively correlated with the height of bankside trees and the bank.[6]

Calopteryx virgo (Beautiful Demoiselle) (Figs 16, 17, 18) has a general appearance similar to *C. splendens*, but it is common on fast-flowing unpolluted rivers and streams with a stony bottom, so they rarely occur together.[7] The species has a predominantly southern and western distribution in England, Wales and Ireland with outposts in the Lake District, North York Moors and western Scotland. Adults are on the wing from mid-May to early September. The species does not breed in polluted sites or those which have suffered from bankside clearance of trees and emergent plants. This species is *semivoltine* in the New Forest.[8]

Lestidae – Emerald Damselflies

There are only two resident species of Lestidae in Britain and Ireland, *Lestes sponsa* and *L. dryas*, but these have recently been supplemented by two vagrant species, *L. barbarus* and *L. viridis*, from continental Europe. Adult Lestidae are relatively large zygopterans. The bodies are metallic green, usually with pale blue *pruinescence* at the base and tip of the abdomen in males. The wings are unpigmented. Unlike other damselflies, which rest with their wings closed over the abdomen, Lestidae hold their wings half open when perched (Fig. 19). They breed in standing water that usually supports a dense growth of submerged and emergent aquatic plants amongst which the eggs are laid and the larvae live. Tandem pairs of *L. sponsa* adults often form away from the breeding site[9] and copulation in *L. sponsa* and *L. dryas* may last 30–60 minutes.[10] The pair stay in tandem throughout oviposition which may continue with the pair being fully submerged for up to 30 minutes.[10] Eggs are often laid above water and can

FIG 19. The habit of perching with the wings held half open is characteristic of Lestidae, as seen in this male *Lestes dryas* (Robert Thompson).

FIG 20. Larva of *Lestes sponsa* in stadium F-0. Like other Lestidae, this species has conspicuously banded caudal lamellae (Robert Thompson).

withstand desiccation. Lestidae are the only British zygopterans that overwinter in the egg stage. The larvae are large and hunt prey actively. This makes them vulnerable to predation by fish. All lestid larvae, except *Austrolestes colensonis* in New Zealand,[11] develop rapidly and complete development in a few months. This enables them to take advantage of temporary pools that dry out in late summer and so are fish-free. The larvae have large caudal appendages that are lamellate and characteristically banded (Fig. 20).

Lestes viridis (Willow Emerald Damselfly) was recorded from a single male adult in Hertfordshire in 1899, but the authenticity of this record has recently been disputed.[12] The first and only fully authenticated record in this country was of a F-0 exuvia collected on the North Kent Marshes in 1992.[13] The species is widespread in most of Europe, although absent from Scandinavia.[14] It breeds in a wide variety of standing and slow-flowing waters that are lined with trees and shrubs, especially willow, into which the female inserts her eggs.[15] The eggs overwinter and larvae develop within three months after hatching in spring.[15] Adults are on the wing from June to November, peak numbers appearing in August and September.

Lestes barbarus (Southern Emerald Damselfly) was first recorded in Britain in Norfolk in July 2002.[16] Subsequently it was recorded in 2003 at the same site and at an additional location in Kent.[17] So far only five specimens have been seen, and none was recorded in 2005,[18] so it is too soon to decide whether the species will become established in England. The Norfolk site was a shallow, muddy coastal dune pool with no submerged vegetation but some emergent plants. This is typical of sites used by the species in continental Europe. The species also breeds in brackish water.[19]

Lestes dryas (Scarce Emerald Damselfly) (Fig. 19) is rare in England where it occurs around the Thames estuary, north Norfolk and at a few sites in the Midlands. It is commoner in Ireland. It favours shallow freshwater or brackish-water pools and ditches,[20] which may dry out in late summer and support dense emergent vegetation, or ponds with naturally fluctuating water levels, such as turloughs in Ireland[2] and some pingos in Norfolk.[21] Such sites are liable to become totally overgrown and eventually permanently dry, so a succession of densely vegetated pools in an area is necessary for the continued local survival of the species. Over-abstraction, nutrient enrichment and overgrazing all threaten the suitability of sites for the species. *Lestes dryas* is on the wing from the end of June until the end of August.

Lestes sponsa (Emerald Damselfly) (Fig. 20) occurs throughout most of Britain and can be common locally. Adults are usually seen lurking amongst dense emergent vegetation near a wide range of standing waters, including ponds, lakes, canals, bog pools and brackish coastal pools. Excessive clearance of aquatic plants from a breeding site can reduce numbers. Adults are on the wing from late June until the end of September.

Platycnemididae – White-legged Damselflies

Platycnemis pennipes (White-legged Damselfly) is the only species of Platycnemididae currently resident in Britain, although two other species occur in western Europe. Males are characterised by their broad white tibiae. The abdomen is white in females and immature males, becoming pale blue in mature males. In Britain, the species typically breeds in slow-flowing rivers and canals supporting dense stands of emergent and floating vegetation. However, in France it commonly breeds in standing water, and in recent years there have been records of this habitat choice in Britain.[22] Late-stadium larvae are easily recognisable by the appearance of the caudal lamellae which have dark patches and a long slender thread at the tip (Fig. 21). The larvae live amongst leaves and detritus at the bottom. Development probably takes two years.[1] Males dangle their legs to display the broad, flattened tibiae when in flight, probably as gestures of threat, but there is no firm evidence that the legs are used in courtship display (Fig. 22). The legs are also used to stimulate the female during

FIG 21. Larva of *Platycnemis pennipes* in stadium F-0. Its caudal lamellae are mottled and each has a long, slender thread at the tip (Robert Thompson).

FIG 22. Male *Platycnemis pennipes* are characterised by their broad white tibiae (Ann Brooks).

copulation, which may last up to 30 minutes.[23] Oviposition occurs in tandem, in groups with the male in the *sentinel position*. Eggs are laid into floating or emergent plants, but the female often descends below the water to continue laying into submerged stems.

Platycnemis pennipes is restricted to southern England where adults are on the wing from mid-May to mid-August. The species is locally distributed on slow-flowing rivers and canals, but can be abundant on well-vegetated, unpolluted waters where the adults perch amongst dense emergent plants, tall grasses and shrubs. The adults have a distinctive bouncing flight, but can be difficult to locate as they meander through the tall bankside vegetation. *Platycnemis pennipes* is vulnerable to pollution, but especially to the clearance of aquatic and bankside vegetation.[23]

Coenagrionidae – Blue and Red Damselflies

There are twelve species of Coenagrionidae currently resident in Britain and Ireland. *Pyrrhosoma nymphula* and *Ceriagrion tenellum* are red and black species, and the following are blue and black: *Coenagrion hastulatum, C. lunulatum, C. mercuriale, C. puella, C. pulchellum, Enallagma cyathigerum, Erythromma najas, E. viridulum, Ischnura elegans* and *I. pumilio*. The family is widely distributed throughout Europe. The British fauna includes a boreal element, comprising *Coenagrion hastulatum* and *C. lunulatum*, and a southern element, including *Ceriagrion tenellum, Coenagrion mercuriale, Erythromma viridulum* and *Ischnura pumilio*.

Coenagrionidae are small to medium-sized damselflies and are strongly sexually dimorphic. Females have more extensive black markings on the abdomen than males and can be difficult to distinguish at species level in the field. Males of the genus *Coenagrion* and *Enallagma* can be distinguished at species level by close examination of the shape of the black marking on the upper surface of the second abdominal segment. Adults of both sexes of the genus *Ischnura* exhibit several different colour forms, some of which are age related (Fig. 92, p.176). Different colour forms also occur in females of *Ceriagrion tenellum*, several *Coenagrion* species, *Enallagma cyathigerum* and *Pyrrhosoma nymphula*.

Adult coenagrionids can be abundant at freshwater sites, sometimes forming aggregations of hundreds of individuals. They typically have a weak fluttering flight, although *Erythromma najas* is more powerful. Males fly close to the water surface or perch amongst emergent vegetation at the water margin. Female coenagrionids may be encountered in fields remote from water. Mating is usually brief, lasting less than ten minutes, although *Ischnura elegans* may remain *in copula* for up to six hours (see p.250). Females oviposit endophytically, either

accompanied by the male in the sentinel position (p.86) (Fig. 50, p.88) or, in
the case of *Ischnura*, alone. Frequently the female descends completely below the
surface of the water to lay eggs on submerged plant stems. Larval development
of most species is completed within one or two years. Most larvae (Fig. 23)
are *claspers* (p.118) and cling to the stems and leaves of submerged plants, but
the larvae of some species, such as *Pyrrhosoma nymphula*, live amongst dead
vegetation at the bottom. Most species have a long *flying season* and an
unsynchronised emergence, having a Type 2 life cycle, although *Pyrrhosoma
nymphula* is an exception (Table 6, p.170).

 Ceriagrion tenellum (Small Red Damselfly) (Fig. 103, p.195) is restricted to
warm, nutrient-poor, unshaded, shallow pools and seepages in acidic bogs or
in calcareous mires, clay pits and slow-flowing shallow streams. Adults fly, while
the sun is out, just a few centimetres above the ground and seem to disappear
as soon as the sun is obscured by a cloud. Despite the red abdomen, they are
surprisingly cryptic as they perch on low rushes and sedges. *Ceriagrion tenellum*
has a patchy distribution in southern England and west Wales, and an isolated
population exists in East Anglia. The species is local, and vulnerable to

FIG 23. Larva of *Coenagrion puella*, a typical coenagrionid, in stadium F-0 (Robert
Thompson).

eutrophication, afforestation, shading, over-abstraction and dredging. The flying season extends from early June to early September. The larvae live in mats of sphagnum moss or debris at the bottom and take two years to complete development.[24]

Coenagrion armatum (Norfolk Damselfly) was last recorded in Britain in 1957.[25] The loss of the species resulted from its breeding sites being encroached by reeds and willows and ultimately drying out.[1] Populations are usually established in moderately eutrophic standing or slow-flowing water with dense submerged and aquatic vegetation. The life cycle has been little studied and the duration of the larval stage is unknown. Adults were on the wing in the Norfolk Broads from late May to mid-July.

Coenagrion hastulatum (Northern Damselfly) (Fig. 3, p.19) breeds in small, shallow pools, often overgrown with emergent vegetation, and so silting-up of sites is a threat. Larvae take two years to develop.[26] The adult flying season is from mid-May until early August.

Coenagrion lunulatum (Irish Damselfly) (Figs 24 & 25) was first discovered in Ireland in 1981[27] and is now known to breed throughout central Ireland in

FIG 24. Like most other British Coenagrionidae, male *Coenagrion lunulatum* have a black abdomen with extensive patches of blue. This species is confined to Ireland (Robert Thompson).

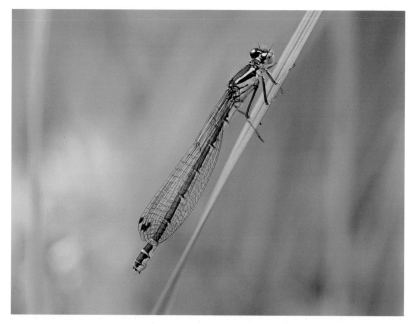

FIG 25. In most female Coenagrionidae the upper surface of the abdomen is almost entirely black, as in this female *Coenagrion lunulatum* (Robert Thompson).

shallow mesotrophic lakes and bog pools with floating plants and sparse emergent vegetation. It seldom flies for long before perching on the floating leaves of aquatic plants.[2] Large breeding populations are restricted to those sites not affected by drainage or nutrient enrichment. Probably due to these causes the species seems to have been lost from 25 per cent of its previously known sites in Northern Ireland since its discovery.[28] The duration of the larval stage has not been studied in Ireland, but is likely to be one year or possibly two.[2] The flying season extends from mid-May to late July.

Coenagrion mercuriale (Southern Damselfly) (Fig. 141, p.301) is rare in Britain and occurs only in shallow, slow-flowing, base-rich streams in parts of southern England and Wales. Adults of this small damselfly are seldom abundant even at stem habitats (Box 6, p.76)[29] and fly a few centimetres above the ground, frequently perching. They do not stray far from the natal stream.[30] High water temperatures in summer and winter are essential for the survival of this species and it avoids stretches that are shaded.[31] Grazing favours this species by preventing the development of vegetation that may shade the breeding sites. The species is also vulnerable to eutrophication, over-abstraction and dredging.

The species is semivoltine in the New Forest[24] (Fig. 90, p.168). First-year larvae live in detritus at the bottom, but in the second year of development they move up into aquatic plants.[32] Adults are on the wing from mid-May to early August.

Coenagrion puella (Azure Damselfly) is common and widespread throughout England, Ireland and southern Scotland. It prefers to breed in small ponds, including garden ponds, with dense vegetation. Adult males are often abundant, weaving through emergent plants or standing sentinel above ovipositing females, their vivid pale blue abdomens like shards of the sky. The species is sensitive to pollution although it tolerates eutrophication, but populations may be reduced by clearance of aquatic plants. Larvae live amongst aquatic vegetation and usually complete development within one or two years.[33] Adults are probably not territorial.[34] They are on the wing from mid-May until late August.

Coenagrion pulchellum (Variable Damselfly) (Fig. 15, p.30) has a scattered and local distribution in England, Wales and southwest Scotland, but is common and widespread in Ireland. It breeds in standing or slow-flowing water having luxuriant growth of aquatic and bankside vegetation and can be eliminated by dredging. It is similar in appearance and behaviour to *C. puella* but slightly more delicate. Larval development is completed in one or two years,[35] and adults are on the wing from mid-May until early August.

Coenagrion scitulum (Dainty Damselfly) was known from two sites in Essex between 1946 and 1953 before catastrophic flooding by the sea rendered them unsuitable.[1] Breeding sites in continental Europe are well-vegetated ponds, lakes and streams and the species also appears to be tolerant of brackish water in coastal marshes.[36] Larvae live amongst aquatic vegetation and probably complete development in one year.[36] Adults were on the wing in England from late May until late June.[1]

Enallagma cyathigerum (Common Blue Damselfly) (Fig. 98, p.185) is widespread and common throughout Britain. It breeds in a wide variety of standing and slow-flowing waters, but tends to prefer those with expanses of open water. Males are often abundant and characteristically skim across the surface of the open water or perch amongst emergent vegetation in groups of hundreds of individuals. The larvae live amongst submerged plants. Development is completed within one or two years,[37] but in the north of its range development may take longer. Males are not territorial. The flying season lasts from May to early September.

Erythromma najas (Red-eyed Damselfly) (Fig. 4, p.20) occurs in southern England, where it can be locally common, but is absent from much of southwest England. It has recently extended its range north and west in Britain. The species favours large standing and slow-flowing waters with floating-leafed plants on which the males perch and fend off rivals. The species appears more robust than other coenagrionids. It flies close to the water surface but rarely comes to the shore, so its distinctive red eyes are best seen through binoculars. Females oviposit into the underside of the leaves of water lilies or use floating mats of dead reeds and rushes. The species may be lost from sites if these plants are removed by clearance, increased flow or boat traffic. The larvae live amongst aquatic plants and take one or two years to complete development.[1] Adults emerge in mid-May and are on the wing until mid-August.

Erythromma viridulum (Small Red-eyed Damselfly) (Fig. 137, p.296) is the most recent addition to the resident British dragonfly fauna. The species was first recorded from Essex in 1999.[38] After a large influx in 2001 it has now spread across much of East Anglia, the southeast of England and the Isle of Wight, and many inland counties including Cambridgeshire, Northamptonshire, Buckinghamshire and Warwickshire. Breeding has been confirmed at several sites. The species has been spreading northwards in Europe recently.[39] This is a colonisation event caused by the expansion of the species' European range rather than a series of migratory landfalls, and further consolidation and expansion inland in Britain is taking place (p.295). The species breeds in eutrophic ponds and lakes with floating-leafed plants. It closely resembles *E. najas* in behaviour and appearance. Mating pairs are attracted to patches of submerged plants, especially *Ceratophyllum* species (hornworts), close to the water surface.[39] Duration of the larval stage is unknown. Adults are on the wing from July to early September.

Ischnura elegans (Blue-tailed Damselfly) is common and widespread throughout most of Britain, but more local in northeast Scotland. It is tolerant of moderate pollution and brackish water and is sometimes very abundant. The species breeds in a wide variety of standing and slow-flowing waters. At nutrient-rich sites it can be superabundant, rising in swarms as the emergent vegetation is parted, although it is less frequent at small garden ponds. The blue tip of the abdomen of this delicate damselfly is in striking contrast to the black of the rest of the abdomen. As an adult, the species is the most tolerant of all British species of bad weather. In exposed northern sites, it is often the only species present. Larvae live amongst aquatic plants and take one or two years to complete development,[40] depending on temperature and food availability.[41] The flying season extends from mid-May to mid-September.

Ischnura pumilio (Scarce Blue-tailed Damselfly) is rare in Britain, having scattered populations in south and southwest England, Wales and Ireland. The species is restricted to warm, shallow, unshaded pools and seepages with little vegetation. Suitable sites are maintained by disturbance, either by the grazing and trampling of cattle or by vehicles in mineral extraction sites. Shading of sites by encroachment of scrub can lead to local extinction.[42] This small, delicate

FIG 26. A male *Pyrrhosoma nymphula* (Robert Thompson).

FIG 27. The female *Pyrrhosoma nymphula* is marked with a greater extent of black than the male (Robert Thompson).

damselfly is rarely abundant or conspicuous, but the sight of the vivid orange *aurantiaca* phase female colour form (Fig. 95, p.178) is arresting. Larvae develop within one year[43] and adults are on the wing from late May to July.

Pyrrhosoma nymphula (Large Red Damselfly) (Figs 26 & 27) is common and widespread throughout Britain and Ireland, breeding in a wide range of standing water habitats including garden ponds. *Pyrrhosoma nymphula* is the only odonate known to breed in Shetland.[44] It is usually the first damselfly to appear in the spring, during late April, and is a welcome sign that the odonatological season has begun, but the flying season can be prolonged such that late-emerging adults can still be present in early September. Larvae live amongst plant debris at the bottom and complete development in two years[45] or occasionally one year.[46]

ANISOPTERA – WARRIORFLIES

Aeshnidae – Hawkers

The family includes eight resident species: *Aeshna caerulea*, *A. cyanea*, *A. grandis*, *A. isosceles*, *A. juncea*, *A. mixta*, *Anax imperator* and *Brachytron pratense*. In addition, the following species are more or less frequent migrants: *Anax junius*, *A. parthenope* and *A. ephippiger*. Aeshnidae includes some of the largest species that occur in Britain. The larva of *Anax imperator* may reach over 55 millimetres in length and the adult has a wingspan of 105 millimetres. Adult *Aeshna* species have blue or green eyes with broad blue or yellow stripes on the sides and upper surfaces of the thorax, and characteristic rows of blue and yellow or green spots arranged in pairs along the upper surface of the abdomen. All species, with the exception of *Aeshna isosceles*, are sexually dimorphic, females having yellow or green abdominal spots and mature males having blue markings. Most species can be distinguished in the field, even when on the wing, by their distinctive markings. The thorax of *Anax imperator* and *A. junius* is green and lacks black markings; the abdomen has a black central upper stripe and the rest of the abdomen is blue in mature males but green in mature females (Fig. 29). Males of these two species can be distinguished only after close examination of the anal appendages and the marking on the vertex which, however, may vary greatly in outline.[47] In both *A. parthenope* and *A. ephippiger* the abdomen is yellow-brown, with a black central upper stripe and a prominent blue saddle at the base.

Hawkers are so-called because of the habit of males of flying persistently when patrolling their prospective breeding sites. That is, they are *fliers* (p.233). In most species, individual males may be present at the same site for many hours, but males of *Aeshna cyanea* may remain for less than 40 minutes at a pool before moving elsewhere, and in this way time-share breeding sites between several males[48] (Fig. 110, p.221). Similarly, males of *A. caerulea* do not remain long at any one pool.[49] Male aeshnids tend to be aggressive, and frequent clashes occur between patrolling males. In the early evening they are often seen over rough grassland and hedges in large mixed-species foraging aggregations when aggressive behaviour is suppressed. Aeshnids do occasionally perch during the day (especially in overcast conditions) by hanging from the branches of trees and bushes (Fig. 30). Mating usually lasts more than ten minutes,[50] and takes place amongst the foliage of bushes or trees or on the ground in long grass. It may last longer in poor weather. Females oviposit endophytically, usually unaccompanied by the male, except in the case of *Anax junius*, *A. parthenope* and *A. ephippiger* which often oviposit in tandem. Eggs are laid in submerged, floating or emergent plants or into rotting wood which may be protruding from the water, overhanging or even several metres away from the water (see p.82). Except in *Anax imperator* and *Brachytron pratense*, the eggs overwinter in *diapause* (Table 1, p.100; Box 16, p.167).

FIG 28. Larva of *Aeshna mixta* in stadium F-0. Aeshnid larvae typically have streamlined bodies, large compound eyes and short antennae (Robert Thompson).

Aeshnid larvae have smooth, streamlined bodies and large eyes (Fig. 28) and are typical claspers (Table 2, p.119), living amongst submerged vegetation and clinging to plant stems. They are active predators, often stalking their prey, which may include small fish and tadpoles. Species take from one to four years to complete development. *Brachytron pratense* and *Anax imperator* are Type 1 or *spring species*, passing their last winter as a F-0 larva in diapause and exhibiting synchronised emergence in spring or early summer, but the other aeshnids are Type 2 or *summer species*, emerging later and in a less synchronised fashion (Table 6, p.170).

Aeshna caerulea (Azure Hawker) occurs in northwest Scotland, and there is an isolated population in southwest Scotland. The breeding habitat comprises mossy bog pools, often in, or adjacent to, woodland.[51] The larvae remain in this stage for three winters.[52] Adults are seldom abundant, but may be seen basking in the sun on boulders or tree trunks, or flying low and fast around remote highland bog pools. They are on the wing from late May until early August.

Aeshna cyanea (Southern Hawker) (Fig. 2, p.18) is essentially a woodland species but is also frequently encountered over garden ponds where it readily breeds. Even in urban areas *A. cyanea* is a common visitor to gardens where its apparent curiosity will allow human observers to savour its rich green and blue pattern as it hovers close by. It occurs throughout England but becomes less frequent in the north, although it is currently expanding its range northwards. There are isolated populations in Scotland. It is a summer species and needs at least two years to complete larval development.[53] Adults are on the wing from July until October and frequently fly after dusk on warm summer evenings.

Aeshna grandis (Brown Hawker) is common in lowland parts of central and eastern England and Ireland but is absent from most of southwest England and Ireland, and from most of Wales and Scotland. It breeds in a wide variety of standing and slow-flowing waters. On a late summer's afternoon the sight of dozens gliding over a wild, uncut meadow, foraging for small insects, with the low sun making their wings shine like gold, can raise the spirits of an odonatologist jaded after a hot day in the field. The life cycle is thought to be completed in two to four years.[1] The flying season extends from June to October.

Aeshna isosceles (Norfolk Hawker) (Fig. 140, p.299) is the least common of the resident British aeshnids, being restricted to the Broads and fens of northeast Norfolk and Suffolk. The vivid green eyes of adult males are not easily overlooked or forgotten. The species breeds almost exclusively in those ditches and dykes that support the floating aquatic plant *Stratiotes aloides* (Water Soldier),[54] and is the only British species closely associated with a particular species of plant, although in continental Europe the association between *Aeshna isosceles* and this plant is not invariable (p.74). *Stratiotes aloides* will not survive in eutrophic sites and so *Aeshna isosceles* itself is vulnerable to this form of pollution. In addition, sea-level rise poses a prospective threat because most of the dragonfly's breeding sites are at low altitude and close to the coast. The life cycle is probably completed in two years.[1] The species is on the wing from early June until mid-July.

Aeshna juncea (Common Hawker) (Fig. 12, p.28) is widespread throughout western and northern Britain but rather local in, or absent from, much of south-east England. It typically occurs at upland pools and lakes on moors and bogs or in woodland. This is an aggressive species which frequently clashes with others of its own and other odonate species as it attempts to dominate the moorland pool it has selected as a breeding site. The larvae take two or more years to complete development.[55] Adults are on the wing from late June until early November.

Aeshna mixta (Migrant Hawker) (Fig. 138, p.297) is common and widespread in southeast England and is spreading north and west. The species was recorded in Ireland for the first time in 2000,[2] and populations have become established in north-east England in the last few years. In the 1930s the species was considered a scarce but regular migrant from southern Europe, having isolated breeding colonies in southeast England.[56] The species breeds in a wide variety of standing and slow-moving fresh and brackish waters. It is frequently seen foraging in large aggregations along sheltered hedgerows or sunlit gardens and glades into the early evening. It avoids acidic pools and so is absent from heathland and bogs. Larval development is completed within a few months[1] and so the species requires warm waters and is likely to extend its range in response to global warming. Adult males at breeding sites are less aggressive than other aeshnids. *Aeshna mixta* is the smallest of the British aeshnids and often forms foraging aggregations in the lee of hedges and trees in which adults dart to and fro and up and down at a height of several metres above ground. The flying season is from late July until early November.

Anax imperator (Emperor) (Figs 29 & 30) is common throughout much of southern England and Wales, although absent from uplands in this area, and has recently expanded its range northwards. It breeds in a wide variety of well-vegetated standing and slow-flowing waters, including garden ponds, which may support large numbers of larvae. The adult's large size and its habit of flying high above the water rather than skirting the edges, sometimes hovering, sometimes gliding or incisively dashing forward, give it an almost regal air that is unmatched by other odonates. The flying season extends from early June until late August. The life cycle is usually completed in two years, but may be completed in one year if larvae have reached their penultimate stadium by the late summer of the first season (p.162).[57]

FIG 29. As in other female Aeshnidae, the abdomen of *Anax imperator* lacks the vivid, bright colours of the male, although sometimes old females can become blueish (Robert Thompson).

FIG 30. A male *Anax imperator*. Like other Aeshnidae he has large compound eyes and hangs vertically with wings outspread when at rest (Robert Thompson).

Anax junius (Green Darner) is common and widespread in North America, but in September 1998 six individuals were recorded in Cornwall and the Isles of Scilly.[58] This is the first time that any *endemic* American species of odonate has been recorded in Europe (Appendix 2). The journey across the Atlantic was probably assisted by the passage of a hurricane passing up the east coast of North America.[59] This species, unlike *A. imperator*, often oviposits in tandem.

Anax parthenope (Lesser Emperor) (Fig. 136, p.295), a migrant from southern Europe, is expanding its European range northwards and was first recorded in Britain in 1996.[60] Since then, adults have been recorded in low numbers almost every year and successful breeding was recorded at two sites in Cornwall in 1999 when F-0 exuviae were found in small, well-vegetated ponds.[61] In Britain it has been seen between June and September at localities as far apart as Cornwall and Orkney and several in between.

Brachytron pratense (Hairy Hawker) (Fig. 134, p.293) has a patchy distribution over southern England, where it appears to be spreading, and Wales. There are a few colonies in northeast England and western Scotland. It is widespread in central Ireland. The species frequents habitats that have a linear margin, including ditches, dykes, and canals that are rich in water plants. The larvae are frequent amongst dead vegetation, and females often lay into floating mats of dead reeds or rushes. This small, blue hawker is usually the first anisopteran of the year on the wing, but often offers only a fleeting glimpse as it zigzags between clumps of emerging plants at the edge of a fenland drainage dyke. The life cycle can be completed in one year,[62] but a two-year larval development time is thought to be usual.[1] Adults are on the wing from early May to late June.

Anax ephippiger (Vagrant Emperor) is a scarce migrant that turns up in Britain in low numbers rather infrequently. It was recorded only five times prior to 1980; between 1980 and 1998 there were eleven records, but it has not been recorded since. This last date coincides with a large increase in the number of sightings of *Anax parthenope*, which closely resembles *A. ephippiger* in flight, so it is possible that some of the earlier records of *A. ephippiger* were misidentifications. The 1971 record of *A. ephippiger* from the Shetland Isles and the Cornish record in 1988 are based on specimens deposited in The Natural History Museum, London. The species breeds in pools that are often temporary and saline, in sub-Saharan Africa and through the Middle East to Pakistan, but has never been recorded as breeding in Britain. Adults undergo long migratory flights and are apparently carried to Britain by strong southwesterly winds.[63] Most individuals arrive in Britain in late summer and autumn.

Gomphidae – Club-tails

Gomphus vulgatissimus (Common Club-tail) is the only species of Gomphidae currently resident in Britain, although ten species are known from mainland Europe. A distinguishing feature of adults of the family is that, unlike other families of European Anisoptera, the compound eyes do not meet on the top of the head (Fig. 31). Adult *G. vulgatissimus* are of medium size and have yellow and black bodies, becoming green and black in mature males, and they have a distinctive swelling towards the tip of the abdomen. Adults are best seen when they are emerging in large numbers from slow-flowing rivers (especially the Thames, Arun and Severn) in early to mid-May. *Gomphus vulgatissimus* is a Type 1 or spring species (Table 6, p.170), and emergence is highly synchronised. After emergence the adults disperse into the hinterland, especially into adjacent woodland, and can be difficult to find.[64] Males perch on shaded, tree-lined stretches of the river, patrolling close to the water surface. Females oviposit alone,

FIG 31. A young female *Gomphus vulgatissimus*. Her eyes do not meet over the top of the head, a feature characteristic of Gomphidae (Robert Thompson).

dipping the tip of the abdomen into the water to wash off the eggs. They usually breed in slow-flowing rivers, but will occasionally breed in standing water where a habitat is situated close to a river.[65] The larvae burrow into the silt and debris on the river bed and are thought to take three to five years to complete development.[66] The larvae are squat and differ from other anisopterans in having an enlarged third antennal segment (Fig. 32).

Gomphus vulgatissimus occurs on slow-flowing rivers in south-central England, the Welsh borders and southwest Wales where it can be locally common. A colony previously known in the New Forest until the 1960s is now probably extinct.[1] Water pollution, dredging and clearance of bankside trees and woodland close to breeding sites may threaten populations. Removal of aquatic and emergent vegetation is not necessarily deleterious and the species is able to survive on rivers severely affected by boating that are no longer suitable for *Platycnemis pennipes*.[66] Probably the surest way to see the adult is to time a visit to

FIG 32. Larva of *Gomphus vulgatissimus* in stadium F-0. This species is exceptional among Anisoptera in having a conspicuously enlarged third antennal segment in the larva (Robert Thompson).

one of the rivers on which it breeds so as to coincide with a mass emergence. On the right morning in May, hundreds of adults can be seen emerging on the bankside within a few hours. Adults are on the wing from early May until the end of June.

Cordulegastridae – Golden-ringed Dragonflies

Cordulegaster boltonii (Golden-ringed Dragonfly) is the only species of Cordulegastridae that occurs in Britain, although another five species are known from mainland Europe. This large, yellow-and-black-striped species frequents small moorland and heathland streams. A distinctive characteristic of adult Cordulegastridae is that the large green eyes meet at a point (as distinct from a line as in the Aeshnidae) above the head. Males (Fig. 10, p.26) and females are similar in colour, but the females have a distinctive, long, stout ovipositor protruding beyond the tip of the abdomen (Fig. 33), justifying the common name for the genus, 'spike-tail', used in North America (and Ireland, where it has never

FIG 33. The long ovipositor of this female *Cordulegaster boltonii* is characteristic of Cordulegastridae, as is the way that the compound eyes meet at a point across the top of the head (Robert Thompson).

FIG 34. The larva of *Cordulegaster boltonii*, here shown in stadium F-0, is a shallow *burrower*, usually living partly buried in stream sediments. The head is similar in shape to that of a libellulid but the abdomen is more elongate (Robert Thompson).

been recorded!). Adult males patrol long stretches of small streams, flying low and fast, close to the water surface, occasionally hovering or perching on overhanging vegetation. The males are not territorial in the strict sense, but will clash with other males of the same species which they encounter on their patrol flights.[67] Females oviposit alone, using their robust ovipositor to thrust eggs deep into the substrate of the stream. The squat larvae typically live partly buried in detritus and gravel (Fig. 34) and probably take up to five years to complete development.[1]

Cordulegaster boltonii is common in southern, western and northern Britain where it breeds in shallow upland or heathland streams with a gravel substrate. It is worth searching for the spectacular larvae, which can be surprisingly abundant amongst gravel. The female is equally arresting when seen working like a pneumatic drill to insert her eggs deep into the substrate. Adults frequently perch amongst bushes of *Ulex* (Gorse) and are obligingly tolerant of the photographer. The species is not seriously threatened within its range, but populations may suffer from plantations of conifers which shade the water and limit larval habitats by reducing organic detritus and emergent plants.[68] Adults are on the wing between the end of May and September.

Corduliidae – Emerald Warriorflies

This family includes three species currently resident in Britain: *Cordulia aenea*, *Somatochlora arctica* and *S. metallica*. A fourth, *Oxygastra curtisii*, formerly bred in Britain, but is now probably extinct here. The family has a predominantly northern and alpine distribution in Europe, which makes the species especially vulnerable to global warming. Adults are medium sized and metallic green with yellow or orange patches on the head and abdomen and bright green eyes (Fig. 35). *Cordulia aenea*, *Somatochlora arctica* and *S. metallica*, which may occur together at some sites, can only be distinguished reliably by close examination of the male anal appendages or female ovipositor. *Oxygastra curtisii* has distinctive orange-yellow spots down the upper mid-line of the abdomen. Male corduliids have a restless, inquisitive flight when at water, patrolling a stretch of the bank and performing frequent bouts of hovering. They usually remain for less than

FIG 35. The male *Cordulia aenea*, with its metallic green and bronze body and bright green compound eyes, is typical of Corduliidae (Robert Thompson).

FIG 36. Larva of *Somatochlora metallica* in stadium F-0. Its long legs and squat body, which are adaptations for hiding amongst leaf litter, are typical of Corduliidae (Robert Thompson).

30 minutes at the water. Mating takes place in the tree tops and is prolonged, sometimes lasting for over one hour.[69] Females oviposit unaccompanied by the male, hovering over the water and rapidly tapping the surface with the tip of the abdomen. Females of *Somatochlora metallica* sometimes alight to deposit eggs into damp moss at the water's edge.[70] Away from water, adult corduliids are often seen feeding in woodland clearings where they may rest, hanging from branches or clinging to tree trunks. Corduliid larvae have squat, broad abdomens, long legs that extend beyond the tip of the abdomen and small eyes (Fig. 36). Corduliid larvae live amongst leaf litter and debris in the shallow margins and so populations are likely to be damaged by dredging and clearance of leaf litter or excessive removal of bankside trees. All are Type 1 or spring species (Table 6, p.170), exhibiting synchronised emergence of adults in spring or early summer.

Cordulia aenea (Downy Emerald) has a local distribution throughout southern and western England, with outposts in northeast Norfolk, western Scotland

and the extreme southwest of Ireland. Larvae probably take three years to complete development[71] and may climb several metres up bankside trees before emergence. Adults are usually encountered at ponds within large woodland blocks between mid-May and mid-July. The bright green eyes are often the first thing that draws the observer's attention to a male as he darts, hovers and pirouettes in small bays along the banks of tree-lined ponds. In Britain, this species has probably declined following nutrient enrichment and the loss of woodland ponds. Its current, patchy distribution in Britain is probably the result of fragmentation of ancient forest.

Oxygastra curtisii (Orange-spotted Emerald) (Fig. 130, p.286) was known from small populations on the River Tamar, on the Cornwall-Devon border, and from the Moors River, in the New Forest, where the last individuals were seen in the early 1960s. The habitat was made unsuitable by sewage contamination and overshading by bankside trees.[72] In Britain the species was known to breed only in slow-flowing rivers, but in continental Europe there are a few records from standing water.[14]

Somatochlora arctica (Northern Emerald) is rare, occurring only in northwest Scotland, and maintaining an isolated population in southwest Ireland. The species breeds in mossy bog pools in open woodland where population densities are low. Larval development is likely to take at least two years.[73] Adults are on the wing from late May until late September.

Somatochlora metallica (Brilliant Emerald) (Fig. 7, p.24) has two centres of distribution, one in southeast England and the other in the Scottish Highlands. It is possible that the northern population may represent a postglacial relic whereas the population in southeast England may be the result of recent colonisation from continental Europe. Genetic analysis may shed light on the origins of these two populations. The southern population appears to be expanding at present.[74] *Somatochlora metallica* is encountered from July to early September at large woodland ponds, lakes and lochs that have extensive margins of moss in Scotland and, in the south, also on slow-flowing rivers and canals sheltered by overhanging trees. The species is similar in appearance and habits to *Cordulia aenea* but seems less furtive, flying faster and further before pausing more briefly to hover, and being less reluctant to enter shaded overhangs. Larvae in southern England probably take two or three years to complete development.

Libellulidae – Chasers, Skimmers and Darters
There are ten species of Libellulidae regularly breeding in Britain and these are supplemented by an additional seven frequent or infrequent migrant species,

some of which have bred in Britain. Adult libellulids are small to medium sized with a yellow, blue or red abdomen. Adults of most species are sexually dimorphic. The three species of *Libellula* have a dark patch at the base of each hind wing. The males of *L. fulva* and *L. depressa* (Fig. 38, p.61) develop a blue pruinescence as they mature, but the females remain yellowish. The abdomen is broad and stout in *L. depressa*, but more slender in *L. fulva* and *L. quadrimaculata*. Males and females of *L. quadrimaculata* are similar in colour, remaining brownish throughout life. The two British species in the genus *Orthetrum* have unpigmented wings, and mature males also develop blue pruinescence (Fig. 39, p.63) while the females remain predominantly yellow (Fig. 40, p.63). *Orthetrum cancellatum* is a large species. The male has prominent black markings on the abdomen, which has a conspicuous black tip. *Orthetrum coerulescens* is smaller and lacks black abdominal markings. Mature males in most species of the genus *Sympetrum* have a red abdomen (Fig. 43, p.66) (the abdomen is black in *S. danae* (Fig. 41, p.64), whereas the abdomen of females and immature males is yellow (Fig. 42, p.65). Species of *Sympetrum* (especially females) can be difficult to distinguish on the wing, and individuals often need to be examined at rest or in the hand when details of wing and leg coloration will usually permit identification (Appendix 2). *Leucorrhinia dubia* is characterised by its white face (Fig. 139, p.298). It also has a brown patch at the base of the hind wing. The abdomen is predominantly black, having yellow spots in the female and immature male. These spots become red in mature males.

Libellulidae breed in a wide range of standing and slow-flowing waters. The larvae are squat. Larvae of *Libellula* and *Orthetrum* are shallow burrowers (Table 2, p.117). They have short legs, live buried in the mud, silt and debris on the bottom, and their bodies are clothed with setae to which particles adhere. In contrast, *Sympetrum* and *Leucorrhinia* larvae (Fig. 37) are *sprawlers* (Table 2, p.119). They have longer legs and their bodies are not covered in setae. They live amongst submerged plants. *Sympetrum* larvae have a Type 3 life cycle (Box 16, p.167), completing development within one year, but development in the other genera is more protracted and may take up to three years. Emergence of adults is closely synchronised (in spring) in *Libellula* and *Leucorrhinia* but less synchronised in the other libellulids. Unlike aeshnids, libellulids are *perchers* (p.233). Adult males of most species are strongly territorial and are frequently observed perching, often in large numbers, on tall plants around the edges of ponds and lakes or on the banks of rivers. From there each male makes sallies to chase away rival males, catch prey, or pursue females, before returning to the same perch. Copulation in *Libellula* and *Orthetrum* species is often brief, lasting just a few seconds while in flight,[75] or may be more prolonged and continue for a few

FIG 37. Larva of *Leucorrhinia dubia* in stadium F-0. This species is a sprawler, being squat, having relatively long legs and lacking a dense covering of setae (Robert Thompson).

minutes on the ground or a perch.[76] In *Sympetrum* and *Leucorrhinia* species, copulation is usually longer, lasting from 5–60 minutes,[77] and is completed while the pair are perched on the ground or amongst foliage. Species of *Sympetrum* usually oviposit in tandem, the male swinging the female down to the water to wash the accumulated eggs off the *vulvar scale*. After a few oviposition *bouts* the male releases the female and, like the other libellulid species, guards her while hovering nearby. Eventually the male may fly off, leaving the female to complete oviposition alone (p.86). Eggs laid in late summer by *Sympetrum* species may hatch within a few days, although most enter *diapause* and do not hatch until the following spring (see pp.98–9). However, in most libellulids the first winter is passed in the larval stage (Table 1, p.100).

    Crocothemis erythraea (Scarlet Darter) is common and widespread in southern Europe and well known for its migratory habits. Since 1995 it has been recorded four times in Britain and is likely to reappear. It breeds in a wide variety of standing waters including those that are brackish or slightly polluted. The species is not easily distinguished (even in the hand) from *C. servilia*, a species liable to be imported with aquarium plants from the tropics (Appendix 2).[78]

Between 1980 and 2000 the breeding range of this species has been extending steadily northwards in western Europe.[79]

Leucorrhinia dubia (White-faced Darter) (Fig. 139, p.298) is a rare, resident species breeding in bogs in northwest England and northern Scotland. Its habit of resting on bare ground or low in vegetation makes it difficult to locate at first, but when disturbed it will suddenly fly off in an erratic manner for a short distance before settling again. The larvae (Fig. 37) live amongst submerged or floating mats of moss in bog pools. The species has recently been lost from Thursley Common, a nature reserve in Surrey, its southernmost site in England, apparently due to changes in habitat quality, possibly exacerbated by global warming. The species has a predominantly northern or alpine distribution in Europe and consequently can be expected to contract its range northward as average annual temperatures increase. *Leucorrhinia dubia* is also threatened by the destruction of bogs by commercial peat extraction by the horticultural industry, and by drainage and afforestation. It is likely that larvae require two years to complete development, although some individuals may complete it in one or three years.[80] Adults are on the wing from mid-May to early August.

Libellula depressa (Broad-bodied Chaser) (Fig. 38) is common and widespread throughout southern England and Wales, but has recently increased its range

FIG 38. A male *Libellula depressa*. The blue pruinescence (a waxy secretion) develops as the insect matures (Robert Thompson).

northwards. It breeds in a wide variety of standing water sites, preferring non-acidic, open-water habitats in early *successional* stages with few aquatic plants. It is often one of the first visitors to a newly created garden pond where it will readily breed. The pond becomes less attractive to it as the aquatic vegetation develops, and *L. depressa* will become lost as a breeding species if the plants are not kept in check. The large size and broad, bright blue abdomen of the male makes him conspicuous as he patrols a garden pond. A rustling of wings may reveal a female repeatedly tapping the water surface at the edge of the pond, or she may be encountered as, resembling an enormous hornet, she suns herself on the outer branches of a bush (Fig. 107, p.201). Larvae can complete development in one year[81] but two years are usually necessary.[1] The flying season lasts from mid-May until early August.

Libellula fulva (Scarce Chaser) is restricted to short stretches of a few nutrient-rich, slow-flowing rivers in southeast England where aquatic and bankside growth of plants is well developed. The species is rare in Britain, although it may be expanding its range as water quality improves. A few new colonies have recently been discovered in Kent and on the River Wey in Surrey and Hampshire.[82] This is one of the few species of Odonata in which the female out-shines the male. The sight of the golden-orange abdomen and shining wings of an immature female perching on tall vegetation in the sun makes a rewarding climax to a visit to one of the lush lowland rivers where the species breeds. *Libellula fulva* is adversely affected by overshading, pollution, over-abstraction, dredging and canalisation. Larvae probably require two years to complete development.[1] The flying season extends from late May to early August.

Libellula quadrimaculata (Four-spotted Chaser) (Fig. 111, p.229) is widespread throughout Britain and Ireland, breeding in a wide range of habitats including heathland, moorland, bogs, fens, canals, dykes, slow-flowing streams, gravel pits, lakes and ponds, and even brackish water. It is often abundant where it occurs, and the males are fiercely territorial. Swirling aerial 'dogfights' frequently develop as *conspecific* males clash over hotly disputed territories, or they engage other species, including larger aeshnids. The species is migratory, at least in mainland Europe, and is often encountered far from suitable breeding sites. Larvae probably take two years to complete development.[1] Adults are on the wing from late May until mid-August.

Orthetrum cancellatum (Black-tailed Skimmer) (Figs 39 & 40) is common and widespread in southern England and Wales, and central Ireland, and appears to be extending its range northwards. It is a typical occupant of gravel pits, but breeds in a variety of pools, lakes and slow-flowing rivers. Males typically land on bare patches of ground or dry moss where they bask. Here they make a

FIG 39. The mature male of *Orthetrum cancellatum* frequently perches on dead tree trunks, bare ground or rocks (Robert Thompson).

FIG 40. A female *Orthetrum cancellatum* whose colour resembles that of an immature male (Robert Thompson).

tempting subject for the photographer, but more often than not, as the photographer settles to take the shot, the male will speed away to another basking patch just out of range. The species may be lost from sites in late successional stages. Adults often take relatively large insect prey such as butterflies, grasshoppers and adult Zygoptera. The larvae probably take two or three years to complete development.[83] The flying season lasts from late May until early August.

Orthetrum coerulescens (Keeled Skimmer) (Fig. 5, p.21) is locally common at small pools and streams on bogs, where it has an affinity for even the most subtle flow of water, but is patchily distributed in southern and western Britain and Ireland. It is threatened by encroachment and fragmentation of heathlands, especially in Dorset, and by peat extraction. The males rise from perches around bog pools or clash over the open water, but are drab in comparison to the females with their gold-stained wings. Larval development probably takes two years.[83] Adults are on the wing from early June to late August.

Pantala flavescens (Wandering Glider) is pan-tropical and a regular migrant. It has been recorded in Britain four times, most recently in 1989, but it is unlikely to colonise Britain. The species breeds in small, shallow, often temporary pools, where larvae develop very rapidly.[84]

FIG 41. A mature male *Sympetrum danae*. The habit of perching with wings swept forward on top of prominent vegetation is characteristic of many Libellulidae (Robert Thompson).

FIG 42. The immature male of *Sympetrum danae* has a coloration resembling that of the female (Robert Thompson).

Sympetrum danae (Black Darter) (Figs 41 & 42) is the smallest of the British libellulids. It is widespread and common in northern Britain and Ireland but is local further south where it is most frequently encountered on heathland, moorland and bogs. It has an erratic flight of short duration when put up from low moorland vegetation, but immature males can often be closely approached as they perch in rows on fences, basking in the low, late-summer sun. The species is not threatened nationally, but populations in East Anglia have been severely reduced in the last few decades by agricultural intensification and drainage. Like other *Sympetrum* species, adults disperse widely, and individuals may be seen far from breeding sites. Unlike most other libellulids, males are not strongly territorial. Larvae hatch in early spring and complete development within a few months. The flying season is from mid-July until mid-September.

Sympetrum flaveolum (Yellow-winged Darter) is widespread in Europe and an infrequent migrant to Britain. In some years (notably 1926, 1945, 1955, 1995 and 2006) huge numbers appeared in southeast and eastern England.[85] Aggregations of adults are often encountered amongst tall grasses in meadows. The species breeds in shallow pools and in shallow, well-vegetated margins of lakes. The species has not established any long-term breeding colonies in Britain.

Sympetrum fonscolombii (Red-veined Darter) is primarily a tropical, migratory species whose distribution includes the Mediterranean region and which often migrates into northern Europe. It is a frequent migrant to Britain where it appears in most years, especially in southwest England. Recent major landfalls were recorded in 1992, 1996, 1998 and 2000.[86] Recently, breeding has been sustained over a few years at some sites in Cornwall and Kent[87] but there is no clear indication that the species has become established in Britain. It breeds in a wide variety of shallow, standing fresh or brackish waters.

Sympetrum meridionale (Southern Darter) has been recorded four times in Britain, most recently in 1901[1] (see Appendix 2). The species is common in the Mediterranean.

Sympetrum pedemontanum (Banded Darter) has been recorded once in Britain, during 1995.[88] It occurs in southern central Europe where it breeds in marshes and is especially frequent in uplands. The species is expanding its range northwards in Europe and so may reappear in Britain in future.

Sympetrum sanguineum (Ruddy Darter) (Fig. 43) has a southeasterly distribution in England, Wales and Ireland, and is currently expanding its range in England

FIG 43. Like *Sympetrum sanguineum*, most mature males of *Sympetrum* species are predominantly red (Robert Thompson).

northward and westward. Suggestions that it may be a relatively recent colonist in Ireland appear to be unfounded, and new records are probably due to increased recorder effort.[2] The species is usually encountered at ponds, lakes and marshes with extensive stands of emergent vegetation and often in woodland where the bright crimson of the male abdomen seems to glow in the semi-shade. Eggs are sometimes laid in vegetation, damp mud or hollows near the water's edge,[89] and do not hatch until they are covered with water in early spring. The species is a vagrant: migrants fly in from continental Europe each summer, and males are often encountered at water bodies where breeding does not occur. The shallow, well-vegetated sites in which the species breeds are likely to be damaged by clearance of emergent plants, dredging and succession of terrestrial plants. The life cycle lasts one year.[11] The flying season extends from late June until early November.

Sympetrum striolatum (Common Darter) (Fig. 1, p.17) is one of Britain's commonest species. It is abundant and widespread throughout most of Britain and Ireland but becomes less frequent in northeast Scotland. Populations in northwest Scotland and western Ireland are more extensively marked with black, leading some authorities to regard them as a distinct species which has been named *S. nigrescens*.[90] However, the evidence for this is not compelling and *S. nigrescens* is probably only a *melanic* form of *S. striolatum*.[91] The species breeds readily in most standing and slow-flowing waters, including brackish water. It is a frequent resident at even small garden ponds where it tolerates the close approach of the inquisitive odonatologist. Demonstrations of territoriality, oviposition, foraging, reproductive behaviour and larval habitat preferences are obligingly provided. Larval development is completed within one year.[92] Adults can be seen from mid-June until as late as December in mild years when prey is still available. They are often seen basking on pale, *insolated* surfaces in autumn. The British population is sometimes supplemented by migrants from continental Europe.[93]

Sympetrum vulgatum (Vagrant Darter) is a rare migrant to Britain, but may be overlooked because of its close similarity to the abundant *S. striolatum*. The species is common and widespread in central and northeast Europe where it breeds in a wide variety of standing-water habitats.

OPPORTUNITIES FOR INVESTIGATION

Few hard data exist on the duration of the larval stages (voltinism) of Odonata in Britain. Some of the information given on voltinism is anecdotal or based on evidence derived from European studies which may not apply to the same species in Britain. The duration of the larval stage in a southern European population of a species is likely to be less than in a northern European population of the same species because rate of larval development is strongly influenced by temperature. Raising larvae in aquaria at home or in the laboratory is unreliable as evidence of voltinism in nature because it is difficult to duplicate outside temperatures and food availability, both of which have a significant influence on larval development rate.

It is not easy to obtain information on voltinism, but it is a subject on which the amateur odonatologist can make a useful contribution because it requires no expensive equipment but only patience, careful observation and field skills. Species emerging within one year of a pond being dug provide unequivocal evidence of a *univoltine* life cycle. The presence of different age *cohorts* in a larval population sampled in late autumn, winter or early spring can also provide useful inferences about voltinism. If larvae are absent in late autumn but very small larvae are present in spring, this suggests that eggs undergo a winter diapause and that larvae develop within a few months during the spring and summer. If only one age class of a particular species is present, this suggests a univoltine life cycle. If larvae in very early stadia are present together with final or penultimate-stage larvae this indicates a two-year or semivoltine life cycle. A three-year life cycle would be indicated if larvae in the earliest stadia were present together with mid-stage larvae and final-stadium larvae. This presupposes that the larvae can be accurately identified in all stages, which for several of the British species is not possible at present.

CHAPTER 3

Habitat Selection and Oviposition

THE HABITAT

T HOSE WHO STUDY Odonata soon become aware that each species, as larva and adult, frequents a particular kind of habitat (Box 4). An adult male of *Brachytron pratense* characteristically patrols the margins of reeds flanking static or slowly flowing water, and the larva clings tightly to floating or submerged stems of reeds or plants of similar diameter. Dragonflies do not exhibit parental care in the strict sense. The closest they come to doing so is when the female, sometimes guided by her male partner, lays her eggs in a site favourable for development of their progeny.

Some species of Odonata, probably only a few, exhibit *philopatry*, returning when reproductively mature precisely to the water body whence they emerged. The Palaearctic *Lestes barbarus* does this,[1] but many Odonata apparently disperse widely across the countryside seeking water bodies that meet their needs. The arrival of many species of Anisoptera and Zygoptera at ecologically isolated ponds[2] and the rapid colonisation by Odonata of newly constructed water bodies are consistent with this conclusion, although most individuals of some other species (e.g. *Coenagrion mercuriale*) appear to stay close to the emergence site throughout adult life.[3] Having arrived at a water body, adults seem to choose whether to localise there or to move on. Many of the adults seen by Jochen Lempert[2] arriving at an ecologically isolated pond departed after briefly approaching it closely.

Thus *habitat selection* is a regular feature of the odonate behavioural repertoire. Indeed, it is difficult to imagine a behavioural trait that plays a more important role in contributing to the *inclusive fitness* of a species. As we shall see

....

BOX 4

A PLACE TO LIVE

The habitat of a species (literally its dwelling place) varies with space
and time, over a spectrum of levels of scale, complexity and heterogeneity.
Plants play a major role as components of a dragonfly's biotic environment, especially for species that use plants as egg-laying substrates (Box 7,
p.80). So it can be clarifying to apply different terms to different levels of
habitat complexity according to the plantscape – the architecture and
texture of plants, at the level of the community and at the level of the
foliage structure of individual plants. No consensus exists regarding
appropriate terms to describe levels within this hierarchy, but we use the
following terms in this book: at one end of the scale is the *biotope*, an area
having a characteristic association of plants and other organisms (the
biota), for example, a marsh, a waterlogged peat bog, a willow carr, a
stream. A habitat is a place within a biotope where a given species lives.
A habitat may be subdivided from a functional point of view into places
where different activities are centred; so one can speak of an oviposition
habitat, foraging habitat and so on. The term *microhabitat* is usefully
applied to an animal's chosen surroundings at the most intimate level –
for example, the deposits of gravel, sand or silt in which a larva burrows,
or the matrix of submerged foliage amongst which a larva sprawls. So,
whereas a larva's habitat may be a lake margin, its microhabitat may be
the surface of fine silt at a depth of 1–2 metres in the *littoral* zone. Quite
another concept is the *niche*, which combines behavioural and ecological
parameters with the physical habitat. A species' niche is its functional role
and position in an ecosystem. It might also be termed metaphorically its
profession or occupation. For example, the niche of a larva of *Lestes sponsa*
could be described as that of an active, surface-living, plant-dwelling,
predominantly *diurnal*, intermediate predator with a high thermal
coefficient for growth and an aversion to water bodies occupied by fish.

....

in Chapter 5, larvae of different species are closely adapted in many respects to
different kinds of habitat and microhabitat; it follows that their prospects of
survival will depend to a large extent on the eggs from which they originated
being placed in a habitat that suits them.

HABITAT SELECTION

Where habitat selection is concerned, it is useful to distinguish between two properties of a habitat: *ultimate factors* and *proximate cues* (Box 5). All British species of Odonata develop in water, be it flowing or static. So we have no need to consider here cues that might be used by those tropical species that develop in tree cavities or in moist leaf litter on the forest floor.[5] The received hypothesis, due largely to Hansruedi Wildermuth,[6] sees habitat selection as a stepwise process involving successive binary decisions, of increasing precision. At each stage, the searching adult will be making a choice based on a proximate cue. A challenge for the investigator is to discover, for each species, the nature of these proximate cues. An exciting advance towards this end has been the discovery[7] that some insects find their aquatic habitats on the basis of reflection-polarisation patterns of skylight visible on water surfaces.[8] Polarised *ultraviolet light* is the critical stimulus, reception of which is mediated by microvilli in the compound eyes.[9] Odonata are among the aquatic insects able to detect such stimuli.[10] There is little doubt that the first proximate cue to be perceived by a searching dragonfly is the presence of a water surface, detected through a response to the polarisation of light reflected from a horizontal surface.[11] By analogy with findings from other aquatic insects, this response would allow the dragonfly to discriminate between different kinds of water body. This is because the sensitivity maxima of the reflection-polarisation receptors of some aquatic insects occupy different parts of the visual spectrum that correlate with patterns of reflected light characteristic of different kinds of aquatic habitat.[12] Furthermore, the reflection-polarisation pattern visible at the water surface varies, among other things, according to the depth of the water body, the material composition of the bottom and the dissolved organic materials, and so can convey useful information about the suitability of a site for a searching dragonfly.[13] There is a physical basis for the process by which a species is attracted to (or *avoids* in the case of a *teneral* adult) an aquatic habitat. Anyone who has flown in a light aircraft low over wetlands facing the sun when it is near the horizon will know how conspicuous the smallest patch of surface water can be (even to the human eye which lacks polarisation receptors). So a dragonfly, flying towards the sun, especially at dusk,[13] would have a superb sensory mechanism for locating surface water. A response to the wavelength of reflected light can also permit Odonata to recognise plants used as oviposition substrates, on the basis of light reflected from floating leaves, as in *Erythromma najas*,[14] or from the shape of leaf margins, as in *Pyrrhosoma nymphula*.[15] The experiments

....

BOX 5

ULTIMATE FACTORS AND PROXIMATE CUES

When the attributes of a habitat that play a role in habitat selection
are being analysed it is helpful to distinguish between so-called ultimate
factors and proximate cues. Ultimate factors are those properties of
the environment that exert selection pressure that maintains a specific
kind of behaviour. An example would be predation over evolutionary
time that affects larval survival. Predation correlates, among other things,
with the presence of submerged aquatic plants that provide refuges
from predators. The plants could provide proximate cues – features of
the environment detectable by adults and to which they respond when
choosing a habitat. Proximate cues are presumably reliable indicators
of ultimate factors and represent signposts guiding the choice of a habitat
in which a species' inclusive fitness will be enhanced. An example of a
proximate cue for habitat selection by a species of *Calopteryx* would be
current speed, used by the female (and perhaps also the male) when
choosing a site for copulation and therefore also for subsequent
oviposition. Current speed correlates with, among other things, the
susceptibility of eggs to *parasitism* by minute wasps.[4] In this case, it has
been suggested that current speed, the proximate cue, is being used
as an indicator of an ultimate factor, parasitism risk, which affects the
inclusive fitness of the ovipositing female and her male partner, who
are unable to detect the level of potential parasitism directly.

....

leading to these conclusions have greatly increased our understanding of the
crucial, early stages in habitat selection. It is no exaggeration to say that a
response to polarised light is the most important mechanism that guides
Odonata in their selection of habitats and oviposition sites.[16]

The determining role played by horizontal reflection polarisation in habitat
selection explains how dragonflies sometimes alight, or oviposit, on unsuitable
substrates, such as the bodywork of cars,[17] reflections from which are strongly
polarised,[18] and oil lakes by which dragonflies (such as *Aeshna mixta, Anax
imperator* and *Sympetrum vulgatum*) can be deceived, attracted and trapped.[19]
The observation of *Cordulegaster boltonii* striking the surface of an asphalt road
with its abdomen[20] presumably has a similar explanation. It is not uncommon

for riverine dragonflies to be deceived by roads: Hansruedi Wildermuth watched a male of the riverine aeshnid, *Boyeria irene*, searching intensely for females along the border of a road that had structures resembling those at streams.[21]

The occasional occurrence of some normally riverine Odonata in standing water[22] may result from agitation of the water surface that might make it resemble flowing water. Some Odonata are notoriously catholic in their habitat choice: *Aeshna cyanea* larvae have been found in small coastal pools just below the splash zone.[23]

Here, sounding a cautionary note, we should mention a remarkable observation of an adult *Cordulegaster boltonii* (an obligate stream-dweller) following precisely, for more than 100 metres, the course of a stream that had been totally enclosed within a culvert hidden beneath pavement.[24] Clearly much remains to be elucidated about proximate cues that dragonflies use for habitat selection.

Having arrived at a water body, the dragonfly must exercise choice based on features that we know empirically to be correlated with its ecological tolerance, such as the size and shape of the water body, the disposition of emergent plants around the margin, the degree of shading, the riparian ground cover (which may comprise meadows or woodlands), and floating plants or algal mats. Mowing of riparian meadows lowered the density and changed the species composition, density and *dispersal* rate of zygopterans occupying a lowland brook near Freiburg.[25] This result of habitat modification emphasises the great importance of terrestrial habitats for dragonfly assemblages and therefore, one supposes, for habitat selection.

Some species exhibit a wide range of ecological tolerance, that is to say they are *eurytopic*. By definition, they exercise little further choice once they have located a body of water. Among British Odonata, eurytopic species include *Enallagma cyathigerum* and *Ischnura elegans*. To learn more about the later steps (if any) in habitat selection, we must look at so-called *stenotopic* species, namely those with a narrow ecological tolerance. It is from such species that the notion derives that some species occur exclusively in habitats possessing certain attributes. Although the concept is appealing to the tidy minded, and although (in field experiments) some species do indeed exhibit marked and highly predictable selectivity when choosing oviposition substrates, few if any species comply strictly with this concept. In field experiments *Platycnemis pennipes* can exhibit marked and highly predictable selectivity when choosing an oviposition substrate (e.g. flower heads of the water lily *Nuphar lutea*)[26] but this may reflect little more than the alternatives offered in the choice experiment, because this species can sometimes be abundant at sites where this water lily is absent. For many years it was supposed that the Palaearctic *Aeshna viridis* reproduced only in habitats containing the Water Soldier, *Stratiotes aloides*, a floating plant with spiny leaves in which females oviposit and larvae dwell. A survey by Oliver Leyshon and Norman Moore revealed that *Aeshna isosceles* is also closely associated with this plant.[27] As with *A. viridis*, the association, though strikingly close, is not invariable. In a survey at Castle Marshes, Barnby, Suffolk, during 1991–2, F-0 exuviae of *A. isosceles* were found in nine dykes and sections with *S. aloides* and in none without. Exuviae were confined to dykes having a high density of *S. aloides*, and all exuviae were found within 1 metre of an *S. aloides* plant, many being attached to it. Likewise, most adult male and female *A. isosceles* were observed on dykes containing abundant *S. aloides*, and oviposition was confined to dykes having a dense population of this plant. Interestingly, *A. isosceles* is virtually confined to water bodies with *S. aloides* in Britain but not on the continent of Europe. The reason for the close association between dragonfly and plant in Britain is unknown. However, abundance of *S. aloides* indicates unpolluted water and therefore a rich aquatic *invertebrate* fauna.[28] Thus it may be that, at the edges of its range (as in Britain), or in areas of low background productivity, the presence of *S. aloides* is a useful proximate cue indicating a rich source of prey for larvae. In Britain, *A. isosceles* is now restricted to a few grazing marshes which are relatively isolated from polluted water.[29] In the Netherlands and Germany, where *Aeshna viridis* is associated with *S. aloides*, if such habitats are left unmanaged, in due course they become unsuitable for continued occupancy by *S. aloides* because this plant represents a successional stage. As it happens, farmers harvest the *S. aloides* for pig food and by doing so arrest ecological succession and thus secure the continued occupancy of water bodies by the plant and therefore also by *A. viridis*![30] Exceptions to the association between *A. viridis* and *S. aloides* exist, notably in the Netherlands[31] and in the eastern Palaearctic where the species is associated with willow bushes.[32] So the concept of linkage to a certain plant species still remains theoretical if considered in the absolute, at least as far as Odonata are concerned, although several species, in temperate and tropical regions, show a very high correlation between habitat occupancy and the presence of a given species of plant.[33]

One result of stenotopy is that a species having very circumscribed habitat requirements will, by definition, encounter less competition for space and other resources. By the same token a stenotopic species will probably be more vulnerable to habitat modification. An extreme example is the small, delicate coenagrionid *Nehalennia speciosa*, now a severely threatened, continuously declining, vanishing relic in mainland Europe. It occupies an unusually narrow ecological niche, analysed in detail by Rafal Barnard and Hansruedi Wildermuth,[34] and exhibits poor dispersal.

We conclude that a neat, mechanistic explanation of the correlation between the occurrence of certain species and habitat type remains elusive, supporting the realist's dictum that 'the only thing that fits a pigeon hole is a pigeon'. Be this as it may, in Britain the presence of *S. aloides* may well be a proximate cue for *A. isosceles* for a stem habitat (Box 4, p.70).

The fact remains that species of Odonata can be usefully associated with certain habitat types if these are categorised at the appropriate level of detail. For example, as described in Chapter 2, each of the following habitat types in Britain has its own characteristic assemblage of Odonata: lowland rivers, streams and upland rivers, bogs, moorland and lowland wet heath, levels, fens and grazing marshes, and ponds and gravel pits.[35]

An intensive study of discrete populations of *Coenagrion mercuriale* in Britain has shown this species to be associated with several habitat features, the most important of which are a channel substrate consisting primarily of silt, wide underwater ledges, and in-channel emergent dicotyledons and bankside monocotyledons; and its presence is negatively associated with bankside trees.[36] Although this generalisation applies to habitat selection by *C. mercuriale* in Britain, it is not necessarily valid throughout the species' range. In continental Europe this species can be found in habitats of at least two kinds: calcareous spring mires in the foothills of the Alps and meadow streams and ditches.[37] So *C. mercuriale* may occupy what appear to be very different types of habitat in different parts of its range, and the same is true of *Ceriagrion tenellum*, the distribution of which is limited by winter cold in the north-eastern part of its range.[38] This heterogeneity of habitat selection may be one evolutionary route to population isolation and subsequent *speciation*. The process may begin with the occurrence within a species' range of habitats that are unevenly suitable for survival, perhaps across stages of the life cycle. *Oxygastra curtisii*, for example, is found only in lakes in Switzerland, but in southwest Europe almost exclusively in running water.[39]

When species are found to be occupying what appear (to the observer) to be very different habitats, it can be salutary to bear in mind that there may be some attribute common to both types of habitat that has escaped notice. For example, *Ischnura pumilio* in Britain was formerly thought to be acidophilic because it seemed to be restricted to acid seepages. Then populations were found in seepages in chalk pits, after which it was concluded that its habitat requirement was shallow, warm water.[40]

Another example of a species that appears to have more narrowly constrained

BOX 6

METAPOPULATIONS

Aquatic habitats occupied by dragonflies vary considerably in the opportunities they offer for reproduction and population maintenance. This realisation underlies the concept of the *metapopulation*, as a group of populations within which population dynamics operates at two levels: within patches and between patches.[54] One subpopulation may go extinct, later to be re-established by colonisation from another subpopulation. A study of *Aeshna subarctica* by Klaus Sternberg[55] illustrates the way in which habitats of varying suitability contribute to the reproductive potential of a species. Components of metapopulations in southwestern Germany exist in three kinds of habitat, designated according to the opportunities they offer for reproduction.

1) Stem habitats (Fig. 44) function as distribution centres, their large ('source')[53] populations being self-supporting for many years.

2) Secondary habitats represent population reserves, their small ('sink')[56] populations being self-supporting only for some years and depending on immigration to survive; for *Lestes viridis*, a species that breeds in temporary as well as permanent water bodies, temporary ponds contain *sink populations* in dry years and are quickly recolonised after the local population has been extinguished.[57]

3) *Latency habitats* (also harbouring sink populations) are the least productive (of emerging adults), being inhabited mainly by larvae. Adults (usually only females) are found sporadically. Such habitats contribute to the stability of a metapopulation by providing stepping stones for the colonisation of other habitat types.

Survival of a metapopulation of *Aeshna subarctica* depends on intensive interaction and exchange among several subpopulations occupying different types of habitat. The concept of metapopulations has important implications for nature conservation, especially in regard to habitat management and to the interpretation of distribution records.

FIG 44. The Fish Pond, Wokefield Common, Berkshire, viewed from the northern end in late May 1953. At that time it was a stem habitat for *Anax imperator* and *Pyrrhosoma nymphula*. In 1952 more than 4,300 individuals of *A. imperator* and several hundred *P. nymphula* emerged from it. The expanse of water in the foreground covers a sward of Shoreweed, *Littorella uniflora*; in the middle distance are floating mats of Marsh St. John's Wort, *Hypericum elodes*; and beyond them is a large patch of Broad-leaved Pondweed, *Potamogeton natans*. Most emergence of *A. imperator* took place on the oak trees and willow bushes at the southern end near the dam. (From Corbet.[58]) (Photo S. Beaufoy.)

habitat associations in Britain than in the rest of its range is *Platycnemis pennipes*. In Britain the species is restricted to slow-flowing rivers, whereas in northern France it is more widespread. Large populations can be found on ordinary farm ponds in Brittany. A similar 'edge-of-range effect' is found in other insect groups (Chapter 2).

The occurrence of *Calopteryx splendens* appears to be positively correlated with the height of riverside vegetation, and to be negatively correlated with the height of bankside trees and the bank.[41]

When flying above water, both sexes of *Calopteryx dimidiata* (a Nearctic species closely related to the British species of *Calopteryx*) can detect oviposition substrates that are completely submerged.[42] This raises the possibility that searching adults might be able to detect the presence in a water body of submerged predators, such as fish or frogs. Because fish are major predators of odonate larvae, especially Zygoptera, an ability by the ovipositing female to detect fish would seem to be of high selective value. In North America, though apparently not in Europe, there are species assemblages of Odonata (especially in the genus *Enallagma*) that are confined *either* to lakes with fish *or* to lakes without fish – the so-called 'winterkill' lakes[43] – and, correlated with the fact that their main predators are fish in the former and anisopteran larvae in the latter, the innate antipredation behaviour of their larvae differs accordingly.[43] Yet, curiously, it seems that searching adults of species inhabiting fishless lakes cannot discriminate between lakes with and without fish,[44] despite the obvious selective advantage of doing so. At the present state of our knowledge, differences in species distribution among lakes are provisionally attributed not to active selection of different 'lake types', but to the low propensity of adults to disperse from their natal lakes,[45] coupled, presumably, with poor survival in lakes with fish.

When one reflects on the wide range of microhabitats occupied by larvae, whose morphology and behaviour differ according to whether they are burrowers, claspers, *hiders* or sprawlers (p.121), it is remarkable that adults seem to make an appropriate choice so frequently. Both sexes do so by choosing a *rendezvous*, and females, sometimes with male assistance, do so by choosing an oviposition site, which may or may not share properties with that rendezvous.

Certain species offer us strong clues about habitat choice. Examples are to be found among so-called 'species pairs', both members of which occupy rather similar habitats, but seldom occur together, such as *Calopteryx virgo* and *C. splendens*, and, in Germany, *Cordulegaster boltonii* and *C. bidentata*. Early studies by Rudolf Zahner[46] suggested that *C. splendens* differs from *C. virgo* in avoiding streams less than 60 centimetres wide, or free water with an area of less than 0.5 metre. Both species, typically but not invariably, avoid lakes (perhaps acting on an area assessment) and, by analogy with *congeneric* species (such as *C. haemorrhoidalis*),[4] females of both probably use current speed as a cue during the precopulatory courtship display.

Proximate cues that serve for habitat selection can be inferred by noting the common or invariable attributes of habitats occupied by the species in question. On this basis, *Enallagma cyathigerum* is inferred to need standing water with vertical structures along the shoreline (perhaps used for oviposition and emergence).[47] Hansruedi Wildermuth believes this species to be restricted to water bodies with a rather large water surface, with patches of vegetation occupying no more than an area of about 10 x 10 metres.[48] In some places, *Erythromma najas* apparently needs floating Yellow Water Lily, *Nuphar lutea*, or White Water Lily, *Nymphaea alba*, shallow water (no more than 4 metres deep), marginal reeds and woodland close by.[49] However, other studies have revealed that floating mats of algae or *Potamogeton natans*, Broad-leaved Pondweed, can also be suitable. *Erythromma viridulum* needs fine-leaved, submerged vegetation, parts of which must reach the water surface.[50] For *Coenagrion mercuriale* it appears that the main proximate cues are water velocity and the nature of the aquatic and bank vegetation.[51] Habitat selection by *Gomphus vulgatissimus* may depend on water velocity which is itself a correlate of sediment particle size.[52] Females of *Onychogomphus uncatus* and *Ophiogomphus cecilia* oviposit in running water in slowly flowing stretches, where relatively fine sediment will accumulate.[53]

CHOICE OF OVIPOSITION SUBSTRATE

Species that oviposit *endophytically* (Box 7) can easily be seen to discriminate among the substrates into which they place their eggs, using the numerous sensory receptors on the ovipositor.[59] A degree of discrimination probably exists also in species that oviposit *exophytically*, although this may be less obvious. For example, an ovipositing female of *Libellula depressa* touches the water surface with the tip of her abdomen many times before starting to oviposit, presumably testing the substrate, which may be floating plants, especially algae. The laid eggs then form discrete clumps resting on the vegetation.[60]

In nature, egg-laying females of endophytic species pay attention to a wide range of substrates (usually plants). On the other hand, they show a high level of discrimination during choice experiments. For example, although ovipositing females of *Platycnemis pennipes* have been seen to associate in nature with at least 30 species of plant,[61] in choice experiments they exhibited a strong preference for ovipositing in flower heads of the Yellow Water Lily, *Nuphar lutea*, discriminating with respect to colour, age, size, and verticality of the bloom.[26] Several factors may contribute to this apparent paradox. If a preferred substrate is hard to find, a female may recognise a hierarchy of progressively less-favoured substrates on which she may land and probe; further, as Andreas Martens and others have stressed, a female seen to make oviposition movements on a substrate is not necessarily laying eggs there. It is not always possible to distinguish between simulated and actual oviposition by simple observation. Among *Platycnemis pennipes* ovipositing in flower heads of *Nuphar lutea*, 89 per cent of apparent oviposition activity resulted in actual oviposition. On Spiked Water-milfoil, *Myriophyllum spicatum*, this value was 83 per cent. For the rest of the time spent on these plants, females probed without laying.[61] On the whole, very brief visits to a substrate did not result in oviposition there. But for stays of more than 40 seconds the duration of oviposition behaviour correlated closely

....

BOX 7

OVIPOSITION

Depending on the species and the substrate, dragonflies lay eggs (oviposit) in various ways, most of which are encountered in British species. The three main ways in which eggs are laid are:

1) endophytically, the eggs being inserted into plants or other substrates, (Figs 45 & 46), such as mud, using the valvulae of the ovipositor;
2) exophytically, the eggs being washed off the tip of the abdomen (Fig. 47) onto the water surface; and
3) *epiphytically*, the eggs being stuck to vegetation at or above the water surface.

British Odonata that oviposit endophytically comprise all Zygoptera and all Aeshnidae. Functionally, *Cordulegaster boltonii* also belongs in this category because it thrusts its eggs into sand or mud at the edge of a stream, using a hyperdeveloped, sclerotised ovipositor. Species that oviposit exophytically comprise all Libellulidae and Corduliidae, and *Gomphus vulgatissimus*. Sometimes the two species of *Somatochlora* oviposit epiphytically by placing eggs on the surface of moss near the water's edge. Some libellulids in other countries possess bilateral, projecting foliations on the eighth abdominal tergite which the female uses, when ovipositing exophytically and in flight, to scoop up a drop of water and flick it, together with some eggs, toward or onto the bank. In some such species, this behaviour places the eggs above the prevailing water level, thus delaying hatching until the water level rises and submerges them. No British species has yet been recorded as ovipositing in this way, though it is possible that species of *Orthetrum* may occasionally do so.

....

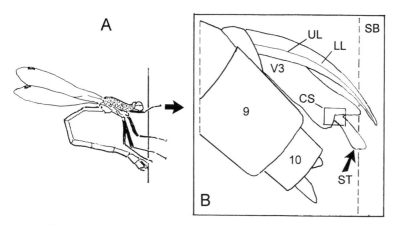

FIG 45. Diagram of component parts of the endophytic ovipositor of *Lestes sponsa* when in contact with an oviposition substrate, such as a plant stem (accompanying male not shown). A) posture of female (body length about 38 mm); B) placement of ovipositor (much enlarged); CS, location of campaniform sensilla; LL, lower leaves of ovipositor; SB, substrate; ST, stylus; UL, upper leaves of ovipositor; V3, third valvulae; 9, 10, abdominal segments. (Redrawn after Matushkina and Gorb.[59])

FIG 46. *Aeshna grandis* ovipositing endophytically into a decaying log (Robert Thompson).

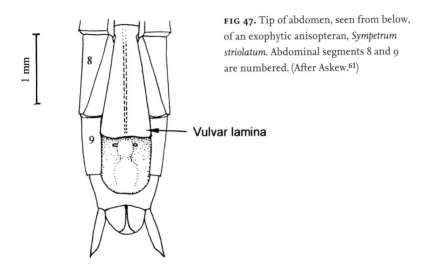

FIG 47. Tip of abdomen, seen from below, of an exophytic anisopteran, *Sympetrum striolatum.* Abdominal segments 8 and 9 are numbered. (After Askew.[61])

Vulvar lamina

1 mm

with the total number of eggs laid.[62] Simple observations of oviposition movements do not necessarily constitute a record of reproduction at a site or of substrate choice.

Our understanding of substrate choice is confounded by actions that appear to be wayward or maladaptive. There are bizarre examples, mostly of female aeshnids, laying eggs (or at least performing oviposition movements) in manifestly unsuitable substrates that happen to be close to a pond. A female *Aeshna cyanea* laid at least one egg in a brown, woollen, knitted pullover worn by Roderick Dunn, then Secretary of the BDS, as he sat beside a pond;[63] and another female *A. cyanea* was seen making oviposition movements upon a rubber boot worn by Sally Corbet, another member of the BDS, as she stood near a pond.[64] Hansruedi Wildermuth, the distinguished Swiss odonatologist, standing barefoot by his garden pond, received attention from a female *A. cyanea* who set about ovipositing in his ankle. She tickled him but did not penetrate, showing that she was probing, not ovipositing.[65] A fourth female of *A. cyanea* was seen by Mike Parr, then President of the Worldwide Dragonfly Association, making oviposition movements upon the rump of his dog (a beagle called Oscar), as the latter lay on mown grass by a pond's edge.[66] Interestingly, Oscar exhibited noteworthy indifference throughout. However, it would be premature to conclude that *A. cyanea*, when using anomalous substrates, chooses only those associated with odonatologists. This species often lays in decaying wood near pond margins. Perhaps the award for the most bizarre, inappropriate substrate should go to the female *A. cyanea* seen by Bernard Schmidt probing the skin of a male Yellow-bellied Toad, *Bombina variegata*. As soon as the probing commenced the toad submerged, washing the dragonfly into the water whereupon she was grasped by a conspecific male who copulated with her.[67] Another observation deserving mention involved an aeshnid making oviposition movements on the back of a carp protruding above the water surface at Trentham Park, near Stoke-on-Trent.[68] The dragonfly, which was photographed but not closely examined, could have been *A. cyanea*. We can expect to encounter further observations of this kind. It is to be hoped that, in some cases, it may be possible to discover whether or not eggs have actually been laid in such apparently unsuitable substrates.

The anomalous oviposition substrates we have described may share certain textural properties with decaying wood, although it is not obvious what these properties might be. What could be the selective value, if any, of such substrate choices? We need to understand the ultimate factors that correlate with the

FIG 48. A tandem pair of *Lestes sponsa* before ovipositing endophytically into the stem of a Horsetail, *Equisetum* (Robert Thompson).

FIG 49. *Sympetrum sanguineum* ovipositing exophytically, in tandem (Robert Thompson).

choice of oviposition substrate. A knowledge of how *prolarvae* reach the water after the eggs hatch, about which we know almost nothing at present, should illuminate this question.

ARRANGEMENT OF LAID EGGS

It has long been known that the laid eggs of Zygoptera are arranged in patterns characteristic of a given species.[69] Matushkina and Gorb have investigated the sensory systems that regulate the positioning of eggs in an egg set – the eggs laid during a bout.[59] The ovipositor is richly endowed with sense organs, including campaniform sensilla (usually associated with strain detection) which occur on the upper and lower leaves of the ovipositor and at the base of the style (Fig. 45, p.81). *Lestes sponsa* lays up to four eggs in each incision, adjusting the angle of each to the direction of the egg line so that this angle diminishes with each successive egg laid. The angle of the whole egg line, which is usually related to the orientation of fibres in the substrate, is regulated by the styli. Many eggs can be laid by many females in a single plant stem, and it has been suggested that regular positioning may help to keep eggs of successive sets apart and so reduce damage to eggs laid previously.[59] Egg sets can be arranged in one of three patterns: irregular; regular simple; and regular complex, where several eggs occupy one incision. Such arrangements probably reflect physical properties of the oviposition substrate.[70] Egg sets of Zygoptera have been found in dicotyledonous leaves from the Cretaceous period (about 90 million years before present).[71]

GUARDED OVIPOSITION

During guarded oviposition the female's last copulation partner remains close to her while she oviposits. If he retains his grip on her head (as in Anisoptera) or *prothorax* (as in Zygoptera), the behaviour is termed 'contact guarding', resulting in 'tandem oviposition' (Fig. 50). If the male relinquishes his grip but hovers near the female, the behaviour is termed 'non-contact guarding'. Among British species, tandem oviposition occurs in all Zygoptera except the two species of *Calopteryx*, *Enallagma cyathigerum*, *Ischnura pumilio* and *I. elegans*; it occurs *facultatively* in certain Libellulidae and *Anax parthenope*. All species that oviposit in tandem sometimes also do so alone. The species of *Calopteryx* engage in non-contact guarding, and in *Enallagma cyathigerum* the oviposition flight begins in tandem and then the female eludes the male by descending beneath the water surface to oviposit while he remains above, hovered or settled, often close to the stem she used for her descent.

Unattached males can be aggressive towards tandem pairs, trying to dislodge the male partner, sometimes even submerging to achieve a takeover.[72] *Lestes sponsa* males exhibit unusually possessive guarding during oviposition. This may reflect several circumstances that bear on *sperm competition* (pp.253): high female receptivity after copulation; high male capacity to resist takeover; high male density and *operational sex ratio*; and a short interval between copulation and oviposition.[73] Several species of Anisoptera, mainly Libellulidae, exhibit guarded oviposition, the choice of mode being facultative:[74] when potential interference by conspecific males is high, the tandem mode is liable to be adopted, but when such interference is low, non-contact guarding is more common.[75] One obvious consequence of tandem oviposition is that the accompanying male, because of his physical position, is preventing any rival from usurping him as parent of the eggs the female is laying. If the accompanying male can prevent his female partner from copulating again before she has laid most or all of her current *clutch* of eggs, he can sometimes virtually ensure that it will be his sperm that fertilises her eggs. His status as father of her current progeny can, however, be jeopardised if she postpones oviposition after copulating with him because, by about 24 hours after copulation, the sperm in her storage organs becomes mixed so that the sperm she receives *last* ceases to enjoy priority for fertilising any eggs that are then laid.[76] So another benefit to the male that may accrue from contact or non-contact guarding may be that after copulation he can induce his partner to oviposit promptly. Such a function of guarding has not yet been demonstrated unequivocally for Zygoptera, but the male of some Anisoptera (such as *Orthetrum coerulescens*) has been seen to nudge his partner immediately after copulation in a way that induces her to begin ovipositing.[77] Ingenious field experiments, conducted by Andreas Martens and Gunnar Rehfeldt of Braunschweig University, have revealed other selective benefits of guarded oviposition. In several species of small Zygoptera, namely *Platycnemis pennipes, Coenagrion puella, C. pulchellum, Pyrrhosoma nymphula* and *Ceriagrion tenellum*, the male adopts the 'Agrion' or *sentinel position* when the female is ovipositing (Fig. 50). This posture has several consequences that may enhance the fitness of both partners:

- the male greatly extends his field of vision, thus being able to detect predators (such as frogs) sooner;
- the tandem pair can alight on (and therefore use) smaller areas of substrate than would otherwise be the case because the male requires no horizontal space for himself;
- by analogy with the *obelisk posture*, the vertical posture of the male may reduce his thermal gain under bright sunlight, perhaps meeting a physiological need for species that oviposit during the heat of the day; and
- the vertical posture may offer greater protection from takeover by rival males than the horizontal posture adopted by certain Anisoptera.[78] When libellulids contact guard during exophytic oviposition, the male himself contributes to the oviposition manoeuvres by making movements that lower and raise the female. An example is *Sympetrum striolatum*, in which the active role of the male can be demonstrated by observing the flight of a male in tandem with a *dead* female.[79]

The other mode of post-copulatory guarding is non-contact guarding, in which the male stays close to, but not linked to, his most recent copulation partner while she oviposits, although he may not remain with her during the whole bout of oviposition. The flexible nature of this behaviour, often seen in species of *Sympetrum*, presumably reflects the trade-off for the male between protecting his genetic investment in the progeny of the guarded female and being free to respond to mating opportunities with new females.[80] A female whose guarding partner leaves her may oviposit more slowly thereafter.[81]

The Japanese coenagrionid *Pseudagrion pilidorsum* sometimes continues to contact guard his mate while she submerges, but balances contact and non-contact guarding according to the need to defend his territory (above the water surface) from other males.[82] The male of the European *Enallagma cyathigerum* hardly ever accompanies his mate when she submerges; he normally releases the female as soon as she submerges unless there is strong harassment from other males, in which case he may retain the tandem grip until he becomes completely submerged.[82]

It is rare among Zygoptera for the female always to oviposit alone, although this is the case in most species of *Ischnura*, including the two that occur in Britain. The reproductive behaviour of *I. elegans* is anomalous in another respect: females exhibit aggressive behaviour toward males that encroach on their oviposition sites.[83] A remarkable type of guarding, quite unlike anything so far described in this chapter, is shown by *Sympetrum depressiusculum*, a Palaearctic species that exists in high-density populations in southern France. There males form tandems with females away from water at nocturnal roosting sites in the early morning (where presumably females are relatively easy to find and grasp) and retain their grip until about three hours later when copulation and oviposition (in tandem) ensue.[84] This type of association has been termed 'precopulatory guarding' and has been interpreted as a means whereby, when competition for receptive females is intense, a male that finds a female can sequester her until a time of day when the ambient temperature has risen enough to permit copulation and oviposition. This type of guarding has not yet been recorded in any British species of dragonfly, although in one British species, *Lestes sponsa*, males have been seen to form tandems away from water and then to escort females to the oviposition site.[73] The behavioural difference between populations may perhaps reflect the number of perching (or roosting) sites close to the water's edge.

Non-contact guarding occurs regularly among the British species of *Calopteryx*, and has been reported occasionally among aeshnids. There is an example purportedly involving *Anax imperator* in continental Europe,[85] but this record has subsequently received critical scrutiny.[86] The North American migrant, *A. junius*, regularly oviposits in tandem and occasionally makes landfall in western Europe.[87] *Anax junius* is not easy to distinguish from *A. imperator* except in the hand. The possibility cannot be dismissed that the anactines seen ovipositing in tandem by Balança and Visscher were not *A. imperator* but *A. junius*, which at that time had not yet been recorded from Europe. (It might also have been *A. parthenope!*) This possibility must remain hypothetical because no voucher specimens were retained. Among aeshnids worldwide, guarding of either kind is rare and facultative.[88]

GROUP OVIPOSITION

Females sometimes oviposit in conspicuous conspecific groups. A participating female may do this with or without a male in tandem. Such groups can comprise many individuals which, although very close to one another, show little or no interaction. Sometimes *Lestes sponsa* does this at a density of more than ten tandem pairs per stem.[89] British species that routinely exhibit group oviposition include *Coenagrion puella, C. pulchellum, Platycnemis pennipes* (Fig. 50). *Erythromma najas, E. viridulum* and *Pyrrhosoma nymphula.*[15, 90] It has also been witnessed, perhaps as an exception, in *Aeshna grandis.*[91] In the species of Zygoptera the accompanying male is often in the sentinel position. Theoretically there are two quite different ways in which such aggregations of females could come about.

First, many females, acting independently, could each be attracted to the same highly suitable oviposition site. Second, each new arrival could come because she had been attracted to the presence of conspecific females (or tandem

FIG 50. *Platycnemis pennipes* ovipositing endophytically, exhibiting tandem and group oviposition (Steve Cham).

pairs) already there. By ingenious use of models and by skilful experiment, Andreas Martens has shown that aggregations of ovipositing *Pyrrhosoma nymphula*,[15] *Platycnemis pennipes*,[92] *Coenagrion mercuriale*[93] and *Coenagrion puella*[94] arise because tandem pairs are positively attracted to pairs already at the site. The phenomenon and its behavioural explanation are securely founded, and this mechanism of aggregation may well apply to other species too. For example, tandems of *Coenagrion mercuriale* land preferentially on a substrate where a single motionless male is in the sentinel position.[93] It is interesting to speculate about ways in which such behaviour might enhance inclusive fitness. Gunnar Rehfeldt has listed two, both of which serve an antipredation function:

1) species that aggregate occupy water bodies frequented by frogs so that group oviposition may enhance survival because the presence of tandems may indicate a low risk of predation by frogs;[95] and
2) if several pairs are together in a group, a successful frog is likely to catch only one pair at a time, thereby alarming the rest who can then escape.[96]

UNDERWATER OVIPOSITION

Predation risk is not confined to species that oviposit above the water surface. Species employing the third mode – underwater oviposition – risk predation by fish, newts and aquatic insects, including beetles (such as *Cybister*, Fig. 51), waterbugs (such as *Notonecta*) and even conspecific anisopteran larvae.[98] Underwater oviposition is the primary mode in *Enallagma cyathigerum* in which the oviposition flight begins in tandem and ends with the female submerging by climbing down a plant stem (p.85). Her male partner may accompany her under water, but usually remains above the surface. When she reappears, he or another male grasps her.[99] A female *E. cyathigerum* may descend as far as 1 metre beneath the surface.[100] During submergence she probably obtains oxygen from the physical-gill action of the air bubble surrounding her (presumably unwettable) body and wings. Her fore wings, shielded by the closed hind wings, remain dry so that she can take off, perhaps with assistance from a male, after regaining the surface. Sometimes a female briefly interrupts oviposition to visit the surface, presumably to replenish the air in the bubble that invests her body. Several species, including *Enallagma cyathigerum*, that oviposit under water make rocking movements while submerged or when experiencing oxygen deprivation, flexing and extending the legs at the coxal joints on alternate sides. Peter Miller interpreted such movements as preventing the accumulation of an unmixed

FIG 51. Predation during oviposition. A larva of the Diving Beetle, *Cybister lateralimarginalis*, attached to the abdomen of a female *Aeshna grandis* which it had grasped while the latter was ovipositing. (Photograph by J. Ott.[97])

boundary layer of oxygen-depleted water around the body.[99] Most oviposition by
E. cyathigerum witnessed by Miller was into green stems of submerged *macrophytes*
where high oxygen levels could be expected as a product of photosynthesis.

After completing a bout of oviposition, a female *Enallagma cyathigerum* rises
to the surface simply by floating upwards, using for lift the buoyancy of the air
bubble around her. Once at the surface, she makes herself conspicuous to
searching males by flexing and extending her abdomen repeatedly; she usually
lies on her side, whereupon a male almost always grasps her, turning her *dorsal*
side uppermost and either carrying her away in tandem or towing her to a
support as a prelude to a brief flight in tandem before trying to copulate with
her. Females not assisted in this way probably drown because they seem unable
to rise from the surface unaided.[99] As far as the male is concerned, his 'rescue'
behaviour will be rewarded if the female still contains unlaid eggs, accepts
copulation and resumes oviposition soon afterwards, although Peter Miller
found that almost half the females surfacing spontaneously after oviposition
contained no eggs ready to lay and that only about 25 per cent contained at
least 50 residual eggs and so would have offered a paternity opportunity for a
rescuing male.[99]

Underwater oviposition has both costs and benefits. A cost is lowered survival
through predation or drowning. Possible benefits include *thermoregulation* by
evaporative cooling, freedom from interference by searching males, freedom to
choose an oviposition site, a heightened assurance that the laid eggs will not be
subject to desiccation after a fall in water level, and a reduced likelihood that the
eggs will be parasitised by Hymenoptera (p.104).

Until recently it was assumed that only Zygoptera oviposited under water.
Now it is known that at least two species of Australian Aeshnidae can do so,[101]
but it is a rare event in Anisoptera. In Japan, *Aeshna juncea* ovipositing in mud
has been seen to submerge completely except for the head and wings.[102] *Aeshna
grandis* will back down into the water to the level of the hind wings.

PREDATION

We may expect predation to be greater on dragonflies ovipositing while settled
than on those doing so in flight. The main predators of species ovipositing
endophytically are frogs, fishes, birds (such as wagtails) and certain aquatic
insects, including anisopteran larvae.[98] The tandem position does not necessarily
protect the female from predators that approach from *beneath* the water surface
because the female's abdomen often probes the underside of a floating leaf. As we

have already seen, guarded oviposition, especially in the sentinel position, serves as anti-predation behaviour as far as predators visible from above the surface are concerned. Underwater oviposition involves an obvious trade-off between freedom from male interference on the one hand, and increased exposure to attack by aquatic predators, especially fish and waterbugs (such as *Notonecta*), on the other. The anti-predation value of tandem oviposition is illustrated by ovipositing females of *Coenagrion puella* when harassed by *Notonecta*. Most solitary females that were grasped were killed, and those solitary females who escaped left the site, whereas females ovipositing in tandem remained.[103]

Females preoccupied with oviposition may be especially susceptible to predation. Hornets, *Vespa crabro*, have been seen to prey on aggregated tandems of *Sympetrum sanguineum*.[104]

DIEL PATTERN

Once a female has been inseminated and is ready to oviposit, she risks being interrupted by interference from searching males. One strategy, as we have seen, is to oviposit in tandem. Another is to oviposit under water. With the exception of *Anax parthenope*, neither option seems to be available to female aeshnids which (in British populations at least) are not known to oviposit in tandem. Moreover, aeshnids, with some notable exceptions, differ fundamentally from most Zygoptera and Libellulidae in that several days elapse between copulation and oviposition.[105] A female bent on oviposition runs the risk of being detected and grasped by a searching male when she arrives at an oviposition site. It is probably to avoid or mitigate such interference that, in some habitats, females of *Aeshna cyanea* prefer to oviposit early or late in the day when males are not present. At one such habitat in southern Germany, receptive females arrived at the rendezvous, which was also an oviposition site, throughout the day, whereas most of the non-receptive females (namely those coming *solely* to oviposit) arrived in the evening, after most males had departed.[106] Likewise, at a habitat in the south-eastern Alps, females of *Aeshna juncea* oviposited in small numbers throughout the day but showed a clear peak of abundance during evening twilight when no male was present.[107] Non-receptive females of *Cordulia aenea* have been observed to oviposit late in the day or during overcast weather when fewer males are present at water.[108] In Germany, females of *Aeshna mixta* and *A. cyanea* oviposit in the early morning, thereby escaping the attentions of conspecific males, but no such strategy is exhibited by *Coenagrion puella* or *Ischnura elegans*.[109] This raises the possibility that *endothermic* species can use this strategy whereas Zygoptera cannot. The *diel* periodicity of ovipositing *Anax imperator* coincides with that of males, but females possess effective means of rejecting males:[110] they flex the abdomen downwards, almost at right angles, as they fly away close to the water surface. Some coenagrionids behave likewise. David Thompson has pointed out that this posture constitutes an 'honest signal' to males that the female is a poor prospect for mating because it can only be adopted when her abdomen is devoid of eggs.[111] Evidently pursuing males quickly get the message! Non-receptive females of some corduliids exhibit unequivocal escape behaviour. Females of *Somatochlora arctica* and *S. metallica* were seen arriving inconspicuously at small water bodies, flying very low and ovipositing at hidden places amongst plants. As soon as one was detected by a male she fled from the water towards adjacent forest, followed by the male. Sometimes, when a male came very close, a female would plunge into riparian sedge and feign death, whereupon her pursuer would stop and hover at the site, apparently unable to locate her.[112]

RATE

The rate of oviposition (the number of eggs laid per unit time) correlates with the oviposition mode. Endophytic species, as might be expected, lay eggs relatively slowly, at about 1–22 eggs/minute.[113] The rate may vary according to the type of substrate. Five species of Coenagrionidae have been observed to lay at between 2.0 and 7.1 eggs/minute.[114] Exophytic species, by contrast, may lay at rates greatly exceeding 1,000 eggs/minute. It has been demonstrated that the rate in exophytic species is positively correlated with environmental temperature,[115] and one may assume that the same is true for endophytic species. Another factor that can influence oviposition rate in exophytic species is persistence of the tandem link: in *Sympetrum sanguineum* the rate declines after the transition from contact to non-contact guarding.[81] The suggestion by Wesenberg-Lund that exophytic oviposition (clearly a derived evolutionary condition) may have been selected for partly in response to predation risk[116] becomes even more plausible when one reflects on the extent to which exophytic oviposition reduces the *duration* of oviposition and the concomitant exposure to hazard. Early advantages of endophytic oviposition may have included the positioning of eggs in a microclimate free from extremes of temperature and humidity and in an environment relatively free from the risk of predation. A well-developed ovipositor was a feature of the first recognisable progenitors of dragonflies, the Protodonata, known from lower Upper Carboniferous deposits laid down more than 300 million years ago.[117]

FECUNDITY

The total number of fertile eggs laid by a female during her lifetime equates to her *fecundity*, also known to evolutionary biologists as her *lifetime reproductive success* (LRS), a term which suitably emphasises the quantitative nature of her inclusive fitness, measured by her numerical and genetic contribution to the next generation.

During a female's life she lays eggs discontinuously, in successive pulses or *episodes*, typically separated by intervals of 1–5 days. In a study of *Sympetrum danae*, for example, the interval between successive episodes averaged 4.7 days and ranged from 1 to at least 20 days.[118] Interepisodal intervals estimated for other British species were 1–3 days for *Aeshna cyanea*,[119] 1 day for *Calopteryx virgo*[120] and 1–17 days for *Coenagrion puella*.[121] Some of the higher recorded values for this interval may be overestimates: the female concerned may have been visiting (and ovipositing in) other habitats unknown to the observer between successive sightings and so may have avoided notice and registration. Weather permitting, we would expect a general estimate of 1–5 days for the interclutch interval to be realistic.

If one knows the average number of eggs laid during each episode, known as a clutch, and also the number of episodes (which depends on a female's expectation of life), one can estimate the lifetime egg production – a direct measure of fecundity. The calculation requires extensive data of high quality and so is unlikely to become available for more than a very few species. The work of Michael Banks and David Thompson has provided such data for *Coenagrion puella* in Britain.[121] Their results, which they have analysed in depth, reveal that the mean number of clutches per female was 3.85 (maximum 15) and that potential fecundity for long-lived females exceeded 4,000 eggs during two consecutive years at a medium-sized pond in The Wirral, England. Clutch size, which varied with ambient temperature, body size and interclutch interval, ranged from slightly more than 100 to 400. Depending on the weather during the flying season, and especially the degree to which sunny days were clumped, fecundity varied between years by a factor of 10. Chance played a dominant role in determining fecundity because a female who began her reproductive life during an unbroken succession of sunny days produced many more eggs than a female whose reproductive life coincided with cloudy weather. Unsurprisingly, the same dependence of fecundity on weather exists in *Calopteryx virgo*.[119] We conclude from these two careful studies that generalisations regarding LRS in

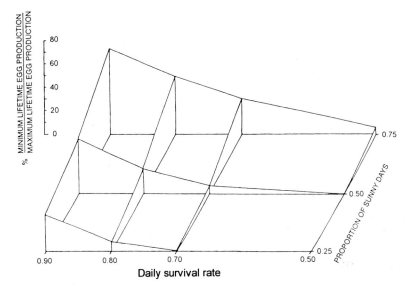

FIG 52. The effect of daily survival rate and the proportion of sunny days on lifetime egg production by *Coenagrion puella*, derived from a simulation model (sample size 30 for each simulation). (After Thompson.[122])

a changeable temperate climate will always be elusive, depending as they do on local conditions, especially the weather.

A simulation model based on his studies of *Coenagrion puella* enabled David Thompson[122] to construct the framework of dependence shown in Fig. 52. Two dependent variables have a major effect on interyear variation in lifetime egg production: reproductive life span and number of clutches.[121] The pre-eminent importance of life span is evident also from a study of LRS of *Lestes sponsa* in Belgium.[123] The use of clutch size in estimating LRS can be subject to error when eggs fail to hatch, either because they have not been fertilised or because they have been parasitised. For example, 22.4 per cent of eggs laid by the continental lestid, *Sympecma paedisca*, were parasitised by the wasp *Anagrus*,[124] whereas water mites consume laid eggs of zygopterans and libellulids.[125]

OPPORTUNITIES FOR INVESTIGATION

This chapter has highlighted topics likely to be rewarding for future investigation, and the cited sources describe approaches and methods that are appropriate. For investigators with suitable opportunities, a project likely to be of great value in increasing understanding of odonate biology in general is the estimation of LRS. The studies of *Calopteryx virgo* by Claire Lambert[120] and of *Coenagrion puella* by Michael Banks and David Thompson[121] provide worthy models to follow. As with most field research on Odonata, a prerequisite for success is a favourable study site. This should be a stem habitat (Box 6, p.76) inasmuch as it should support a continuous succession of large populations, and it should be readily accessible and possess a vegetation structure sufficiently robust to resist being downgraded by frequent visits. Such habitats exist, though their numbers are decreasing, and they have sometimes become famous among odonatologists as foci for studies that have acquired benchmark status because of the rich information they have yielded.

For investigators who lack the opportunities to study LRS or other topics that require daily visits to a site throughout the flying season, there are many other useful projects to be pursued. For example, it would be rewarding to conduct tests in the field on choice of substrates by ovipositing females, especially by those that lay eggs endophytically. Again, one needs access to a habitat where one can count on finding many ovipositing females. We learnt on p.82 how *Aeshna cyanea* will sometimes lay in bizarre, unnatural substrates near a pond. Presumably primary attributes of an acceptable oviposition substrate for most endophytic species are substrate texture, position with respect to the water's edge, perhaps colour, and orientation with respect to the sun's azimuth. All these variables are susceptible to experimental manipulation. There are many different kinds of plastic materials, including polystyrene products, of varying rigidity, that have a sponge-like texture and could be exposed in various positions as surrogate oviposition substrates. If presented in the form of moveable tiles, or plaques, they could readily be monitored for the presence of eggs. The feasibility of this approach has already been demonstrated in laboratory studies, using polystyrene to harvest eggs of the North American coenagrionid *Argia moesta*.[126]

Surrogate substrates could also be used to explore further the distinction between apparent and actual oviposition and thus to document further the relationship between a female's length of stay and the number of eggs that she lays. Studies using surrogate substrates could also have value as a means of obtaining eggs (for which the exact time of laying was known) for laboratory studies of the role of temperature in determining the rate of *embryogenesis* and diapause development – areas of developmental biology that have been neglected in British Odonata, about a seventh of which have eggs in which diapause is obligate (p.99). Eggs of known provenance could also provide material for taxonomic studies of egg morphology and of early larval stadia, two topics that urgently need documentation. And, with appropriate arrangements, one might tackle the elusive question of how prolarvae of species that oviposit near, but away from, water make their way there before *moulting* to the second stadium.

The matter of whether ovipositing females can detect the presence of fish in a water body could be approached by constructing similar, adjacent ponds, some with and some without fish in them, and monitoring the result.

CHAPTER 4

The Egg and the First Two Larval Stadia

THE ROLE OF THE EGG IN THE LIFE CYCLE

THE DRAGONFLY EGG provides a bridge between the adult and the larval stages. Because eggs of most species are small and difficult to find in the field, this stage is usually the last to be investigated. Yet it has an important role to play in the life cycle, mainly by determining the season at which larvae begin their development. For example, eggs of some species, usually those laid in spring or early summer, develop promptly and directly after being laid, completing embryonic development in about a month and then hatching. Others, by contrast, show delayed development such that hatching is postponed for several months. This is likely to happen in eggs laid in late summer or autumn which are then liable to overwinter in that stage. Such a pattern of development is achieved by the egg undergoing diapause. Diapause is not the same as *dormancy* or quiescence, states that can be induced by environmental conditions (e.g. temperature and food) being unfavourable for development at the time. Diapause is a state of suspended development that may occur in any stage of the life cycle (egg, larva or adult) and that typically constitutes an *anticipatory* response to unfavourable environmental conditions. Species like *Lestes sponsa* or *Aeshna cyanea* that habitually lay diapause eggs will typically lay eggs of this kind long before the onset of winter. Such eggs then develop very slowly during the autumn and winter, hatching the following spring, after the water temperature has reached a level at which larvae can survive and forage. We know something about how this pattern of development is regulated in *L. sponsa*, from experiments conducted at controlled temperature.[1] After being laid, eggs need a period of about two weeks (at normal summer temperatures) to reach a stage at which the embryo is almost fully formed and has assumed its final orientation inside the eggshell. The embryo now enters diapause, a physiological state which is completed most rapidly at a temperature characteristic of late autumn in Britain, actually about 10°C. By the time that this next stage has been completed, the ambient temperature has fallen below that at which hatching can occur. In this way the eggs, after completing diapause, are obliged to postpone hatching until spring, at which time they hatch synchronously, producing larvae that then grow rapidly. The situation revealed in the eggs of L. *sponsa* shows diapause to differ from normal development by having a thermal optimum close to 10°C, which is much lower than that for normal (i.e. non-diapause) development.[1]

The existence of a diapause in the egg has a large impact on the pattern of larval development and therefore on the life cycle as a whole. One obvious effect of an egg diapause is that the earliest larval stadia, which are assumed to be the most susceptible to low temperature, escape winter temperatures. Species having diapause eggs begin larval development, more or less synchronously, in spring, whereas those having non-diapause eggs hatch in summer or autumn, typically in a staggered fashion that reflects the temporal dispersion of oviposition. We shall see on p.119 that larvae from late-hatching eggs can be at risk from heavy predation from their older, larger conspecifics.

Among the British species an egg diapause, if it occurs, is usually obligate, meaning that it is an unvarying feature of the life cycle. In a few species, however, diapause is optional, or facultative, occurring in some years and not in others. The distribution of egg diapause among the British species is shown in Table 1. These data should not, however, be regarded as the last word, because in some genera (e.g. *Somatochlora*) it has been shown, by careful experiment, that the existence of diapause in the egg depends on the date in summer when the egg is laid. Thus *Somatochlora alpestris* and *S. arctica* lay diapause *and* non-diapause eggs, the proportion of diapause eggs increasing as the summer advances,[2] showing that the diapause is facultative. It has long been known that the egg diapause in some species of *Sympetrum* is facultative, an example being *S. striolatum*,[3] in which, likewise, the incidence of diapause depends on the date when the egg is laid, and also *S. sanguineum*,[4] but for these two species experiments to determine the factors involved still have to be performed. In Japan, which is home to many species of *Sympetrum*, several species are known that exhibit facultative diapause in the egg.[5]

TABLE 1. The incidence of delayed embryonic development in British Odonata.

FAMILY AND SPECIES	DELAYED DEVELOPMENT	DIRECT DEVELOPMENT
Aeshnidae		
Aeshna caerulea	X	
A. cyanea	X	
A. grandis	X	
A. isosceles	X	
A. juncea	X	
A. mixta	X	
Anax imperator		X
Brachytron pratense		X
Calopterygidae		X
Coenagrionidae		X
Cordulegastridae		X
Corduliidae[a]		X
Gomphidae		X
Lestidae	X	
Libellulidae		
Leucorrhinia		X
Libellula		X
Sympetrum danae	X	
Other *Sympetrum* spp.[b]		X
Platycnemididae		X

Note: Various sources, including those listed by Corbet[6] and Sternberg and Buchwald.[7]

[a] All three species show direct development, but in Germany the proportion of diapause eggs laid by *Somatochlora arctica* increases steadily as the summer progresses.[2]

[b] In *Sympetrum sanguineum* and *S. striolatum* the typical pattern of embryonic development is unclear. In these species both direct and delayed development have been recorded.

EXTERNAL MORPHOLOGY AND OVIPOSITION MODE

Eggs are usually either spindle-shaped and several times longer than wide, or ellipsoid to subspherical (Fig. 53). In general, eggs of the former type are laid endophytically and the others are laid exophytically (Box 7, p.80). Eggs laid endophytically tend to be pushed into an incision in the substrate and positioned so that the *anterior pole* faces the outside, sometimes projecting very slightly outside the substrate. A hazard that such eggs presumably face is that of being sealed inside the stem or leaf by overgrowth of the plant tissue. The eggs of several species that oviposit endophytically are furnished with a cap, funnel or bladelike projection (Fig. 54), apparently formed from the outermost layer of the eggshell, which seems to prevent the plant tissue enclosing the egg and so provides a conduit through which the hatching prolarva can pass when the egg hatches. Such a projection is especially well developed in eggs of *Anax*, Calopterygidae, Coenagrionidae and Platycnemididae. In *Anax* the bladelike cone is apparently formed by the outer eggshell sliding away from the inner eggshell as the egg is placed into the substrate.[8] A close examination by Steve Cham of hatching in *Ischnura pumilio* has shown that the cap at the anterior pole does indeed facilitate the passage of the prolarva during hatching.[9] Also at

FIG 53. Shapes of dragonfly eggs. (a) *Aeshna isosceles* (1.5 mm long); (b) *Pyrrhosoma nymphula* (0.9mm); (c) *Sympetrum danae* (0.7mm); (d) *Libellula depressa* (within a gelatinous matrix) (0.9mm). (a) and (b) are laid endophytically and (c) and (d) exophytically. ((a) from Gardner;[10] (b) from Gardner and MacNeill;[11] (c) from Gardner;[12] (d) from Gardner.[13])

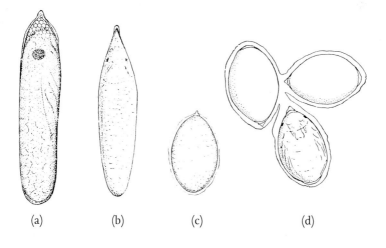

(a)   (b)   (c)   (d)

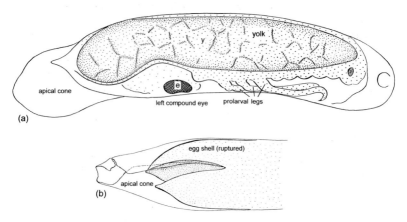

FIG 54. The egg of *Anax imperator* (length excluding apical cone 1.8 mm). (a) showing the apical cone, the yolk mass, the left compound eye (e) and the prolarval legs; (b) the anterior end after hatching, showing the ruptured egg shell and cone through which the prolarva has passed during *eclosion*. ((b) after Corbet.[14])

the anterior pole of the egg are two or more conical or nipple-shaped projections containing canals (*micropyles*) through which sperm travels before penetrating the thin envelope enclosing the egg cell. Fertilisation takes place as each egg passes down the uterus during the act of oviposition.

Eggs of some exophytic species are invested by a gelatinous matrix which sometimes has adhesive properties. In riverine gomphids (e.g. *Gomphus simillimus*), this covering appears to enable the eggs to adhere to the substrate promptly after being laid and so avoid being swept downstream.[15] Curiously, no such investment has been found on the egg of *Gomphus vulgatissimus* in which it might have been expected. The egg of the other exophytic riverine anisopteran in Britain, *Cordulegaster boltonii*, lacks a gelatinous covering, but this is not surprising because the ovipositing female thrusts each egg into sediment near the bank, where the egg is protected from dislodgement by the current.

EMBRYONIC DEVELOPMENT

The appearance of the egg changes markedly during embryonic development. Immediately after it has been laid, the egg of most species is milky white or pale yellow, and in unfertilised eggs it remains this colour until decomposing. Usually, however, a very high proportion (often 100 per cent) of laid eggs are fertile. After having been demonstrated in the laboratory in a Japanese gomphid,[16] *parthenogenesis* in the Odonata has been confirmed to occur naturally, and to be widespread among populations of *Ischnura hastata* on the Azores,[17] a place where its existence had long been suspected because of the Islands' isolation, and because collections there consisted only of females.[18] Adolfo Cordero and colleagues surmise that parthenogenetic *I. hastata* may have been infected by a novel endosymbiontic bacterium able to cause this mode of reproduction.[19] Parthenogenesis has not been detected in any other species of odonate, or in North American populations of *I. hastata*, although *Wolbachia*, bacteria able to induce parthenogenesis in their arthropod *hosts*, have been found in several species of tropical Odonata,[20] but, interestingly, not in *I. hastata*.[19] It is not known whether *Wolbachia* is associated with the role reversal of the sexes that is a conspicuous feature of species of the Polynesian pseudagrionine genus *Nesobasis*.[21]

The fertile egg soon darkens, and after a few days the developing embryo becomes visible inside, the first, most conspicuous signs of development being the pigmented compound eyes. Thereafter, under appropriate lighting and magnification, the legs, labium and abdomen become visible and then the embryo undergoes *blastokinesis* (or katatrepsis), abruptly reversing its orientation within the egg shell. After blastokinesis the embryo's head is at the anterior end of the egg, in the position in which hatching will later take place. Species with diapause eggs differ according to whether blastokinesis occurs after winter (Type 1) (e.g. most species of *Aeshna* and *Sympetrum danae*) or before winter (Type 2) (e.g. most species of *Lestes*).[22] The ecological significance of this dichotomy is not understood. In the North American *Sympetrum vicinum*, the eggs of which exhibit facultative diapause, eggs laid early in autumn, at a water temperature above 14°C, conform to Type 2, whereas those laid later, in colder water, conform to Type 1.[23] In *S. vicinum*, as in *Lestes sponsa*, diapause development proceeds most rapidly at intermediate temperatures. Species whose eggs exhibit direct development (i.e. which lack diapause) typically hatch four to six weeks after being laid at seasonal ambient temperatures (e.g. *Brachytron pratense* in three weeks;[24] *Cordulegaster boltonii* in 24–43 days[25]).

SURVIVORSHIP

The point at which within-generation survival begins to be determined is the number of laid, fertilised eggs that hatch. Egg mortality after hatching is caused by predators and parasites. Very little is known about predators of dragonfly eggs

BOX 8

PARASITOIDS OF DRAGONFLY EGGS

A *parasitoid* is a parasite that invariably kills its host and so, in this respect, resembles a predator. Odonate eggs that are laid endophytically are especially vulnerable to parasitoids which can attain high levels of incidence. Egg parasitoids consume the host from within in the stage in which it is attacked (i.e. very soon after oviposition), and so prevent its subsequent morphological development. Egg parasitoids of Odonata belong to two superfamilies of Hymenoptera: Chalcidoidea and Scelionidea. Most belong to the Chalcidoidea, in which three families and about ten genera are represented.[29] This topic has received relatively little attention by researchers and so it is likely that many more host-parasite associations remain to be discovered. Some egg parasitoids, such as the eulophid wasp *Tetrastichus polynemae*, can act as a *hyperparasitoid*, developing at the expense of a parasitoid already in a host egg. Adult females of the parasitoid walk or swim under water to locate the host egg in which they oviposit by thrusting the ovipositor deep into the victim.[30] Some egg parasitoids (e.g. Mymaridae) are among the smallest of insects (Fig. 55), the adults being only 0.2 millimetres long, which is smaller than some Protozoa. Even the smallest Zygoptera are available to them as hosts. Some Trichogrammatidae can mate inside the host eggshell, doing so on the day of emergence[30] and thus completing the whole life cycle in seven to ten days.[31] Recorded rates of odonate mortality due to Chalcidoidea range between 12 and 95 per cent.[32] In a species of *Polynema*, an egg parasitoid of *Calopteryx virgo*, usually only one parasitoid larva develops per host egg, and if more than one parasitoid larva occupies a host egg, only one parasitoid individual completes development there.[33] Some such parasitoids, mainly Chalcidoidea, employ elaborate strategies to locate the eggs of the host: mature female wasps sometimes travel around with the host, clinging to its body, and so being well placed to find eggs promptly after they have been laid.[34] Wasps of the latter type are mainly Scelionidae.[35] Only females have this phoretic relationship with their dragonfly hosts which likewise are predominantly (perhaps exclusively) females. Such an association would enable the scelionid to attack the host egg immediately after it had been laid, and so before the host embryo began to develop and before any protective covering accompanying the egg had had time to harden.[35] This, it seems, would be a much more effective way of exploiting the host than having to search for the laid eggs (as some chalcidoids do) and thus sustaining a delay. Very little is known about this fascinating relationship, perhaps partly because, when the female host is captured, the parasitoids probably drop off and so escape detection.

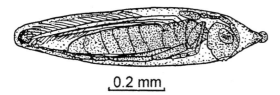

0.2 mm

FIG 55. An adult female of the trichogrammatid parasitoid wasp *Hydrophylita aquivalans*, from right side, inside the egg of a coenagrionid, *Ischnura verticalis*. The wasp has used its mandibles to make a hole in the eggshell through which it will pass when emerging, before swimming to the water surface using its wings as oars. (From Davis.[36])

to which presumably eggs laid exophytically are more vulnerable, although the eggs of a West African species of *Malgassophlebia*, laid exophytically within a gelatinous investment, are subject to predation by drosophilid larvae;[26] and water mites consume laid eggs of zygopterans and libellulids.[27] As far as is known, mortality during embryonic development is caused largely by parasitism, mainly by minute wasps which act as parasitoids of eggs laid endophytically (Box 8). Parasitoids of dragonfly eggs can exert heavy mortality: 22.4 per cent of eggs laid by the continental lestid *Sympecma paedisca* were killed by the parasitoid wasp *Anagrus*.[28]

HATCHING

Several hours before the eggshell ruptures, the embryo can be seen making peristaltic movements of the oesophagus, synchronised with rhythmic contractions of the dilator muscles of the pharynx. Thereafter, hatching differs in the two suborders. In Zygoptera the embryo swallows amniotic fluid, supposedly causing water to enter the egg through the micropyles. Increase of pressure ruptures the inner eggshell along a line of weakness and distends the *vitelline membrane*, pushing the anterior pole away from the egg (Fig. 56). Continual swallowing, accompanied by abdominal distension, causes the embryo to move forward so that its head occupies the chamber formed by the bulging vitelline membrane. At this time the anterior tip of the egg often projects visibly from the oviposition substrate. The prolarva then slides out of the egg, passing through an anteriorly placed cone if one is present (Fig. 56), its exit apparently being eased by posteriorly directed tiny teeth on the head and thorax as well as spines on caudal appendages. The embryo's continual, active intake of water, through mouth and probably also anus, and the arching of its head and thorax, enable the prolarval *cuticle* to split on the head and thorax, exposing the stadium-2 larva, which quickly makes its exit, often leaving the exuvia of the prolarva still attached to the now-empty eggshell. The process of hatching, as described here, takes about 20 minutes in *Calopteryx virgo*,[37] but some Coenagrionidae apparently complete the process more rapidly.[17] Visible swallowing movements in *Coenagrion puella* cease immediately after the moult to stadium 2.[38]

In Anisoptera the eggshell is typically ruptured by an egg burster, a sclerotised crest on the head of the prolarva. The egg burster, which is on the *frons* of endophytic species and on the top of the head of exophytic species,

FIG 56. Successive stages (a–c) during egg hatching in *Enallagma cyathigerum*. At the anterior end of the egg, water enters through the micropyle and distends the vitelline membrane which ruptures the eggshell and forms a vesicle into which the hatching embryo pushes its head. Later the embryo, by swallowing water, will rupture the vesicle and leave the egg. (After Degrange.[37])

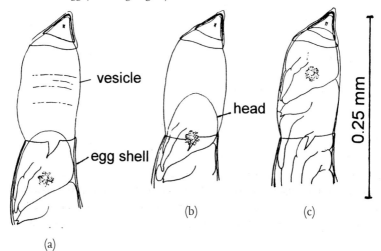

produces a slit that may extend around the egg. The prominent 'frontal horn' on the stadium-2 larva of *Anax imperator* may represent the relic of the egg burster.[39]

About 30 seconds to a few minutes after the moult to stadium 2, the main dorsal tracheal trunks fill rapidly with gas, starting in the midgut region and spreading backward and forward. The gas, initially carbon dioxide,[40] is soon replaced by nitrogen and oxygen and can then perform a respiratory function.

The precise stimuli that trigger hatching are unknown for British species. For eggs that are submerged, ambient temperature exceeding a threshold may be the stimulus. For eggs positioned out of water, and by analogy with certain tropical species, wetting may be the trigger, as it is for *Ischnura pumilio*.[9] For British species it is not known if hatching follows a diel periodicity.

THE PROLARVA AND STADIUM 2

There are persuasive grounds for regarding the prolarva (Box 9) as a true stadium, as we do here.[41] Some observers have been reluctant to regard it as a stadium partly because of its extreme brevity: it often lasts less than a minute and seldom as long as five minutes, although it can greatly postpone moulting if obliged to seek water from a distance. When having to travel to water, the prolarva of the New Zealand lestid, *Austrolestes colensonis*, can delay the first moult for almost nine hours.[42] On reaching water, the prolarva of the Japanese aeshnid *Aeschnophlebia longistigma* floats for three to five minutes and then moults, but it can survive as a prolarva for 14 hours if it fails to reach water within that time.[43] Some other odonates, including the primitive Japanese *Epiophlebia superstes*, can jump over a dry substrate as prolarvae, sometimes covering in one leap a distance about 100 times their own length.[44] Prolarvae travel more effectively on a firm surface: those of the Japanese aeshnid *Planaeshna milnei* can travel nearly 20 centimetres at each jump over land but much less than 1 millimetre over water.[45] The European lestid *Lestes viridis* oviposits in the woody branches of the willow *Salix aurita* growing beside a pool. When the eggs hatch, most prolarvae drop directly onto the water of the pool, but some land on the ground, in which case they jump around until they alight on water.[46] For endophytic species that habitually oviposit away from water, one may suppose that mortality during the prolarval stage is typically high. For exophytic species that lay eggs in clusters, such as *Libellula depressa*, prolarvae from late-hatching eggs may suffer predation from their more precocious siblings who have already entered stadium 2 and so are able to attack them.[13]

BOX 9

THE PROLARVA

The first larval stadium, usually very brief, is the prolarva.[41] In appearance it somewhat resembles an Egyptian mummy, the limbs and mouthparts being barely delimited from the rest of the body (Fig. 57). It can wriggle and jump but not walk, swim or feed. Its duration, which can vary from a few seconds to several hours, seems to depend on when it reaches free water, at which time it moults promptly to embark on the second larval stadium – the first mobile, feeding stage. Sometimes the prolarval exuvia may remain attached to the eggshell, as in many species that oviposit exophytically. If the prolarva has to travel to reach free water, moulting can be postponed and the prolarval exuvia may be left floating on the water surface. Few people have observed the behaviour of prolarvae travelling to water from oviposition sites remote from water. The reduced form of the odonate prolarva has a parallel in the first stadium of certain grasshoppers and cicadas and may serve to facilitate smooth emergence from the egg by a larva whose long legs might otherwise get entangled with the edges of the opening in the eggshell.

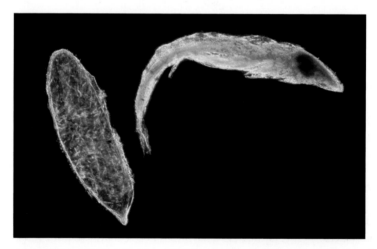

FIG 57. The egg (left) and prolarva (right) of *Anax imperator* from the collection of Eric Gardner. The length of the egg, including the apical cone, is about 2.2 mm (The Natural History Museum).

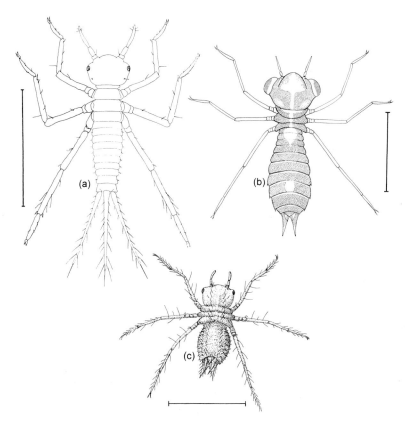

FIG 58. Stadium-2 larvae of (a) *Coenagrion mercuriale*; (b) *Anax imperator*; (c) *Sympetrum striolatum*. Scale lines 1.0 mm. ((a) after Corbet;[47] (b) from Corbet,[14] (c) from Corbet.[48])

The first larval moult discloses stadium 2, this being the first stage that most odonatologists recognise as a dragonfly larva (Fig. 58).

OPPORTUNITIES FOR INVESTIGATION

It is not known how prolarvae from eggs hatching away from water locate the water, but it is likely that they possess some means of orientating towards it. The ability of a prolarva to locate water if it hatches away from it must have very high survival value. Although prolarvae seldom exceed 1 millimetre in length, and are therefore inconspicuous, a description of their behaviour during the journey from hatching site to water could be highly informative and could perhaps indicate how this orientation is being accomplished. In Britain an obvious candidate for such a study would be *Aeshna cyanea*, which is notorious for laying eggs in substrates which are sometimes a metre or more from water. By analogy with *Austrolestes colensonis*,[42] it is assumed that the prolarva makes its way to water by skipping around on land first. Accounts of the behaviour and orientation of prolarvae during this episode would fill long-standing gaps in our knowledge of this brief but fascinating developmental stage. This might be achieved by marking the positions of extra-aquatic eggs, determining the diel periodicity of hatching, and then waiting to observe some of the later eggs hatching. Alternatively, it would not be difficult to position laid eggs in a laboratory situation so that the passage of prolarvae towards water could be recorded. One should allow for the possibility that prolarvae, like adults, possess a sense that allows them to orient towards a horizontal water surface by perceiving the reflection of polarised light.

Endophytic oviposition away from water might reduce parasitoid attack on eggs. This merits investigation.

Little is known of the temporal pattern of oviposition in the field, but such information would throw light on the population dynamics of larvae of species that lay non-diapause eggs. The provision of surrogate oviposition substrates, to be examined and replaced daily, would make possible acquisition of such data, as well as providing a supply of eggs, the exact age of which was known, for experiments.

Other fruitful topics for investigation include the relationship between temperature and rate of development in diapause and non-diapause eggs. This would throw light on the nature of facultative diapause and its role in seasonal regulation. The requisite apparatus need not be elaborate: containers in which both temperature and daylength could be regulated, and a supply of eggs, the species and age of which were known. Parallel studies in the field would also contribute to our understanding of life cycles. The confinement and regular inspection of eggs (of known age and origin) in nature would yield information about egg survival and rate of embryonic development under natural conditions. It might also yield information about the frequency of parasitoid infection and the identity of the parasitoids involved.

Another informative project would be to capture ovipositing females of Anisoptera with a net of very fine mesh. As described above (pp.104–5), sometimes, by a lucky chance, adult scelionoid wasps (minute egg parasitoids) are caught on ovipositing Anisoptera. Catching adult Anisoptera with a fine-mesh net might reveal other phoretic organisms of interest, as might observing them carefully through a short-focus telescope. Using both techniques, Klaus Sternberg found five female adults of the minute milichiid fly, *Desmometopa* sp., running around on the head of an adult *Cordulegaster boltonii* (p.194),[49] apparently sharing the dragonfly's last meal, something that the egg parasitoids may also do when their energy supplies become depleted. Because of the way that odonatologists usually catch adult dragonflies, with robust manipulation of a wide-mesh net, such minute 'hitchhikers' are liable to escape notice. Further study of this relationship could not fail to be rewarding.

CHAPTER 5

The Larva: Survival Under Water

THE ROLE OF THE LARVA IN THE LIFE CYCLE

THE LARVA IS THE only stage in the life cycle in which significant growth in size occurs. Being confined to water, the larva has evolved in directions quite different from those of the adult. Larvae show much greater diversity in body shape and behaviour than adults, a reflection of their occupancy of different microhabitats, which in turn appears to reflect adaptations to reduce predation, mainly by fish, but also by larvae of other dragonflies. In Britain the larval stage occupies an environment that is relatively well insulated against extremes of temperature. From this refuge, the time of emergence to the less protected adult is regulated by the larva's responses to seasonal variables such as daylength and temperature (p.172). The ways in which such regulatory responses enable each species to position the adult stage at a constant and characteristic time of year (p.169) are marvellous to behold, and to unravel them provides a continuing challenge for the investigator.

RESPIRATION

Comparative morphology tells us that the form of the respiratory system in dragonfly larvae – a network of gas-filled tubes, or *tracheae* – shows that they have descended from terrestrial ancestors that must have breathed through paired apertures, or spiracles, on the thorax and abdomen.[1] Throughout most of the larval life the spiracles are closed, and the tracheae fill with gas, spontaneously, early in stadium 2. The routes by which oxygen passes from the water to the tracheal system differ markedly in the two suborders.

In Zygoptera most respiratory exchange occurs via the three caudal appendages, often called caudal lamellae when they are leaflike, at the tip of the abdomen. The caudal lamellae have a large surface area, and are richly supplied with fine branches of the tracheal system. The lamellae also function as fins and for enhancing swimming speed during escape behaviour. Being large and conspicuous, they need to be camouflaged. Each lamella has a breaking joint at the base, allowing it to become detached readily if grasped by a predator, enabling the larva to escape, rather in the manner of a lizard jettisoning its tail.[2] The lamellae are not essential for respiration: a larva can survive without them, at least until dissolved oxygen in its surroundings becomes seriously depleted. Some respiratory exchange occurs also through the surface of the body, especially via parts that are richly tracheated, like the *wing sheaths*. The shape and relative size of caudal appendages change greatly during larval development:[3] in the earliest stadia they are relatively large and often spearlike, bearing long setae which are assumed to be sensory (Fig. 59). Small larvae readily use them for aggressive or defensive display, whipping them forwards to jab at a potential adversary, of the same or another species. Such behaviour is evident as early as stadium 2 in larvae of *Calopteryx splendens*.[4] During the last four or five stadia of

FIG 59. Middle caudal appendage of three species of Coenagrionidae, viewed from the right side, showing the change of shape during development. (a) *Coenagrion mercuriale*; (b) *Pyrrhosoma nymphula*; (c) *Ceriagrion tenellum*. Left, in approximately stadium 7 (body length 3.5mm); right, in the final stadium. (From Corbet.[3])

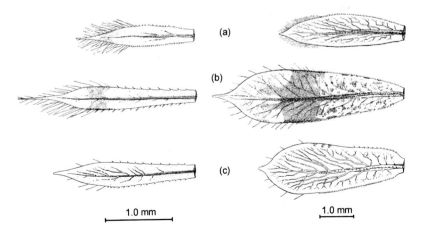

(a)

(b)

(c)

1.0 mm

1.0 mm

many species of Zygoptera, the appendages diminish in size relative to abdomen length and become progressively more leaflike (Fig. 59), presumably coming to play a larger role in respiration and emergency locomotion.

In Anisoptera, gaseous exchange occurs across the richly tracheated inside wall of the rectum which is typically furnished with elaborately patterned gills arranged in bunches or tufts (collectively known as the *branchial basket*). The rectal epithelium is irrigated by pulsating movements of the abdomen which draw in and expel water from outside. The requisite changes in pressure are effected by a transverse, muscular diaphragm inside the abdomen. The diaphragm performs other vital functions besides respiration: by increasing the strength and frequency of pulsations the larva can expel water from the anus so vigorously that it can swim by jet propulsion to elude predators, to chase prey and, occasionally, to hover, head uppermost, just beneath the water surface to forage (Box 10). Sometimes the diaphragm helps forcibly to eject faecal pellets, which, for reasons unknown, can be propelled for 30 centimetres or more away from the larva's body.[5] Another vital function that relies on the diaphragm is the sudden extension of the labium during prey capture (Box 10).

....

BOX 10

OPERATION OF THE LARVAL LABIUM DURING PREY CAPTURE

The larval labium as developed in Odonata is a highly specialised organ found only in this order. It derives from the fusion of the second maxillae to form a robust, hinged extensible organ consisting of two parts, the postmentum and prementum[9] (Fig. 60).

The prementum bears two palpi, each armed with a moveable hook; and the palpi open like pincers to grasp the prey. The explosive protraction (extension) of the labium results from its being an energy-storage mechanism, not unlike that causing the leap of a flea, locust or click beetle. Its successful operation requires the precise co-ordination and rapid operation of three processes: contraction of the abdominal diaphragm (in Anisoptera) or the abdomen (in Zygoptera), which increases internal pressure of the *haemolymph*; simultaneous closure of the anal valve (to prevent exhalation); and release of the mechanism that locks the labium in the resting position.[10] The primary flexor muscles of the labium, together with a locking device, keep it in the resting position

while energy is stored before protraction. Release of the locking
mechanism causes explosive protraction of the labium, enabling the
moveable hooks on the labial palpi to open and then grasp the prey (Fig.
60) whereupon the captured prey is drawn back to the mouth by muscular
action which restores the labium to the resting position, folded and
locked beneath the head.[10] The time taken to achieve full protraction has
been recorded as about 15 msec in some Anisoptera[11] and 40 msec in some
Zygoptera.[12] The co-ordination achieved by Anisoptera when operating
this mechanism is remarkable: sometimes larvae of Aeshnidae and
Libellulidae can be seen using jet propulsion to hover (in a jerky manner)
just below the water surface while simultaneously using the labium to
catch small prey, such as mosquito larvae or microcrustacea, that have
assembled beneath the surface. At other times the ascent can appear
relatively smooth: Sandra Sell was amazed to see a late-stadium larva of
Anax imperator rise vertically to the water surface, with no visible means of
support, to use the labium to capture a fly that had settled above it.[13]

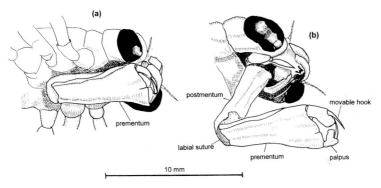

FIG 60. Head of an aeshnid larva, viewed obliquely from beneath right side,
(a) with labium in resting position and (b) a few milliseconds after the onset of
the labial strike. In (b) the locking mechanism holding the prementum in the
resting position under the head has just been released, allowing blood pressure
built up by the muscular abdominal diaphragm to launch the labium towards
the target. The labial palps will be opened just before the target is engaged.
(Modified from Weber.[14])

FORAGING

Dragonfly larvae are catholic feeders, taking predominantly living prey which they detect, visually or by touch, and usually by its movement. Their default mode is to ambush prey as it swims or crawls within range of the labium which is then extended, extremely rapidly, to grasp the prey and draw it back to the mouth, where it is crushed by the mandibles (Box 10). Selection pressure on the rapidity of labial extension has probably been intense: in an aeshnid this may happen so fast that a small tadpole does not initiate a startle response (thus alerting conspecifics) until *after* being struck by the labium.[6] As ambush foragers, like spiders and praying mantids, dragonfly larvae are using energy in a very efficient way,[7] at least as long as suitable prey organisms continue to come close to a larva's perch. Their prey not infrequently includes dragonfly larvae, of their own as well as other species. This intra-odonate predation is most likely to occur when larval density is high, when prey is in short supply, and when the largest and smallest larvae differ in size by two or more stadia.[8] Thus, when emergence is poorly synchronised and when oviposition (and therefore egg hatching) are temporally dispersed, intra-odonate predation (either *intraspecific* or *interspecific*) can be expected to be most pronounced. One effect of this will be to reduce the size range of the surviving larval population, as the smallest larvae suffer disproportionately from predation.

Cannibalism (i.e. intraspecific predation) may be a decisive factor for survival.[15] *Brachytron pratense* larvae of all sizes show active sibling cannibalism when prey is scarce.[16] Temporal priority (reflected in size differences) confers dominance on larger larvae and may cause smaller larvae to show anti-predation behaviour.[17] If larvae of different size (or age) cohorts were to occupy different microhabitats, this might serve to mitigate intraspecific predation; and, as mentioned later (pp.119–121), the banding pattern of larvae of *Anax imperator* and some other aeshnids may make them less visible to older conspecifics in semivoltine populations.

Although it is realistic to regard dragonfly larvae as primarily ambush foragers, they sometimes show remarkable versatility in their foraging behaviour. To obtain a balanced perspective of their foraging capabilities, we can consider some of their opportunistic behaviour. For example, although many experiments have shown that the ways in which prey *move* plays a major role in their detection and capture, some species, such as *Anax imperator*,[18] are able to detect, recognise and capture prey that is virtually immobile or moves extremely slowly, such as a snail, and then stalk and capture it. Thereafter the sequence of actions larvae use to manipulate and ingest the prey depends on the prey type (Fig. 61): for example, a caddisfly larva inside its case will be handled differently from a snail in a shell. Even more surprising perhaps is the finding that certain zygopteran larvae (e.g. the New Zealand coenagrionid *Xanthocnemis zealandica*) may return to feed off the carcass of another zygopteran larva, rather in the manner of a fox or jackal coming back to scavenge for second helpings.[19] Aeshnid larvae sometimes vary the ambush feeding mode by actively stalking prey. This behaviour, which aeshnids are most likely to adopt when hungry,[19] can be well observed when tadpoles are available as prey. The aeshnid larva is alerted to the tadpole's presence each time the latter wriggles and then, when the wriggling stops, seems to remember where the tadpole was and stalks it accordingly. Christine Blois[18] and Richard Rowe[20] have shown how the predatory sequence can be recorded and analysed in a systematic way and have thereby revealed the scope that exists for fruitful studies of behaviour in this field (Fig. 61).

At the family level, species, especially among Anisoptera, segregate as larvae into broad categories within which eye structure, larval shape, behaviour, microhabitat and growth rate are correlated. This diversity has led to larvae being classified into types, based mainly on eye specialisation and behaviour.[21] Another classification can be based on behaviour, morphology and microhabitat occupancy (Table 2). These two classifications, which do not conflict, provide a template against which we can assemble information about larval behaviour and ecology.

Taking into account only Anisoptera, we may consider examples of the four main categories. These should not be regarded as discrete, exclusive categories, but rather as foci, among which larvae move and towards which they gravitate depending on prevailing environmental conditions, as determined by the array of microhabitats that are available, prey availability, predator pressure, etc. Notwithstanding this generality, certain species of *Cordulia* and *Somatochlora* exhibit behaviour that combines features of more than one type,[23] and this may be true of corduliids in general. *Somatochlora flavomaculata*, depending on its microhabitat, which can be submerged vegetation as well as semiliquid peat mud, can show leg movements characteristic of sprawlers *or* shallow burrowers.[24] In general, the behavioural types offer opportunities for niche differentiation leading to compromises in which microhabitat use, voltinism and sensitivity to predation by fish are highly correlated.[25] Foraging mode depends partly on prey availability and activity: for example, in experimental situations, *Coenagrion hastulatum* and *Aeshna juncea* used the ambush mode when prey density was high, but the active mode when it was low or prey were sedentary.[25] Among anisopteran larvae four focal categories have so far been recognised (Table 2).

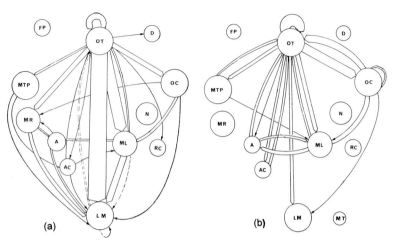

FIG 61. Flow diagrams showing precapture behavioural sequences for an F-0 larva of *Anax imperator* with (a) a larval caddisfly, *Phryganea* sp., and (b) an aquatic snail, *Limnaea* sp., as prey. Solid lines denote successful, and broken lines denote unsuccessful, labial strikes. The width of bars and linking lines is proportional to frequency, only values exceeding 1 per cent being shown. Capture of a caddisfly larva is characterised by a relatively simple, brief phase between orientation of the head (OT) and labial protraction (LM); capture of a snail includes an initial, extended, preparatory phase that entails orientation of the head (OT) and body (OC) interrupted by slow walking (ML) and spells of immobility (A). Postcapture sequences for the two prey types (not shown) also differ markedly. Other abbreviations: AC, body (of predator) moves forward horizontally but legs retain their position on the substrate; D, larva turns away from prey and abandons precapture sequence; FP, prey escapes; MR, larva walks rapidly over substrate; MT, larva uses fore legs to groom antennae, mouthparts and legs; MTP, legs trample substrate; N, larva swims; and RC, walks backward. (After Blois.[18])

Claspers, typically aeshnids (Figs 62 & 63), usually cling tightly to a stem or stick. The body is typically elongate, and the compound eyes are large and prominent. *Brachytron pratense* (Fig. 63) is a good example of this type and, when in the resting position, the dark larva is well camouflaged. Species of *Aeshna* adopt much the same position, being greenish if they are amongst water plants, but they are much more flexible in their choice of substrates. *Aeshna cyanea* (Fig. 64), for example, can occasionally be found in rock pools[26] or even cement tanks[27] that are almost devoid of perches. Claspers that occupy perches near the water surface (e.g. *Anax imperator*) typically have large compound eyes and respond promptly and actively to movement, readily stalking or pursuing

TABLE 2. Categories of larval Anisoptera in relation to behaviour, morphology and microhabitat occupancy (from Corbet[22]).

1. Clasper:	compound eyes large, symmetrical; active; abdomen elongate; a visual forager; clings to vegetation near water surface: for example, *Aeshna cyanea*.
2. Sprawler:	compound eyes small, less symmetrical; active; abdomen squat; a visual and tactile forager; occupies vegetation near water surface: for example, *Sympetrum striolatum*.
3. Hider:	3.1 compound eyes small, asymmetrical; sedentary; abdomen squat, setose; a tactile forager; occupies fine detritus: for example, *Libellula depressa* sometimes.
	3.2 compound eyes small, asymmetrical; sedentary; abdomen squat, setose; a tactile forager; lives amongst coarse leaf litter: for example, *Cordulia aenea*.
4. Burrower:	4.1 **shallow burrower:** compound eyes small, asymmetrical; sedentary; abdomen elongate, setose; a tactile forager; lives amongst fine stones or sand; legs perform digging movements: for example, *Cordulegaster boltonii*; *Libellula depressa* sometimes.
	4.2 **deep burrower:** no British example.

Note: These designations are focal points rather than discrete categories. Under different circumstances or in different stages of development, larvae of a given species may move from one category to another.

potential prey if it fails to come near enough to grasp with the labium (Box 10, p.114). Odonatologists who keep *A. imperator* in a glass-fronted aquarium will become accustomed to a larva turning its head to track the movements of anyone passing nearby. Such active species tend also to grow more rapidly than others and to forage more aggressively. A counterpart among the Zygoptera (which do not on the whole conform to the types in Table 2) are larvae of lestids which are more responsive to movement and grow more rapidly than coenagrionids of similar size, under identical experimental conditions.[28] Like larvae of *A. imperator*, those of lestids occupy perches near the water surface, where the water is usually warmest and the light intensity highest. It is noteworthy that in Britain *A. imperator* can be semivoltine, requiring two years to complete larval development.[29] This means that larvae in the earliest stadia have to exist alongside larvae a year older which, as aeshnids, would not be averse to making a meal of them.[30] Close to the water surface, where such larvae live, the incident

FIG 62. Larva of *Aeshna caerulea*, a clasper and sprawler, in stadium F-0. The wing sheaths cover the first four abdominal segments (Robert Thompson).

FIG 63. Larva of *Brachytron pratense*, a clasper, in stadium F-0 (Robert Thompson).

FIG 64. Larva of *Aeshna cyanea*, a clasper and sprawler, in stadium F-o. It is shown in stalking mode. Excellent stereoscopic vision serves aeshnid larvae well when they are capturing prey (Robert Thompson).

light forms a mottled pattern of light and shade caused by the ripples on the surface. In their first year, larvae of *A. imperator* are strikingly banded with black and white, but they lose this pattern when they graduate to the larger size cohort.[31] It is tempting to regard this age-dependent pattern as camouflage that helps to protect them from predation by the senior size cohort. It may be no coincidence that early stadia of several *Aeshna* species, most of which are semi- or *partivoltine*, are mottled with black and white. A similar progression occurs in some other aeshnids.[32]

A second category, **sprawlers**, are squat in shape and typically have a spoon-shaped prementum. They sprawl, usually with the legs extended laterally, amongst macrophytes, close to the water surface. Examples are species of *Sympetrum* (Fig. 65), known for their capacity for rapid growth.

Hiders, typified by Corduliidae, are somewhat similar in shape to sprawlers, but tend to be less active and to hide amongst leaf litter and detritus near the bottom. The setae on the body of some hiders gather particles from the sediment and help to camouflage the larva; other hiders are smooth and their bodies do not accumulate detritus. The larvae develop much more slowly than do sprawlers. *Sympetrum striolatum*, a sprawler, can complete larval development in little more than three months,[33] whereas *Cordulia aenea*, predominantly a hider,[34] and a

FIG 65. F-0 larva of *Sympetrum striolatum*, a sprawler (Steve Cham).

smooth one, may often require three years or more for the same purpose.[35]
Larvae of *Libellula quadrimaculata* and *Orthetrum coerulescens*, the bodies of which
are invested with setae, sometimes behave as hiders and sometimes as burrowers.

Species in the last category, **burrowers**, are squat, dark, and often thickly
invested with hair-like setae, and use their legs to cover the body with sediment.
As in sprawlers and hiders, the prementum is spoon-shaped, except in *Gomphus
vulgatissimus*, in which it is more or less flat. The shape of the legs, and the
movements they make, are well suited for digging, especially in *G. vulgatissimus*.[36]
The species of *Libellula* and *Orthetrum* found in Britain are mainly shallow
burrowers and, especially in *L. depressa* and *O. coerulescens*, achieve additional
camouflage when fine silt adheres to the setae on the dorsal surface. *Libellula
fulva*, however, is also a sprawler, living amongst plant debris at the bottom
of ponds like *Cordulia aenea*. Its possession of dorsal spines seems to indicate
that it is a sprawler more than a burrower.[37] *Cordulegaster boltonii* (Fig. 67) also

FIG 66. F-0 larva of *Cordulia aenea*, at different times a hider, sprawler and shallow burrower (Steve Cham).

FIG 67. F-0 larva of *Cordulegaster boltonii*, a shallow burrower which is widespread in Europe. The tips of the pointed compound eyes and the *anal pyramid* project slightly above the sediment when the larva is buried, a posture typical of a cordulegastrid larva (Hansruedi Wildermuth).

belongs in this category,[37] inhabiting silt that accumulates near the margins
of streams. This species is not regarded as an obligate burrower; it occupies a
variety of cryptic microhabitats, changing its preference according to the stage
of development.[37] The larva is large and ponderous, and it can lend zest to a
field trip to see a fully grown one clamber out of a mud sample. This example
reminds us that not all odonate larvae can be expected to fit neatly into the focal
categories that have been identified in Table 2. For example, some *Somatochlora*
larvae combine behavioural and morphological features of sprawlers, shallow
burrowers and hiders.[37] Also, the activity mode varies with hunger and density
or availability of prey.[19] Burrowers tend to have conical compound eyes that
project dorsally, extending above the surface of the sediment, and when at rest
they point the tip of the abdomen upwards, presumably to avoid inhaling silt
with the respiratory current. In Britain all burrowers are classified as **shallow
burrowers** because they rest just below the surface of the bottom sediment, but
in other countries, notably tropical Africa, there are genera (e.g. *Neurogomphus*)
whose larvae burrow deeply, having a narrow, cylindrical abdomen terminating
in a long, slender respiratory siphon that may occupy up to one third of the total
body length.[38] Such larvae are classified as **deep burrowers**. Larvae of burrowers
select their substrates according to particle size, the smallest larvae of *C. boltonii*
occupying much finer sediment than do larger larvae.[39] Larval development of
C. boltonii may take three or more years,[35] so this arrangement may reduce the
likelihood of predation by larger larvae on their smaller conspecifics. In one of
the few studies of the diet of *Cordulegaster* larvae,[40] no conspecific larva featured
among the gut contents.

Diets of larvae are very diverse and include almost any animal that is palatable
and not too large to handle. The diet during the last few stadia of *Aeshna juncea*,
A. caerulea, *Somatochlora arctica* and *Leucorrhinia dubia* in a northern bog included
Cladocera and larvae of *Chaoborus*, Chironomidae and Trichoptera.[41] Larvae in a
population of *Pyrrhosoma nymphula* (Fig. 68) studied by John Lawton near Durham
began by eating small Crustacea such as *Daphnia* and *Chydorus*, the lower limit
of prey length being about 0.8 millimetres, and then, as they grew larger, fed on
progressively larger prey, including small Crustacea (copepods and ostracods),
chironomid larvae and oligochaete worms.[42] Occasional items included other
Zygoptera, water mites and dipteran larvae. Different prey items present different
costs and benefits to the predator. For example, *handling time* can vary from five
or six seconds for an F-0 larva of *Cordulia aenea* or *Leucorrhinia dubia* consuming
Cladocera or Copepoda[43] to 19 minutes for an F-0 larva of *Aeshna juncea* eating
the case-bearing trichopteran *Limnephilus pantodapus*.[44] The largest claspers
sometimes catch and eat small fish. One of the obstacles to be overcome when

FIG 68. Larva of *Pyrrhosoma nymphula*, a clasper, in stadium F-o. Its swollen wing sheaths show that it is in an advanced state of metamorphosis. The specimen illustrated is in an alert mode and may have detected a prey item or a conspecific (Robert Thompson).

larvae are being reared in captivity is to find a ready supply of living prey, tailored in size to the size of the larvae. For larger larvae this is seldom difficult because a wide variety of animals can be used, including mosquito larvae and *Artemia*, the brine shrimp. For the smallest dragonfly larvae, whose prey is little known, cultures of large Protozoa are likely to serve the purpose well.

Many investigators use the voided faecal pellets (each conveniently enclosed in the sloughed peritrophic membrane) as a source of information about the prey of larvae. This method has much to recommend it, not least because larvae do not have to be killed, and because the pellets can be conveniently stored for later inspection, each labelled with the size of its originator. An added advantage is that the investigator quickly becomes adept at recognising prey organisms from inspection of minute and triturated body parts, an admirable though arcane skill that unfortunately has little practical application beyond the realm of freshwater biology and palaeoecology!

After the mandibles have fragmented the prey, the gizzard in the midgut grinds the prey into small parts. A larva taken from the field can be measured, kept until a faecal pellet is voided, and then released.

The stadium-2 larva is usually endowed with yolk derived from the egg, which is visible as a glistening, pale cream bolus occupying the midgut, and which may exempt the larva in that stadium from having to capture prey. After its yolk has been exhausted, in stadium 3 and beyond, the larva must obtain all its energy from its prey.

A continuing challenge faced by all organisms is to achieve a positive energy balance: in the long term their energy intake must equal or exceed their energy expenditure. Attempts to elucidate the way in which animals meet this challenge constitute the field of ecological energetics.[45] A truly remarkable feature of animals, especially opportunistic predators like dragonflies, is that they continually make appropriate choices as to how they should direct their activities so as to husband, and use, energy effectively. Energy acquisition through feeding need not always exactly match simultaneous energy expenditure (through growth and movement) because an animal can sometimes compensate for a temporary deficit by drawing on its own stored food reserves.

A quantitative estimate of the energy acquired and the energy expended at the level of the individual or the population is termed an *energy budget* (Box 11). The first energy budget calculated for an aquatic invertebrate animal was constructed by John Lawton for an odonate, the semivoltine *Pyrrhosoma nymphula*, in northern England, at the level of a population (Table 3) and a representative individual (Fig. 69).[46] The species is consistently semivoltine throughout Britain,[35] and Lawton's study covered two years.

The reasoning underlying the estimation of an energy budget is explained in Box 11.

A noteworthy feature in Table 3 is that population energy flow was similar in two year classes in which larval population dynamics (as expressed in average numbers/m², mortality rates, and numbers emerging) differed considerably.

The energy efficiency of foraging (i.e. food energy consumed divided by energy expended during its collection) for *P. nymphula* (1.6–3.6) is very low

BOX 11

ENERGY TRANSFORMATION

Energy is the capacity to do work, which includes growth. Plants typically obtain their energy by capturing solar energy and transforming it (by photosynthesis) into chemical energy which is stored in the form of simple organic compounds. Animals obtain their energy by consuming plants (if they are herbivores) or other animals (if they are carnivores). The chemical energy acquired by an animal can all be accounted for as growth, respiration and excretion.

The amount of energy an animal acquires per unit of food intake depends on its *assimilation efficiency* (AE), expressed as a percentage of dry weight of food consumed – (dry weight of faeces produced)/(dry weight of food consumed). Most species of dragonfly that have been studied have an AE exceeding 70 per cent.[47] *Pyrrhosoma nymphula*, in stadium 2, can achieve an AE of about 95 per cent and in stadium F-0 this value falls to between 75 and 90 per cent, depending on the type of prey.[46] The high AE of dragonflies perhaps compensates for their low feeding rate, a reflection of their default lifestyle as sit-and-wait predators. The energy content of food assimilated is conventionally expressed in joules (J), and can be estimated from its dry weight or by combustion, thus making it possible to compare the energy content of widely different substances. Energy consumed by respiration can be assessed by measuring the amount of carbon dioxide evolved. By such techniques the energy budget during larval life can be determined. The values in Table 3 and Fig. 69 show how energy was allocated by two successive year classes in a larval population of *P. nymphula*.

compared with that of many other animals, for example a bumblebee (4.4–20.2) or a largemouth black bass (3.8–10.3).[48] Lawton interpreted this low value as follows: larvae were feeding conservatively, in that at no time were they feeding at close to their maximum daily rates, but this was still (just) a viable food-gathering strategy because of the very high efficiency with which the food was being assimilated in this species (87.8 per cent) and the low energy cost of being an ambush-type predator.[49]

The dry weight of a population, which is expressed as its *biomass*, is a

TABLE 3. Energy flow[a] in a larval population of *Pyrrhosoma nymphula* in two successive year classes. (From Lawton[46])

	YEAR	
CATEGORY OF ENERGY FLOW	1966–7	1967–8
Consumption	35.57	35.91
Growth	16.55	15.08
Respiration	13.31	15.41
Exuviae	2.10	1.26
Faeces	3.61	4.16

Note: [a] (kJm²/year)

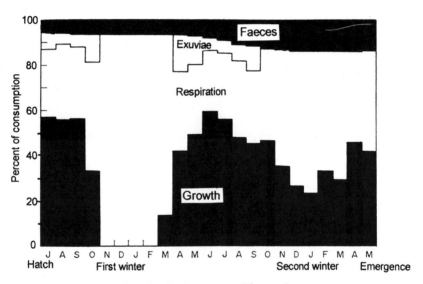

Months in two-year life cycle

FIG 69. Monthly energy utilisation for growth, respiration and production of exuviae and faeces as a percentage of consumption in a representative larva of *Pyrrhosoma nymphula* during its two-year development in nature. Based on pooled data from both year classes in two ponds in northern England. (After Lawton.[46])

measure of central importance in studies of biological productivity, itself a criterion of richness much used by ecologists when comparing habitats. Analyses of this kind make it possible to determine the proportion of macroinvertebrate biomass contributed by dragonflies in a community of freshwater organisms. For example, a population of *Leucorrhinia* larvae in acidified fishless lakes accounted for about 50 per cent of the total biomass of macroinvertebrates down to a depth of 6 metres.[50] Usually predators make up a smaller biomass than their prey, but sometimes the biomass of odonate larvae exceeds that of their prey, indicating that they are playing a major role in regulating their prey.[51] In such a case stability is maintained because the prey has a much higher turnover rate than the predator. This enables the predator to survive on a relatively low prey biomass.

Among invertebrates, odonate larvae are large, obligate predators and so can be expected to have considerable impact on community structure. When *Cordulegaster boltonii* larvae invaded an acidic, spring-fed stream this species became the new top predator. Food-web complexity changed markedly, presumably as a result of the opportunistic foraging style of *C. boltonii*, its large size range and the dietary shifts during its development.[52] It reduced the abundance of the former top predator, the trichopteran *Plectrocnemia*, and the stonefly *Nemurella*. Global warming is thought to have triggered the invasion, which perhaps gives us a foretaste of what will happen if *C. boltonii* ever becomes established in Ireland.

Odonate larvae have often been (uncritically) promoted as promising agents of biological suppression of insect pests (e.g. mosquitoes). But, for compelling reasons,[53] such introductions are unlikely to be effective, except in the very short term, and in closely confined habitats, such as treeholes[54] or artificial water-storage containers.[55]

INTERACTIONS WITH OTHER ORGANISMS

The main groups of organisms likely to be associated with larval Odonata in Britain are reviewed in this section. A more extensive account is given elsewhere.[56]

Comments on some of the organisms listed in Box 12 may help the observer to recognise them and understand the nature of the association.

BOX 12

THE MAIN GROUPS OF ORGANISMS LIKELY TO BE ASSOCIATED WITH LARVAL ODONATA IN BRITAIN

Epibionts include algae, Protozoa, Rotifera, bivalve molluscs and tube-dwelling chironomid larvae attached to the outside of the body, as well as the early stages of mites that are later ectoparasites of adults after emergence.

Pathogens are presumably present, but virtually nothing is known about them.

Parasites include Protozoa (Sporozoa, Gregarinida) that inhabit the gut and can be carried over to the adult stage, and several major groups of invertebrates (especially Trematoda, Cestoda and Aschelminthes) that use odonate larvae as intermediate hosts in a parasite life cycle that is completed by reproduction in a *definitive host* that is usually an habitual predator of odonate larvae, such as a fish, amphibian or bird.

Predators. Apart from Odonata (of their own and other species) the main predators of dragonfly larvae are fish and birds and perhaps amphibians, as well as some of the larger aquatic beetles (Coleoptera) and bugs (Hemiptera: Heteroptera).

Epibionts

The juvenile, dispersal stage of the freshwater mussel *Dreissenia polymorpha* sometimes attaches to the outside of larvae of Gomphidae, Corduliidae and Libellulidae[57] and is found on F-o exuviae after the carrier has emerged. Attachment to such a site presumably results in the premature death of the mussel. The attachment of larval cases of chironomids to larvae of *Gomphus vulgatissimus*[58] and *Somatochlora metallica*[59] may reflect a need by some *commensal* organisms for a secure substrate and, in flowing water, for a substrate that does not get buried in silt and that consistently faces upstream.[60]

Parasites

Larvae ingest sporocysts of gregarine Protozoa which develop in the host's gut to form immature sexual forms, or gamonts, each of which can attain a length of 0.8 millimetres.[61] In a severe infection, gamonts come to pack the larva's gut and seriously impair digestion, causing malnutrition and sometimes death.

When the density of gregarines reaches 300–500 per host, the gut wall can rupture, killing the host.[62] *Enallagma cyathigerum* has been recorded as a host of gregarines.[62] Gregarines are found also in the gut of adults, sometimes, perhaps, having been carried over from the larval stage. The gregarine burden in adults is inversely correlated with survival of both sexes of the North American coenagrionid, *Enallagma praevarum*.[63]

Adult *Calopteryx haemorrhoidalis* infested by gregarines exhibit lower *mating success*, and the intensity of their wing pigmentation is negatively correlated with their parasite load.[64] This finding may indicate how a potential partner could assess the reproductive fitness of a potential mate (by monitoring the intensity of wing pigmentation). Gregarines infest *Calopteryx splendens* early in the *prereproductive period* and are more numerous in older hosts. Infested adults accumulate less fat during the prereproductive period and consequently are less able to secure and maintain territories later.[65]

Parasites include several other major groups[66] and commonly infest both larvae and adults. Infestation often occurs during the larval stage. For example, metacercariae of the digenetic trematode *Haematolaechus* (a fluke) invade zygopteran larvae at the base of the caudal appendages or the intersegmental membranes.[67] Invasion of Anisoptera commonly takes place through the rectum, presumably being assisted by the inhalation that serves the respiratory system. When cercariae are invading the rectum, dragonfly larvae (e.g. *Sympetrum*) have been seen first to suspend respiratory movements for several seconds, then to exhale vigorously, and finally to try to catch and eat the cercariae.[68]

Many genera of digenetic trematodes are found as internal parasites of odonate larvae and, if the larva survives, are carried over at emergence to the host's adult stage. Occurrence of trematodes in Odonata is sometimes correlated with the presence in the vicinity of genera of molluscs that form the trematode's first intermediate host. The odonate larva is typically the second intermediate host. The metacercariae form cysts inside the larva, sometimes assuming the appearance of galls located in muscular or fatty tissue. The parasite's life cycle is completed when a vertebrate predator such as a fish, frog or bird ingests the dragonfly larva. An unpleasant fluke infection of poultry, which can be fatal to the birds, is caused by a species of *Prosthogonimus*. It is now known that birds can contract this parasite by consuming adult dragonflies but, in the 1920s, long before this fact was established,[69] folk wisdom maintained that, to prevent infection, birds should be denied access to the water's edge when dragonflies were emerging there or when adults were present in large numbers.[70] *Libellula quadrimaculata* is known to be a host, and its intermittent occurrence at very high density and its propensity for mass *migration* are thought to make it a formidable disseminator of this parasite. In countries where dragonfly larvae form part of the human diet (e.g. in Southeast Asia), humans may contract the flukes by ingesting uncooked dragonfly larvae.[71] The effect of trematode infection on the survival of larval or adult dragonflies is unknown and would be difficult to determine, partly because it may sometimes be indirect, as when a parasitised individual becomes more vulnerable to predation by virtue of its weakened condition,[72] and partly because the dragonfly may be harbouring other kinds of debilitating parasite. Similarly, some tapeworms, which are ingested as eggs by odonate larvae, form cysts within the odonate larva and then complete the life cycle in a predatory bird such as a heron.

Predators

Predators of odonate larvae, apart from other Odonata, aquatic beetles and Hemiptera, are mainly vertebrates. Many species of bottom-feeding fish consume large numbers of larvae[73] and predators of less importance include amphibians (frogs and newts), reptiles (snakes), water birds (such as kingfishers and herons)[74] and leeches.[75] In the tropics, crocodiles, especially when young, consume large anisopteran larvae, often when these are emerging at the water's edge at night.[76]

There is little doubt that fish are the most influential predators of odonate larvae. Odonate biomass is greater in fish-free waters, although there is no correlation between fish presence and odonate species richness.[77] The impact of fish varies according to the species of Odonata, presumably reflecting the dragonfly's antipredation behaviour. For example, in Swedish lakes the abundance of larvae of *Aeshna juncea* and *Leucorrhinia dubia* correlates negatively with the presence of fish, but for *Coenagrion hastulatum* and *Libellula quadrimaculata* there is no correlation, and for *Erythromma najas* and *Cordulia aenea* this correlation is positive.[78] We have observed that the introduction of Rudd, *Leuciscus erythrophthalmus*, into a garden pond was followed by a sustained drop in the numbers of *Sympetrum striolatum* (a sprawler) but no noticeable change in the numbers of *Pyrrhosoma nymphula* (a cryptic clasper) which continued to be abundant.

Predation of larvae by other Odonata (of the same or different species) can be substantial, contrary to early assumptions. In some species, for example *Ischnura elegans*[79] and *Pyrrhosoma nymphula*,[46] intraspecific predation is virtually nonexistent, but records from North America show that it can be heavy in *Aeshna juncea*, in populations where a three-year life cycle obliges larvae of different size cohorts to coexist[80] and where populations of coexisting species have contemporaneous components differing widely in size.[81] Evidently cannibalism (i.e. intraspecific interodonate predation) can be expected when larvae of different sizes coexist in time and space. Experiments in the laboratory and in field cages show that, under such circumstances, a size difference of two or more stadia renders such predation highly probable.[80] Zygopteran larvae seem to be more vulnerable than Anisoptera to intra-odonate predation, especially if fish are absent. In middle North America, where there are numerous species of *Enallagma*, including *E. cyathigerum*, their larvae are subject to predation, either by fish (where these are present) or by large Anisoptera (such as *Anax*) in habitats that lack fish.[82] In North America the antipredation behaviour exhibited by larvae of *Enallagma* differs in lakes with and without fish, depending on the kind of predator they are exposed to. In lakes containing fish, larvae respond to a predator's approach by becoming immobile and thus escaping the attention of fish, whereas in lakes without fish, where the top predators are Anisoptera, *Enallagma* larvae have developed much greater swimming speeds and enhanced physiological ability to fuel strenuous activity.[83] This equips them well to swim away, a strategy which helps them to escape from an anisopteran larva but which would invite capture in the presence of a fish. This dichotomy of antipredation responses in North American species of *Enallagma* larvae reflects the selective pressure exerted on them by predation and, considered alongside other studies, emphasises the protection they gain by occupying submerged water plants.[84] Interestingly, this relationship is not necessarily reproduced among European populations of *E. cyathigerum* which, unlike North American populations of this species, can coexist with fish,[85] although they sometimes suffer high predation as a result[86] and appear to have developed (or retained) rapid swimming as an antipredation response.[87] This difference between Old World and New World populations of '*E. cyathigerum*' is less surprising now that it has been recognised that they may not have the same evolutionary history.[88] It may be significant that, in two populations where larvae of *E. cyathigerum* in Britain were coexisting with fish (trout), the larvae were concentrated in dense swards of Shoreweed, *Littorella uniflora*.[89]

We suppose that larvae and adults of the beetle *Dytiscus*, and of aquatic bugs (*Nepa, Notonecta, Ranatra*) prey on larvae, especially Zygoptera, but there are few records. We have seen the aquatic bug *Ilyocoris* consuming larvae of *Coenagrion puella* in a garden pond.

The intensity of predation on *Coenagrion puella* larvae by the backswimmer *Notonecta* was much reduced under experimental conditions when larvae were provided with refuges in the form of artificial water plants. Presumably water plants also serve an important function for ambush foragers – as perches from which to forage. These considerations emphasise the importance to larvae of finding and defending favourable perches. They may well allow us to interpret the aggressive behaviour that Zygoptera larvae show, apparently in defence of their perches. Such behaviour is complex and stereotyped. A North American species of *Ischnura* exhibits more than 40 discrete behaviours when close to conspecifics,[90] larvae of *Pyrrhosoma nymphula* exhibit 17[91] and those of the diminutive *Agriocnemis pygmaea* 25.[92] These behaviours include face-to-face staring, side-to-side swinging of the abdomen and jabbing by the caudal lamellae. Such ritualistic confrontations typically end with one adversary moving away. This behaviour must result in larvae becoming spaced out among perches, and in selection for vigour in aggressive display. In larvae of *Ischnura elegans* face-to-face staring leads to increased success in intraspecific larval encounters.[93] (The vanquished larva in such an encounter vacates the field.) Curiously, intraspecific aggressive behaviour, which exhibits so rich a repertoire in larval Zygoptera, has seldom been recorded between larvae of Anisoptera, although large larvae of the North American *Anax junius* stare fixedly at each other, sometimes for many minutes at a time.[94]

As we have seen, zygopteran larvae typically escape from predators by swimming to avoid Anisoptera and by adopting immobility to escape notice by fish. Larvae of some Anisoptera have other defensive behaviours in reserve if actually grasped or touched by a predator. These entail one of three strategies. Initially, a larva will try to wriggle free. Then, if it is a robust anisopteran such as *Aeshna cyanea*, it may try to pierce its attacker using the sharp caudal appendages (paraprocts) which for this action are tightly closed, forming a three-sided spike that can draw blood from a human finger.[95] Also the labium or mandibles may be used to nip an attacker. Finally the larva may feign death by adopting a stiffly immobile posture which is likely to be maintained, despite further physical interference, for several to many minutes, as, for example, in *Brachytron pratense*.[96] The hypothesis that reflex immobilisation has been selected for by the intensity of predation by fish receives support from the finding that larvae of *Leucorrhinia dubia* from *fishless* habitats in Sweden, when subjected to a simulated fish attack, exhibited no reflex immobilisation but tried to escape, whereas larvae of three other anisopteran genera feigned death under the same conditions.[97] British species that sometimes feign death are listed in Table 4. This form of antipredation behaviour has been investigated thoroughly in species in Japan[98] and Europe.[99] This condition entails a marked prolongation of the brief immobility, lasting only a few seconds, that is often an immediate response to physical disturbance, especially in species that coexist with fish. The posture adopted (Fig. 70) tends to be characteristic of the family. Death feigning, or reflex immobilisation (RI) (or *thanatosis*), has so far been recorded in eleven families, all

TABLE 4. British species that exhibit reflex immobilisation (RI) as larvae. (After Wildermuth.[99])

SPECIES	POSTURE CATEGORY	DURATION OF RI (RANGE IN SECONDS)	
		IN WATER	ON LAND
Aeshnidae			
Brachytron pratense	clasper	up to 1,800	>3,600
Cordulegastridae			
Cordulegaster boltonii	shallow burrower	?	?
Corduliidae			
Cordulia aenea	sprawler	2–330	
Somatochlora metallica	hider/sprawler	5–679	90–>3,600
Libellulidae			
Libellula quadrimaculata	shallow burrower	?	?
Orthetrum cancellatum	shallow burrower	?	?
O. coerulescens	shallow burrower	?	?

but three of which are Anisoptera. Immobilisation tends to last longer if the larva is out of water. In species of *Somatochlora*, RI is exhibited by larvae in stadium 2[99] and so presumably occurs throughout larval life.

Death feigning has been recorded in only three families of Zygoptera, including Coenagrionidae.[98] Sometimes larvae of *Pyrrhosoma nymphula* will remain immobile for several minutes, in a flexed position, often lying on their backs, after being disturbed.

The mere presence of a predator can entail costs for a zygopteran larva, even if it avoids being eaten. A larva of *Pyrrhosoma nymphula* can detect the presence nearby of a larva of *Aeshna juncea* by waterborne chemical stimuli, with the result that the *P. nymphula* larva forages less. The *A. juncea* larva is chemically labelled by its diet,[100] a phenomenon found in some predatory fish such as Pike, *Esox lucius*,[101] and in this way zygopteran larvae can be warned of its proximity.[102] The discovery that zygopteran larvae detect some predators chemically rather than visually has far-reaching implications for our understanding of their ecology, behaviour and foraging success. One may wonder whether adults retain this sensory ability, enabling ovipositing females to detect the presence of fish.[103]

A zygopteran larva can increase the likelihood of escaping from a predator by voluntarily relinquishing a leg or one or more of its caudal lamellae – a process termed *autotomy*.[104] This may allow a larva to escape to live another day, but it is not without cost. Loss of a lamella by *Lestes sponsa* increases the probability of its

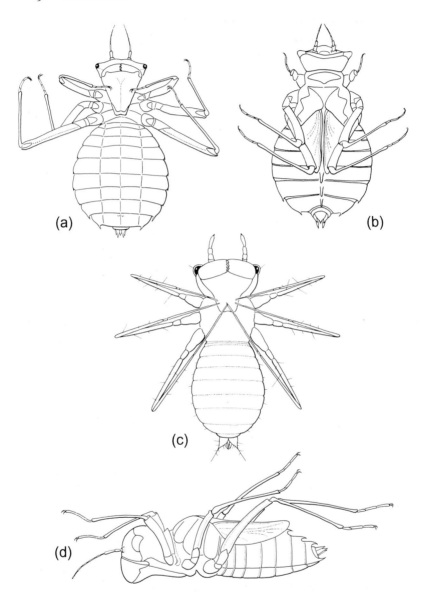

FIG 70. Postures adopted by *Somatochlora* larvae during reflex immobilisation, viewed from below (a, c), above (b) and left side (d). (a, b) *S. metallica*, stadium F-0, length 25mm; (c) *S. alpestris*, stadium 2, length 1.2mm; (d) *S. flavomaculata*, stadium F-0, length 22mm. (After Wildermuth.[99])

being eaten by conspecifics or preyed upon by the Backswimmer, *Notonecta*, and it also reduces hunting success by the deprived larva.[105]

SURVIVORSHIP

There have been several systematic studies of survivorship of larvae in the field. These have produced values for survivorship (i.e. the number of larvae surviving the larval stage as a percentage of the numbers entering it) ranging from 0.2 per cent (for the Japanese subspecies *Cordulia aenea amurensis* over the five-year larval period)[106] to 16 per cent (for *Pantala flavescens* over the three-month larval period in Indiana, USA).[107] Most values obtained, however, lie well below 10 per cent. The corresponding value for *Pyrrhosoma nymphula*, during a two-year larval period in a fish-free habitat in northern England, was 0.2 per cent.[108] An unsurprising implication of such findings is that a long larval life decreases survivorship. Survivorship during the larval stage sometimes shows a disproportionate decline shortly before emergence, while larvae are undergoing metamorphosis.[109] In a dense population of *Anax imperator* only 46 per cent of F-0 larvae survived during the month before emergence.[29] In the European gomphid *Onychogomphus uncatus*, mortality of overwintering F-0 larvae can be 99 per cent.[110] In a high-altitude population of *Aeshna juncea* only 2.5 per cent of hatched larvae were still alive after three years.[111]

The functional role of odonate larvae in aquatic ecosystems depends primarily on whether or not they coexist with fish. If fish are present, the fish are usually the top predators, and Odonata occupy an important intermediate role in the food web, preying on a wide variety of smaller invertebrates, as well as on each other. When fish are absent, the larger Anisoptera, such as aeshnids, can be the top predators and the behaviour of Zygoptera (especially) may be modified accordingly. Species-rich communities of Odonata can exhibit great stability in the relative abundance of constituent species from year to year.[112] Given the complex interactions between odonate larvae and other organisms, not to mention the annual fluctuations in physical factors, such stability is remarkable, reminding us that the ways in which populations are regulated remain poorly understood. Studies of the composition and dynamics of larval odonate assemblages are few, not least because they need to be searching and long term, and to entail protracted studies of a detailed nature. Although some-times the relative numbers of species can vary widely, the high stability of some populations that have been studied (in relatively unchanging habitats)[112] indicates that regulation is taking place. The mechanism for such regulation remains obscure, although one can assume that, because it is density-dependent, it must be driven predominantly by interaction among conspecifics which, in practice, means cannibalism.

PHYSICAL FACTORS

Odonata are primarily a warm-adapted group and their abundance and species diversity diminish with increasing latitude and altitude. British Odonata constitute an impoverished, marginal, northern European fauna, subject to yet further reduction by virtue of being an island fauna.[113] Within the British Isles the species diversity of Odonata decreases from south to north,[114] as one would expect of a group experiencing temperature limitation. However, it is unclear at which stage or stages the limitation acts, and careful work would be needed to determine this. The limitation need not necessarily operate in the aquatic stages; it might be mainly a weather-mediated effect of inclement conditions experienced by adults. Many species of larvae can survive being frozen into blocks of ice, but the habit of moving into deeper water during winter must often enable larvae to avoid being frozen. It is unlikely that larvae in Britain ever encounter the upper temperature threshold for survival which, for species that have already been acclimatised to high temperatures in hot *lentic* habitats, is close to 45°C.[115] Anecdotal evidence suggests that larvae of several species can survive the absence of surface water in a larval habitat.[116] Such larvae have been found in minute pockets of water (e.g. *Aeshna cyanea*),[117] in humid cavities under stones (e.g. *Ischnura elegans*),[118] or in the dry gravel bed of a pond (e.g. *Libellula depressa*).[119] A libellulid larva found frozen within a layer of humus in a dried-up swamp swam actively after having been thawed out in water.[120] In an alpine pond in Colorado, under snow cover, a larva of *Somatochlora semicircularis* retained the capacity to rehydrate and then behave normally after nine months in dry moss without free water.[121]

Two correlated physical factors that determine habitat distribution of British species are water movement and dissolved oxygen. Species typically segregate into those inhabiting standing (lentic) and flowing (*lotic*) water respectively. Species of *Calopteryx* and *Cordulegaster* are almost never found in standing water, and *Gomphus vulgatissimus* and *Platycnemis pennipes* only occasionally,[122] whereas many species are virtually confined to standing water. A few, such as *Pyrrhosoma nymphula* and *Libellula quadrimaculata*, can often be found in both types of habitat and, as discussed in Chapter 2, it is not uncommon for several other species to occupy both lentic and lotic habitats. No British species occupies shallow, rapidly flowing streams with a rocky bottom, a habitat occupied by *Boyeria irene*, *Caliaeschna microstigma* and *Epallage fatime* in mainland Europe and by several species of dragonfly in North America. In running waters, water movement and the resulting particle-size of sediment are likely to determine the micro-distribution of burrowing larvae.[123] In running waters that show wide seasonal fluctuations in depth, larvae may take refuge deep in the sediment during the season of low water.[121] In standing waters, odonate larvae (especially Anisoptera) are found predominantly in shallow water less than 1 metre deep,[124] but larvae of both suborders may occur in deeper water if rooted water plants are present. In New Zealand, larvae of the corduliid *Procordulia grayi* and the coenagrionid *Xanthocnemis zealandica* occur down to a depth of 19 metres (in Lake Waikaremoana) in places where there are stands of water plants.[125] In the River Main, Germany, larvae of *Gomphus vulgatissimus* occur between depths of 0.8 and 5.2 metres, but most often between 2.5 and 3.0 metres.[126] In *Cordulegaster boltonii* the preference of larvae for coarse sediment increases during larval development, except during F-0 when the trend is reversed. Larvae are usually totally buried except for the protruding antennae and anal pyramid (Fig. 67, p.123).[37]

Four species of *Cordulegaster* that occupy streams in southeast Saxony, Germany, are segregated along a stream: *C. bidentata* and *C. insignis* are confined to springs and the headwaters of their outflow streams, whereas *C. boltonii* and *C. picta* occur from the springs down to larger streams and rivulets. This complementary distribution reflects the different ways in which the two pairs of species avoid downstream drift after spates.[127] Among British species *Calopteryx splendens* and *C. virgo* exhibit a complementary distribution in watercourses.

Interest has focused on the potential usefulness of Odonata as indicators of water quality and therefore on the effects on their survival of different kinds of pollution. Because pollutants seldom act singly, acute effects of individual additives are difficult or impossible to assess in the field. The main additives that pollute fresh waters are erosion products, industrial effluents, farm runoff (including pesticides) and domestic sewage. Because odonates are obligate predators, pollutants affect field populations indirectly, via the susceptibility of their prey, as well as directly, through their own exposure. One commonly used measure of organic pollution of fresh waters, including eutrophication, is the *biochemical oxygen demand* or BOD. This is defined as the amount of oxygen (expressed as parts per million or mg/litre) taken up by a sample during the first five days of decomposition at 20°C. Domestic sewage has a BOD of about 200 mg/litre. Work in North America has shown that only one species of *Ischnura* occurred where the BOD exceeded 10 mg/litre.[128] It is likely that species of

Ischnura are exceptionally tolerant of pollution. After a major pollution incident in April 1985, involving spillage of the organophosphate insecticide 'Dursban 4E' (active ingredient chlorpyrifos) into an Essex river, all species of odonate larvae were eliminated, although all had returned (presumably by recolonisation) within about 14 months.[129] The first odonate species to become re-established was *Ischnura elegans*, which is consistent with the report that this species is often the only odonate to persist in polluted waters.[130] Where organic pollutants are concerned, it may often be the heightened BOD that dominates the acute effect. Some larvae, for example *Calopteryx* spp.,[131] possess stereotyped behavioural responses that help them to mitigate the effects of low oxygen availability in the short term, but they are still affected by the mortality of other organisms on which they depend for food. Sometimes the deleterious effects of high BOD can be offset by fortuitous human activities: *Gomphus vulgatissimus* in a heavily polluted lake in Germany was able to survive where turbulence caused by boat traffic increased the amount of dissolved oxygen.[132]

Pollutants include metals and pesticides, and their effects can be severe. For example, high concentrations of tin, such as are found in mine tailings, are associated with serious deformity among emerging adults, especially of *Aeshna cyanea* and *Pyrrhosoma nymphula*.[133] Tin was used as a constituent of antifouling paints (as tributyltin) on boats until a Europe-wide ban in 1987, and was a serious pollutant in the Norfolk Broads. Apparently lead is accumulated in considerable amounts in the midgut, fat body, rectum and cuticle of exposed larvae,[134] although its harmful effects, if any, in those organs are unknown. The effects of individual pesticides can only be determined from monofactorial experiments in the laboratory which may bear little relation to conditions in the field. However, by combining evidence from laboratory tests and field trials, certain provisional conclusions can be drawn about the effects on Odonata of a pollution incident. First, Odonata are often promptly affected by diminution of their prey. Second, the direct toxicity to Odonata larvae of insecticides probably follows approximately this sequence, in decreasing order of severity: organochlorines, organophosphates, rotenone, carbamates, insect growth regulators, microbials, surfactants and plant oils.[135] Pyrethroids, which can cause massive invertebrate mortality for miles downstream of even a small spillage, deserve a prominent place in this list.

So, one may ask, can odonate larvae serve reliably as indicators of the type and quality of habitats? Subject to the qualifications we have recognised, it can be concluded that:

1) Odonata can be useful as bioindicators, but mainly as one among a mosaic of correlated habitat attributes that together indicate 'water quality' and stages of ecological succession, including degradation caused by human impact; and

2) the use of species assemblages, rather than individual species, strengthens this usefulness by rendering less fragmentary the correlation between habitat and Odonata, and by buffering that correlation against the effects of some small deficiency in the array of physical and biotic conditions needed by each species, and against intraspecific variation.[136] When Odonata are enlisted as bioindicators, one must remember that they need more than pollution-free water.

OPPORTUNITIES FOR INVESTIGATION

Perhaps the greatest obstacle to progress in our understanding of the behaviour and ecology of larvae is the difficulty (often the near impossibility) of identifying to species larvae in early stadia, despite the relative paucity of the British fauna. All over the world larvae still tend to be the Cinderellas of odonatology: more effort is required to find them, they are less attractive to photographers, and they are often difficult to identify. Nevertheless, ecologically the larva is probably the most influential stage in the life cycle. In Britain, as in most temperate latitudes, it lasts far longer than the egg or adult and has intimate links with the reproductive habitat. At present larvae in the first few stadia are extremely difficult to distinguish to species. In some genera of Libellulidae and Aeshnidae, stadium-2 larvae bear characteristically shaped protuberances on the top of the head.[137] If such features exist in any British species, they might prove useful for identifying early stadium larvae.

There is an urgent need for keys to earlier stadia. To rectify this will be a mammoth task, involving the raising of many species from the egg to the final larval stadium, and the search for diagnostic characters which, in early stadia, may prove elusive. Fortunately, a few species (e.g. *Anax imperator*, *Pyrrhosoma nymphula*) can be identified in all stadia by their shape, posture and colour pattern, but for the great majority of species this is impossible. Moreover, even if the information on external morphology *does* become available, as it has for several species of North American *Enallagma*, there is still no guarantee that effective keys can be constructed.[138] Only for larvae of Norwegian dragonflies does a key exist which comes near to this ideal and this, the product of expert and painstaking work over many years,[139] is unlikely to be duplicated elsewhere.

There is, however, a way forward, available to anyone with access to simple laboratory facilities. This entails the use of cellulose acetate gel electrophoresis, the apparatus for which can be readily packed and transported for use in the field.[140] The trace, or imprint, so obtained is unique to larvae (and adults) of each species, regardless of stadium. To develop this method so that it could be used routinely would probably represent the most valuable contribution that could be made at present to our knowledge of larval behaviour and ecology. An approach offering similar promise for identifying early-stadium larvae is to detect the presence of species-specific proteins in the homogenates of thoracic muscles.[141]

Building on the secure foundation that such an advance would provide, other topics that offer rewards for the investigator could be explored with confidence. Examples are studies of voltinism, which are needed to understand the mechanisms of seasonal regulation.

Another potentially fruitful field of study, requiring little more than an aquarium, patience and a video camera with a time-lapse facility, is the way in which some species tailor their foraging and feeding behaviour to different kinds of prey and microhabitat. This constitutes an arena where behaviour has both learnt and innate components, and where analytical studies cannot fail to be rewarding. Furthermore, as recent studies have shown,[19] this approach can reveal the repertoire involved in opportunistic foraging and aggressive behaviour, which must be understood if the complex phenomenon of competition among larvae is ever going to be illuminated.

FIG 71. Design for stationary trap for collecting larvae of Zygoptera. (After Krüner[143].)

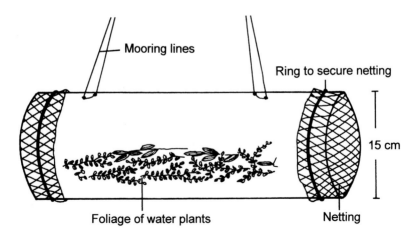

Mooring lines

Ring to secure netting

15 cm

Foliage of water plants

Netting

Related to this topic is the need to know what kind of microhabitats larvae occupy. How do larvae of different species and different posture categories behave in simulated natural microhabitats in an aquarium? Their movements, diel activity patterns, foraging, hiding, and interactions with conspecifics of different ages are all topics worthy of further study. It would also be helpful to discover whether larvae that occupy very small bodies of water depend on terrestrial prey.

The invention of a static trap for larvae[142] (Fig. 71) offers opportunities for monitoring as well as quantifying the activity of larvae in the field. We know of no tests of such a trap in Britain, but in Germany Ulrike Krüner collected larvae of Coenagrionidae and Lestidae by this means.[143]

To determine the prey of larvae and relate this to larval size and microhabitat would require a microscope, patience and skill, but no other specialised equipment. It can be done, without sacrificing larvae, by examining the faecal pellets they void after capture. The contents of the pellets can then be compared with other invertebrates occupying the same habitat, and, if fortune smiles on the investigator, identified.

CHAPTER 6

Larval Development and Emergence

GROWTH

L ARVAL DEVELOPMENT IS punctuated by a variable number of moults (Box 13).

The final stadium (F-0) varies little in size, any variation in the number of stadia being compensated for by the *growth ratio* between stadia that precede F-0. Because the number of stadia can vary, it is inappropriate to designate the degree of intermediate larval development by stadium number. The head width generally increases at a uniform rate during development, and so is a useful measure of larval size[1] and is commonly used by investigators studying the rate of growth in natural populations. Body length can also be useful for those who lack the facility to measure head width, but it is subject to wider variation because the abdomen may be unusually extended before a moult (Fig. 72) and telescoped at some other times.

Species of Odonata differ with regard to their growth rate when exposed to identical conditions of temperature, daylength and food. For example, lestids usually grow more rapidly than do coenagrionids.[2] Such differences correlate with the categories of lifestyle described in Table 2, p.119; for example, the higher foraging rate of *Lestes sponsa* correlates with a high growth rate.[3] Growth rate can also be affected by variables such as temperature and prey availability, and by responses to daylength that play a crucial role in seasonal regulation of the life cycle (p.167). Growth rate of *L. sponsa* can be depressed by the mere presence of a predator (*Aeshna cyanea*), a nonlethal effect that is perhaps caused by a lowering of the assimilation efficiency and/or by raised metabolic rate,[4] or perhaps by a judicious curtailment of foraging behaviour.

BOX 13

GROWTH AND MOULTING

Arthropods (including dragonflies), whose bodies are typically enclosed in a hard, inelastic integument, increase in size by undergoing successive moults (or *ecdyses*) (Fig. 72). Within a few hours after each moult, while the cuticle of the larva (or adult) remains pale and soft (i.e. while the animal is still teneral, Fig. 72), the body dimensions can increase by a factor of about 25 per cent if the larva (or adult) can swallow water (or air) to inflate the body (and wings). A short time before a moult, the epidermis separates from the cuticle of the existing stage and begins to secrete the new cuticle of the forthcoming stage. This process, termed *apolysis*, marks the beginning of the *pharate* condition in the moulting cycle. The interval between successive apolyses is termed an *instar* and the interval between successive moults is called a stadium. Odonata pass through 8–18 stadia (average 12.4) between the egg and adult stages, the first stadium being known as the prolarva[1] (p.107). The number of stadia can vary within a species and even among siblings originating from eggs of the same *batch* laid on the same day. The last few stadia are numbered backwards from the final stadium (F-0) thus: F-1, F-2, etc. During the last days of F-0, changes in morphology, physiology and behaviour take place in anticipation of the final moult (emergence) which will disclose the adult. These changes constitute metamorphosis. Some of them are visible externally and can provide a means of predicting when an individual will emerge, notably those occurring in the compound eyes, the wing sheaths and the prementum of the labium (Fig. 73).

During the last four or five stadia the rudiments of the wing sheaths become visible externally and increase in length greatly at each moult. Indeed the interstadial growth ratio of the wing sheaths is close to 1.75, compared with the corresponding value of about 1.25 for other parts of the body.[1] This means that wing-sheath length usually provides a reliable criterion for recognition of the last three stadia, giving information that is essential for inferring the ways in which the life cycle is regulated (p.172). Occasionally one finds a stadium intermediate in dimension between F-1 and F-0,[5] but this is very rare.

In the rest of this chapter many of the species references are to *Anax*

FIG 72. Larva of *Aeshna cyanea*. The pale, soft cuticle shows that it has recently moulted to stadium F-1 (Robert Thompson).

imperator. This is because a thorough study was made of the ecology and behaviour of this species at a stem habitat (Box 6, p.76), the Fish Pond, in southern England in the early 1950s.[6] Although this study provided a great deal of information not easily obtained for other species, the temptation to regard it as representative of all species or all populations of *A. imperator* in Britain should of course be resisted.

METAMORPHOSIS

Changes associated with metamorphosis are conspicuous and easy to categorise in aeshnids (Fig. 73) where they can be used to track the progress of metamorphosis in a larval population and also to predict when emergence will begin. Metamorphosis in British species is almost always followed within weeks by emergence. The only known exception is *Cordulegaster boltonii*, a spring species, in which a few larvae in a population in southern Spain showed signs of incipient metamorphosis in autumn.[7] In the latest stages of metamorphosis, normally encountered only a few days before emergence, the internal tissues of the labium

FIG 73. Heads of F-0 larvae of *Anax imperator*, from above, showing progressive changes associated with metamorphosis. (a) expansion of the compound eyes towards the midline (dorsal view); (b) retraction of the adult labium within the larval prementum (pm) (ventral view). (From Corbet.[6])

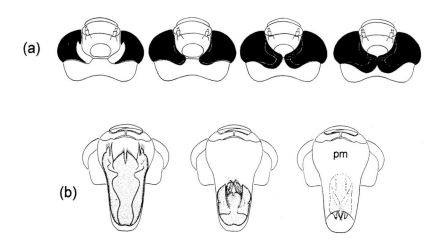

retract within the prementum, passing across the labial suture and finishing up in the postmentum. In all species of British Odonata this progression can usually be seen, without extending the labium, using a hand lens, and can be put to good use in field studies. The easiest way to determine whether metamorphosis has begun is to note the orientation and swelling of the wing sheaths.[8] Such changes can usually be detected with a simple hand lens or even the unaided eye, in Zygoptera as well as Anisoptera. Strictly speaking, metamorphosis has not been completed by the time of emergence: some of the body muscles and their nerves do not complete the transformation until several days after emergence.[9]

EMERGENCE

When an individual is ready to emerge its first action is to select an emergence support. Larger Anisoptera (e.g. *Anax imperator*) do this several days in advance, swimming towards the water margin at night.[2] Zygoptera, which, weather permitting, emerge in mid-morning, swim towards the shore in daylight, possibly orientating by following a positive temperature gradient in the surface water.[10] Frequently an individual will find a suitable support, usually the upright stem of an emergent water plant, before reaching the water's edge, but, if not, it will often leave the water and clamber over the ground in search of a support. An individual of *Pyrrhosoma nymphula*, engaged in such an overland journey, was seen to meet a spider around the side of a grass tussock.[10] Remarkably, the dragonfly whipped the tip of its abdomen forwards and jabbed its pointed caudal lamellae at the spider, which promptly withdrew. This event is noteworthy because the dragonfly, although adopting a familiar larval display posture (p.113), was at the time no longer a larva but an adult enclosed in a larval skin (i.e. a *pharate* adult). *Anax imperator* larvae sometimes travel up to 6 metres from the water's edge before selecting an emergence support, and up to a height of 5 metres;[2] once an individual of *A. imperator* crossed a grassy meadow and passed several trees and a fence before emerging more than 30 metres from the nearest water.[11] *Cordulegaster boltonii* sometimes travels far before emerging,[12] F-0 exuviae having been found *in situ* up to 6 metres above and 4.2 metres away from a stream margin.[13] Some libellulids in other countries have been seen to travel more than 40 metres before moulting.[14]

Once an individual has selected a position, head upwards, on an emergence support, and before starting to moult, it usually swings the abdomen and legs in a characteristically jerky manner, apparently to verify that it is securely anchored

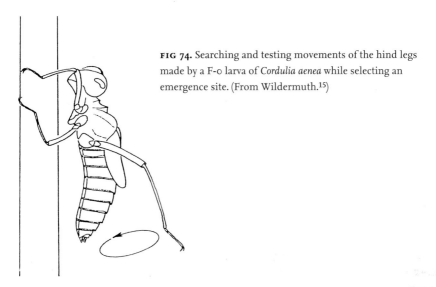

FIG 74. Searching and testing movements of the hind legs made by a F-0 larva of *Cordulia aenea* while selecting an emergence site. (From Wildermuth.[15])

and not too close to any object that might impede its forthcoming transformation, during which its expanding wings could be permanently damaged if they touched anything. After *Cordulia aenea* has ascended a potential emergence support it makes 'searching' movements with the fore and mid legs. Then, while stationary, it makes circling movements with the hind legs (Fig. 74). Only then does it clasp the support tightly and begin to moult. If disturbed during the testing process, it descends and chooses a new support.[15] When emergence supports are in short supply, it can happen that the earliest individuals to select their emergence supports are unable to complete the final moult because individuals arriving slightly later clamber over them and use them as emergence supports. Such interference can be a major source of density-dependent mortality.[2]

Sometimes exuviae (usually, it seems, of Zygoptera) are found *in situ* but upside down[16] (Fig. 75). This is unexpected and so far unexplained. In some cases, but certainly not all, such an exuvia may have become inverted (perhaps by wind) after the adult has vacated it.

When emergence has been completed, the exuvia (Fig. 76) of the F-0 larva remains on the emergence support. The value of the exuvia as a tool for quantitative ecological studies cannot be overstated. Exuviae of most British species can be determined to species[17] and, except in strong wind or rain, they remain *in situ* for several days. They provide the most secure evidence that a generation has been successfully completed in a habitat. Also, if exhaustive

FIG 75. Inverted emergence of *Ischnura elegans* (Robert Thompson).

FIG 76. The collection of F-0 exuviae from around the edge of a pond is a good way of establishing which species are breeding and the size of the emerging population (Robert Thompson).

collections are made at short, regular intervals (preferably daily), exuviae reveal precisely the temporal pattern of emergence, or *emergence curve*, an extremely informative ecological parameter (Box 15, p.163). Additionally, they can be used to determine the size of the population at emergence. Moreover, because their sex can be determined, exuviae provide a reliable measure of the sex ratio at emergence,[18] a valuable baseline for interpreting sex ratios encountered later among mature adults at the reproductive site.[19] Exuvia collections are the method of choice for characterising the emergence curve of Anisoptera, but they are less suitable for Zygoptera whose exuviae are small and inconspicuous, more easily dislodged by wind and rain and sometimes telescoped to an extent that renders them very difficult to find or identify. For Zygoptera it can be more effective to record the presence of teneral adults.[20] To apply this method rigorously, the investigator needs to take into account the diel periodicity of emergence so as to detect adults before they leave the emergence site on the *maiden flight*. Another advantage of this method is that the teneral adult can be confined for 24 hours, while the cuticle hardens, and then given an individual mark from which its exact postemergence age can be known whenever it is resighted (Appendix 2).

The successive stages of emergence are described in Box 14.

During stage 1 of emergence an anisopteran changes from employing aquatic to aerial respiration, losing the use of its rectal breathing apparatus and relying on the thoracic spiracles. During emergence, the exuvia, clinging securely to an emergence support, is usually vertical, head uppermost, or nearly so. Exceptions to this are *Gomphus*, which often emerges on a horizontal surface, and those individuals of other species which appear to emerge upside down.

During most of stage 2, the head, thorax and legs are out of the exuvia and the body is attached to it only by the posterior part of the abdomen, which remains inside the exuvia. The emerging individual remains immobile for a relatively long time in this position which is accordingly referred to as the resting stage. During the resting stage the head, thorax and legs hang downwards (the hanging type (Fig. 83) as in Aeshnidae, Calopterygidae, Cordulegastridae, Corduliidae and Libellulidae), or they face upwards and forwards (the upright type, (Fig. 84), as in Coenagrionidae, Lestidae and Platycnemididae), or horizontally and facing forwards, as in Gomphidae. During stage 3 the wings and abdomen attain their full size. The end of stage 4 (Fig. 82) often cannot be precisely determined, partly because takeoff in a flight-ready individual may be postponed until it receives the appropriate stimulus or until the ambient temperature permits spontaneous flight. For example, on warm nights in southern England, newly emerged adults of *Anax imperator* attain flight readiness well before sunrise, but do not take to the wing until dawn twilight.[6] Completion of stages 1–4 may take an hour or

BOX 14

THE STAGES OF EMERGENCE

It is useful to distinguish four stages of emergence.

1. The dragonfly is completely out of the water but the cuticle has not yet split (Fig. 77).
2. The cuticle of the head and thorax has split (Fig. 78).
3. The abdomen of the adult has been withdrawn from the exuvia (Fig. 79).
4. The wings and abdomen are expanding. The stage ends when the abdomen and wings have attained their full size and (in Anisoptera) the wings have opened and the dragonfly is flightworthy (Figs 80, 81, 82).

FIG 77. *Libellula depressa* in stage 1 of emergence (Robert Thompson).

FIG 78. *Libellula depressa* in stage 2 of emergence (Robert Thompson).

FIG 79. *Libellula depressa* in stage 3 of emergence (Robert Thompson).

FIG 80. *Libellula depressa* early in stage 4 of emergence (Robert Thompson).

FIG 81. *Libellula depressa* late in stage 4 of emergence (Robert Thompson).

FIG 82. *Orthetrum coerulescens* at the completion of stage 4 of emergence. The teneral adult is ready to fly (Robert Thompson).

considerably more in Britain, but can vary widely, probably depending on ambient temperature. Emergence of *Gomphus flavipes* in Germany took between 15 and 59 minutes.[21] In Britain, emergence of Zygoptera probably takes between one and two hours (e.g. 83 minutes in *Erythromma najas*),[22] whereas large Anisoptera probably take two to four hours (e.g. more than three hours in *Aeshna juncea* at high altitude[23] in Japan and about three hours at night in *Anax imperator*[6]). At low latitudes emergence can be completed more rapidly: a small gomphid, *Paragomphus genei*, by Lake Tchad, at 13°N, emerging by day in sunlight, completed stages 1–4 in 20 minutes,[24] and another gomphid, *Crenigomphus renei*, by Lake Albert at 0–2°N, emerging after dark, did so in 30 minutes.[25]

In Britain many species emerge in mid-morning, but some of the largest Anisoptera leave the water close to sunset, complete the moult by about midnight and then remain on the emergence support, presumably in stage 4, until dawn

FIG 83. *Cordulia aenea* during the resting stage of emergence. An example of the hanging type (Steve Cham).

FIG 84. *Pyrrhosoma nymphula* during the resting stage of emergence. An example of the upright type (Ann Brooks).

twilight, when they take off for the first time (i.e. perform the maiden flight) (Fig. 85). The maiden flight of a large dragonfly like *Anax imperator* during a synchronised emergence is a memorable sight. At the first glimmer of morning light, just before the last bat returns to roost, adults begin to vibrate their wings, supposedly to warm the thoracic muscles and prepare them for flight.[26] After some minutes of wing-whirring, clearly audible to the human observer, an adult walks slowly to the top of its emergence support and then, after increasing its wingbeat frequency, it becomes airborne.[6] The air temperature in Britain at dawn in May and June (when *A. imperator* emerges) can be as low as 6–10°C and thus well below the normal threshold for spontaneous flight. One may assume that an extended period of warm-up by wing-whirring is a prerequisite for the maiden flight in species that have committed themselves to nocturnal emergence at high latitudes. It seems that this activity may be stimulated by light of a certain low intensity. To judge by observations made in southern England, an early maiden flight is of high selective value as a means of reducing predation by birds: about ten minutes after the first wave of newly emerged adults had left the emergence sites at the Fish Pond (Fig. 44, p.77), Blackbirds,

FIG 85. Normal diel periodicity of emergence of *Anax imperator*, illustrated by counts of larvae entering the four successive stages of emergence (Box 14). Asymptotic values for stages 1–3 differ because of mortality. The maiden flight (end of stage 4) at sunrise, for which a different sampling area was used, is much more closely synchronised than evening emergence. The air temperature (upper frame) remains permissive for emergence until midnight. (From Corbet.[6])

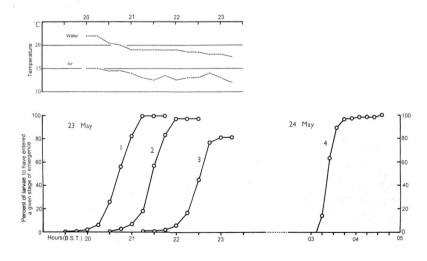

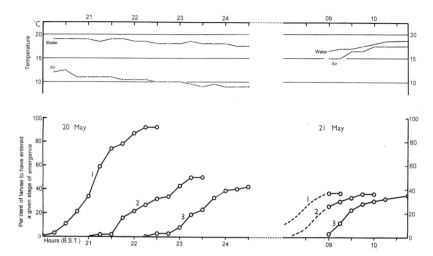

FIG 86. Diel periodicity during divided emergence of *Anax imperator*. Conventions as in Fig. 74, p.149. Asymptotic values of stages 1 and 2 in the evening differ primarily because of the return to water of about 40 larvae at 22:30 h, after the air temperature had fallen below 10°C; those of stages 2 and 3 differ because of mortality. Most larvae which had returned to water emerged between 09:00 and 10:00 h the next morning, presumably when the air temperature again became permissive. (From Corbet.[6])

Turdus merula, began to harvest stragglers that had failed to depart in the first tranche.[6]

Species of *Anax*, in Europe and North America, modify the emergence pattern when nights are cold (below about 10°C), thus avoiding being exposed on emergence supports, unable to fly, early the next morning. What happens then is that, at sunset, individuals leave the water as usual, but if the air temperature is below about 10°C they postpone the final moult and return to the water (which will still be warmer than the air). Having lost their ability to use jet propulsion, they swim awkwardly, waggling the abdomen from side to side, in the manner of a zygopteran larva. They then leave the water again in mid-morning the following day, when the air temperature has become permissive. This modification of the normal diel periodicity of emergence is termed *divided emergence* (Fig. 86) and has been observed in *Anax imperator* in Britain,[6] in *Anax junius* in southern Ontario[27] and *Orthetrum cancellatum* in northeast Spain.[28] In northern Britain, in exposed sites, *Aeshna caerulea* emerges between noon and early afternoon.[29] Such a habit probably greatly increases predation risk, this being the warmest time of the day, albeit in a cold, windswept habitat.

Recreational boating can reduce survival by causing waves, threatening the stability of emergence supports,[30] and dislodging emerging adults.

Once airborne, an adult *A. imperator* rises to about 3 metres above any obstacle and then flies away, on a horizontal course directed away from the water; if such an adult encounters a reflective surface in its way (such as a wet sealed road) it veers away from it.[6] It is not known whether such a negative response to water during the maiden flight is general among Odonata, but anecdotal observations suggest that it is. Adults within 24 hours of emergence (i.e. in a teneral condition) have not yet hardened the body and wings and so are ill-equipped to defend themselves against robust physical contact with mature conspecifics who might harass them if they remained at or near the emergence site. The maiden flight of *A. imperator* can vary in length between 20 and at least 200 metres.[6]

To leave the emergence site promptly and decisively when stage 4 has been completed must be of survival value for a teneral female. Searching males of *Aeshna juncea* hover low over vegetation and try to grasp teneral females at the emergence site before the latter can embark on the maiden flight.[31] This is how immature females can sometimes bear copulation marks.[32]

Mortality during emergence is relatively easy to study because the whole population is localised around the margin of a habitat and because the evidence of mortality is often clear. The Blackbirds that preyed heavily on *Anax imperator* during emergence at the Fish Pond could not have been more obliging in this regard: after collecting a teneral adult from its emergence support, a bird would take the dragonfly to a nearby 'anvil' and remove the wings before carrying it away to its nest.[6] The anvil was a patch of bare, hardened soil in a sheltered place, and the dismembered wings remained *in situ* for several hours. (In this case the investigator was fortunate that ants were not taking the wing fragments away.) Wings or fragments of wings of Anisoptera can be readily assigned to fore and hind, and left and right wings. So it was straightforward to estimate from the wings that remained on the anvil the minimum number of adults involved. Such estimates yielded the values for this species shown in Table 5.

Mortality from all causes, but especially failure to moult and to expand and harden the wings, is strongly density-dependent and therefore likely to be exacerbated by the synchronisation of emergence. As might have been expected, almost all the annual (emergence) mortality of *Anax imperator* occurred during the first, synchronised peak of emergence. Whatever benefits may accrue from synchronised emergence, we encounter here a definite cost. In a population of *Coenagrion mercuriale* mortality during emergence was 4.9 per cent, the main cause being deformity,[33] a condition often caused by overcrowding or wind. High mortality in one emerging population of *Pyrrhosoma nymphula* was due to

TABLE 5. Per cent mortality during annual emergence due to three causes.

SPECIES	CAUSES OF MORTALITY[a]					TOTAL EMERGING
	1	2	1+2	3	1+2+3	
Anax imperator[2]	1.4	6.2	7.6	9.7	11.4	7,312
Leucorrhinia dubia[34]	1.6	6.8	8.4	0.2	8.6	1,287
Pyrrhosoma nymphula[35]	0.8	1.6	2.4	0.9	3.3	1,981
Pyrrhosoma nymphula[36]	–	–	6.2	21.8	27.9	1,099

Notes: [a] Causes: 1) failure to moult; 2) failure to expand and harden the wings and therefore to fly; 3) predation.

individuals losing their grip on *Iris* leaves that were too wide for them to grasp securely.[37]

Values in Table 5 for *Pyrrhosoma nymphula* (derived from different habitats in different years) show that predation by birds can vary greatly. Factors such as the location of the emergence site in relation to the feeding territories of insectivorous birds, the size and visibility of the dragonfly, its diel periodicity of emergence, and the weather at the time of the maiden flight will all influence the level of mortality during emergence. It is clear that, for some combinations of circumstances, such mortality can be heavy. In *Anax imperator* about 90 per cent of an annual emergence group survived emergence although, during divided emergence, almost 50 per cent of a day-group died, mainly from bird predation.[6] *Lestes viridis* employs several strategies that greatly reduce mortality due to rain at the time of emergence: larvae can postpone emergence during rain for up to 14 hours at the emergence site, or by at least one day in the water; larvae choose emergence supports under leaves and oblique stems that provide the teneral adults with a degree of protection from rain; and during rain most larvae choose better protected sites for emergence.[38] We may expect such adaptations to be found among other odonates also.

Usually neither sex emerges significantly before the other but, if either does so, protandry (earlier emergence of males) is more frequent. The disparity is liable to be increased if there is a second emergence peak, in which females can predominate.[6] From a comprehensive review of exhaustive exuvia collections, it can now be said that the overall sex ratio at emergence is approximately 50 per cent males, but varies considerably among habitats and among years, males usually being slightly more numerous in Zygoptera, and females in Anisoptera.[18]

VOLTINISM

Determining the voltinism of a species, that is the number of generations it completes in a year, is a prerequisite for inferring the mechanisms by which seasonal regulation is achieved. It has long been recognised that, for each species, the flying season occurs at a characteristic time of year, but it is only during the last 50 years or so that odonatologists have tried to find out how this regularity comes about. The first serious attempts to study voltinism in European species were made by the Danish biologist Carl Wesenberg-Lund in the early twentieth century.[39] He showed that some species regularly complete the life cycle in one year (being univoltine), whereas others required two or more years to do so, being semivoltine or partivoltine. His work was taken much further by Paul Münchberg who in the 1920s recorded the voltinism of several species in Germany.[40] It was not until the early 1950s that attempts were made to determine the responses to physical factors that determined voltinism and the timing of the flying season.[41]

The temporal pattern of emergence, known as the emergence curve (Box 15), is disproportionately valuable for the understanding of seasonal regulation.

Characterisation of the emergence curve, year after year, in a population in which larval development is being monitored, makes it possible to infer when, and in what stages, developmental arrest is occurring (Fig. 88). In the population of *Anax imperator* studied in the Fish Pond most larvae were semivoltine, passing their second and last winter in diapause in the final stadium, but a few (sometimes about 10 per cent) grew so rapidly during their first summer that they managed to complete growth in one year, entering F-0 just after their first winter and proceeding without diapause to metamorphosis and emergence.[6] These precocious, univoltine individuals emerged about 25 days after the larger, semivoltine component and were responsible for a small, second peak in the emergence curve (Fig. 89) in which females predominated. The life cycle of *Pyrrhosoma nymphula* closely resembles that of *Anax imperator*, and its emergence curve also features a second peak in a similar position.[5] In the populations studied, *A. imperator* and *P. nymphula* both spent their last winter in F-0 in diapause and showed a highly synchronised emergence the following spring. There is a causal relationship between these two attributes. The final-stadium diapause enables laggards to catch up with more advanced larvae, in the manner of cars accumulating at traffic lights when the traffic light shows red. By early spring, diapause has been completed and all larvae are ready to respond synchronously to the rising temperature that stimulates the onset of

BOX 15

THE EMERGENCE CURVE

In a water body where the margin allows exhaustive collections of F-o exuviae of an identifiable species to be made daily throughout the emergence season, the exact numbers emerging daily can be recorded.[6] If these numbers are plotted cumulatively, the percentage of the annual emergence that has already taken place on each day can be computed in due course. Such a plot takes the form of a curve of characteristic shape which reveals a distinct dichotomy between species that exhibit a highly synchronised emergence (spring species or Type 1 species) and those in which, by comparison, emergence is temporally dispersed (summer species or Type 2 species). The form of these emergence curves correlates closely with the mechanism of seasonal regulation used by each type of species,[42] *Anax imperator* being a Type 1 species and *Aeshna cyanea* being a Type 2 species (Fig. 87). Highly synchronised emergence reflects the fact that all larvae in the senior cohort passed the previous winter in F-o and

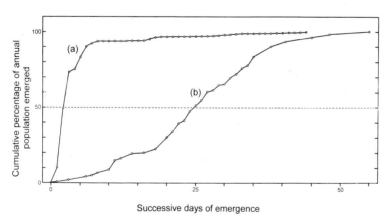

Successive days of emergence

FIG 87. Emergence curves of (a) a Type 1 species, *Anax imperator*, and (b) a Type 2 species, *Aeshna cyanea*, showing the different degrees of synchronisation. In *Anax imperator* 50 per cent of the annual population had emerged by the third day, whereas in *Aeshna cyanea*, this value was not reached until the 25th day of emergence. (After Corbet and Corbet.[42])

so were all ready to respond synchronously to the rising temperature in spring when they embarked on metamorphosis together. Type 2 species, in contrast, spent their last winter in F-1 and so had to pass through stadium F-0 in spring before embarking on metamorphosis and emerging. Thus they accumulated more temporal variation and their emergence was less synchronised.

To facilitate the objective comparison of the timing of emergence between species, habitats and years, we can compare the first and last days of emergence, the day by which 50 per cent of the annual emergence has taken place (abbreviated as EM_{50})[43] and the period within which 90 per cent of the annual emergence takes place (EM_{90}).[44] If the exuviae are retained for examination, they can be used to investigate correlations between time of emergence and sex ratio and linear dimension, both of which sometimes correlate with seasonal emergence time.[45]

metamorphosis. Then, like the cars being released when the traffic light turns to green, the whole population can respond simultaneously. The first peak of emergence is explosive, the EM_{50} value (Box 15) being reached after only three days. This causal relationship led to an ecological classification of the British dragonflies, based on the stage in which larvae spend their last winter and the degree of synchronisation of emergence.[41] Because the type with the more synchronised emergence tends to emerge earlier than the other type, the two types were called spring and summer species respectively. They correspond to life cycles of Types 1 and 2 described in Box 16. Although larvae of summer species resume development in their last spring in several stadia, there are ways in which they can reduce temporal variation before emergence. One mechanism was recognised theoretically in 1957[46] and subsequently validated by laboratory experiment.[47] It entails each successive developmental stage having a higher temperature threshold for its onset than its predecessor, so that the most advanced larvae are held back until the rising temperatures of spring reach their temperature threshold, by which time the less advanced larvae will have caught up with them. A second mechanism is the 'light-growth effect'[48] whereby the rate of development is accelerated in response to longer daylengths, so that, as the season progresses, larvae develop more and more rapidly.[49] An intriguing theoretical consequence of this effect, yet to be confirmed experimentally, is that, between the spring equinox and the summer solstice, growth rate will correlate positively with latitude so that development rate in Type 2 species would enable emergence date to compensate for latitude.[50] The existence of such a mechanism

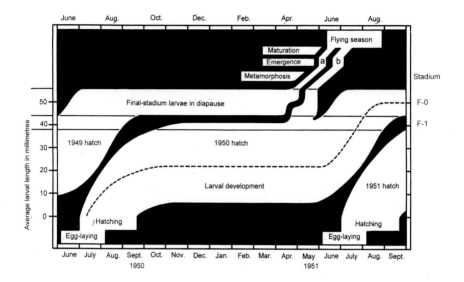

FIG 88. Seasonal development of *Anax imperator* in a stem habitat (see Fig. 44, p.77) in southern England. The broken line approximates to the average growth rate of larvae hatching from eggs in 1950. The extent of the white areas indicates the upper and lower limits of larval size in that age group and in those hatching in 1949 and 1951. Most of an age group enter F-0 in August one year after hatching, spend the winter in diapause and emerge early the following year (emergence group a), thus conforming with the typical Type 1 life cycle (Box 15). The few precocious larvae that enter F-0 before 1 June forgo diapause and emerge later the same year (emergence group b), thus conforming to the typical Type 2 life cycle. (From Corbet.[6])

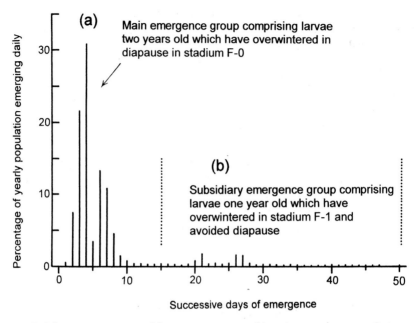

FIG 89. The two components of the emergence curve of *Anax imperator* (corresponding to groups (a) and (b) in Fig. 88 when Type 1 and Type 2 life cycles respectively coexist in the same population. The lack of synchronisation among individuals in group (b), which can comprise 5–10 per cent of the annual emergence, is conspicuous. (After Corbet.[51])

would help to explain how some dragonflies living close to the Arctic Circle can emerge almost as early as their southern counterparts.[50]

It is often possible to infer the voltinism of a population (p.162) by analysing the sizes of larvae in a sample and making allowance for the time of year, and then using the result as a baseline against which to compare further samples taken at other times of year. To take a simple example: searching for larvae immediately after the end of the emergence period can be informative. If no larvae can be found, the species is almost certainly univoltine. (If all larvae found are in the final stadium and showing signs of metamorphosis, the emergence period has clearly not finished and the species is likewise univoltine.) If smaller larvae are present, the species requires more than a year to complete a generation, and the size-distribution of the residual larvae will sometimes allow one to infer how many additional years are needed for larval development. A species that shows the last type of distribution is *Cordulegaster boltonii*, which evidently requires three or more years to complete a generation in Britain.[52]

Since 1971, meticulous research in Sweden by Ulf Norling[53] has greatly increased our knowledge of the way in which responses by larvae contribute to seasonal regulation. It had been recognised since the 1960s that there are three types of life cycle among British and northern European dragonflies. This classification, recently modified and reformulated,[50] remains valid, although more is now known about the larval responses that maintain the regularity of the life cycles involved. In Table 6 the British species are assigned to the three types of life cycle (Box 16).

Because not all larvae in a population develop at the same rate, it can happen that cohort-splitting takes place so that two Types of life cycle (1 and 2) may coexist within the same habitat, as in *Anax imperator,*[6] *Pyrrhosoma nymphula*[5] and *Coenagrion hastulatum.*[54] Cohort-splitting is evidently commonplace, especially in partivoltine species (i.e. those that take more than two years to develop), and those in which the oviposition season is extended.

....

BOX 16

LIFE CYCLES AND SEASONAL REGULATION

Dragonflies in Europe and Britain exhibit three kinds of life cycle, each being maintained by different regulatory responses. Examples among British species are listed in Table 6.

The Type 1 life cycle, typified by spring species
By spending the last winter before emergence in the final larval stadium, in diapause, such species can respond promptly and simultaneously to rising temperature in spring. So they tend to emerge early and synchronously. The eggs typically develop directly, hatching about one month or less after being laid, although some *Somatochlora* in Germany are facultative in this respect, developing directly if laid early in the summer, but overwintering as eggs if laid later.[55] The possibility that species of *Somatochlora* and perhaps some libellulids show similar responses in Britain cannot be discounted.

The Type 2 life cycle, typified by summer species
Because they spend the last winter before emergence in one or more late stadia preceding F-0, such species typically emerge later than Type 1 species and with less synchronisation. The eggs of *Aeshna* species typically

overwinter in diapause. Despite commencing growth in their last spring in more than one stadium, Type 2 species can improve their synchronisation of emergence by using a system of rising temperature thresholds that enable retarded larvae to catch up with more advanced ones[56] (Fig. 90).

The Type 3 life cycle. Obligatorily univoltine species.
These species represent a subset of Type 2, distinguished by being invariably univoltine. They typically, but not invariably, overwinter as eggs in diapause. Larval development is completed in two or three months in spring and early summer, and adults die in late summer (Fig. 91). The larvae tend to have relatively high thermal growth coefficients.

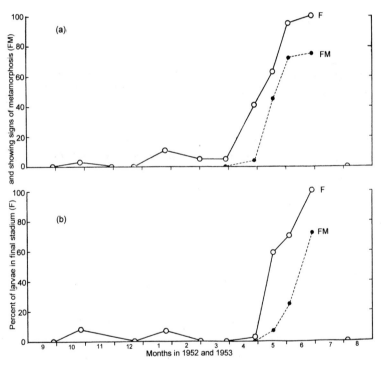

FIG 90. Larval development in two Type 2 species: (a) *Coenagrion mercuriale*, and (b) *Ceriagrion tenellum*. Both species are semivoltine. Most individuals enter F-o in spring and then proceed promptly to metamorphosis as a prelude to emergence in early summer. (From Corbet.[46])

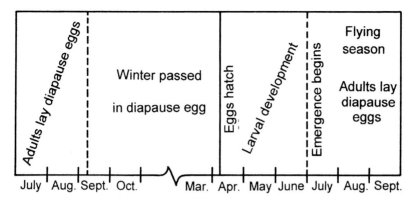

FIG 91. The life cycle of *Lestes sponsa*, a Type 3 species. (After Corbet.[57])

SEASONAL REGULATION

Research in Sweden by Ulf Norling[60] has revealed two strands in the seasonal regulation of Odonata in temperate latitudes based on two discrete events that can both act, though at different seasons, to ensure that emergence is positioned at an appropriate time of year[58] (Box 17).

It appears that, on the whole, emergence begins later at higher latitudes but, as mentioned above, observations suggest that some kind of compensating mechanism is operating such that northerly populations emerge earlier than would be expected from a latitude-temperature gradient alone.[50] Another factor to be taken into account is that certain northern species (e.g. *Coenagrion hastulatum*) may differ from southern species (e.g. *C. puella*) in having a lower temperature optimum for growth.[59] The situation is further complicated by the fact that the thermal optimum for growth may change seasonally, in a manner that is considered adaptive. Any latitude-compensation mechanism which entails a change in growth rate will bear a survival cost in the presence of a predator able to depress foraging activity and growth efficiency. Even so, larvae of *Lestes sponsa*, induced to grow rapidly, balanced this trade-off differently, by taking more risks when a predator was present. The higher predation cost was to some extent offset by the higher growth efficiency.[60]

In patterns of seasonal regulation we see evidence of the ways in which odonate life cycles have become adapted for survival at high latitudes. It is recognised that temperate latitudes have been colonised from regions closer to the equator; and the prevailing view is that, compared with other aquatic insects

TABLE 6. Types of life cycle found in British Odonata.[a]

TYPE 1 (SPRING SPECIES)

Anisoptera
  Aeshnidae
    Anax imperator
    Brachytron pratense
  Cordulegastridae
    Cordulegaster boltonii
  Corduliidae
    Cordulia aenea
    Somatochlora arctica[b]
    S. metallica[c]
  Gomphidae
    Gomphus vulgatissimus
  Libellulidae
    Leucorrhinia dubia
    Libellula depressa
    L. fulva[d]
    L. quadrimaculata
    Orthetrum cancellatum
    O. coerulescens
Zygoptera
  Calopterygidae
    Calopteryx virgo
  Coenagrionidae
    Erythromma najas
    Pyrrhosoma nymphula

TYPE 2 (SUMMER SPECIES)

Anisoptera
  Aeshnidae
    Aeshna caerulea[e]
    A. cyanea
    A. grandis
    A. juncea
Zygoptera
  Calopterygidae
    Calopteryx splendens[f]

TABLE 6. – *cont.*

TYPE 2 (SUMMER SPECIES) – CONT.

Coenagrionidae
  Ceriagrion tenellum
  Coenagrion mercuriale
  C. hastulatum
  C. puella
  C. pulchellum
  Enallagma cyathigerum
  Ischnura elegans
  I. pumilio[g]

TYPE 3 (OBLIGATORILY UNIVOLTINE SPECIES)

Anisoptera
  Aeshnidae
    Aeshna mixta
  Libellulidae
    Sympetrum danae
    S. sanguineum
    S. striolatum
  Zygoptera
  Lestidae
    Lestes dryas
    Lestes sponsa

[a] Entries are provisional pending further study from habitats over a range of latitudes. Sources (unless specified) as listed elsewhere.[51] Type 1 species often feature a small Type 2 component, although in a Scottish population of *Aeshna caerulea* neither component appeared to dominate.[61] In southwestern Germany the life cycle of *A. caerulea* conforms with Type 2.[62] The status of some species remains to be determined. Reports from Sternberg and Buchwald refer to southwestern Germany.[63]
[b] Sternberg (2000) in Sternberg & Buchwald (2000).
[c] Sternberg & Schmidt (2000) in Sternberg & Buchwald (2000).
[d] Sternberg *et al.* (2000) in Sternberg & Buchwald (2000).
[e] Smith & Smith (2000).
[f] Schütte *et al.* (1999).
[g] Sternberg (1999) in Sternberg & Buchwald (1999).

BOX 17

MECHANISMS OF SEASONAL REGULATION

Strands can be identified in the larval responses that help to regulate
their life cycles and the season of emergence. They operate in autumn
and spring respectively.

Strand 1
*Retardation of larval development in late summer and early autumn so that
the larval population overwinters in an appropriate, cold-resistant stage.* This
process is usually accomplished by the onset of a diapause induced by
a response to daylength (photoperiod). Initially long, and perhaps
sometimes decreasing, photoperiods postpone entry to one or more
late stadia whereupon short photoperiods prevent development from
proceeding further before the onset of winter. This Strand concerns pre-
diapause development and is well developed in the Type 1 life cycle in
which diapause is induced in F-0; it determines the stadium and/or
intrastadial stage in which the last winter will be passed. In *Aeshna caerulea*
larvae reduce food intake as diapause starts in late summer and early
autumn.[64]

Strand 2
*The placement of emergence, in spring and early summer, early in the season
favourable for adult activity and survival.* This Strand concerns post-diapause
development, and is achieved by responses quite different from those
that characterise pre-diapause development. In this Strand, instead of
being retarded (as in Strand 1), larval development is *accelerated* under
long photoperiods. The larval response to photoperiod has evidently
been reversed among larvae that have experienced a spell of low (winter)
temperature and/or decreasing or short photoperiods.

(mayflies and stoneflies), the Odonata retain features of a warm-adapted group.[65]
Although this remains to be verified, it seems that the stages least resistant to
cold are non-diapause eggs and the earliest larval stadia. Life cycles are organised
in such a way that these two stages seldom or never coincide with the winter.
When, as happens very occasionally, small larvae of lestids (Type 3 species) are

encountered in autumn, this may be due to the anomalous premature hatching of diapause eggs, perhaps caused by the stimulus of wetting or submergence.[66] Such happenings are sufficiently rare that they do not challenge the general thesis that mechanisms of seasonal regulation normally ensure that the earliest stadia are *not* exposed to winter temperatures.

We may expect climate change, and especially global warming (p.294), to have a marked effect on the *phenology* of dragonflies. In particular, because ambient temperatures in spring and early summer influence emergence date in all types of life cycle, we can expect emergence to begin earlier, resulting in a corresponding advance of the flying season (p.189). There is already evidence of such an effect. The flying seasons in northwest Germany of *Coenagrion puella, Ischnura elegans, Libellula depressa, L. quadrimaculata* and *Pyrrhosoma nymphula* started 20–28 days earlier in the 1990s than in the 1980s, when temperatures had been lower. A corresponding difference for 17 of the most widespread species in Germany was almost two weeks.[67] Furthermore, a recent and significant northward range expansion has taken place in 14 European species of Mediterranean provenance accompanied in some by a spread to higher altitudes.[68] Some of the routes along which such expansion takes place may reflect those along which central European species came from their postglacial refuges into central Europe.[69] Experience of climate warming in Florida leads one to expect that the flying season of temperate species of Odonata will become longer and that their distribution will expand northwards.[70]

In Britain we can expect range extensions corresponding to those detected in Germany, together with increases in population size and colonisation of biotopes at higher altitudes.

OPPORTUNITIES FOR INVESTIGATION

For researchers with access to laboratory facilities, there is scope for determining the lower temperature threshold for survival of larvae in the earliest stadia and for determining the optimal temperature for the completion of diapause in larvae. From two Type 1 species, *Anax imperator* and *Pyrrhosoma nymphula*, there is anecdotal evidence that the final-stadium diapause has been completed by November[71] and this could easily be verified by removing diapause larvae from the field each month from October onwards and exposing them to the prerequisites for metamorphosis (food and warmth).

It can always be informative to construct emergence curves by making exhaustive, daily collections of F-0 exuviae.[6] To achieve this the study habitat needs to be carefully selected. In particular, it would improve our understanding of seasonal regulation to obtain precise emergence curves for some of the more elusive Type 1 species, such as *Cordulia aenea* and *Somatochlora* spp. Emergence curves, especially if combined with larval samples taken from the same habitat at selected times of year, can inform about patterns of seasonal regulation. Precise characteristics of the emergence curve can also provide a reference point for inferring the duration of the prereproductive period, a feature of special interest if global warming supervenes, especially for species such as *Aeshna mixta* and *Sympetrum striolatum* (p.67), and possibly some lestids.

Gaps in our knowledge of life-cycle types and voltinism remain for several British species (Table 6, p.170). It will be rewarding to fill them and to compare the results with patterns observed for the same species in continental Europe.

CHAPTER 7

Adult Life

MATURATION

THE TENERAL ADULT is reproductively immature. After the teneral stage, which lasts about 24 hours, the adult remains immature for days or months until the *gonads* attain reproductive readiness. During this prereproductive or *maturation period* the gonads develop, the body and wings harden and acquire their mature colours, and adults come to exhibit reproductive behaviour. When the behaviour of an adult is being noted, it is important, where possible, to record its state of maturity. Diagnosis may be difficult or impossible if the body is pale and soft, but it is usually straightforward in the later stages of the maturation period. Body colour is sometimes but not invariably a reliable criterion of sexual maturity.[1] For example, the gonads of male *Leucorrhinia dubia* in a Finnish population matured *before* the body coloration became 'mature'[2] but in a German population of *Lestes sponsa* adults achieved mature coloration after 15 days of life, but did not exhibit reproductive activity until three or four days later.[3] In *Ischnura elegans* the green phase of the male is almost entirely a maturation phase (Fig. 92): only 4 of 709 individuals in this phase were seen mating.[4] More work is needed to establish reliable (preferably external) criteria for determining the physiological age of adults during the maturation period. A suitable model for such an investigation would be *I. elegans* which shows an orderly, time-dependent progression of colour forms during maturation[5] (Figs 92–94). To calibrate these against spermatogenesis and oocyte development would be informative.

In British species the teneral adult is not well endowed with stored fat, and the rate of maturation probably depends on the amount of food an adult can

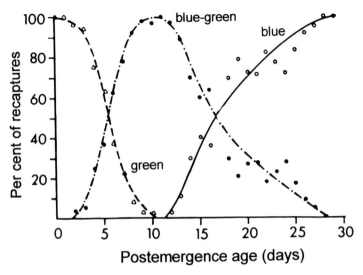

FIG 92. Change with age of thoracic ground colour of *Ischnura elegans* males based on recaptures of individuals marked when teneral or green. Most males in this population became sexually mature about 11 days after emergence, although some males can mate when still green and therefore almost certainly when younger than 11 days. (After Parr.[6])

FIG 93. An immature male *Ischnura elegans*. The thorax becomes blue when the insect is mature (Robert Thompson).

(a)

FIG 94. (a–d) Age-related colour forms of female *Ischnura elegans*. The form *violacea* (a) will develop into either the *andromorph*, formerly known as *typica* (b), or the form *infuscans*, and the form *rufescens* (c) develops into the form *rufescens-obsoleta* (d) (Robert Thompson).

(b)

(c)

(d)

FIG 95. A female *Ischnura pumilio* form *aurantiaca* (Robert Thompson).

obtain during the prereproductive period. It can be assumed that this in turn will be strongly influenced by the weather, in the form of wind, precipitation and temperature, which will determine the opportunities available for foraging. Some individuals begin to forage on their first day as adults: Wesenberg-Lund recorded *Cordulia aenea* doing so.[7] On the other hand, *Calopteryx splendens* and *Erythromma najas* are said not to forage when 'freshly emerged'.[8] The maturation period of *Ischnura pumilio* (Fig. 95) lasts 6–12 days depending on the food intake.[9] *Ischnura elegans*, which can survive in exposed habitats, has been observed to mature in 3 or 4 days in one habitat[10] and in 10 or 11 days in another.[11] It is common for adults to leave the reproductive site (usually also the emergence site) during the maturation period, but *I. elegans* appears to be an exception.[12] The maturation period of *Cordulia aenea amurensis* (in Japan) is prolonged by cool weather.[13] In a Finnish population of *Leucorrhinia dubia* sperm development required 10–14 days during unfavourable weather instead of the usual 4–5 days.[2] The maturation period in British species usually lasts about two weeks, being slightly longer in females than males and considerably longer in large Anisoptera. In one detailed study *Aeshna cyanea* required at least a month to achieve maturity,[14] a finding which conforms closely with information obtained over several years. In a population at 47°23'N the average maturation period of this species over ten years was 50 days.[15]

In species with a maturation period of normal (unextended) duration, males tend to mature more rapidly than females[16] (Table 7).

The duration of the maturation period can be estimated approximately by recording the interval between first emergence and first appearance of mature adults at water, taking note of any inclement weather that might delay maturation (by suspending foraging) during the intervening period. It can be estimated more reliably by marking newly emerged adults to indicate their date of emergence and then noting when each subsequently returns to water. Such a study is labour intensive and time-consuming, but can yield data of high quality. For a population of *Aeshna cyanea* in Germany (Fig. 96) such data show the maturation period to have lasted from about four weeks (for individuals emerging earlier) to about seven weeks (for those emerging later), the duration increasing gradually between these extremes.[14] Whereas the minimum values

TABLE 7. Duration of maturation period in males and females (from Corbet)[16].

DURATION (DAYS)			
SPECIES	PLACE	MALES	FEMALES
Aeshna cyanea[a]	SW. Germany	21–28	35–42
Anax imperator[b]	S. England	7–12	13–16
Calopteryx virgo[c]	S. England	21	28
Coenagrion puella[d]	S. England	13	17
Cordulia aenea[e]	N. Japan	9	16
Pyrrhosoma nymphula[f]	N. England	11	16
Sympetrum danae[g]	Belgium	10	13
		(13)	(14)

Notes:
[a] Kaiser (1970).
[b] Corbet (1957a).
[c] Lambert (1994).
[d] Banks & Thompson (1985); Thompson (1989).
[e] Ubukata (1974).
[f] Gribbin & Thompson (1990).
[g] Michiels & Dhondt (1989b). Values in parentheses derive from the semi-natural conditions of a field cage. The disparity between these and values derived from nature suggests that results from the field are subject to bias.

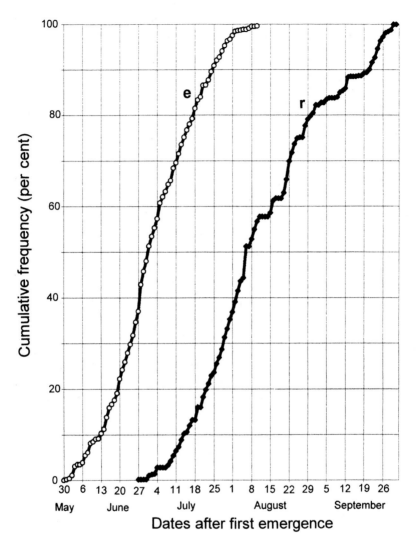

FIG 96. Duration of the prereproductive period of *Aeshna cyanea* throughout the emergence period, as shown by the interval between emergence (e) (*N*=756) and return to the emergence site (r) (*N*= 579) of adults marked as individuals at emergence in Germany. The duration increases greatly, from about four to six weeks, as the season progresses. (After Inden-Lohmar.[14])

are probably realistic, the apparent maximum values may be subject to error due to adults visiting other aquatic habitats in the meantime, and there is no obvious way of investigating this possibility.

In Britain the duration of the maturation period is not likely to play a role in seasonal regulation, but in the Mediterranean region it often does. So, with the prospect of climate change, interest attaches to reviewing some examples of Mediterranean life cycles and thus anticipating some of the changes that may one day occur among British species.

In Algeria, at about 36°N, winters are mild, summers are hot and dry, and autumn is heralded by heavy rain liable to reinstate shallow bodies of water that have become dry during the summer. In such a climate Type 3 species (Box 15, p.163), such as *Aeshna mixta, Sympetrum striolatum* and *S. meridionale*, develop rapidly in lowland lakes and pools and emerge in spring, to be faced with the early prospect of their larval habitats drying up. Immature adults leave the lowlands, ascending to woodland in nearby hills at 500–1,000 metres a.s.l., where they remain for three or more months, feeding and gradually becoming sexually mature.[17] Then, in late September or early October, with the advent of the first heavy rains of autumn, they return *en masse* to the lowlands where they reproduce in the newly replenished ponds. In this life cycle the maturation period serves as a summer diapause, or *aestivation*, stage, maintaining the Type 3 life cycle by postponing reproduction until early autumn, as well as by reducing the risk of eggs being laid in ephemeral bodies of water. One wonders whether British populations of *Aeshna mixta* and *Sympetrum striolatum*, both of which are regularly augmented by migrants from continental Europe, contain individuals with a predisposition to delay maturation, perhaps in response to high summer temperature. One manifestation of this might be that these species would have an exceptionally long maturation period in Britain in years when they were exposed to high temperatures as young adults in summer. In our view, these two species will be worth monitoring closely in this regard. Although Andy McGeeney records *A. mixta* as having a maturation period of only seven to ten days,[18] the relatively late appearance of mature adults in late July and August[19] (more than a month later than *Lestes sponsa* which also has a Type 3 life cycle) seems to indicate a maturation period much longer than this in some years or some places. As for *Sympetrum striolatum*, during one very hot summer in southwest England, adults that emerged in mid-June apparently did not return to water for about two months.[20] In *S. striolatum*, part of the wide variation in time of adult appearance may arise from the bimodal emergence caused by the existence of diapause and non-diapause eggs.[21]

A possible model for what may be happening in British populations of *Aeshna mixta,* and perhaps *Lestes sponsa,* or for what may come to pass as summer temperatures rise, is provided by populations of *Lestes sponsa* in Japan. *Lestes sponsa* is a Type 3 species which needs to avoid ovipositing early in the summer so that its diapause eggs do not hatch in autumn. It achieves this in Japan by increasing the duration of the maturation period in accordance with the ambient temperature in summer.[22] Thus the maturation period lasts about 20 days at all latitudes between about 40 and 58°N, but lengthens progressively south of 40°N to become about 120 days near 34°N. South of 40°N a close correlation exists between the duration of the maturation period and mean annual temperature (Fig. 97). To our knowledge there is no indication that *L. sponsa* exhibits a long maturation period anywhere in Europe;[23] on the other hand, the southernmost limit of its distribution there is 40°N,[24] just the latitude at which in Japan the maturation period begins to lengthen on the north–south gradient. Tantalisingly,

FIG 97. Relationship between duration of the prereproductive period of *Lestes sponsa* and mean annual temperature at 21 localities in Japan between 34°25′ and 58°40′N. Open circles, localities where the onset of the reproductive period is not postponed; filled circles, those in which the onset is postponed. (After Uéda.[22])

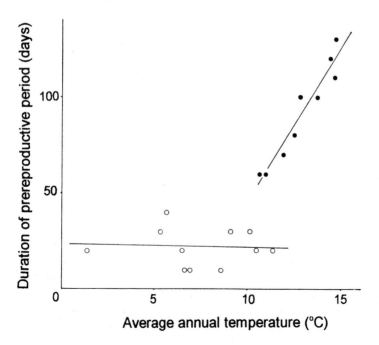

there is an obsolete record of *L. sponsa* from northeast Algeria, at about 37°N, but the species can no longer be found there.[25] Two other species of *Lestes* in northeastern Algeria, *L. barbarus* and *L. viridis virens*, also existing there as Type 3 species, have a protracted maturation period in that area.[26]

In the tropics a long maturation period contributes to seasonal regulation by postponing reproduction during the dry season, which corresponds phenologically to the winter of temperate latitudes. Such a suspension of development is known as *siccatation*, rather than *hibernation* (inactivity during winter) or aestivation (inactivity during the summer).

PHYSICAL FACTORS

Thermoregulation

Odonata, being insects, have been termed 'cold-blooded' or 'poikilothermic', implying that their body temperature, unlike that of 'endotherms', like mammals and birds, closely tracks that of their immediate surroundings. However, Heinrich has pointed out that it is more realistic to regard insects like dragonflies as facultatively endothermic because they can raise their body temperature by their own actions, for example, by wing-whirring.[27] So Heinrich has proposed that dragonflies be termed heterothermic. Were dragonflies to be comprehensively poikilothermic, they would be at a great disadvantage early in the morning or during cold spells during the day because they cannot fly when cold. Fortunately for them, however, they can raise the body temperature above that of their surroundings, enabling them to maintain the thorax at a temperature high enough to permit spontaneous flight. The need to do this is ever-present in temperate latitudes and becomes acute among species that emerge during the night and (to escape from predators) need to leave their emergence supports during dawn twilight when the air temperature is close to its diel minimum. An additional need, rare in temperate regions but commonplace in the tropics, is to prevent the body *over*heating. Sometimes, on a hot summer's day, one can witness British dragonflies reducing their body temperature by evaporative cooling. This involves the intermittent immersion in water during flight. Controversy has attended its physiological function because of its resemblance to exophytic oviposition. The function of this behaviour is less equivocal if a male is exhibiting it, but one cannot exclude the possibility that an adult appearing to immerse itself is drinking, as adults of *Calopteryx* are sometimes known to do.[28] Of course, such behaviour may simultaneously serve both functions (drinking *and* evaporative cooling) and it would be difficult to verify this. But when a patrolling male *Cordulegaster boltonii* (a flier) repeatedly touches the water surface during flight on an exceptionally hot day, it can be assumed that it is drinking and/or wetting the body.

Odonates possess a suite of behaviours directed towards thermoregulation – the process of keeping the body temperature between the lower and upper limits permitting physiological function and spontaneous flight. It lends savour and interest to odonate-watching to recognise these behaviours and to infer how comfortable a dragonfly is in its current microclimate.

Dragonflies commonly roost on surfaces warmed by the setting sun, which of course face west. This places them at a thermal disadvantage the following morning when, as the sun rises in the east, the formerly insolated surfaces are shaded. To raise the thoracic temperature to a value that permits spontaneous flight (about 25–30°C), adults must initially vibrate the wings. This endothermic warming is feasible only in larger species; Zygoptera do not exhibit it. It has been closely studied by Mike May in *Anax junius*, the New World counterpart of *Anax imperator*.[29] After wing-whirring has begun, the thoracic temperature rises rapidly, followed by the temperature of the head and abdomen. At an ambient temperature of about 15°C, after about 13 minutes, the temperature of the thorax (and therefore the wing muscles) peaks at about 29°C. Then the dragonfly tries to become airborne and the head temperature suddenly rises, perhaps reflecting the increased need for visual sensitivity as flight commences. Presumably the temperature differential between different parts of the body is effected by controlled circulation of the haemolymph, which, under different circumstances, can transport heat from the thorax to the abdomen to assist radiative cooling in fliers.[30] Once they can fly, adults can seek out insolated surfaces where they can consolidate the warming process by basking.[31] As the sun appears to circle the sky, perchers (in cool temperate latitudes) systematically move around the margin of a water body so as to remain in sunny spots.[32]

Thereafter they can maintain the thoracic temperature. Fliers do so by flying (which warms the thorax), and perchers by alighting on insolated surfaces or basking with the body orientated at right angles to the incident rays of the sun (ectothermic warming). By such means, adults continually adjust their behaviours through the day so as to regulate the thoracic temperature: if too warm, they seek a shaded resting site. Alternatively, if they wish to remain perched in an exposed site, they point the abdomen towards the sun so as to minimise the incident radiation on the body (minimising the body's shadow). This position is known as the obelisk posture[33] and is rarely seen in Britain. There are variations on this theme. Some Zygoptera use the wings to produce a 'greenhouse' effect in which the wings insulate the body from the cooling effect of winds while admitting solar energy to warm the body beneath.[34] *Lestes viridis* places the wings together, above the abdomen, in a posture unusual for a lestid, which reflects the sun's rays on to the abdomen, thus raising its temperature.[35] A further option is used by species with blue external pigmentation. In hot, sunny weather, the body surface remains pale blue, reflecting solar energy and postponing overheating. In cool weather the blue changes to grey, absorbing energy and thus raising the body temperature. In some species the timing of this colour change is under the control of an in-built 24-hour clock (*circadian rhythm*) so that, when the sun rises, the body is already dark and able to absorb solar radiation more effectively.[36] Female *Enallagma cyathigerum* typically oviposit beneath the water surface, sometimes being accompanied briefly by an attendant male who is initially predominantly blue (Fig. 98). Often, when such a male returns to the surface, his abdomen is no longer blue, but grey (Fig. 99), and so equipped to absorb the sun's rays more effectively. Likewise, if a blue male is confined in a refrigerator for a few hours, he turns grey. Other British species that often exhibit this type of colour change include species of *Aeshna* and *Anax imperator*. The change can be so striking that, in the past, observers have sometimes

FIG 98. A mature male *Enallagma cyathigerum* in the blue phase (Robert Thompson).

FIG 99. An immature male *Enallagma cyathigerum* which when mature will become blue at normal ambient temperatures but grey when cold (Robert Thompson).

interpreted it as denoting a colour form, analogous with the colour phases of *Ischnura elegans* and *I. pumilio* (Figs 92–95, pp.176–178).

A satisfying way of documenting the changing demands of thermoregulation as the day progresses is to monitor the behaviour of individual odonates belonging to species with different temperature preferences. Dagmar Hilfert-Rüppell has done this for several species, some British, occurring near Braunschweig in central Germany.[37] Many British odonatologists will know, from casual observation, that *Ischnura elegans* is one of the British dragonflies most tolerant of low temperature. Dagmar watched adults of *I. elegans* as they resumed activity in the morning. Adults often roost close to water, among fringing *Carex*[38] or on grasses *Juncus* or *Equisetum* at a mean height of about 80 centimetres above ground. They choose a stem that matches their head width, so that they can see an approaching object and yet hide the body behind the stem, sidling around the stem as necessary to remain hidden.[39] As the sun rises, they first orientate the body at right angles to the sun. Then, when warm enough to fly, they move around the pond margin, alighting intermittently in the warmest spots until warm enough to begin reproductive activity over water. Different species typically become active at different times, reflecting their differing thresholds for spontaneous flight and the options available to them for endo- and ectothermic warming.[37]

Although odonates use several different strategies for thermoregulation, sometimes simultaneously, body size and strategy are broadly correlated. Zygopterans and smaller anisopterans, being perchers, are predominantly *ectotherms*, whereas larger anisopterans, mainly but not exclusively fliers, are predominantly endotherms. A few small perchers, including libellulids and coenagrionids, appear to be thermal conformers, showing no obvious attempts at thermoregulation. Others show great versatility, behaving, at different times, as perchers, fliers or hoverers and sometimes switching from one mode to another from day to day.[40] Unlike fliers, perchers (Fig. 100) have to attain the takeoff temperature by passive heat gain by basking (and so, in temperate latitudes, tend to fly only when the thoracic temperature exceeds ambient by about 7°C). The time of first morning takeoff by *Sympetrum* correlates better

FIG 100. A male *Sympetrum sanguineum* soaks up heat radiating from a stone (Robert Thompson).

with incident radiation than with ambient temperature.[41] *Sympetrum striolatum* is a typical percher, but sometimes, in cool weather or the evening, it forages in flight, dancing up and down within a swarm of its prey, resembling a typical flier such as *Aeshna mixta*.

Dagmar Hilfert and Georg Rüppell examined the thermoregulatory behaviour of seven European species, comparing populations in northern Germany (52°15′N) and southern France (43°34′N), recording the lowest ambient temperature permitting spontaneous flight.[42] This value was lower in northern than in southern populations, and in both was lower in September than in May and June, reflecting the fact that thresholds can change during the life of an individual by acclimatisation. The lowest values were found in *Ischnura elegans* (12°C) and *Orthetrum cancellatum* (4.9°C).[42] Both species arrived at water earlier in the day than the other species studied (*Aeshna cyanea*, *A. mixta*, *Lestes sponsa*, *Sympetrum striolatum* and *S. vulgatum*). *Ischnura elegans* and *Orthetrum cancellatum* were probably typical in thermoregulating through perch choice. *Ischnura elegans* crawled from shaded to sunlit spots and pressed its *ventral* surface against the warm vegetation. *Orthetrum cancellatum* first settled on insolated stones or patches of dry grass, sometimes holding the wings horizontally and close to the grass, thus retaining the warm air close to the thorax and reducing heat loss due to convection. As Dagmar observed, such 'warming' sites may feature as a proximate cue in habitat selection: *O. cancellatum* is known to colonise gravel pits which are typically surrounded by perch sites that facilitate thermoregulation. As the diel periodicity of oviposition indicates, females of some species probably have a lower threshold temperature for flight than do conspecific males.[43] In general, Zygoptera have a lower threshold than do Anisoptera, perhaps reflecting their lower wing-beat frequency.[43] As would be expected, the resting sites chosen by perchers (including *O. cancellatum*) are located round the perimeter of a pond according to the apparent position of the sun.[32]

There is a latitude gradient in the minimum takeoff temperature, which is significantly higher in a warmer climate where the temperature at which heat torpor supervenes for perchers and fliers is much higher.[44] Whether or not such differences are partly genetically determined, we may expect dragonflies in Britain to differ in their temperature thresholds for activity from their conspecifics in southern Europe. One implication of this latitude gradient is that fliers should be better represented at the highest latitudes because of their greater thermoregulatory versatility. Provisional analyses support this inference.[29]

Flight activity

In high temperate latitudes adult Odonata are predominantly diurnal, their activity peaking close to noon. A few species (e.g. *Aeshna grandis* and *Anax imperator*) often fly during evening twilight. In *A. imperator* this *crepuscular* phase forms a discrete peak and is not merely an extension of the diurnal activity.[45] Sometimes females of *Aeshna cyanea* visit water, apparently mainly to oviposit, in the late afternoon or early evening, well beyond the normal activity period for both sexes. This may enable them to oviposit free of male interference.

Wind and rain usually inhibit flight of British odonates. Some species, especially *Ischnura elegans*, sometimes fly in a rather strong wind, but perhaps choose lee situations in which to do so.[46] The upper limit of wind speed permitting flight of *Coenagrion puella* is about 8 m/sec (28.8 km/h).[47] Other Zygoptera can continue to fly into a wind of 3.5 m/sec (12.6 km/h)[48] and the corresponding value for Anisoptera is up to 10 m/sec (36 km/h). In Britain rain, or a sudden drop in air temperature, promptly inhibits flight. Surprisingly, a few tropical species appear to fly mainly or only during rain, and others frequently tolerate it.[49]

When the sky abruptly becomes overcast, dragonflies leave the water and move to protected sites amongst vegetation, even when the coincident drop in ambient temperature is slight.[50] Such behaviour can be witnessed during a total solar eclipse,[51] normal activity being resumed promptly after illumination is restored.[52]

In some species in North America and the tropics individual members of a population exhibit, and maintain, idiosyncratic diel activity patterns, and we may anticipate such a phenomenon in British species. In *Lestes disjunctus australis*, for example, some males (about 33 per cent) frequented water throughout the day, others (about 32 per cent) in the morning and afternoon, with a lull near noon, and a third group (about 20 per cent) only in the late afternoon.[53] Together these components made up the diel periodicity of the whole male population at water which was bimodal with peaks in morning and afternoon.

Because larval growth, metamorphosis, emergence and maturation are temperature dependent, we may expect the timing of the flying season, namely the time when reproductively mature adults are active, to reflect local climate and, in particular, the cumulative *growing-degree day* total. One of the most informative ways of portraying the flying season shows relative abundance (Fig. 101). A strength of this method of portrayal is that it reveals, for each species, whether the peak of numbers falls near the beginning of the flying season (as in Type 1 species, such as *Pyrrhosoma nymphula*) or in the middle (as in Type 2

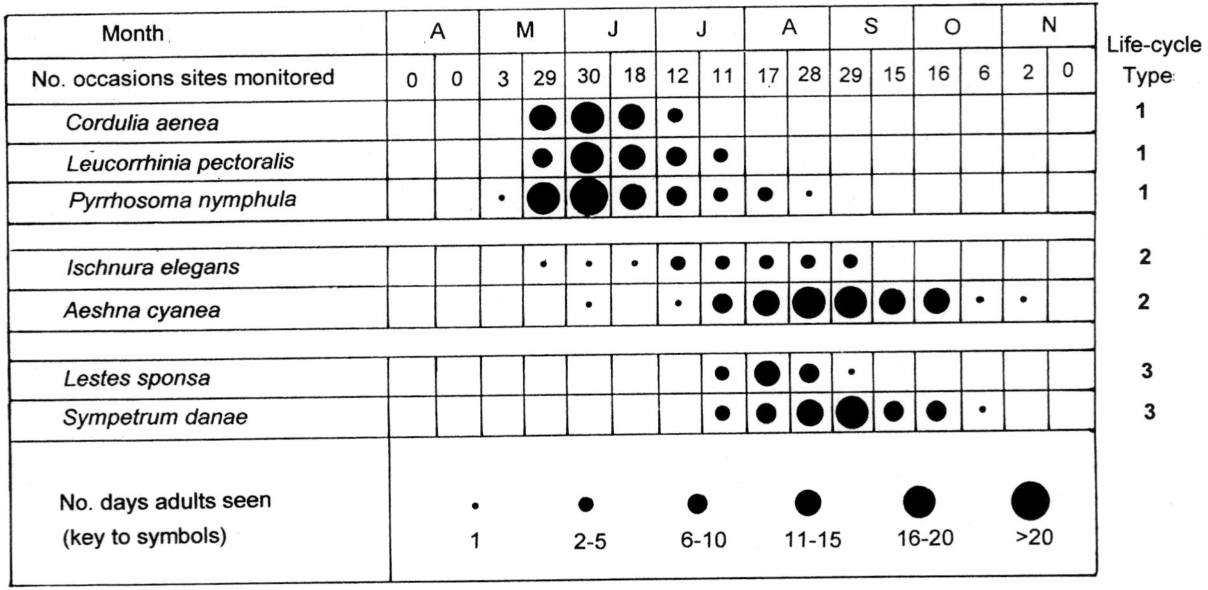

Month	A		M		J		J		A		S		O		N		Life-cycle Type
No. occasions sites monitored	0	0	3	29	30	18	12	11	17	28	29	15	16	6	2	0	
Cordulia aenea				●	●	●	●										1
Leucorrhinia pectoralis			●	●	●	●	●	●	•								1
Pyrrhosoma nymphula			•	●	●	●	●	●	●	•							1
Ischnura elegans				•	•	•	●	●	●	●	●						2
Aeshna cyanea				•	●	•	●	●	●	●	●	●	●	●	•		2
Lestes sponsa							●	●	●	•							3
Sympetrum danae							●	●	●	●	●	●	•				3
No. days adults seen (key to symbols)	•		●				●		●		●		●		●		
	1		2-5				6-10		11-15		16-20		>20				

FIG 101. Flying seasons of dragonflies which have three types of life cycle near Zürich, Switzerland, during nine years. The top row shows the number of days on which sites were monitored in each half-month, and the bottom row an arbitrary scale of abundance based on the number of site-days on which adults were seen during each time interval. Entries in the right margin correspond to life-cycle types defined in Box 15, p.163. (After Wildermuth.[54])

species, such as *Enallagma cyathigerum*). Within Britain, as expected, the flying season of a given species tends to be earlier in the south than the north.

Longevity

One of the first questions people ask about dragonfly biology is 'How long do adults live?' A rough estimate of the maximum length of life can be obtained by comparing the time elapsing between the beginning of emergence and the apparent end of the flying season. In *Coenagrion puella*, daily survival rate is constant and independent of size for mature adults of both sexes and the mean mature life span for males and females respectively is 5.6 and 5.4 days.[55] In this species, in the population studied, daily survival rate independent of age for both sexes, being 0.83 for males and 0.82 for females. However, the asymptotic shape of the survivorship curve for *Pyrrhosoma nymphula* (Fig. 102) shows that the maximum length of life tells one little about the longevity of the bulk of the population. An informative value is the median or life expectancy, namely the time (or age) at which 50 per cent of the population has died. For the survivorship curves shown in Fig. 102 the median values are much less than the maxima which are (for 1951 and 1952 respectively) 32 and 44 days for males and 20 and 37 days for females. These values apply only to adults surviving the initial maturation period of 9–15 days. Like the median values, they emphasise the difference in survival (in the same population) between the two years. Because *Pyrrhosoma nymphula* is a Type 1 species, the peak density will come at the beginning of the flying season and the bulk of the population will grow old together.[56] This being so, it was at one time hypothesised that the selective pressures for longevity would be less on Type 1 species than on species of Types 2 and 3.[57] Insufficient data exist to confirm this, although some of the highest recorded values for longevity in Europe come from aeshnids with a Type 2 life cycle: *Aeshna grandis* in Poland and *A. juncea* in Germany attained post-emergence ages of at least 64 and 70 days respectively,[3] including the long prereproductive period of about 35 days. Potential longevity clearly exceeds these values which depend partly on recapture probability. Post-emergence ages exceeding 80 days have been recorded for captive *Calopteryx splendens*, *Aeshna juncea* and *Anax imperator*.[58] Excluding species in which adult life is prolonged by a diapause, it may be said that the life expectancy during the reproductive period is close to 11.5 days for Anisoptera and 7.6 days for Zygoptera and that durations for the prereproductive period are about two weeks and one week respectively, the maximum being 30 days for both suborders.[59] In *Coenagrion puella* weight is positively correlated with male longevity,[60] as it is in *Sympetrum danae*,[61] although sometimes a finding of this kind is contradicted when a study is repeated in another season.[63] The mean life

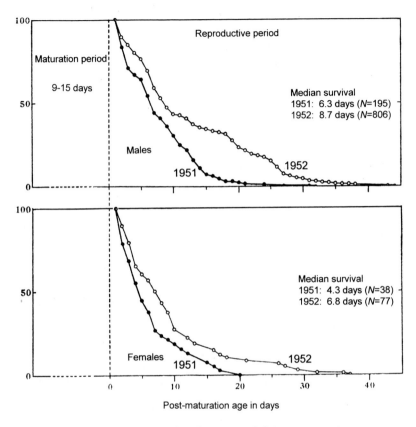

FIG 102. Survival of mature adults of *Pyrrhosoma nymphula* in two successive years at a stem habitat (Fig. 44, p.77). Results are based on the greatest intervals between release and recapture of marked individuals *after* they had returned to water, those recaptured after only one day providing the value for 100 per cent. Survival was lower in 1951, a year that featured a late spring and summer, less favourable weather and a longer prereproductive period. The median values represent the expectation of life on the first day of the reproductive period. Males lived slightly longer than females. (After Corbet.[62])

span of mature adults of *Coenagrion mercuriale* has been estimated to be about a week.[64]

A continuing need is to identify morphological criteria for determining post-emergence age. A promising relationship has been found between the intensity of wing pigmentation and age in *Calopteryx maculata*.[65] This character is used by the European *C. haemorrhoidalis* for mate recognition during courtship,[66] during

which enhanced fitness may accrue from being able to recognise the age
(reproductive quality) of a potential mate.

Flight seasonality

Global warming[67] is likely to change the distribution and faunal composition
of Odonata in temperate latitudes.[68] At present, species richness (i.e. the number
of species in a given locality) in Britain is correlated positively with mean air
temperature, in summer, though not in winter.[69] Thirty-seven species of resident
British Odonata have extended their range northwards during the past 40 years.[70]
Observed and anticipated effects of global warming on the phenology of British
Odonata are explored on p.294 and p.295.

In northern Europe the flying season of 11 species of dragonfly now peaks
earlier than it did in 1980. *Pyrrhosoma nymphula* (a Type 1 species) shows the
strongest effect, having advanced its flight peak by 17 days. *Aeshna grandis* (a Type
2 species) has done so by about 14 days. For most of the 11 species the shift in
flight peak is strongly correlated with increasing spring temperatures at a site,
especially in May.[71]

Jürgen Ott, studying trends in Germany and mainland Europe, is thoroughly
monitoring changes in the dragonfly fauna that are correlated with steadily
rising temperatures there. Such changes include earlier seasonal emergence,
more rapid larval growth, increased voltinism and change in species
composition, favouring eurytopic species over ecologically sensitive (*stenotopic*)
species: the former include *Aeshna affinis*, *Anax parthenope*, *Boyeria irene*, *Lestes
barbarus*, *Orthetrum brunneum* and *Sympetrum fonscolombii* and the latter include
species such as *Coenagrion hastulatum*, *Leucorrhinia dubia*, *Orthetrum coerulescens*
and *Sympetrum flaveolum*.[72]

BIOTIC FACTORS

Adults, like larvae, are used as a resource by commensals, parasites and predators
(Box 12, p.130).

Commensals

Commensals are seldom observed because they are usually so small, and probably
also because they often escape when a dragonfly is netted. The benefits they gain
from attachment to the dragonfly adult include transport and food. Very few
observations exist of commensals of British species. One of the most interesting
observations is due to Klaus Sternberg, who closely watched a male *Cordulegaster*

boltonii in Germany.[73] When the dragonfly was settled and not feeding, minute flies of the milichiid genus *Desmometopa* were seen on the coxae, legs and sides of the thorax, usually remaining on the thorax when the dragonfly was flying. While the dragonfly was feeding (and settled) the flies were active around the mouthparts, sucking the already masticated, fluid-covered prey and dabbing at the dragonfly's mouthparts after it had ingested its meal. They nimbly avoided being crushed by the dragonfly's jaws or being swept off by cleaning movements of its legs by running quickly away or by making short flights. We have already mentioned (Box 8, p.104) the scelionid wasps that are parasitoids of the eggs of endophytic Odonata and that are sometimes phoretic on ovipositing adults with the prospect of being already close to the female when eggs are laid. In the phoretic phase they are behaving like commensals.

Endoparasites

Internal parasites that are carried over from larvae to adult dragonflies (namely Protozoa, Trematoda and Cestoda) have been described on p.131. Such endoparasites are very widely distributed in adult Odonata. Infection of *Calopteryx splendens xanthostoma* with eugregarine Protozoa during the prereproductive period reduces the ability of adults to accumulate fat, and consequently diminishes their ability to acquire and maintain territories when they attain maturity.[74] It can be assumed that most endoparasites lower the viability of their hosts, but it is difficult to identify their impact because parasitised hosts cannot readily be recognised without dissection and because parasites of different kinds may interact with one another.

Ectoparasites

Most observers of Odonata will have noticed the bright red or orange ectoparasitic mites (Acarina) attached to the ventral surface of the thorax and abdomen (especially of Zygoptera) (Fig. 103). They belong to three families of water mites, or Hydrachnida (also known as Hydrachnellae or Hydracarina). The life cycles are complex, involving parasitic and free-living phases.[75] Most belong to the genus *Arrenurus*, at least 55 species of which parasitise Odonata, but three other genera are involved.[76] *Arrenurus cuspidifer*, infesting *Ischnura* in southern France, can serve as an example. The egg, laid under water, hatches in one to three weeks, releasing a minute six-legged larva that swims freely and seeks out a final-stadium *Ischnura* larva, to which it attaches phoretically, favouring one at a late stage of intrastadial development. On pharate F-0 larvae of *Pyrrhosoma nymphula* these minute mite larvae (less than 1.5 millimetres wide) attach by preference to the back of the head, in the deep groove between the head and

FIG 103. A male *Ceriagrion tenellum* carrying a heavy load of parasitic mites on his thorax (Robert Thompson).

thorax, this being one of the few places on the body surface immune from the grooming movements employed by the dragonfly larva.[77] Some mite larvae may locate and cling to a host just after its moult to F-0; some may attach beneath the wing sheaths of *Ischnura elegans*[78] and on the compound eyes at the bases of the antennae in *Coenagrion puella*.[79] When viewed through a hand lens, the clustered mite larvae at this stage resemble a dusting of red pepper. As the dragonfly emerges, the mite larvae transfer to the teneral adult, very promptly, moving rapidly during stage 2 of emergence and taking up positions on the dragonfly's body that are characteristic of the species of mite. Here they quickly penetrate the cuticle before it hardens. They may even transfer to the adult during stage 1 of emergence, entering the F-0 exuvia through the ecdysial aperture to do so. Up to 30 seconds (but no longer) after the host's ecdysis, mites will abandon an injured host, but thereafter are committed to the attachment. Having inserted the mouthparts, they then steadily imbibe the host's haemolymph through the stylostome, a tube ensheathing the mite's mouthparts. Over a period of several days, this feeding causes the mite's body to swell and adopt a characteristic appearance, becoming shiny, red and almost spherical (Fig. 103). Initial loads of *Arrenurus cuspidifer* on *Ischnura elegans* can reach 150 mites per host. When the ectoparasites have attained their full size, after a period approximating to the maturation period of the host, they are ready to drop off the host's body and enter the water. In *Coenagrion puella*, and probably other coenagrionids, the stimulus that induces detachment is the proximity of water:[79] if a flying adult approaches to within 25 centimetres of the water surface, fully grown mites are stimulated to drop off their host. *Arrenurus cuspidifer* mites detach from *Coenagrion hastulatum* and *C. puella* during host oviposition, regardless of their host's sex.[80] This is consistent with the finding that males of *Coenagrion mercuriale* in tandem carry fewer mites than do single males.[81] When a mite has detached from a dragonfly, it may leave behind it part of the stylostome and often a brownish scar.[82] Once in the water, the six-legged larva, now engorged, completes its development.[83]

Each species of parasitic mite tends to attach to a specific part of the host's body and to have a characteristic appearance, enabling an experienced observer to recognise the species by eye, or at least with a hand lens. Likewise, for mites that attach only at emergence, the approximate time that the mite has been attached to the immature dragonfly can be judged by the state of the mite's engorgement and, because the host's burden of mites becomes less with each visit to water, the number of attached mites is broadly correlated with the host's post-emergence age.[85]

For most species of *Arrenurus*, all the mite larvae that will transfer to a host do so at the time of emergence and thereafter enlarge synchronously until they drop off. Arnold Åbro found that in Norway all *Arrenurus* larvae on *Coenagrion hastulatum* and *Enallagma cyathigerum* attached synchronously and only at the time of the host's emergence, whereas on *Lestes sponsa* and *Pyrrhosoma nymphula* some mites attached at emergence but most did so later, when the hosts visited water for reproduction.[84] So, in the latter two species, the mite-load actually *increased* with post-emergence age. This means that, for such species, the degree of engorgement of a dragonfly's mite load (assessed by the mites' size and surface texture) does not necessarily correlate with the host's post-emergence age.

Absence of mites does not necessarily mean that they have already dropped off; there are usually some adult odonates that remain unparasitised. In *Pyrrhosoma nymphula*, a Type 1 species (Box 16, p.167) with a large, early, synchronised peak of emergence, followed about 25 days later by a small second peak,[86] the onset of the second peak can be marked by an abrupt increase in the proportion of adults carrying small mites.[87]

Much of what is known about the effects of mite parasitism on adult Odonata derives from recent work by Jens Rolff.[88] On *Coenagrion puella, Arrenurus cuspidator* reduces the body fat of males and reduces the fecundity of females,[89] and impairs host fitness by draining nutrients,[90] although parasitism does not lower ejaculate volume or mating success.[89] *Coenagrion puella* bearing mites are more likely to disperse,[91] which must have a large effect on the host's population dynamics because in some populations of *C. hastulatum* and *C. puella* parasitism can reach 100 per cent.[92]

Other kinds of water mite sometimes found as ectoparasites of dragonflies belong to the Hydraphantidae and Limnocharidae. The former parasitise species of *Coenagrion* and *Ischnura* and the latter species of *Anax, Enallagma, Gomphus, Lestes, Leucorrhinia* and *Sympetrum*.[76] Larvae of the Hydraphantidae and Limnocharidae are primarily terrestrial and encounter the adult dragonfly by crawling or running on the surface film of water. After attachment they engorge on the host and then transform to the nymphochrysalis, either on the host or after dropping off.

Other ectoparasites of adult Odonata, almost invariably attached to the wings, are flies of the genera *Forcipomyia* and *Pterobosca* in the (mainly Holarctic) family Ceratopogonidae. The circumstances attending their attachment are unknown. The females attach to the bases of the host's wings, apparently without inflicting serious injury, remaining there for several days imbibing haemolymph while the parasites' oocytes mature.[93] It appears that sometimes attachment occurs close to emergence: adults of *Forcipomyia paludis*, recorded only on dragonflies, were found on teneral adults of *Aeshna isosceles, Ceriagrion tenellum* and *Libellula quadrimaculata*.[94] Infested adults presumably suffer from the loss of haemolymph, especially if infestations are high: an adult *L. quadrimaculata* carried 171 *Forcipomyia paludis*.[95]

Predators

Because Anisoptera are such agile, powerful fliers, virtually the only effective predators on mature adults are birds, mainly raptors and bee-eaters, that can match or better the dragonflies' powers of flight. Zygoptera, being weaker flyers, are vulnerable to a wider range of aerial predators (Fig. 104). In a study of *Calopteryx haemorrhoidalis* in southern France, the main predators were found to be wasps, Anisoptera (especially *Orthetrum cancellatum*) and spiders (Araneidae).[96] It is likely that predation on adults of both suborders is greatest at the time of emergence, before and during the maiden flight, at roosting sites on cold mornings[97] and during oviposition, especially among species that oviposit endophytically. In Britain, the Hobby, *Falco subbuteo*, has days when (as an

FIG 104. A Willow Warbler, *Phylloscopus trochilus*, proffers an adult male *Ischnura elegans* to its nestlings (Robert Thompson).

alternative to small passerine birds) it concentrates on Anisoptera, such as *Leucorrhinia dubia* and *Libellula quadrimaculata*, snatching them in the air in a masterly display of agility. Eleven species of Odonata have been recorded as prey of the Hobby.[98] It has been estimated that a juvenile Hobby would need to consume 75–90 *Aeshna mixta* or 200–250 *Sympetrum striolatum* in order to meet its daily energy requirements.[99] The celebrated ethologist, Niko Tinbergen, gave an exciting and detailed account of the behaviour of a Hobby feeding on a population of *Libellula quadrimaculata* in the Netherlands.[100] Speeding from its nest to a source of dragonflies about 2.5 kilometres away, the bird would sweep its prey out of the air and return with it, flying at about 150 km/h. In this case the bird flew to a chosen destination to collect its prey, but sometimes falcons, like perchers among dragonflies, behave as sentinel foragers, selecting an observation perch and then darting out from it, flycatcher fashion, to intercept a passing dragonfly. We seldom witness large, overland migrations of odonates in Britain, but in the New World, where such migrations are commonplace, raptors (which may be migrating themselves at the same time and on the same flyway) often prey on aggregations of dragonflies, drifting in and out of the moving cluster of insects to assuage their hunger. Many other kinds of predators take their toll of adults, mainly when these are perched. They include insectivorous plants, such as *Drosera* (Fig. 105), which often capture coenagrionids, and spiders (Fig. 106) in whose webs adults may get entangled when alighting on vegetation. Adults that fall on to the water surface, often as a consequence of being defeated in a territorial clash, often fall prey to aquatic Hemiptera: Heteroptera, such as *Notonecta* and *Nepa*, foraging just beneath the surface. Adult Robber flies, Asilidae, also operate from a perch and can easily catch Zygoptera and small libellulids (such as *Sympetrum*) in flight.[101] Among Amphibia and Reptilia, frogs and crocodiles sometimes catch mature adults at the surface of the water, although, mercifully, crocodiles do not concern us in Britain. We should also mention the toll taken sometimes on roosting adults by foliage-gleaning insectivorous bats which apparently use echolocation to detect their prey.[102]

Hornets, *Vespa crabro*, sometimes take large dragonflies as prey, attacking them in flight or when ovipositing: Steve Cham watched a Hornet kill an active male *Aeshna cyanea*, dismember it and return later to feed on the carcass.[103] Likewise, one sunny day another active male *Aeshna cyanea* was caught and decapitated by a Hornet. The Hornet then removed the whole dragonfly piece

FIG 105. Zygoptera, such as this male *Coenagrion puella*, are often trapped by Sundew plants, *Drosera* (Robert Thompson).

FIG 106. This crab spider, *Misumena vatia*, has ambushed a male *Coenagrion puella* (Ann Brooks).

by piece.[104] On another occasion a Hornet brought down a flying female *A. cyanea*, stung it and then removed the exoskeleton of the thorax and consumed the contents.[105] Hornets' chances of success are greater when dragonflies are relatively inactive: ovipositing females, especially when flying in confined spaces, and roosting adults are more than usually vulnerable to attack.[103] Hornets also take Zygoptera.[106] Sometimes the roles of attacker and target are reversed, as when two male *Libellula depressa* were seen to harry a queen Hornet,[107] perhaps mistaking the Hornet for a conspecific female (Fig. 107). The Common Wasp, *Vespa vulgaris*, may prey on emerging tenerals of *Aeshna cyanea*, which resist attack by wing-whirring,[108] and on adult *I. elegans* at the emergence site.[109] Other predators of Odonata include other dragonflies, usually the larger Anisoptera.

To judge from the sensory perceptions of humans, many dragonflies use camouflage, or *crypsis*, as a means of reducing predation risk. This they achieve by a combination of colour, pattern, posture, choice of resting site and immobility. All human dragonfly watchers will be familiar with the experience of watching a 'patterned' dragonfly, such as *Cordulegaster boltonii* or *Aeshna mixta*, alight and then losing sight of it almost instantly because it has become almost invisible against its chosen background. Other antipredation behaviours are brought into play when a settled adult is grasped or struck by a predator. If it can escape, it is liable to fly swiftly upwards and away, and not return to the site of the attack for an hour or more. If it is held by the attacker, it will struggle violently and may swing the abdomen dorsoventrally, even to the extent of making thrusting movements downwards and forwards, as if trying to probe the attacker with the tip of the abdomen. These resemble the precursors to stinging movements made by some bees and wasps, and can be discouraging to a human handler. Such movements may have led Dr Samuel Johnson, the celebrated lexicographer, to define dragonfly as 'a fierce stinging fly'.[110] Also, if appropriately positioned, a large anisopteran may use its formidable mandibles to try to bite its handler, even managing to puncture the skin of a human finger. Sometimes, after being

FIG 107. The female *Libellula depressa* resembles a Hornet, *Vespa crabro* (Robert Thompson).

handled, adults of both suborders may drop to the ground and exhibit a behaviour known as reflex immobilisation, thanatosis, or death feigning, remaining immobile and unresponsive to stimuli for many minutes. This has been observed in *Enallagma cyathigerum* and *Ischnura elegans*.[111] Resumption of activity is usually spontaneous.

The antipredation behaviours described above are probably not predator-specific, being induced by the close approach of any unfamiliar, large object; but a North American species of *Calopteryx* exhibits a predator-specific response which we may expect to find in British species of this genus. A very large North American gomphid, *Hagenius brevistylus*, preys frequently on adults of *Calopteryx maculata*, which it readily captures in flight. Both species were active in a stream-side population in southwest Virginia. When female *C. maculata* became aware of the presence within 3 metres of a perched *H. brevistylus*, they remained perched and immobile, neither feeding nor wing-clapping (possibly a thermoregulatory behaviour),[112] for a period exceeding two hours while the predator was present. Within 30 minutes of the latter's departure, however, they resumed their normal activity.[113] Such predator-specific avoidance behaviour is presumably innate and implies a long and close association between predator and prey, both of which inhabit running water. In Europe, in places where species of *Calopteryx* habitually encounter vertebrate or invertebrate predators,[114] similar antipredator responses may exist.

The evolution of discrete flying seasons is often interpreted as a form of ecological partitioning which reduces competition between species assumed to be sharing one or more finite resources, such as space, food, or freedom from physical interference. To sustain such a notion it is necessary to identify a limited resource and also to observe competition taking place. Norman Moore has thrown light on this matter, showing that, among similar-sized Anisoptera sharing a habitat, a dominance hierarchy exists, such that one species regularly expels one or more others after an interspecific midair clash at a reproductive site.[115] For example, at ponds he observed in southern Britain, Norman found that a male *Aeshna cyanea* would almost always expel a male *Sympetrum sanguineum*, and that a male of either *Lestes sponsa* or *Libellula quadrimaculata* would almost always expel a male *Sympetrum striolatum*. Notwithstanding the elevated status of *L. sponsa* in this hierarchy, it was usually the smaller of two competing species that was ousted. This investigation revealed a rare example of competition in action. More commonly, competition is a notional phenomenon that is accepted intuitively but can seldom be demonstrated. The dominance hierarchy maintained among dragonflies localising over a single body of water imposes a fitness cost on those that are being denied access because they are deprived of potentially valuable time at the reproductive site during favourable weather. In other words, it is a clear-cut example of interference competition. This being so, we may infer with confidence that the staggering of flying seasons has selective value.

DISPLACEMENT BY FLIGHT

Being superbly competent fliers, adult dragonflies can be expected to exhibit outstanding powers of dispersal. Evidence that they do so is widespread and convincing. A newly constructed pond is rapidly colonised by several species, even if it is several kilometres from the nearest source of immigrants. Not surprisingly, little is known about the nature of this dispersal behaviour. What we do know derives largely from an ingenious project devised by Jochen Lempert,[116] working in Hamburg. He chose a small, isolated pond replete with insectivorous fish and containing a few species of dragonflies, which included *Coenagrion puella* and *Ischnura elegans*. Jochen spent many hours each day at the pond, recording the behaviour and species of arriving dragonflies. Very large numbers of adults (including 18 species of Anisoptera and 9 species of Zygoptera), mainly mature, arrived over a long period, at the remarkable rate of one every four to five minutes. Arrivals during one year included more than 1,600 *Sympetrum*. Adults were marked on arrival, allowing Jochen to establish that about 4 per cent stayed for two or three days and 2 per cent for four to seven days, and that more than 50 per cent of *Sympetrum danae* left within two hours, suggesting that some males could have visited more than one pond in a day. Some arrivals continued on their way without even descending close to the water surface, suggesting that they were detecting key properties of the habitat from a height of several metres.

The picture that emerges from these well-documented observations at the pond in Hamburg is that of a countryside overlain by a blanket of dispersing dragonflies several metres above the ground. If, as Lempert found, most of these are mature, then it is reasonable to assume that a high proportion had been expelled from a reproductive site by inter- or intra-specific competition, underlining the heavy cost of occupying a low position on the dominance hierarchy. Are members of this travelling blanket of dragonflies reducing the randomness of their paths by navigating? Certainly, as they approach a water body, their ability to detect the horizontal polarisation of light will enable them promptly to detect it and, especially near the beginning and end of the daylight period, when the sun appears low in the sky, they may use its reflection to detect ponds. Wind direction may also influence their course. We know also, from work of Klaus Sternberg in southwestern Germany,[117] that large numbers of Anisoptera and Zygoptera (more than 29 and 8 species respectively), almost all mature, were found moving singly or in small groups along rivers, especially those with wooded margins. Only about 25 per cent of these species normally occupied running water. Some stopped from time to time but others (especially older aeshnids and corduliids) proceeded non-stop. Thus it appears that travelling odonates orientate visually to linear features of the landscape. It is important to emphasise that the species represented in these studies by Lempert and Sternberg were not those normally regarded as migratory (Box 18). Notwithstanding these findings, mark–recapture studies of discrete populations show that the great majority of individuals move only short distances during their lives as mature adults.[118] In a population of *Coenagrion mercuriale* studied by David Thompson, 70 per cent of mature adults (mostly males) travelled less than 50 metres during the flying season and 85 per cent travelled less than 100 metres. A few travelled much further, covering more than 1.25 kilometres.[119] Average distances travelled during a lifetime were greatest among individuals from parts of the habitat where density was least and with less pronounced underwater ledges and with deeper water.[120] Indeed, molecular genetic evidence indicated that adults of this species are highly sedentary, moving very little and then only to neighbouring sites.[121] Interhabitat movement of *Ischnura elegans* is usually very restricted, but a few individuals, both immature and mature, can cover long distances.[122] Some of these must be founders of new colonies.

It is useful to distinguish between trivial and non-trivial flights. Trivial flights are relatively brief, short-range movements associated with an obvious, immediate goal, such as thermoregulation, escape, foraging or reproduction.[123] Non-trivial flights, which normally play a major role in the maintenance of the life cycle, are longer, straighter, and undistracted by such immediate goals. Four kinds of non-trivial flight have been distinguished. Each performs a different ecological function (Box 18). One of these is migration, a term best used (in a zoological context) to mean spatial displacement of adults to a new reproductive site.

Non-trivial flights (at least of Types 3 and 4) can be seen as adaptations to habitat discontinuity. In Britain we are only likely to witness Types 1, 2 and occasionally (near the southern and eastern coasts) Type 4. Flights of Type 3 are associated with Mediterranean-type climates that feature long, hot summers during which aquatic habitats become unsuitable for oviposition. In Algeria *Aeshna mixta* and some species of *Sympetrum* show Type 3 flights, moving to

BOX 18

TYPES OF NON-TRIVIAL FLIGHT PERFORMED WITHIN A SINGLE GENERATION: A PROVISIONAL CLASSIFICATION (FROM CORBET)[124]

Type 1. Maiden flight
This, a one-way flight from the emergence site to the first resting site, can vary in length between 1 and at least 500 metres. It is undertaken by the teneral adult and occurs only once per generation. This flight appears to be orientated away from water. All Odonata exhibit it.

Type 2. Commuting flight
A two-way flight practised daily, weather permitting, between the roosting sites and the foraging and reproductive sites. In that each flight has an apparent goal, probably dictated by an adult's physiological state, commuting flights share properties with trivial flights. Flights can vary in length between a few metres and more than a kilometre, as in *Aeshna caerulea*.[125]

Type 3. Seasonal-refuge flight
A two-way flight between the emergence site (or its vicinity) and a refuge that offers a benign environment in which foraging and reproductive maturation can take place during the hot, dry summer.[17] A regular feature of certain species in Mediterranean climates, it has not yet been detected in Britain but may be in prospect as a consequence of global warming.

Type 4. Migration
A one-way flight between the emergence site (or its vicinity) and a new reproductive site. As far as is known, it may be obligate or facultative, and occurs only once per generation. Distances covered may extend to several thousand kilometres, depending on the strength and direction of high-level winds within which travel often takes place. Although migratory dragonflies may reach Britain, many originate in the tropics where they inhabit ephemeral pools fed by seasonal rains. The transient nature of their habitat requires that they translocate every generation, their flights being directed by rain-bearing winds. While migrating, adults roost at ground level every night, ascending on morning thermals to regain the high-level winds and descending again in the evening.[31]

sheltered upland sites as immatures in early summer and remaining there in diapause until summer's end, when the first major falls of rain cause them to become reproductively mature and to return to the newly filled ponds in the lowlands.[17] The same species sometimes appear in Britain as cross-Channel immigrants. We provisionally interpret this behaviour as Type 3 flights that have become diverted, rather than as genuine Type 4 flights. However, this remains an open question.

We still know very little about the nature and ecological significance of the different kinds of flight made by dragonflies. For example, the position in the provisional classification in Box 18 of the flights witnessed by Lempert[115] and Sternberg[116] remains unclear.

Only occasionally do long-distance migrants appear in Britain. Examples are *Anax ephippiger*, *Pantala flavescens* and *Anax junius*. The first two species are tropical-centred and are well known as occupants of temporary pools in semi-arid regions and as inveterate migrants, travelling long distances on weather fronts to places where rain is about to fall. Sometimes such flights become diverted so that the travellers end up in severely unsuitable destinations. For example, in 1900, a living adult of *A. ephippiger* turned up in Iceland[126] and, in 1998, several adults of a North American species, *A. junius*, arrived in vigorous condition at sites in southwestern Cornwall, close to the Atlantic seaboard,[127] and again, in 2003, at least one adult of this species made landfall on the coast of France near the mouth of the River Loire.[128] These *A. junius* arrived in September, the month when this species flies south in large numbers in North America, especially along the Atlantic coast.[129] Examination of wind patterns immediately before the arrival supported the inference that their transatlantic flights had been assisted, or perhaps determined, by large-scale frontal systems travelling from west to east.

The late Allen Davies, an enthusiastic and expert odonatologist, used to relate how, one misty autumn evening, he was presented with a specimen of a tropical migrant dragonfly that had arrived near his home in Pangbourne in the Thames Valley. Allen's son, who had hitherto resolutely resisted his father's enthusiasm for odonatology, arrived home from the railway station one evening carrying a moribund specimen of *Anax ephippiger*, which he had noticed lying on the pavement and had brought home out of consideration for his father. Unknown to the collector, Allen had never before encountered a British specimen of this species! This incident emphasises the generalisation that information about dragonfly migration tends to derive from disconnected, chance events which, if good fortune prevails, can be witnessed by observers who can place them in biological context.

Initial attempts to systematise records of this kind have so far met with failure. Many thousands of adult *Anax junius* have been marked as they begin their autumn migration south from Ontario,[130] but so far not one has been recaptured, unlike adults of the Monarch Butterfly, *Danaus plexippus*, whose flight paths have been revealed in this way. A valuable component of success in such a venture is to know in advance the migrants' chosen roosting sites on their journey south. These were known for Monarch Butterflies but not for *Anax junius*. So numbers of Monarch Butterflies first marked in Ontario were resighted further south and their migratory routes tracked. Comparable information for dragonflies is awaited. However, the outlook is promising, on two counts. First, the success of using biogeochemical markers, in the form of trace element concentrations and stable isotopes, to infer the geographical origins of migrating animals, including insects,[131] offers promise for tracing the autumnal movements of *Anax junius* in North America, as well as the origins of those adults arriving at high latitudes each spring. This exciting technique exploits the discovery that the relative abundance of certain stable isotopes follows a distinctive pattern across the North American continent and that these values are reflected in the subsequent isotopic composition of the animals that have fed there. This method has been used successfully to infer the northerly origin, in Canada and the northeastern USA, of migrant Monarch Butterflies at their overwintering refuges in Cuba and central Mexico.[132] Second, the recent discovery that a migrating *Anax junius* can be furnished with a microtransmitter and then tracked by land and by air for several days and hundreds of kilometres on its autumnal, southerly journey[133] has opened the prospect of following adults even further, until they reach the latitudes where the species is believed to spend the northern hemisphere winter. The recent study revealed that migrating adults, tagged in September and October 2005 in New Jersey, USA, migrated, on average, every 2.9 days, making an average net advance of 58 kilometres in about six days in a generally southerly direction, and that they migrated exclusively during daytime, but only after two nights of successively lower temperatures, which were followed by cold, northerly winds that aided the dragonflies' southward migration.

In the 1940s *Aeshna mixta*, the appropriately named Migrant Hawker, was known in Britain as an uncommon migrant from southern Europe,[134] but it has since greatly extended its range from foundation populations in the southeast to become established in southern England southeast of a line from about Hull in the north to Bristol and Cornwall in the southwest, and its range is still expanding (p.48). Near the south coast of Cornwall, *A. mixta* gives the strong impression to insect watchers of being an intermittent cross-Channel migrant:

many days in late July or in August will pass without any adults being sighted and then suddenly a group of immature adults will appear, foraging several metres above the ground, sometimes on a day marked also by the abrupt appearance of Clouded Yellow and Painted Lady Butterflies (*Colias croceus* and *Pyrameis cardui*). Such observations do not constitute *proof* of migration, but are indicative of the kind of circumstantial evidence with which naturalists often have to be content when building up an impression of the migratory proclivities of a dragonfly.

As we have seen, mark–recapture studies of small, stable populations of Zygoptera reinforce the impression that most adults stay close to their natal pond.[118] Mature adults of *Coenagrion mercuriale* in a New Forest population dispersed less than 25 metres on average and did not colonise sites more than about 1 kilometre away.[63] When such adults dispersed they tended to move along a watercourse, few being found more than 4 metres from water, and they seemed disinclined to cross areas of apparently unsuitable habitat.[135] In seven species of British Zygoptera neither age nor sex correlated with the tendency to disperse.[136] What we discover about dispersal of dragonflies is likely to depend on what we look for, as Lempert's observations in Hamburg illustrate. His unique study illustrates a valuable maxim: that, by remaining watchful for a long time in one place, an informed observer can sometimes learn a great deal about animal behaviour.

OPPORTUNITIES FOR INVESTIGATION

Material in this chapter suggests several lines of investigation that could readily be pursued by naturalists in the course of their field work without recourse to specialised knowledge or equipment.

Commensals

In view of the recent, fortuitous discovery that a large anisopteran (*Cordulegaster boltonii*) may carry on the outside of its head, thorax and legs minute flies living as commensals and sharing its prey (see p.111), observers are encouraged to take special steps to determine the prevalence of this association. In the past, it may have been overlooked largely because such dragonflies were caught with a coarse-mesh net which allowed any commensals to escape before detection. In future the use of a fine-mesh net, coupled with observations of perched, feeding adults made with a close-focus telescope, should illuminate this area of dragonfly biology. The same techniques should throw light on the frequency with which adults of parasitoid Hymenoptera accompany endophytic Anisoptera while they are ovipositing (Box 8, p.104).

Dominance hierarchies

Research by Norman Moore has shown that dragonflies localising at a single body of water exhibit a dominance hierarchy characterised by certain species consistently expelling others after a physical clash.[137] By recording the fate of adults recognisable as individuals after a clash, the careful observer can provide valuable information to confirm and extend our knowledge of dominance hierarchies, which may differ according to such factors as the type of habitat, the time of year and the presence of females. For such studies to be incisive, participating dragonflies would need to bear marks enabling them to be recognised in flight as individuals.

Dispersal patterns

The observations by Lempert at an isolated pond in Hamburg have revealed how much can be learnt about cross-country travel by dragonflies.[116] For the investigator willing to devote many hours each day to recording the species of dragonflies arriving at an isolated pond, and their behaviour on arrival, a study of this kind is certain to be fruitful. Likewise, Sternberg's finding that many species use watercourses as flyways when dispersing[117] suggests that systematic observations by streams and rivers could be informative. Where dragonfly dispersal is concerned, we know so little that hard data of almost any kind are certain to enlarge our perspectives.

Until recently, attempts to track dragonflies dispersing from the larval habitat have been frustrated by the lack of a method for marking F-0 larvae with a label that remains identifiable in the adult after emergence. Until now, the only method available has been to collect tenerals at the emergence site, retain them until the cuticle has hardened and then apply an external mark. Mike and Marion Parr have shown that one can safely mark tenerals of Anisoptera by applying a date-specific coding of small paint spots on the wings[138] but Carlo Utzeri[139] found that longevity can be reduced, in Anisoptera, according to the number and position of the paint spots applied for identification. So, besides being labour-intensive, marking can impair a dragonfly's survival. An alternative approach, to render a larva or adult radioactive, requires expensive equipment and special safeguards.

CHAPTER 8

Foraging in Flight

D<small>RAGONFLIES ARE EFFICIENT</small> predators throughout life, but it is as adults that their skill and virtuosity in this role are most conspicuous. They are the insect counterparts of the most agile raptors among birds, and their aerial supremacy never fails to thrill the human observer.

When examining the endowment that enables dragonflies to excel as aerial predators, we should beware against attributing their mastery to just one or a few features. It is the smooth integration of *all* their properties that makes possible the aerobatics that we so admire. The aerial agility of Odonata is by no means a recent phenomenon: Palaeozoic odonatoids showed adaptations to aerial predation on a wide size-range of prey, closely paralleling modern Odonata in shape and wing design.[1] Palaeontologists regard the wings of Odonata as homologous with the leaflike gills of larvae of mayflies (Ephemeroptera), the insect order most closely related to Odonata. The development of flight was undoubtedly a key event in early insect evolution and has proved to be one of the most far-reaching in the history of the earth.[2]

In the opinion of Stanislav Gorb, the dragonfly wing represents an early masterpiece of evolution and the dragonfly 'one of the most skilled pilots in the insect kingdom'.[3] The wings are large and liberally endowed with properties that combine rigidity and flexibility. The nodus, a conjunction of veins halfway along the leading edge, permits elastic tension along that edge, as well as strong twisting, and can act as a shock absorber.[4] The *pterostigma* serves as an inertial regulator, raising the critical gliding speed.[5] Microstructures on the wing surface have an aerodynamic role by regulating airflow over the wings.[6]

Three remarkable attributes of dragonflies contribute disproportionately to their pre-eminence as aerial predators. Though present in all Odonata, these three attributes are much better developed in Anisoptera, in which wing-loading is greater[7] and which in consequence excel in agility. The first is the composition of the load-bearing network of veins which contain resilin, an elastic protein[3] which can store energy. Resilin enables grasshoppers and fleas to leap. These rubber-like veins of dragonflies are arranged so that the wing reacts as a whole, and in an elastic manner, to aerodynamic forces, and they enable changes in wing shape to respond appropriately.[4] The second vital attribute that equips dragonflies as aerial predators is the power of sight and optical resolution. The structure and design of the compound eyes[8] is almost ideal for the needs of an aerial predator. The compound eyes are large, typically occupying almost the whole of the head in aeshnids, and they possess great acuity. This is determined by the angles between adjacent units (*ommatidia*) that compose the compound eye (Fig. 108). The smaller this angle, the greater the distance at which small objects

FIG 108. The compound eyes of dragonflies contain a large number of facets that endow them with acute resolution. The division between the upper and lower part of the eye is clearly visible in this adult *Somatochlora arctica* (Robert Thompson).

can be resolved. With respect to the sizes of the units (and therefore the angles between them) the compound eye is differentiated into dorsal and ventral areas, each containing zones (the *acute zones*) where visual acuity is enhanced. Large, migratory aeshnids have the greatest number of *facets*. The North American aeshnid *Anax junius* can have more than 28,000 ommatidia in each compound eye,[9] and boasts by far the smallest interommatidial angles among insects (0.24° in the dorsal acute zone, a value to be compared with 25–57° in some primitive, wingless insects).[9] Resolution is enhanced by spectral and polarisation sensitivity.[9] The properties of this remarkable compound eye enable dragonflies to make the most of their visual environment. On the other hand, each tiny lens of the compound eyes has low resolution, prompting D.E. Nilsson to comment that 'It is only a small exaggeration to say that evolution seems to be fighting a desperate battle to improve a basically disastrous design.'[9] The third remarkable structure, unique to the Odonata, is the *head-arrester system*, the structure and properties of which have been skilfully elucidated by Stanislav Gorb.[10] This system, which comprises the organs of the head and neck, is unique among arthropods. First described in 1950 by Mittelstaedt,[11] it involves fields of tiny, hair-like structures (*microtrichia*) on the posterior surface of the head and on the neck. The arrester ensures that the head remains immobile during foraging or tandem flight, apparently saving the head insertion from violent mechanical disturbance and at the same time stabilising the insect's gaze (Fig. 109). It is absent in larvae. Its presence in adults probably reflects the evolutionary pressures imposed by aerial copulation and aerial predation. Though found in all Odonata, its structure differs according to family. Its ubiquity in dragonflies implies that it originated early in their evolution.[12] The head-arrester system of Odonata especially *Ischnura elegans* and *Pyrrhosoma nymphula*, has been described in detail with respect to its functional morphology and ultrastructure.[13]

In this chapter we distinguish hunting (foraging) from processing the prey after it has been captured (feeding). The term foraging, an umbrella term to describe hunting, embraces a fascinating variety of options available to dragonflies for improving the efficiency of their food-gathering (p.217). Because dragonflies are usually large enough to enable an observer to see, and interpret, their actions, an analysis of their foraging behaviour provides a rich insight into the flexibility that a dedicated insect predator can command. It also serves to remind one of the tightrope that the adult dragonfly negotiates when having to 'decide' daily (indeed almost from minute to minute) how much of its energy to allocate to foraging and how much to reproduction, each of which entails an energy cost as well as an opportunity cost. To witness an aggregation of dragonflies 'frenzy-foraging' in flight is to be a privileged spectator at a display

FIG 109. The head-arrester system allows the orientation of the head of this male *Aeshna cyanea* to remain independent of that of the thorax during banked flight (Steve Cham).

of aerial virtuosity with few equals in the animal kingdom. Such vivid memories include a mercurial group of *Aeshna mixta*, perhaps hungry after a cross-Channel flight, catching flying ants over the lawn of a Cornish garden on an afternoon in late July. Sheer virtuosity!

FORAGING MODES

The major dichotomy that partitions foraging modes is that between midair foragers and gleaners. Midair foraging is the better-known mode, perhaps partly because it is more conspicuous. It is the mode that was being used by the *Aeshna mixta* just mentioned. It requires perception, and integration, of information about the movements, size and shape of the prey. When a percher, like *Calopteryx*,

Libellula or *Sympetrum*, hunts from an observation post, we classify this as midair foraging because both predator and prey are in flight when the latter is captured. Gleaning, in contrast, involves the detection and capture of sessile (but living) prey. It requires perception, not of movement, but of form and perhaps colour. It also requires competent distance estimation and an ability to hover in a controlled way. Odonatology would benefit from more observations about gleaning behaviour. One reason is that this might reveal possibilities for using small Zygoptera for suppressing pests of greenhouse crops, such as aphids, by augmentative release, rather in the manner that parasitic Hymenoptera have been successfully employed for this purpose.[14] This approach has potential because it is feasible (though challenging) to rear small Zygoptera in captivity[15] (and easier to do so than rearing parasitic Hymenoptera) and because it avoids the need to employ synthetic broad-spectrum biocides. Moreover it is possible, but not yet confirmed, that Zygoptera can be habituated to certain kinds of prey and thus 'taught' to prey selectively on a target pest.

Odonata have a well-earned reputation for being generalised predators. A celebrated exception is the Neotropical family Pseudostigmatidae, species of which specialise on spiders which they pluck from webs while in flight.[16] The process of capture involves an elaborate hovering routine and of course an advanced ability to recognise spiders. This should encourage observers to look for an ability to recognise prey types among other, less specialised gleaners. Occasionally *Ischnura elegans* has been seen to glean a spider from its web and to show deftness in avoiding entanglement.[17] Indeed, ischnurans seem to show a degree of specialisation in taking prey from spiders' webs.[18] There may be more to gleaning than meets the eye.

The opportunism shown by some dragonflies is remarkable, even for so-called generalised predators. An 'aeshnid-like dragonfly' was seen in Holland munching on the porridge-like remains of a slug on an asphalt road.[19] Another striking example of predatory versatility is illustrated by the female *Enallagma cyathigerum*, presumably engaged in underwater oviposition, gleaning Willow Aphids, *Tuberolachnus salignus*, while submerged.[20] It consumed seven or eight aphids in five minutes. Ken Tennessen watched a male of the North American *Enallagma exsulsans* dart repeatedly towards Waterstriders, *Gerris* sp., that were poised on the moving water surface of a large riffle in Alabama. After about 20 unsuccessful sallies the dragonfly secured a Waterstrider and flew to the bank where it perched to consume its prey.[21] Ken noted that, if the dragonfly did not surprise the gerrid and capture it immediately, he retreated and tried another one.

The dichotomy between fliers and perchers does not correspond neatly with that between midair foragers and gleaners, although most observers have the strong impression that gleaning is more prevalent among Zygoptera, which are predominantly perchers. Some perchers use the mid-air mode when foraging, but fliers seldom if ever use the gleaning mode.

On the whole, and although exceptions exist, foraging takes place away from the reproductive site. Therefore, because reproductive activity tends to centre on the warmest time of day, in Britain at least, foraging usually occurs before and after this,[22] except during the prereproductive period when the immature adults do not visit the reproductive site. As soon as the ambient temperature permits spontaneous flight in the morning, and until it ceases to do so in the evening, dragonflies not engaged in reproductive activity are likely to devote time to foraging. The observant naturalist will know where best to look for dragonflies foraging in the midair mode, for example, in warm lee sites where small Diptera habitually swarm.

The structure of the compound eye of dragonflies favours the detection of movement, especially *above* the dragonfly. (The size and arrangement of the ommatidia on the ventral surface of the compound eye is better suited to the perception of form, rather than movement.) Thus dragonflies foraging in the midair mode almost always approach a target from below. Indeed, the swift, darting, upward movement that characterises the approach to prey is one of the hallmarks of foraging flight and a useful criterion for recognising what a dragonfly is doing, and sometimes what it is feeding on. When a dragonfly launches itself from a perch to intercept passing prey, it approaches the latter obliquely, making allowance for the distance to be travelled, the speed of its own flight and that of its target. By analysing video images of the approach flights of perchers (libellulids), Anthea Worthington and Bob Olberg are throwing light on the remarkable powers of information-processing possessed by perchers in the southern USA.[23] In suitably expert hands, the ciné and video camera provide valuable tools for observing the intimate details of foraging behaviour. By this means Georg Rüppell has discovered that, when foraging from a perch, *Calopteryx haemorrhoidalis* uses the wings as well as the legs to improve the probability of prey capture.[24]

DIETS

If confined for a few hours in captivity, adult dragonflies, like the larvae, usually void faecal pellets. For an investigator with skill, experience and great patience, these can yield information about the dragonfly's recent diet. The few such published studies have yielded useful information but, with the knowledge we now possess, it is unlikely that further analyses of faeces will justify the effort required. This is because the clear pattern that emerges is that the prey of midair foragers (and perhaps also of non-specialist gleaners) consists predominantly of small insects.[25] Sometimes a dragonfly can be found with its mouth crammed with small flies (Diptera). Because insect fragments in the faeces have already been triturated and macerated during their passage through the dragonfly's gut, they have acquired a grim uniformity of appearance that thwarts the forensic odonatologist. Often on-the-spot field observations can more readily give information about a dragonfly's current prey. As with the detection of commensals, the use of a fine-mesh net can be rewarding, especially as sometimes a dragonfly captured foraging may still have prey between its legs or mandibles. In the now-classic inventories of prey of Odonata by Campion and Hobby, most prey items were Diptera, comprising representatives of at least eleven families, and the prey included other insects such as wasps, honeybees, bumblebees, butterflies, moths, caddisflies, alderflies, winged ants and other Odonata.[25]

CAPTURING, HANDLING, SUBDUING AND PROCESSING

The legs are long and well armed, especially in Anisoptera, and it is commonly supposed that they are used to grasp the prey. This is certainly so in species of *Calopteryx* in which the legs, liberally furnished with long spines, are positioned to form a net in front of the head during prey capture, while the densely pigmented wings are orientated so as to present a visual barrier, discouraging prey from escaping.[24] Surprisingly, however, close observation has revealed that aeshnids, corduliids and lestids often, and perhaps usually, use the mouthparts alone to capture small prey.[26] The legs tend to be used when capturing larger insects, but it is not always possible for the observer to identify their role precisely, because they may also be used later to subdue the prey. Odonates often carry a large prey item to the ground to consume it, perhaps making it easier to subdue. Ken Goodyear reports the remarkable observation of an adult *Lestes sponsa*, resting on a sprig of heather, holding a large tipulid, *Tipula melanoceros*, it had captured.[27] The dragonfly held the prey firmly by the second abdominal segment, thus preventing the tipulid from beating its wings, and then advanced slowly into thick heather, pushing the prey before it; a few minutes later the prey was dead and being consumed. This sequence of actions comes close to tool-using! Although large prey is often brought to a perch or the ground to be consumed, small prey is often consumed while the dragonfly is in flight. When *Aeshna mixta* is foraging on flying ants, the shower of dismembered wings that descends shows that the ants are being processed and presumably ingested in flight. Sometimes Anisoptera foraging in a dense swarm of small Diptera may be catching prey more quickly than they can ingest it, as shown by a bolus of prey remaining between the mandibles: a male *Aeshna mixta* was once encountered with his mouth crammed with small black midges.[28] Confronted with a situation like this, some animals, ourselves included, would arrange to store the excess against subsequent need. It seems that dragonflies sometimes hoard food in this way (Box 19, F). Benno Hinnekint has seen *Ischnura elegans*, *Orthetrum cancellatum* and *Sympetrum sanguineum* hoarding food regularly in the form of a meatball.[29] *Sympetrum sanguineum* hoarded up to eight *Drosophila* at a time, keeping the meatball inside its mouthparts, instead of beneath them as *Ischnura elegans* did.

INCREASING PREDATORY EFFICIENCY

Optimal foraging theory predicts that natural selection will produce foraging behaviours that maximise the net rate of energy gain.[30] Our intuition makes this outcome almost axiomatic. It would seem impossibly costly in terms of energy for dragonflies to seek prey (which typically has a clumped distribution) at random. Our qualitative experience roundly supports this intuition. Dragonflies possess several strategies for focusing their foraging behaviour in places where the predator-prey encounter rate is very high, and perhaps maximal. It lends interest to field observations to try to interpret foraging behaviour against this theoretical template. Dragonflies worldwide employ at least twelve strategies that seem to serve this purpose. Because species in the tropics are less restricted in their diel periodicity of flight than species in higher latitudes, we can witness more of these strategies in tropical species. It is worthwhile to take note of them because such strategies may appear among dragonflies in Britain during unusually warm weather, or when global warming begins to become manifest. There are three main categories of strategy (Box 19, A–C), each being expressed in several forms.

Most of the strategies listed are self-evident, but three deserve comment. Strategy B.1 is unlikely to be witnessed often in Britain because the ambient temperature near sunrise and sunset is seldom high enough to permit foraging, although it would be worth examining the flight style of occasional crepuscular foragers, such as *Aeshna grandis* and *Anax imperator*, to see if they are employing this tactic. Similar in principle is the habit of perchers, like *Calopteryx* species,

BOX 19

STRATEGIES THAT ARE ASSUMED TO INCREASE FORAGING EFFICIENCY (FROM CORBET)[31]

A. Foraging where prey are concentrated in space and time
    A.1. At a temporary prey concentration caused by:
        A.1.1. swarming of prey
        A.1.2. prey aggregating at a source of attraction
        A.1.3. a localised thermal
        A.1.4. a lee situation.
    A.2. At a persistent prey concentration caused by a light gap in forest.
B. Increasing capture success by:
    B.1. facing the rising or setting sun
    B.2. facing into the wind
    B.3. taking prey by surprise.
C. Foraging where resting prey have been made to fly by physical disturbance caused by:
    C.1. the foraging dragonfly
    C.2. a large, slowly moving object.
D. Foraging for exceptionally large prey.
E. Defending a foraging site from exploitation by other predators.
F. Hoarding food.

that almost always face the sun when in the foraging mode, so that passing potential prey appears to them in silhouette. Strategy C.1, witnessed by Stephen Cham and Clive Banks,[32] though not yet by us, must be exciting to watch. The observers were attracted by a rustling sound emanating from a dense patch of Stinging Nettles, *Urtica dioica*, partly warmed by the rising sun. The sound they heard was being made by the wings of a male *Aeshna grandis* brushing against the nettle stems amongst which it was flying. As the dragonfly repeatedly entered the patch, large numbers of resting chironomids were disturbed and made to fly. Each *A. grandis* would intermittently hover, then catch and consume a chironomid before continuing on its way. The chironomids in the patch constituted a concentrated source of potential food for the dragonfly but, being on the underside of leaves, they were relatively inaccessible for a midair forager unless they could be made to fly. The dragonfly, which was one of three conspecifics behaving similarly, continued to forage in this way for almost 20 minutes. Its behaviour was obviously strategic and not accidental. Strategy C.1 may have developed from the habit of gleaning stationary prey from tree trunks, exhibited by many species of large Anisoptera,[33] when the mere act of prey capture would stimulate neighbouring prey individuals to fly. Strategy C.2 has so far been detected only in the tropics and almost exclusively among Anisoptera of the subfamily Sympetrinae.[34] It occurs over open grassland and entails the foraging dragonflies assembling around large mammalian herbivores (usually cattle or antelopes) as they wander through the grass. The dragonflies are clearly using the animals as 'beaters' which disturb the small insects resting low amongst the grass stems during the heat of the day and thereby make them available to the midair foragers. The dragonflies are behaving very much as Cattle Egrets, *Bubulcus ibis*, do. The ecological context for this behaviour is that the Sympetrinae typically frequent shallow pools, often in open country where most small winged insects are likely to be resting during the day in the relatively humid environment close to the ground, making them unavailable to dragonflies foraging in the open air above them. As British summers become hotter and drier it will be interesting to see whether any of our libellulids, especially species of *Sympetrum*, show signs of adopting strategy C.2. The most conspicuous exponent of strategy C.2 is the Afrotropical sympetrine *Brachythemis leucosticta*, whose behaviour led to the discovery and analysis of this type of *accompanying behaviour*. It is one of the most widespread of Afrotropical libellulids and uses large, slowly moving objects, not its prey, as the stimulus for accompanying.[35] This behaviour, which is characteristic of this species almost everywhere, is a stirring testament to the versatility of foraging strategies exhibited by Odonata.

Strategy E remains controversial. When Douglas St Quentin conducted his pioneer field studies on territorial behaviour he assumed that clashes between adult dragonflies over water constituted attempts to defend a foraging area.[36] In general, these were probably related to reproductive, rather than foraging, behaviour, but in a few instances aggressive interactions between individuals have been reported at a foraging site.[37] Examples should be sought away from water among individuals clearly in the foraging mode and showing no signs of reproductive behaviour.[38]

ENERGY BALANCE

Adults, like larvae, need to maintain a positive energy balance (Box 11, p.127). Adults differ from larvae in three significant respects:

1) they expend relatively much more energy on food gathering than larvae do;
2) the opportunity cost of doing so is much higher (in terms of time unavailable for reproduction); and
3) options (to forage or reproduce) are much more constrained by the weather, especially at high latitudes.

This means that each day, especially during the reproductive period, an adult is faced with decisions that have far-reaching consequences: when and for how long to forage, or to reproduce. Being free from this dilemma, prereproductive adults probably consume more food than do mature adults.[39] Teneral adults of *Calopteryx splendens* and *Erythromma najas* consume less than do post-teneral immatures,[40] but both *Calopteryx virgo*[41] and *Cordulia aenea*[42] have been seen to forage during their first day as adults. The ability of adults to survive without food is highest just after emergence and then declines steadily thereafter.[43] Such a capability would help to mitigate the deleterious effects of inclement weather at the time when adults are least able to fly robustly. During the prereproductive period, adults can gain more than 100 per cent of their weight at emergence, depending on the weather[44] which affects foraging opportunities to a critical extent.

The remarks above imply that foraging and reproductive activity are mutually exclusive as far as time allocation is concerned, and sometimes this appears to be so. However, a spectrum exists between two extremes: at one extreme are species that often forage while reproductively active at the rendezvous, for example, *Orthetrum coerulescens*;[45] and at the other are those that hardly ever do so, for example, *Aeshna cyanea*,[46] *Cordulia aenea*[47] and *Sympetrum striolatum*.[48] Occupying an intermediate position in this spectrum is *Libellula quadrimaculata*.[49] Little is known about time allocation in non-territorial species. There is no clear distinction between patrol and foraging flights of *Cordulegaster boltonii*: a male may patrol for a whole day, during which it may perch or forage for short periods.[50]

The sexes differ slightly in the strategies they adopt when trying to maintain a positive energy balance, because of the different ways in which they achieve reproductive success, males by patrolling or active defence of a territory and copulation, and females by converting energy into eggs and by ovipositing. Furthermore, a bout of reproductive activity costs much more energy per unit time for a flier than for a percher,[50] and so will require a proportionately larger prior investment in foraging, which is itself more energetically costly in the flier mode. One estimate, for a libellulid percher, *Pachydiplax longipennis*, studied in Florida by Fried and May, was that the energy expended on territorial defence

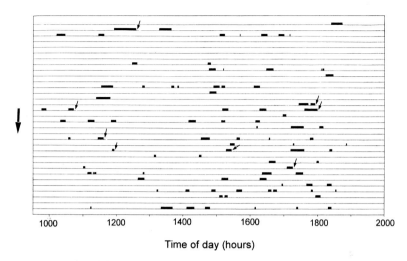

FIG 110. Times and durations of visits to a pond in Germany made by a single marked male of *Aeshna cyanea* from 1 August (top horizontal line) to 2 September (bottom horizontal line) 1967 inclusive. Sloping arrows mark the beginning of copulations which were completed away from water. (After Kaiser.[51])

(about 150 joules per day) amounted to about 85 per cent of assimilable energy obtained per day.[52] This does not seem to leave much of a safety margin if inclement weather curtails foraging activity. Indeed, Fried and May speculated that on some days during their reproductive life, individuals replenish energy reserves by reducing or eliminating their period of territorial defence and concentrating on feeding.[52] It is therefore not surprising that a flier such as *Aeshna cyanea* interposes foraging between relatively brief visits to the rendezvous during permissive weather (Fig. 110).[51]

ECONOMIC IMPORTANCE

For considerably more than a century, biologists have given thought to harnessing the foraging activity of dragonflies to suppress insects that are troublesome to humans, by their numbers and/or activity. The first serious exploration of this idea surfaced in a book by Lamborn.[53] This attractive volume, embellished by a fine, hand-coloured frontispiece of *Anax junius*, was a collection of essays on this topic submitted in response to an advertised competition. The rationale behind the competition was the need to suppress disease-carrying mosquitoes that were threatening the construction of the Panama Canal. Since then, and up to the present day, advocates of *biological control* of mosquitoes using dragonflies continue to present their case, sometimes marketing Anisoptera larvae to augment existing populations in places where mosquitoes are too abundant for human comfort. As long ago as the 1940s, however, a skilled observer in Florida noticed that, even when large Anisoptera had assembled to forage on swarms of stableflies, *Stomoxys calcitrans*, and mosquitoes (probably *Aedes* spp.), no noticeable reduction in prey density resulted.[54] This is not surprising. As mobile, generalised predators, dragonflies are never likely to depress the numbers of one prey type sufficiently to meet comfort thresholds defined by humans. As soon as a prey type begins to fall in abundance and become more difficult to secure, the predator will switch to others that are easier to obtain. To be able to switch is a great asset for a generalised predator but a fatal drawback for a biological control agent in an open system.

The demonstration that adult Anisoptera were lowering the numbers of insect pollinators near a pond in Florida[55] neither contradicts the preceding statements, nor does it demonstrate the potential of dragonflies as biological control agents. To be effective, a biological control agent must maintain its prey below an economic threshold defined by humans, which is usually very low.

However, there *are* situations in which dragonflies can seriously reduce the numbers of their prey. They arise when either the prey or the dragonflies are confined in a closed system. They deserve close scrutiny, if only to arrest the flow of impracticable suggestions that dragonflies in open systems have potential as biological-control agents. The first concerns predation by large Anisoptera on hives of Honey Bees, *Apis mellifera*.[56] Although *Aeshna cyanea* was reported to have destroyed nearly half the Honey Bees in one district of the USSR,[57] the definitive study of this phenomenon was conducted in bee yards along the Mississippi River in Louisiana in the 1940s and involved two large species of aeshnid with a proclivity for assembling close to hives: *Anax junius* and *Coryphaeschna ingens*.[56] Local beekeepers called these dragonflies 'bee-butchers', apparently without exaggeration. If each such dragonfly has a notional consumption rate of 50 per cent of its own body weight per day, it is simple to estimate that a dragonfly feeding thus could kill 100 bees in 20 days. So a hive of 50,000 workers could be exterminated in 20 days by 500 dragonflies, or in 10 days by 1,000 dragonflies.[58] It follows that the reported impact on bee yards is entirely credible. The five prerequisites for such dramatic bee mortality are listed in Box 20. The frequently encountered proposals to suppress mosquitoes by enhancing local populations of dragonflies meet none of these requirements.

The second situation in which dragonflies are effective at suppressing prey

BOX 20

PREREQUISITES FOR DRAGONFLIES TO BE ABLE TO DECIMATE HONEY BEES IN FLORIDA (FROM CORBET)[58]

- bees are spatially concentrated (in hives);
- hives are spatially concentrated (in bee yards);
- dragonflies, being highly mobile, can aggregate from a wide area;
- dragonflies can temporarily specialise on one kind of prey;
- dragonflies are large enough to capture and kill the bees; and
- the dragonflies' flying season coincides with the time when the prey is active and vulnerable.

insects, although not an example of foraging in flight, deserves mention because of the ecological principles it illustrates. It was devised in the late 1970s by Anthony Sebastian, a medical entomologist working in Burma (now Myanmar). After exhaustive preparation, and by following a rigorous protocol, Sebastian successfully suppressed the population of the Yellow-Fever Mosquito, *Aedes aegypti*, in a suburb of Rangoon (now Yangon) throughout the rainy season, the time when the mosquito was transmitting dengue fever and dengue haemorrhagic fever to humans. The numbers of the mosquito were driven down to levels lower than normally attainable by application of conventional pesticides, and low enough to interrupt disease transmission during the rainy season. This situation was a special case because it involved a closed system which Sebastian was perceptive enough to recognise. He reared and released half-grown larvae of a libellulid, *Crocothemis servilia*, into domestic water-storage containers in which a very high proportion of the mosquito population was developing. The prerequisites for success in this case (Box 21) were restrictive, but by no means unique in tropical countries.[59]

A key component of this successful enterprise was that the predator–prey interaction was taking place in a *closed* system. Ancillary advantages of this innovative approach are that it used local resources and involved active co-operation of the local community, and its implementation did not entail use of synthetic chemical pesticides or expenditure of foreign exchange. It is occasion for regret that this discovery has not been exploited.

BOX 21

FACTORS THAT MADE POSSIBLE THE
SUPPRESSION OF *AEDES AEGYPTI* IN MYANMAR
BY THE AUGMENTATIVE RELEASE OF
DRAGONFLY LARVAE

- ability to secure eggs of an exophytic dragonfly that is reproductively active throughout the year;
- ability to raise dragonfly larvae from eggs;
- knowledge that four F-2 larvae of *Crocothemis servilia* will promptly consume all mosquito larvae and pupae in a domestic water-storage container of standard size;
- concentration of a high proportion of the mosquito population as larvae and pupae in domestic water-storage containers;
- knowledge that the dragonfly larvae are able to survive for several weeks without food;
- willingness of local householders to have half-grown dragonfly larvae placed in their water-storage containers; and
- willingness of local householders to allow regular monitoring of mosquito density in their houses.

OPPORTUNITIES FOR INVESTIGATION

Qualitative information about the behaviour and prey of gleaners and the prevalence of gleaning would help to build a balanced perspective of foraging behaviour. Such observations could probably be made more effective by presenting targets of real or simulated prey for gleaners. (Coenagrionids will repeatedly try to glean a gall from a leaf.)[60] While such observations were in train, thought could be given to their possible application for biological control of glasshouse pests, including those in butterfly farms and other insect display houses. Also, more information is needed about the prey taken by midair foragers and about the foraging strategies they employ to secure it. In particular it would be useful to find examples among British species of strategies C.1, C.2 and E in Box 20.

The most rewarding topics probably lie in the field of ecological energetics, building on the pioneer work of Mike May and others.[61] When a percher is making foraging sallies from a perch, its success rate in catching prey can be determined by a patient observer equipped with short-focus binoculars. So far it seems that success rates vary widely – from 2 to 90 per cent.[62] The success rate for a single male *Sympetrum striolatum* was 28 per cent while making an average of 0.96 sallies per minute, the maximum duration of a single sally being 5 seconds.[63] The duration of foraging-only flights of *Orthetrum coerulescens* varied between 1 and 11 seconds, showing an average of 2.7 seconds and a mode of 2 seconds.[64]

Little is known about the aggressive interaction between conspecifics at foraging sites, or 'fights at the dinner table' to use the terminology of Baird and May.[65] Keen observers, watching individually marked adults at foraging sites, could throw light on this.

Scope also exists for enlarging the inventory of large prey taken by Odonata.

CHAPTER 9

Reproductive Behaviour

INTRODUCTION – THE FUNCTIONAL FRAMEWORK

THE ADULT STAGE of the life cycle in British Odonata is relatively brief, lasting only a few weeks for most individuals. Each individual therefore has only a short time to pass its genes on to the next generation and so a large part of adult life is spent maximising the chances of meeting and mating. An extraordinary, complex and fascinating array of reproductive strategies has evolved in response to this strong selection pressure. Reproductive behaviour has a temporal and spatial dimension. Spring or Type 1 species (Box 16, p.167) synchronise their emergence which ensures that most of the adult population is on the wing at the same time. Reproductively mature males increase their chances of meeting females by congregating at water at the time that females are most likely to arrive to oviposit, which in Britain is usually for a few hours either side of solar noon. But, as we shall see, some males are '*sneakers*' and adopt other strategies to meet females; this enables them to forestall their more conventional rivals. At the water's edge, the males of many species of Anisoptera and some zygopterans stake out territories at prime oviposition sites from which they attempt to exclude rival males and so further increase their chances of reproductive success. Competition even persists during the act of mating when the male attempts to remove or displace the sperm of rivals stored within the female's reproductive tracts before delivering his own. Once mated, the male may continue to guard the female during oviposition to prevent usurpation by other males while his own sperm retains precedence for fertilising the eggs his partner is about to lay. The challenges posed by each stage in the reproductive process have been tackled in different ways by different species. We shall view this behavioural diversity in terms of a cost-benefit analysis: a useful approach adopted by evolutionary biologists. In this chapter we shall see how this diversity has been generated.

First, it is useful to identify the essential components of the reproductive process in order to place the elements of reproductive strategy in temporal context.

The encounter

Mature males and females must meet in time and space. Both genders must be able to recognise a suitable rendezvous site. Males may become more or less attached to this site and, in order to improve their reproductive success, may attempt to exclude other conspecifics from it by using a variety of interactive repertoires. The rendezvous site thus often becomes the arena for *sexual selection* on males. At the rendezvous, males search for females.

- *Recognition.* Males and females must be able to recognise each other as conspecific to reduce costly interspecific interactions resulting from mistaken identity.
- *Sperm transfer.* Sperm must be transferred from the male reproductive organs to those of the female. The male may attempt to give a competitive advantage to his sperm by removing or displacing sperm received by the female from former partners (p.246).
- *Guarding behaviour.* Sexual selection continues to operate after mating and results in traits that males use to exclude rivals from access to their recent mates (pp.252).
- *Oviposition.* Fertilised eggs must be laid in a site suitable for larval survival and successful development (Chapter 3).

ENCOUNTER BETWEEN THE SEXES

The rendezvous

For reproduction to be successful it is essential that males and females of the same species meet at the same time and the same place. For most species of dragonfly the rendezvous is the oviposition site. However, for a few British species the rendezvous may occur elsewhere. For example, males of *Sympetrum danae* search for females during the morning away from water where and when over three-quarters of matings occur.[1] *Lestes sponsa* has a similar strategy and pairs arrive at the water in tandem, having already copulated.[2] Males of *Enallagma cyathigerum* may intercept females up to 800 metres from the oviposition site.[3] In southern France, Peter Miller noticed that males and females of *Ischnura elegans* meet at the nocturnal roosting site (away from water) one hour after sunrise and begin copulating within 20 minutes.[4]

Males tend to arrive at the oviposition site earlier in the day than females. This allows territorial species to select and defend high-quality oviposition sites before females arrive. The rendezvous thus serves as an arena for sexual selection as a result of male–male competition, as a site for copulation, and also as an oviposition site.

The precise location of the rendezvous may be determined by the time of day. For example, as a different part of a pond receives direct sunlight and other parts become shaded, so the place defended by a male *Sympetrum striolatum* shifts to that part that is in full sun. Similarly, the time of day that the male is present may alter with the season. At Steve Brooks' garden pond, male *S. striolatum* are present for several hours before and after solar noon during July, but by late August they appear for only about one hour preceding solar noon because for the rest of the day the pond is in shade. Even the age of the individual may determine when it is present at the rendezvous: young female *Aeshna cyanea* are present there earlier in the day than are older females.[5]

Site attachment

The males of most species of Anisoptera and also calopterygid Zygoptera show *site attachment* to a varying extent. They return repeatedly over a prolonged period to the same site and defend this site against incursions by conspecific males or even Odonata of different species. Within this site (the territory) the holder dominates other members of the same species and has prior access to females. The extent to which the territory is fixed in time and space varies and may depend on the number of interactions with other males and females or on exposure to sunlight. In some species, for example *Libellula quadrimaculata* (Fig. 111), the dominant male may tolerate subordinate males within the territory.[6] The vigour with which the male defends the territory can vary with time and between species, and may depend, among other things, on the density of mature males. Territorial behaviour results in males becoming localised on a particular site and spaces them out through that site. Holding a territory becomes increasingly beneficial to the holder as the site gets more crowded and competition for females intensifies.[7]

The degree of site attachment is usually related to male density. Species that occur at low male density at the rendezvous (such as Aeshnidae and Cordulegastridae) typically exhibit weak site attachment, whereas those that

FIG 111. A male *Libellula quadrimaculata* surveys his territory from a vantage point near the edge of a weedy pond (Robert Thompson).

occur at high male density (such as Libellulidae, Corduliidae and Calopterygidae) exhibit strong site attachment. Site attachment often intensifies as the season progresses because male–male interactions and the frequency of female visits increases. Physical factors may also influence the intensity of site attachment.

Those sites, such as clumps of emergent plants or discrete embayments along the shore, which provide landmarks or clearly defined boundaries, tend to intensify site attachment.[8] Odonata evidently have a good topographical memory and spatial awareness: individual males of *Orthetrum cancellatum* (and those of the Mediterranean species *Calopteryx haemorrhoidalis*) remain loyal to the same site even after being absent for a few days following bad weather.[9] Interactions with predators may also influence the strength of site attachment: for example, a male *Calopteryx haemorrhoidalis* is more likely to vacate a territory if attacked by a frog or spider early in its territorial occupancy than a male that has occupied the territory for more than three hours without being attacked and has courted females there; he may remain on site even if attacked later.[10]

Localisation

The first stage of site attachment is *localisation*. On arriving at water, the male surveys the area for its potential to provide suitable oviposition sites. Soon the male will localise at a suitable site where he establishes his territory. *Cordulia aenea amurensis*, the Japanese subspecies of the British Downy Emerald, will localise on a territory within two minutes of arriving at water.[11] Utzeri and Dell'Anna studied localisation behaviour in *Libellula depressa* and found that when a newly mature male first arrives at water he does not show strong site attachment. Instead he frequently changes perches, moving around the pond, engaging with other males and searching for females.[12] However, after his first successful copulation, the male guards the female during oviposition by hovering close by, and subsequently localises on the copulation site and defends this against other males. If there are no subsequent matings over the next day or two the male abandons the territory and resumes searching behaviour, only establishing another territory at the next successful copulation and oviposition site.[12] In this case the male's territory is being selected for him by the female's choice of oviposition site, and the male has to learn which site to defend. Wandering *L. depressa* males are therefore likely to be either unmated and naïve, or older males that have experienced low mating success. In some species the age of the male influences the degree to which he becomes localised at a specific site. Young male *Leucorrhinia dubia* range far and wide, but become increasingly localised at a small part of a pool as the season progresses.[13] Similar behaviour was found in *Orthetrum coerulescens*.[14] On the other hand, although site attachment initially increases in *Calopteryx virgo* (Fig. 112), as the flight season draws to a close males once more begin to show weaker attachment to a particular site.[15]

FIG 112. A male *Calopteryx virgo* localised on a leaf in a sunny spot overhanging a stream (Robert Thompson).

Site fidelity

Most dragonfly species remain at a single pond or group of ponds throughout the reproductive period.[16] However, the length of time a particular male occupies the same territory, even if the species shows high *site fidelity*, can range from a few minutes to many days depending on the species or the individual. Some of the record holders, which can be said to show high site fidelity, include *Calopteryx virgo* (recorded intermittently for 40 days at the same territory),[15] *Aeshna cyanea* (38 days),[17] *Orthetrum cancellatum* (15 days)[18] and *Calopteryx splendens* (13 days).[19] While a male is holding a territory his mating success is enhanced,[20] although the length of time a territory is held and the mating success this achieves must be offset against the energy costs expended in holding it.

The same male of *Aeshna cyanea* in Germany visited a small pond one to eight times a day on 26 days during a 33-day period, each visit lasting up to 40 minutes.[17] His absences from the territory might have been due to bad weather, foraging or presence at other territories. The same territory may be shared by several males during the course of a day. A small bay at the edge of a

FIG 113. A male *Cordulia aenea* patrols the edge of a woodland pond (Steve Cham).

large woodland lake in southern England was occupied and defended almost continuously by different male *Cordulia aenea* (Fig. 113) from 12:38 to 17:03 hours solar time (where solar noon falls at 12:00 h) on 2 July 1994.[21] The bay was left unoccupied when not illuminated by direct sunlight. During the period that the bay was occupied it was shared between seven different males, each one being present for 1–21 minutes (average 10 minutes) at a time. Three of the males appeared in the territory only once during the day, but two others occupied this or the adjacent bay twice during the day; one male reoccupied the bay on three occasions and one male was resident on four different occasions.

Attributes of a territory

The size of a territory is not necessarily related to the body size of the species occupying it or to its flight mode (i.e. whether it is a percher or flier), but there is a tendency for large fliers to have large territories and for small perchers to have small ones. Some of the largest territories recorded in British species include those of *Orthetrum cancellatum* which may patrol a water margin 10–50 metres in length,[18] *Cordulegaster boltonii* which may patrol part of a stream 5–10 metres in length[22] and *Aeshna mixta* whose territory may cover an area of 10 m².[23] The size of the territory can be modified by the physical nature of the terrain (e.g. the presence of landmarks, well-defined bays, clumps of vegetation and the density of perches). Territory size is also inversely proportional to the density of conspecific males and is related to the exposure of the site to direct sunlight. Males of Cordulia aenea patrol the edges of woodland ponds. The size of the area they patrol appears to be related to the number of males present at the pond because when a male meets another male he turns and flies in the opposite direction.[21] Thus, as the number of males present at the pond increases, so the length of bank patrolled by any one individual declines. At high male densities, during the peak of the flight season and towards the middle of the day in fine weather, each territory is limited to one small bay that can be surveyed by a male hovering near the middle of the territory.

Most species of Odonata require a site to be exposed to direct sunlight before they will begin to localise on a territory, and if only a small part of a site is exposed to direct sunlight then the territory will be smaller and confined to that patch. Males of most species will leave a territory when it becomes shaded,[24] although the central European Somatochlora meridionalis has been seen to accelerate through sunlit spots while patrolling shady banks.[25] Some territories appear to attract more ovipositing females than do others, but this is not always related to an obvious physical attribute.[26]

Searching behaviour of males – fliers and perchers

At the rendezvous site a male spends much of his time in either non-aggressive flight, searching for females or, if the species shows site attachment, defending the area against other males. Searching behaviour may take the form of surveying the area from a perch, making brief forays from the perch, or patrolling the site. As we have seen, the searching behaviour of Aeshna cyanea may consist of one to eight flights of up to 40 minutes each at the same site per day.[17] In contrast, Oxygastra curtisii may undertake a continuous single search for several hours.[27] Searching modes used by males may be categorised into a number of types. The first is between perchers (typically Libellulidae and Zygoptera) and fliers (typically Aeshnidae, Cordulegastridae and Corduliidae) in which the male may respectively 'sit and wait' or patrol; this category includes species that are either localised on a particular site or non-localised. The main outcome of the patrol flight is to increase the chances of a male meeting a female. Hidenori Ubukata noted that the patrol flight of male Cordulia aenea amurensis, the Japanese subspecies of C. a. aenea, was similar to the pre-mating flight of the female of that subspecies, and that both increased the chances of meeting a mate.[28]

The patrol flight of a dragonfly tends to be directional (either linear or circular), steady, moderately fast and close to the water. An individual flies to and fro along the same beat or repeatedly returns to the same perch. The ambient light conditions determine the height of the patrol flight which is lowest in shade or towards dusk and higher in bright light. Sometimes the patrol flight will include bouts of hovering while the dragonfly inspects places where females may be resting or ovipositing. Such places are often in the shade, and hovering appears to improve visual discrimination[29], so increasing the likelihood of the male detecting a female. The frequency of hovering bouts tends to increase as light intensity decreases. Hovering may also help to advertise the presence of the male to a female. Hovering consumes a lot of energy and tends to decrease in frequency towards the end of the period spent in the patrol flight. The patrol flight can also include elements of display, for instance when the abdomen is raised in *Cordulia* or *Oxygastra*[30] or turned upwards in *Calopteryx*.[31]

Another apparent function of the patrol flight is to monitor the distribution of neighbouring conspecific males.[32] Indeed, the amount of time spent patrolling by male *Sympetrum striolatum* increases after repeated encounters in rapid succession with other males.[33] The patrol flight may also include periods of foraging, although, as already noted, these two activities are usually segregated.

The precise mode of searching behaviour may be determined by the physical nature of the habitat. After vegetation at the rendezvous had been trimmed, the patrolling behaviour of the central European corduliid *Somatochlora flavomaculata* changed.[34] Similarly, the southeast European *S. meridionalis* displayed three modes of patrolling depending on the location of the rendezvous. At a shaded stream males patrolled continuously along its whole length and sunny spots were avoided; at a meadow margin shaded by trees males localised on a small shaded area and chased off intruding males; and at a group of small pools males inspected areas with overhanging trees and bushes.[25] Male density may also influence patrolling behaviour (p.239).

AGGRESSIVE BEHAVIOUR

Males of species that show site attachment respond aggressively towards conspecific males, and sometimes towards other species, that invade their territory. Aggressive behaviour reduces the flight range of other conspecific males or displaces them from a defended area.[35] Such aggression is directed towards intruders entering the area, but it may also take place while a male is noncontact guarding an ovipositing female. Aggressive behaviour takes different forms depending on the response of the intruder. The outcome of such disputes is often predictable: the territory holder usually wins, although under some circumstances the intruder may displace the resident male. The effect of aggressive behaviour is to space out males at the rendezvous site. Aggressive behaviour also sometimes occurs between females, which may give the winner improved access to foraging or oviposition sites (e.g. in *Aeshna juncea*, *Anax imperator*,[36] *Ischnura*[37] and *Sympetrum*[38]).

Repertoires

Even in species that do not appear to show site attachment, such as *Coenagrion puella*, males may engage in pursuit that can result in either or both males leaving the rendezvous.[39] Such interactions can be difficult to observe and interpret. In species that show overt site attachment, aggressive behaviour is more obvious. If the defender remains perched it may take the form of a threat display (p.236), but usually a resident male takes off and attempts to drive the intruder away. Threat behaviour is most vigorous and effective near the centre of a territory and as the residence time of the male increases.[40] Males are usually able to recognise conspecific males and direct such threat behaviour towards them. But males will sometimes begin to attack a female, only to modify this behaviour by forming a tandem when the female is recognised as a potential mate rather than a threat. Faulty recognition of potential mates occasionally results in the defending male forming a tandem with another male or a female of a different species.[41] Such instances usually occur in conditions of low light intensity or where there has been an accumulation of sex drive after a period of low mating success.

Using high-speed film to analyse the behaviour of species of *Leucorrhinia*, Ilmari Pajunen established that there was a hierarchy of aggressive behavioural acts.[42] This hierarchy has subsequently been witnessed in other Odonata, although the complexity of the repertoire varies. *Leucorrhinia* appears to occupy an intermediate position.[43] Four modes of behaviour have been identified in *L. caudalis*, an Eastern European species closely related to *L. dubia*, namely approach, chase, threat and fight, although the sequence may vary and be repeated. The approach flight is rapid and direct and comes from below or from the side. This differs from the approach that a male makes to a female before forming a tandem, which is usually from above. If the two antagonists recognise each other as conspecific males, a chase follows which may extend beyond the limits of the territory. The pursuing male keeps below and behind the intruder and makes no attempt to catch him. If the intruding male turns to face his pursuer instead of fleeing, the two contestants begin threatening each other by repeatedly darting towards each other, although no contact is made. This results in a circling or spiralling interaction which punctuates the chase. Circle and spiral threats occur when both males show strong site attachment. Threat may develop into fight when one or both contestants attempt to grasp or bite the head or thorax of the opponent. Such escalating behavioural modes are exhibited more or less elaborately by many other species of Odonata. Where a species has brightly coloured patches on the face or abdomen these are often prominently displayed during the interaction, and the white legs with enlarged tibiae are conspicuously trailed by male *Platycnemis pennipes* when confronting other males. Threat displays and physical interactions may also be elicited by intruding tandem pairs, copulating and ovipositing pairs, or while a male is non-contact guarding an ovipositing female.

A more complex repertoire of aggressive interactions is adopted by *Calopteryx virgo* (Fig. 114).[44] When a territorial male approaches an intruder he may engage in frontal threat, in which both males face each other, hovering and changing position to the side or rear, but maintaining the same distance apart. During this display the abdomen is arched upwards and the head and thorax are inclined. In reversed threat the territorial male slowly retreats from the intruder in a characteristic undulating flight during which the abdomen is curved upwards and the head and thorax are held horizontally. Sometimes the antagonists adopt lateral threat in which they fly side by side. Two forms of chase behaviour may occur. In the first the territorial male pursues the intruder at the same height and maintains a distance of 10–15 centimetres behind. In the second type the males face each other and wheel in a tight circle before finally breaking off in a short chase. The final type of aggressive behaviour, which may continue for 30–60 minutes, is termed rocking flight, in which both males rise and fall together, flying erratically and frequently changing direction. Fighting has not been observed in *C. virgo*, although occasional, accidental clashes do occur. *Calopteryx splendens* behaves in a similar way, but stroke frequency and orientation of the wings differ between the modes of aggressive display, and are an important component in this form of communication.[45]

FIG 114. Representative flight postures of male *Calopteryx virgo* during (a) normal flight; (b) mutual frontal threat; (c) one-sided frontal threat; (d) reverse threat; and (e) rocking flight. (After Pajunen.[44])

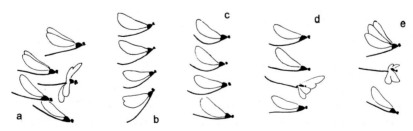

Perched male Odonata, especially Zygoptera, may react to an intruding male conspecific by flicking, clapping or lowering their wings, or by jerking, lowering, raising or curving the abdomen to expose the coloured segments. The characteristic raised abdomen of patrolling corduliids[46] may serve as a form of threat or territorial declaration.

Fighting appears to be the most primitive form of inter-male interaction because it is seen in species that have the simplest interactive repertoires. Fighting is almost nonexistent in those species that have the most complex repertoires of inter-male interaction. Fighting, or even accidental clashes, can result in serious injury, especially to the legs and wings, and can be fatal. An antagonist can be forced onto the water where it may drown. *Aeshna cyanea* may attempt to ram an opponent[17] and male *Pyrrhosoma nymphula* may try to force a rival into the water or mud by pushing from above.[47] *Leucorrhinia dubia* may try to grasp his antagonist's thorax with his legs.[48] Recipients of an attack may attempt to defend themselves by stretching their fore legs above the head and thorax.[49]

Interspecific interactions

Whereas most aggressive interactions are between individuals of the same species, territory holders sometimes react to intruders of different species. Such a response is usually provoked by species that are similar in size and colour, for example, *Anax imperator* (Fig. 115) versus *Aeshna juncea* or *Pyrrhosoma nymphula*

FIG 115. A male *Anax imperator* cruises over his territory searching for receptive females and ready to chase intruding males (Steve Cham).

versus *Ceriagrion tenellum*.[36] However, at high male density *Cordulegaster boltonii* (a large black and yellow species) has been observed to expel a perched male *Orthetrum coerulescens* (a smaller blue species) from its territory.[50] Usually a resident male will maintain its territory when challenged by a male of a different species, although *Aeshna cyanea* is usually expelled by *Anax imperator*.[36]

Outcome of interactions

Almost all interactions are quickly won by the resident male, for example, in *Pyrrhosoma nymphula* the resident male can be victorious 97.5 per cent of the time.[47] So, we may ask: under what conditions is the resident defeated? Males that have recently and frequently copulated are at a disadvantage,[51] as are those that are exceptionally old or young, whereas site familiarity or proximity to the centre of the territory is an asset.[52] Displacement may occur when the resident male is otherwise engaged in copulation or aggressive interactions,[53] contact guarding an ovipositing female,[54] or chasing a female.[55]

Territorial disputes escalate when there is ambiguity regarding the identity of the territory holder.[56] Escalation may occur if the original territory holder is engaged in fighting or mating when the interloper arrives and has time to localise on the territory. Ambiguity may occur if the boundaries of the territory change, for example, as different parts of the rendezvous site become illuminated directly by the sun during the course of the day. If several males enter the territory simultaneously, escalation can occur.[57] As the duration of the dispute increases, the chances of success of the original territory holder decline. In the North American species *Calopteryx maculata*, the resident male won 81.5 per cent of disputes that were resolved within ten seconds, but longer disputes could continue for several hours, leaving the resident male at a disadvantage. In prolonged disputes the contestant with the greater body size and larger energy reserves was often victorious. The greater ratio of flight muscle weight to body weight, the greater the chances of mating success.[58] However, in *Pyrrhosoma nymphula* size has no apparent effect on success, and resident males won 117 out of 120 observed disputes, even though the resident was smaller than the interloper on 56 occasions.[47] Studies on *Calopteryx splendens xanthostoma* from southern Europe revealed that both contenders in an escalated dispute can exhaust 40–50 per cent of their energy reserves, so that only young pre-territorial males, which typically have a high fat content, are likely to displace a resident territorial male.[20] It follows that, once a male has been displaced, he is unlikely to gain a new territory by escalated dispute because of his lowered energy reserves.

Density effects

As the density of males increases at the rendezvous site, there is an increase in the intensity of site attachment and localisation.[59] Aggressive interactions tend to intensify in *Aeshna cyanea*[60] but have been shown to decrease in *Calopteryx splendens*[61] and *Leucorrhinia dubia*.[48] As male density increases, the size of each defended territory decreases,[62] as does the duration of occupation.[17,65] The decrease in territory size under these circumstances reflects an increase in energy expended because the territory has to be defended more frequently. In these conditions males may show less inclination to leave the territory in order to guard ovipositing females or chase rivals.[63] In *Cordulia aenea* the distance a male patrols along the edge of a pond declines as the number of males present at the pond increases (Fig. 117).[64] Other density effects include an increased intensity in the guarding of ovipositing females by males of *Enallagma cyathigerum*[66] and *Sympetrum danae*[67] and an increased likelihood of underwater oviposition by female *Calopteryx virgo*.[44]

When all the available territories at a rendezvous are occupied there is an increase in the number of non-territorial males perched around the pond. Eventually, as the number of males continues to rise, less favoured ponds within the area come to be occupied.[68] An increase in non-territorial males has been demonstrated in *Calopteryx virgo*,[44] *Libellula quadrimaculata*[6] and *Orthetrum*

FIG 116. Two relationships that operate the feedback mechanism that regulates density of *Aeshna cyanea* males at water. a) the number of males at water does not increase linearly (dashed line) in proportion to the arrival rate of males; b) the average duration of visits declines abruptly as the arrival rate of males rises to ten per hour. (After Kaiser.[60])

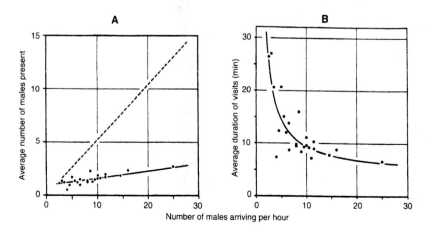

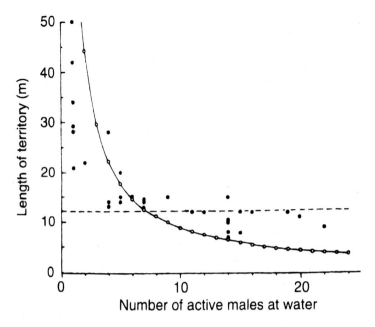

FIG 117. The quantitative relationship between the density of mature males of *Cordulia aenea amurensis* (the Japanese subspecies of the European *C. aenea aenea*) at water and territory formation. When the number of active males in the study area exceeded eight, all males became territorial, causing displacement and spacing of newcomers. The dashed line denotes the average length of territory. (After Ubukata.[28])

coerulescens[69] when there are no longer any territories available. The increase in non-territorial males of *Cercion calamorum* leads to an increase in the number of females that are intercepted on the way to the oviposition site and a decrease in the number of successful matings by territorial males at the rendezvous.[70]

High densities of males can eventually lead to a breakdown in territorial behaviour as the territory-defending males are overwhelmed (e.g. in *Leucorrhinia dubia*,[13] *Calopteryx virgo*[72] and *Enallagma*[72]). This leads to so-called 'swarming behaviour' during which males *en masse* may pursue a single female. Swarming behaviour can also occur at low male densities if there are insufficient perches at the rendezvous or if the arrival rate of females is so high that they prove to be in excess of requirements.[73]

ALTERNATIVE REPRODUCTIVE BEHAVIOUR

In some cases a territorial male will tolerate the presence of other males within or close to the boundaries of his territory. The resulting groups of males may form a dominance hierarchy with a distinct 'pecking order', or there may be a single dominant male with an array of subordinate males that cruise the fringes of the territory. Other males may adopt a non-territorial strategy and search for females away from the rendezvous. There is a tendency for the number of territories with associated *satellite* and subordinate males to increase as the density of males at the rendezvous site increases.[70]

Dominance hierarchies

A consequence of a dominance hierarchy is that it will reduce the number and frequency of territorial disputes, which can be costly in terms of energy expended and can result in serious injuries to the contestants. A territory can be occupied by several males in which one (the 'territorial male') is dominant.[74] The dominance hierarchy in the North American species *Plathemis lydia* (*Plathemis* is a genus closely related to *Libellula*), which was studied by Campanella and Wolf,[75] serves as an illustration of this strategy. As the male matures he rises in the dominance hierarchy; and the higher the male's status the closer he gets to dominating at the optimal time in the day for mating (i.e. 11:00–14:00 h). *Alpha* status is attained midway in reproductive life when the male is dominant during the part of the day that is optimal for mating. As the male passes his prime so does he begin to descend the hierarchy. In *Libellula quadrimaculata* and *Orthetrum coerulescens*, satellite males remain perched around the territory.[76] They do not chase intruders and are not noticed by the territory holder. However, if the dominant male is removed, he is promptly replaced by a satellite.[58]

Shared occupancy

A territory may be occupied and defended by several males that show no strong dominance hierarchy.[77] For example, subordinate male *Sympetrum striolatum* occupy positions just outside the territory of the dominant male. When the dominant male copulates, the subordinate that is perching closer to the territory than the other subordinates takes over the territory. Other males can be regarded as *wanderers*. Whereas territory holders remain perched for over 92 per cent of the time that they are at the pond, and only 4.4 per cent of them make patrol flights, wanderers spend 80 per cent of the time that they are at the pond patrolling.[33]

Non-territorial modes

Up to six alternative non-territorial strategies were recognised in populations of *Calopteryx splendens*,[78] none of which included an element of courtship display. These strategies appear to represent a range of options that may be adopted by non-territorial males:

- *bank lurkers* grasp females as they warm up or pass by;
- *pursuers* chase females for up to 50 metres;
- *roosting site attackers* search for females as they roost either in the early morning or evening, during overcast weather or in light rain;
- *sneakers* prowl the edge of the territory;
- *stealers* attack and split tandem pairs; and
- *water lurkers* search oviposition sites and form tandems with females that are submerging or surfacing and may even pursue females underwater.

Many other species (including *Libellula quadrimaculata*,[6] *Sympetrum striolatum*,[33] *Calopteryx virgo*[71] and *Orthetrum coerulescens*[14]) adopt non-territorial behaviour, especially during times of high male density, and any particular individual appears to be capable of switching from one strategy to another.

RECOGNITION AND VISUAL COMMUNICATION

Like humans, dragonflies are primarily 'visual' animals. As far as is known, they recognise the species and sex of their partners using visual cues, some of which odonatologists can readily appreciate, and some of which can be detected only by experimental analysis. For recognition to be an effective component of reproductive behaviour, it must involve an exchange of signals, the meaning of which is understood by each participant. In other words, it must involve communication, a sequential process, requiring that a mature male can recognise:

1) a mature, conspecific male (in order to try to defend a territory);
2) a mature conspecific female;
3) a receptive female;
4) and that a female can recognise a conspecific male.

In the first of these three steps it is widely accepted that recognition is primarily visual and based on clues such as flight style, size and colour (including ultraviolet reflection and optical density)[79] and pattern. Humans, whose powers of visual discrimination are far inferior to those of dragonflies, employ all these cues to recognise flying dragonflies (often to species), except ultraviolet reflection for which humans lack receptors. Biologists have a tendency to adopt a reductionist approach when addressing questions of this kind, and to seek to identify discrete cues on which recognition is based. Sometimes this approach can be fruitful, but it can nevertheless be useful to bear in mind that the milieu (type of vegetation, degree of shade, speed of current, etc.) in which one dragonfly perceives another may also help it to recognise a receptive conspecific in its preferred surroundings. Often, however, the role of specific cues can be conspicuous, as when a mature male *Pyrrhosoma nymphula* repeatedly 'buzzed' a perched *Libellula quadrimaculata* whose thorax bore a blob of bright red paint,[80] and when a male *L. depressa* patrolling over water tried to seize a Hornet, *Vespa crabro*, which in size and coloration resembles a female *L. depressa*.[81] The use of models can demonstrate that size and posture serve as clues for intraspecific recognition.[82] Intimate knowledge of the internal structure of the compound eye makes it possible to visualise the retinal image produced by different patterns, and, by this means, the essential elements of images that release reproductive behaviour can be inferred.[83] Much can be learnt also about cues that release different behaviours by recording the 'mistakes' made by territorial males when responding to intruders,[84] although care must be exercised to distinguish reproductive behaviour from actions, such as foraging, that may have a non-reproductive function. When trying to locate a potential mate, male anisopterans often seem to respond first, and from a distance of several metres, to the cue for 'anisopteran' and then, at closer range, to cues that require greater discrimination and that may be diagnostic for their own species. For example, a male *Libellula fulva* attacked every anisopteran that approached, but subsequently was able to recognise conspecifics.[85] A perched, tethered female of *Aeshna cyanea*, with wings fluttering, attracted males of three families and six species of Anisoptera (*A. cyanea*, *A. grandis*, *A. juncea*, *Cordulia aenea*, *Libellula quadrimaculata* and *Somatochlora metallica*).[86] It is noteworthy that males of the six species attracted to the tethered female *Aeshna cyanea* have difficulty in recognising conspecific females.[87] At close range, details of the pattern on body or wings probably enable a male to decide whether or not to proceed in his attempt to secure a copulation partner. It is in the male's interest *not* to form the tandem link with a heterospecific female; so it is not surprising that sometimes formation of a heterospecific tandem link is prevented by physical incompatibility between the shape of the superior abdominal appendages of the male and that of the female's head (in Anisoptera)[88] or the dorsal surface of the prothorax of the female (in Zygoptera).[89] Sometimes receptive females seem to advertise their presence by flying in a conspicuous way. In his now-classic study of reproductive behaviour in two North American libellulids, Merle Jacobs[90] observed that when all males of *Perithemis tenera* had been removed from a pond, females behaved conspicuously, visiting oviposition sites and making oviposition movements there. Similar behaviour is shown by female *Sympetrum striolatum* in Britain.[91] This is merely an extreme example of the often distinctive flight style adopted by receptive females when they first arrive at water. On arrival at water a virgin female of the Japanese subspecies *Cordulia aenea amurensis* performs a brief 'pre-mating' flight, at a characteristic height above the water in the Pondweed (*Potamogeton*) zone, during which her posture differs from that of a patrolling male: her abdomen is held at a different angle and her flight is slower and more sinuous.[92]

Species recognition sometimes depends on details of colour pattern and morphology, as in *Coenagrion puella*,[93] and in a habitat where illumination is poor, such as tropical rainforest, it may depend predominantly on physical contact.[94] When several colour forms coexist, as in *Ischnura elegans*,[95] it appears that males choose to mate with the commonest form of the female and that females choose to mate with the commonest colour form of the male.[96] *Ischnura elegans* females with male-like colouring have reduced opportunities to mate and therefore also reduced costs of mating.[97] The angle of approach by male *I. elegans* can determine their success in recognising colour forms of the female.[98] The selective advantage of colour forms remains controversial.

Experiments using a small electric fan to attract males of the Japanese cordulegastrid *Anotogaster sieboldii* showed that they cannot initially distinguish between rotating objects and conspecific females, suggesting that it is the wing-stroke frequency of a flying female (equivalent to a rotation frequency of 20–25 Hz) that is a recognition cue for a male.[99] Naoya Ishizawa suggests that there may be other species of dragonfly that respond to rotating objects.[100] There may, however, be more to this response than meets the eye: *A. sieboldii* responds to the flickering reflection of sunlight from a small waterfall and also to an operating television set! The situation is ripe for experimentation.

Territorial male *Cordulia aenea* have been seen to approach tandem pairs of *Pyrrhosoma nymphula* from above, presumably mistaking the tandem for a conspecific female.

To resist a mating attempt by a male, female Odonata adopt characteristic 'refusal' postures.[101] In zygopterans and aeshnids these often entail the female flying with the posterior half of the abdomen flexed ventrally at a right angle (the so-called 'hockey-stick posture'). David Thompson[102] has pointed out that only females empty of eggs are physically able to adopt this posture and that it could be of selective value to males to recognise this, and, by doing so, avoid a fruitless attempt at mating.

A matter of close relevance to a male's reproductive success is whether he can recognise (as an individual) a female with whom he has just copulated. It would be a waste of a male's seminal investment to expend effort and sperm by copulating again with the same female. This question is not easily answered, but the burden of evidence so far favours the inference that a male *can* sometimes recognise a female with whom he has just copulated, though perhaps not until he attempts tandem formation.[103] Males of *Calopteryx haemorrhoidalis*, however, often guard non-mates.[104]

The means by which females recognise males as conspecific are less well understood, and in any case difficult to infer, partly because their refusal postures, which are well known,[103] may be exhibited on account of a female's physiological unreadiness for copulation and not only when she recognises that an approaching male is not a conspecific. It is much easier to interpret the behaviour of a female in species in which male courtship normally precedes copulation. Among British Odonata, courtship has been confirmed only in the two species of *Calopteryx*. The courting male responds to the proximity of a female by raising his abdomen and spreading his wings. If the female is receptive she alights near him whereupon he performs an aerial dance, fluttering backwards and forwards and from side to side in front of her, his wings beating with a frequency characteristic of courtship.[105] If the female remains receptive (perched and immobile) the male lands on her wing tips (probably using the conspicuous *pseudopterostigma* as a target) and then climbs down the costal edge of her wings until he reaches her thorax, whereupon he fastens his superior abdominal appendages to her prothorax, securing her in the tandem position. If this stage is reached, the female nearly always accepts the male by curling her abdomen forwards and upwards so that its tip engages with his secondary genitalia, thus allowing copulation to proceed. It has been suggested that the male *Platycnemis pennipes* courts the female,[106] but, even though courtship has been recorded in a tropical platycnemidid,[107] it is by no means certain that the conspicuous display by the male of his flattened white tibiae serves this function in *P. pennipes*.[108] It may only function to advertise his presence to conspecific *males*.

PRECOPULATORY TANDEM

The precopulatory tandem position provides the pair with relative freedom from physical interference by conspecific males. Even though a rogue male may try to grasp the female, such an attempt will be seriously impeded by the presence on the female's head or prothorax of her partner's appendages. So takeovers of females in tandem are rare, although the persistence of the intruding male may lead to his grasping the head or prothorax of the tandem male, resulting in a temporary and unstable threesome. Such an outcome, which lends weight to the adage that 'two's company but three's a crowd', is relatively frequent in species of *Sympetrum* and Corduliidae. The intruding male sometimes belongs to another species, though hardly ever to another genus.[109]

Soon after tandem formation the male, by flexing his abdomen downwards and forwards, transfers sperm from his genital pore, situated on the ventral surface of abdominal segment 9, to his sperm vesicle, the sperm-storage reservoir in the secondary genitalia on the ventral surface of abdominal segments 2 and 3. This action, known as *intramale sperm translocation* (IST), almost always occurs *after* precopulatory tandem formation, although in about 5 per cent of such translocations witnessed in two species of North American *Enallagma* IST took place *before* tandem formation.[110] Occasionally copulation proper, entailing insemination, ensues without IST having been witnessed. In such cases the sperm vesicle may have been adequately charged before a previous copulation and so may not need replenishing. Generalisations about the time that IST occurs will always be elusive, partly because it may vary, partly because it may be extremely brief, and partly because it may have taken place out of the observer's sight. For example, it may occur in flight and take less than a second in *Orthetrum cancellatum*.[111]

COPULATION

Copulation begins when the genitalia of the sexes interlock and the '*wheel position*' is adopted (Figs 118 & 119). At this point a truly remarkable phenomenon occurs. Before inseminating his partner, the male uses his penis to displace any sperm in her sperm-storage organs. He may do this by hooking the sperm out of her body using recurved hooks or horns on the surface of his penis (Fig. 120) or by using his penis to push or flush the sperm into recesses in the female's body where it is unlikely to be used when she next lays eggs. Having displaced the sperm of rivals, the copulating male then inseminates his partner, transferring his own sperm from the sperm vesicle, along a duct within the penis, to the sperm receptacle within the female from which she will draw on it to fertilise the eggs she lays during the next 24 hours or so. After that time any sperm in her body will have become mixed, and the priority enjoyed by the most recent sperm will have been lost.[112] By displacing rivals' sperm the male

FIG 118. *Pyrrhosoma nymphula* copulating amongst heather (Robert Thompson).

will have given his own sperm priority over theirs provided that he ensures that his mate lays her complement of eggs promptly, and certainly within the next 24 hours. By achieving this, the male will improve his own fitness by winning the battle of sperm competition, ensuring that he will be the father of the forthcoming batch of eggs.

The discovery that a copulating male displaces rivals' sperm before inseminating his mate stands as one of the most significant in the history of

FIG 119. *Brachytron pratense* copulating on a stem of Meadowsweet (*Filipendula*) (Robert Thompson).

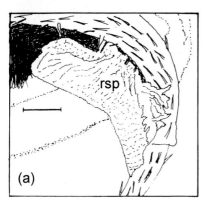

(a)

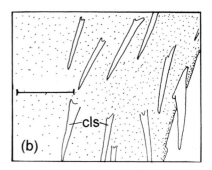

(b)

FIG 120. Drawings from scanning electron micrographs of tip of penis of the coenagrionid, *Ischnura ramburii.* (a) clump of rivals' sperm (rsp) caught on the comb-like spines; and (b) comb-like spines (cls) enlarged. Scale lines (a) 20 μm; (b) 5 μm. (After Waage.[113])

odonatology.[114] The discovery was made by Jonathan Waage during an elegant experiment using *Calopteryx maculata*, a close relative in North America of the British species of *Calopteryx*.[115] With his hypothesis of sperm displacement in mind, Waage combined rigorous field observation (observing the male's body movements during copulation) with microanatomical examination of penis structure and the female's sperm-storage organs, using scanning electron microscopy to reveal that:

1) before copulating, females often carry substantial amounts of sperm;
2) during copulation this sperm is progressively expelled or removed by the male before insemination; and
3) such sperm displacement is 88 to 100 per cent effective.

Waage detected clumps of sperm lodged among the backwardly pointing spines on the hornlike processes at the tip of the penis (Fig. 120). Since Waage's discovery, which was inspired by his acquaintance with work by Geoffrey Parker on sperm competition in the Dungfly, *Scathophaga stercoraria*,[116] sperm displacement has become a cutting-edge topic in odonatology, to which British researchers, such as the late Peter Miller[117] and his former doctoral student Mike Siva-Jothy,[118] have made distinguished contributions. Knowledge of sperm displacement has provided an essential and wonderfully informative context in which to interpret the reproductive behaviour of Odonata. It is evidently a prime target of natural selection. One aspect of Waage's discovery[115] has proved to be very useful for observers trying to interpret the sequence of events during copulation. Two stages can be recognised during copulation of *Calopteryx*, and also during the copulation of *Enallagma cyathigerum*[119] and *Ischnura elegans*.[120] During stage I, which is characterised by active rocking or undulatory movements of the male's abdomen, the male is removing or displacing rivals' sperm. During the much briefer stage II, the male's abdomen is immobile, as he inseminates his mate. The correspondence between the movement (or immobility) of the male's abdomen and his handling of sperm has proved to be invariable, and so the external movements serve to inform an observer of what is happening and thus obviate the need for postmortem examination. Such inference is unfortunately impracticable for those species that copulate in flight and very briefly (see below).

The duration of copulation varies widely among families. Although it also varies widely between species, certain broad patterns can be discerned. The minimum recorded duration of copulation in British Zygoptera is less than five minutes, except in the Platycnemididae. It is also less than five minutes in British Anisoptera, except in Aeshnidae and Cordulegastridae.[121] The Libellulidae, in particular, complete copulation very rapidly, some species being able to do so in less than ten seconds. In Britain and elsewhere species of *Libellula* and *Orthetrum* perform at this level. Several extrinsic factors can prolong copulation.[122] Among physical factors these include low light intensity, high wind and low temperature. Among biotic factors they include youth of the male, as in *Orthetrum cancellatum*,[123] earliness of copulation in a sequence of copulations, as in *Calopteryx splendens*,[124] disturbance by other males, as in *Ischnura pumilio*,[125] female virginity, as in *Calopteryx splendens*,[124] a low likelihood of encountering a female in a given site, as in *Orthetrum cancellatum*[118] and *Sympetrum danae*[126] and earliness in the day, as in *Enallagma cyathigerum*,[127] *Ischnura elegans*,[120] *Lestes sponsa*[128] and *Sympetrum danae*.[126] In *Sympetrum danae*, in which copulation may last for 20 minutes, 95 per cent of the eggs are fertilised by the last male.[129]

Ischnura elegans presents a remarkable exception to the general pattern described above. In a population studied by Peter Miller (in southern France) copulation (or at least the wheel position) lasted for an average of 324 minutes[120] – much longer than had been recorded for any other dragonfly. Miller hypothesised that protracted copulations might allow males to transfer more sperm or other substances to females, or they might enable males to displace more of the sperm of rivals (although in some other dragonflies most of the sperm of rivals can be displaced in relatively brief copulations). *Ischnura pumilio* also sometimes remains *in copula* for several hours, depending on the time of day.[130] Aside from the needs of sperm transfer, a determining factor may well be that longer copulations in *I. elegans* may allow males to guard females until these are prepared to oviposit in the afternoon after 16:00h.[120] Another possibility suggested by Miller is that protracted copulation in *I. elegans* enables the male to secure a female early in the day and so prevent takeovers by other males before the female is prepared to oviposit. According to this last hypothesis, protracted copulation is a form of guarding, enabling a male to be proactive in securing a mate and then to sequester her until she oviposits. This last hypothesis would be consistent with the knowledge that copulation in *I. elegans* is exceptional in being frequently interrupted by extended, inactive pauses which contribute significantly to its long duration.

Copulation duration in Odonata varies widely within and between species[121,122] though correlating positively with the paternity expectation of the male,[123] the extent of disturbance during copulation[124] and the previous mating experience of the female.[125] During stage 1 of copulation, the number of abdominal movements of the pair correlates positively with the stage's duration[126].

Copulation duration in *Orthetrum cancellatum* can be distinctly bimodal, exhibiting modes at about 15 minutes and 21 seconds. The bimodality correlates with different degrees of sperm removal, long copulations resulting in almost 100 per cent removal versus 10–15 per cent removal in short copulations. The difference in copulation duration relates to the site of copulation and to the age of the male. At oviposition sites males who secure copulations are relatively old and copulate only briefly, whereas at foraging sites males who secure copulations are relatively young and copulate for long periods.[127] A consequence of this difference is that males defending a territory, by copulating only briefly, increase their opportunities for mating with a greater number of females (at a favoured oviposition site) whereas males that encounter females away from favoured oviposition sites will mate with fewer females but achieve greater sperm displacement with each one.

During copulation the male can apparently displace rivals' sperm in four distinct ways:

1) by sperm removal (physical withdrawal of stored sperm)[128],
2) by sperm repositioning (packing of rivals' sperm to sites where its use will be least likely)[129],
3) by female sensory stimulation to induce sperm expulsion[130], and
4) by sperm flushing (displacement of sperm using the copulating male's sperm).[131]

A mated female stores sperm in the *bursa copulatrix* and the *spermathecae*, both of which receptacles are situated close to the vagina. When the male's penis pulls out sperm, it often does so only from the bursa because the penis cannot always reach the spermathecae, which accordingly may act as a sperm cache for sperm from previous matings. By using sperm from the spermathecae to fertilise her eggs, a female may be exercising post-copulatory choice among mates.[132] However, it seems that males of some *Calopteryx* species (such as *C. haemorrhoidalis*) are equal even to this ploy; during copulation the *aedeagus* of the penis of the male stimulates mechanoreceptive sensilla which elicit contractile activity around the spermathecae which then eject sperm, probably to the bursa where sperm can be removed by the spines on the head of the penis.[133] In *C. haemorrhoidalis* the width of the aedeagus is positively correlated with the amount of sperm ejected by the female spermathecae. Female *C. splendens* adopt a characteristic post-copulatory posture during which they wipe off the sperm mass that has been received during the penultimate copulation and then ejected. This removes sperm from between the valvulae of the ovipositor and thus prevents the dislodged sperm from obstructing oviposition.[133] The role of the spermathecae and associated glands in sperm storage, and subsequent fertilisation of the eggs, have been described for *Pyrrhosoma nymphula* by Arnold Åbro.[134]

The number of times a male mates in a day may be said to reflect his sex drive, which in turn appears to be hormonally driven. In *Calopteryx splendens* a male that has secured a copulation early in the day exhibits enhanced sexual activity thereafter during the same day.[135] Such behaviour, as in *Libellula depressa*,[136] seems also to be linked to the site where early copulations were obtained. A copulating female dragonfly is sometimes less than single-minded, feeding at the same time, for example, on another dragonfly[137] or a bumble bee (*Bombus*).[138]

The male of some Anisoptera signals to his copulation partner when the copulation should terminate – *Aeshna cyanea* and *A. mixta* by wing-clapping and touching and *Sympetrum striolatum* by wing-lifting.[139]

At very high densities of males, most copulations of *C. haemorrhoidalis* are forced, not being preceded by courtship. Some such coerced females may have already mated. They evidently trade copulation for protection from harassment that would impede oviposition, in a strategy that Adolfo Cordero has called 'convenience polyandry'.[140]

POST-COPULATORY BEHAVIOUR

As we have seen, the priority (for fertilisation) won by a copulating male through sperm displacement is time-limited because his sperm and that of previous rivals mixes completely within about 24 hours after copulation. So it is strongly in his interest that his mate should oviposit promptly after copulation and certainly within the next 24 hours. It is therefore not surprising that the male often remains with his copulation partner, 'guarding' her, at least until she begins to oviposit. He may do this by continuing to hold her in tandem (contact guarding), as in Chasers (*Libellula* spp.) and Darters (*Sympetrum* spp.) and many Zygoptera, or he may remain close to her, in a defensive mode, attacking any conspecific male who approaches her (non-contact guarding), as in *Libellula* and *Sympetrum*, and some species of *Calopteryx*.[141] A male's need to remain close to his copulation partner can be seen as critical for his conservation of energy because, in *Calopteryx* at least, he cannot reliably distinguish her from other females.[142] In two species of European lestid, *Lestes sponsa* and *L. virens*, the importance of the male partner's need to safeguard the paternity of the eggs about to be laid by his mate is evident from the fact that postcopulatory guarding is prolonged when there is intense interference by rival males.[143]

It follows that one way in which a female can sometimes choose the father of her offspring is to postpone oviposition after copulation. Although many libellulids begin to oviposit promptly after copulation, some remain perched for a while before oviposition begins. The duration of such post-copulatory rests (PCR) can vary between less than a minute and more than two hours. Among British species, *Orthetrum coerulescens* exhibits PCR, lasting between five seconds and about ten minutes.[144] At present the biological significance of this variation is not understood, although the Millers speculated that the duration of PCR may reflect a female's need to assess predator pressure at the oviposition site, to assess a male's guarding capacity, or to manipulate recently received sperm, either mobilising it for fertilisation or selecting it according to the 'quality' of their mates.[144] In this situation it is not surprising that a male *Orthetrum coerulescens*, having completed copulation, sometimes nudges or rams his perched mate, apparently inducing her to take off and commence oviposition.[144] Such behaviour is readily explained in terms of sperm competition, but leaves one surprised that it is not more widespread. However, not all species are *able* to oviposit promptly after copulation. Sperm originate in the *testes* as 'cloned' lumps, or *spermatodesms*,[145] each spermatodesm comprising several thousand sperm with their heads embedded in a mucoproteinaceous matrix.[146] The female can be inseminated with spermatodesms, as in Aeshnidae and Gomphidae, with free sperm, as in Zygoptera, Corduliinae and Libellulidae, or with both, as in Cordulegastridae.[147] Sperm are transferred during IST and later to the female in clusters in Zygoptera[148] or spermatodesms in *Aeshna cyanea*.[149]

At one time it was thought that about two days had to elapse after insemination before sperm within a spermatodesm could be released, and that this might explain why males of Aeshnidae, Cordulegastridae and Gomphidae do not usually guard their partners after copulation. However, such an explanation is thrown into doubt by recent studies of two species of aeshnid (*Anax junius* and *A. parthenope*) that inseminate with spermatodesms. Both are exceptional among aeshnids in that the male sometimes exhibits post-copulatory guarding.[150] The male enjoys exclusive paternity of the eggs next laid by the female he was most recently guarding.[146] This being so, any relationship that may exist between insemination by spermatodesm, guarding and *sperm precedence* remains to be elucidated.

MATING SYSTEMS

The principal target for selection, both sexual selection and natural selection, is the number of offspring that an individual dragonfly can endow with his or her genes, a measure embodied in the term lifetime reproductive success (LRS) (p.94). Sexual selection is the outcome of intrasexual competition, manifest as male–male competition for copulations (and sperm priority) and in female–female competition for partners and oviposition sites. Natural selection is either interspecific (manifest in competition with other species for space or other resources) or intraspecific (arising from individual differences in fitness). The main components of LRS are the total number and genetic quality of the eggs a female lays during her lifetime, and the total number and genetic quality of eggs that a male fathers during his lifetime. For the female, LRS depends on her longevity, the number of clutches she lays per day, the number of eggs per clutch and the genetic quality of her male partners. For the male, it depends on his longevity, the number of copulations per day, the number of eggs he fathered in each copulation and the genetic quality of his female partners. One might expect both sexes to discriminate among copulation partners. Until fairly recently it was assumed that only males exercised choice of this kind, by selecting females that complied with perceived criteria for fitness. However, in theory at least, there are several ways in which a female can choose the fitness of the father of eggs she lays. To identify these requires a change in mindset, away from the old-fashioned assumption that only males take the initiative when it comes to choosing a partner. Theoretically, the choices available to females are:

1) at what time of day to visit water;
2) whether or not to copulate, and therefore
3) which male to copulate with (and for how long);
4) how many eggs to lay promptly after copulating; and
5) which partner's sperm to use to fertilise her eggs after copulating.

To demonstrate convincingly that a female is pursuing any of these options presents formidable practical difficulties, but will nevertheless be well worth attempting. By enumerating the ways in which each sex can enhance its LRS, the investigator can visualise the different patterns according to which these are combined into strategies that form a *mating system*. The initiative for identifying odonate mating systems lies with Kelvin Conrad and Gordon Pritchard[151] who were inspired to do so by a seminal review, based on birds.[152] The system proposed by Conrad and Pritchard was subsequently modified to place greater emphasis on migration, male territoriality and guarding behaviour, the role of the primary rendezvous and the duration of copulation[153] – all variables that are functionally related. The resulting six mating systems distinguished are listed in Box 22, together with examples of their British exponents.

System 6 seems to represent the most highly evolved condition in the series that leads toward increased LRS for territorial males. Most copulations are obtained by very few males, and many males never mate. It shows the greatest

....

BOX 22

MATING SYSTEMS ENCOUNTERED IN ODONATA (FROM CORBET)[153]

1. **Long-range migration.** Females mate when teneral, the rendezvous being the emergence site, which males control. Some at least of the females then migrate, ovipositing elsewhere after long-range displacement. The LRS of females probably correlates closely with longevity.

British example: probably *Ischnura pumilio*.[154]

2. **Postponed oviposition.** The rendezvous is the oviposition site, where the female typically oviposits, almost always unguarded, on a subsequent visit to water. Males typically patrol and defend a substantial area, but exhibit only slight site attachment. The type of insemination (by free sperm or by spermatodesm) may reflect the habitat.

British examples: Aeshnidae, Cordulegastridae, Corduliidae and Gomphidae.

3. **Hinterland rendezvous.** The rendezvous is not the oviposition site, but is functionally linked to it because the male typically escorts the female to the oviposition site, usually in tandem, either soon after copulation or beforehand, in which case copulation is postponed until the pair reaches the oviposition site. The primary rendezvous is usually away from water, being either a site where receptive females are likely to interrupt their journey to the oviposition site or the nocturnal roost. Sites used for

basking, foraging and roosting all constitute a form of rendezvous frequented by both sexes for other than reproductive purposes. Most females arrive at water already in the wheel position or in tandem.

British examples: *Ischnura elegans*[12] and *Lestes sponsa*.[143]

4. **Nonterritorial; oviposition site rendezvous.** The primary rendezvous is typically the oviposition site. Contact guarding occurs during oviposition. The males are not territorial but control the females' access to the oviposition site. Oviposition is sometimes under water.

British examples: many non-territorial Zygoptera, including *Coenagrion puella* and *Enallagma cyathigerum*.

5. **Long copulation.** Territoriality is well developed. Males defend many, but not all, oviposition sites. Copulation typically lasts for more than 20 seconds. Post-copulatory guarding is without contact.

British examples: *Calopteryx splendens* and *C. virgo*.

6. **Short copulation.** Territoriality is well developed. Copulation typically lasts for less than 20 seconds. Sperm displacement is by 'packing', probably reflecting the very brief copulation.
British examples: species of *Libellula*, *Orthetrum* and *Sympetrum*.

male-to-male variation in LRS, depending on whether a male holds a territory or not, and on how much time he allocates between contact and non-contact guarding. In System 6 the male has greatest control over the female: she can postpone oviposition but eventually must return and oviposit in a territory which may well be still occupied by her most recent copulation partner. Despite the options available to the female for exercising partner choice, evolution of mating systems in dragonflies is seen as being primarily a male-driven process.[147]

OPPORTUNITIES FOR INVESTIGATION

The discovery that searching male Anisoptera are attracted to an electric fan (p.244) offers the prospect of analysing their responses to visual cues with simple and inexpensive equipment. Because of the great advance in our understanding of reproductive behaviour, especially since the discovery of sperm displacement, many questions now await attention. Some of these require elaborate equipment and techniques in the laboratory, but others can be tackled by skilled field observers without such aids. There is great scope for collaboration between field observers and researchers with access to laboratory facilities and specialised equipment, such as scanning electron microscopy and the means for obtaining DNA profiles. In the past, when such collaboration has been achieved, the outcome has been very informative.[155] Light can be thrown on our perception of mating systems by recording the day-to-day behaviour of marked individuals, especially in regard to their mating frequencies in different places (with respect to the primary rendezvous and the identity of their copulation partners). Such information can help to elucidate the extent of female choice in determining the parentage of offspring. The availability of techniques for marking individuals and of short-focus binoculars has transformed the practicability of constructing dossiers of the day-to-day behaviour of individuals. As always, success in such ventures depends largely on the discovery of a stem habitat that facilitates field observation.

Close observation of copulating pairs may reveal the nature of signals from one sex to the other to announce the intention to separate.[139] Here, access to a digital camera equipped with an automatic focus device (Appendix 2) could be especially valuable.

CHAPTER 10

Odonatology in Britain

DEVELOPMENTS UP TO 1960

Providing a taxonomic framework and establishing the British list

The earliest published attempts to distinguish different kinds of dragonfly (they were not called 'species' in those days) were contained in books, both published posthumously, by Thomas Mouffet (published in 1634)[1] and John Ray (published in 1710).[2] Both books were written more than 50 years before zoological nomenclature became standardised with the publication of *Systema Naturae: Regnum Animale* by Linnaeus in 1758. So the names given to dragonflies by Mouffet and Ray did not (indeed could not) conform with the binomial system introduced later by Linnaeus. Thomas Mouffet (1553–1604), a graduate of the Universities of Cambridge and Basle, practised medicine in London and later became a Member of Parliament for Wilton.[3] His book, *Insectorum sive Minimorum Animalium Theatricum (Insects or Very Small Animals)*,[1] was a mélange of truth, folklore and fancy. He recognised, and illustrated, three broad types of adult dragonflies, on the basis of size: *Maximae libellae* (presumably Anisoptera, Fig. 121), *Mediae libellae* (probably Calopterygidae), and *Minimae libellae* (probably Coenagrionidae). He illustrated larvae of Aeshnidae (on pp.321–322), calling them 'water lizards' and apparently not recognising them as larval dragonflies. He also mentioned vernacular names of dragonflies, including (on p.64) 'adders boultes (*sic*), dragonflies and water butterflies'. A large part of Mouffet's book is devoted (not unreasonably!) to spiders, a group of arthropods with which his name came to be popularly associated. This may explain the nature of the probably fictional encounter

66   *Infectorum five*

permagnum facientes. Septem illi nigræ lineæ tranſverſim in dorſo erant pro-
tractæ;muſcis exilioribus inter volandum veſcitur,hirundinum more. Secun-
da huic eſt ſimilis, ſed obſcuro magis colore.Tertia oculos margaritis ſimiles
obtinet, alas item argenteas, quarum extremam fimbriam macula fuſca in-
ficit; corpus luteo,nigroque colore varium,cauda bifurca nigra,duabus quaſi plumis ornata. Quarta luteo eſt colore, latera habens quaſi diviſa in ſex
partes:juxta alarum argentearum exortum macula lata nigra conſpicitur;me-
dio lineis luteis diſtincta:in caudæ extremitate quatuor vel quinque ſpinulæ
apparent. Quinta corpore & capite cæſio,ore nigro, alis argenteis unà macula notatis: in cauda ultima tres ſpinulæ tridentem referentes conſpiciuntur.
Sextæ alæ adnaſcuntur argenteæ, medio ipſarum nigrà maculà inſignitæ : to-
tum corpus nigrum, ſed rarius, item in dorſo atque ventre luteſcens :
Pectus ſcapulæque ex nigro flavóque æquè mixtæ. Subter caudam
duas ſpinulas recuruas trahit; in fine ejus quinque apparent, ſed admo-
dum exiguæ. Septimæ caput,collum & ſcapulæ,fuſco ſunt colore; reliquum
corpus rubet:in muſæo Pennij procreata fuit, ex vermiculo planè illi mihique
ignoto. Octava adhuc brevior,oculis margaritis ſimilibus, toto corpore luteo,niſi ubi lineis tranſverſim ductis notatur. Cauda illi quaſi abſciſſa, in fine
latiuſcula & obtuſa:argentearum alarum ſummitas nigra macula infuſcatur;
inter ſegetes plerumque reperiuntur. *Libellæ mediæ* maximam naturæ ele-
gantiam omni arte majorem commendant.Prima colore eſt elegantiſſimo.

Maximæ Libellæ.

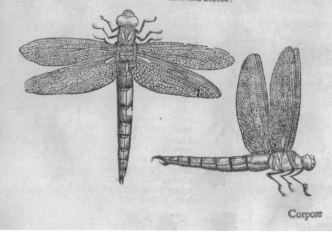

Corpore

FIG 121. On this page of his posthumously published book on 'insects and lesser living
creatures' (1634) Thomas Mouffet illustrated what he termed '*Maximae libellae*', or large
dragonflies.

(between a young girl bearing the name 'Muffet' and an arachnid) given lasting notoriety in a well-known nursery rhyme.

John Ray (1627–1705) was the son of a blacksmith, living in Black Notley in Essex, and best known for his systematic work on plants, fishes and birds. A man possessed of great personal charm and a brilliant mind, he was a Fellow of Trinity College, Cambridge, where he taught Greek, mathematics and humanities, before concentrating on natural history. His output of books on botany, zoology, semantics and philosophy was prodigious and he was elected to a Fellowship of the Royal Society of London.[4] He was a pioneer, setting standards in biology by cataloguing the native flora and fauna through original observation, identification, accurate description and classification. Linnaeus, among others, built on Ray's 'natural system'. Among fellow biologists he was regarded as 'the bright wonder of the age to come'.[3] During his closing, pain-ridden years, Ray concentrated his efforts on describing insects (fortunately for future entomologists), resulting in the remarkable book *Historia Insectorum*,[2] published in 1710 under the aegis of the Royal Society, unfortunately without illustrations. Ray clearly recognised the concept of hierarchies of affinity. He used the word 'Libellula' to serve the function of what would later be termed a genus but, instead of using a single word to designate a species (as in the Linnaean system), Ray used several words which, together, served the additional function of listing diagnostic characters, i.e. constituting what would now be called a species description. He described (on pp.49–53) 23 kinds of dragonflies, distinguishing several categories that broadly correspond to the Linnaean concept of a genus. The page illustrated in Fig. 122 comes from a copy of *Historia Insectorum* formerly owned by the nineteenth-century English entomologist, J.C. Dale (see p.264). Species No. 2 in Ray's list, described by him as '*Libella maxima, abdomine longo tenuiore, alis fulvescentibus*', is almost certainly *Aeshna grandis*. The text of this remarkable book well illustrates the advanced thinking of one of the great pioneers of the systematic approach to natural history.

Naming of the British species according to the Linnaean system began with the publication of *Systema Naturae* in 1758[5] (Fig. 123). There Linnaeus described 18 species of Odonata (which he called Neuroptera), placing them all in the genus *Libellula*. In *Systema Naturae* Linnaeus gave British odonatology a wonderful kick-start by describing ten British species, or about 20 per cent of our present dragonfly fauna. The cumulative graph forming Fig. 124 shows the rate at which the remaining British species were described, from Linnaeus's publication up to the end of the nineteenth century. After 1758, when Linnaeus's names were published, descriptions appeared slowly and steadily, except for intermittent surges of activity, especially in 1764, 1825 and 1840. By 1842 all British species had

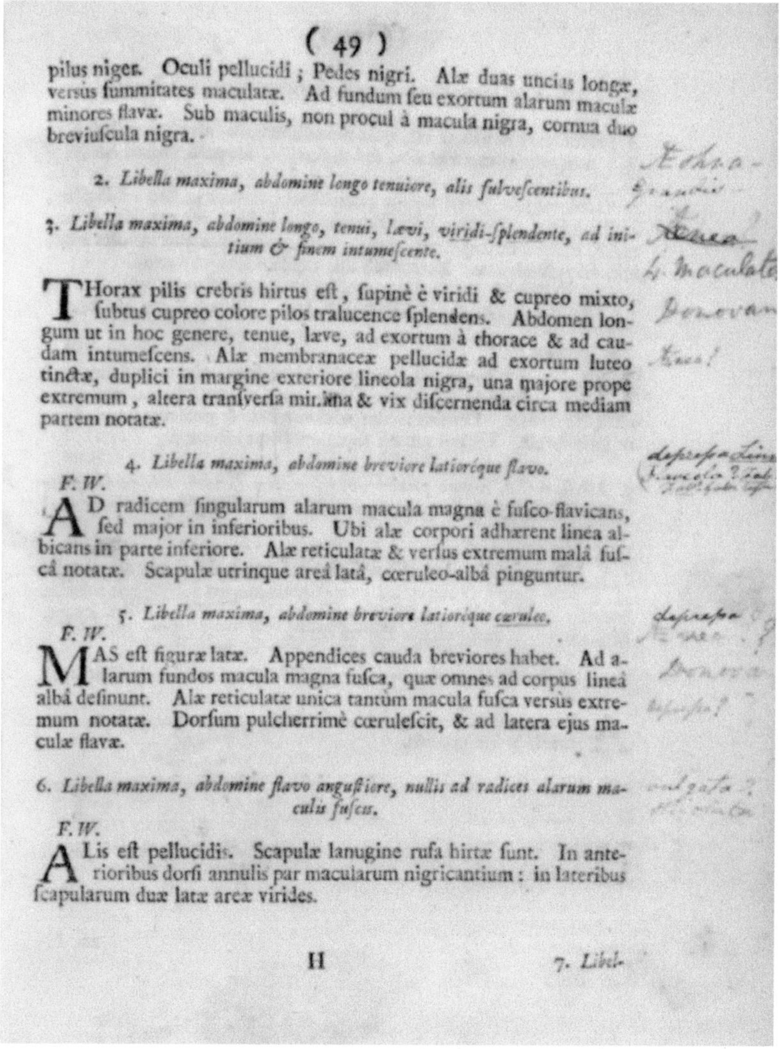

(49)

pilus niger. Oculi pellucidi ; Pedes nigri. Alæ duas uncias longæ, versùs summitates maculatæ. Ad fundum seu exortum alarum maculæ minores flavæ. Sub maculis, non procul à macula nigra, cornua duo breviuscula nigra.

2. *Libella maxima, abdomine longo tenuiore, alis fulvescentibus.*

3. *Libella maxima, abdomine longo, tenui, lævi, viridi-splendente, ad initium & finem intumescente.*

THorax pilis crebris hirtus est, supinè è viridi & cupreo mixto, subtus cupreo colore pilos tralucence splendens. Abdomen longum ut in hoc genere, tenue, læve, ad exortum à thorace & ad caudam intumescens. Alæ membranaceæ pellucidæ ad exortum luteo tinctæ, duplici in margine exteriore lineola nigra, una majore prope extremum, altera transversa minima & vix discernenda circa mediam partem notatæ.

4. *Libella maxima, abdomine breviore latioréque flavo.*
F. IV.

AD radicem singularum alarum macula magna è fusco-flavicans, sed major in inferioribus. Ubi alæ corpori adhærent linea albicans in parte inferiore. Alæ reticulatæ & versus extremum malâ fuscâ notatæ. Scapulæ utrinque areâ latâ, cœruleo-albâ pinguntur.

5. *Libella maxima, abdomine breviore latioréque cærulec.*
F. IV.

MAS est figuræ latæ. Appendices cauda breviores habet. Ad alarum fundos macula magna fusca, quæ omnes ad corpus lineâ albâ definunt. Alæ reticulatæ unica tantùm macula fusca versus extremum notatæ. Dorsum pulcherrimè cœrulescit, & ad latera ejus maculæ flavæ.

6. *Libella maxima, abdomine flavo angustiore, nullis ad radices alarum maculis fuscis.*
F. IV.

ALis est pellucidis. Scapulæ lanugine rufa hirtæ sunt. In anterioribus dorsi annulis par macularum nigricantium : in lateribus scapularum duæ latæ areæ virides.

H

7. *Libel-*

FIG 122. On this page of his posthumously published book *Historia Insectorum* (1710) John Ray provided the first systematic descriptions of Odonata. Here he describes several large Anisoptera, placing each in the 'genus' *Libella maxima*. The marginal annotations, probably by J.C. Dale, an odonatologist and former owner of this copy of the book, apparently represent Dale's attempt to equate Ray's descriptions with their later, Linnaean equivalents. The annotator surmised that this page contained descriptions of *Aeshna grandis* (2), *Libellula quadrimaculata* (3) and the female and male of *Libellula depressa* (4 and 5).

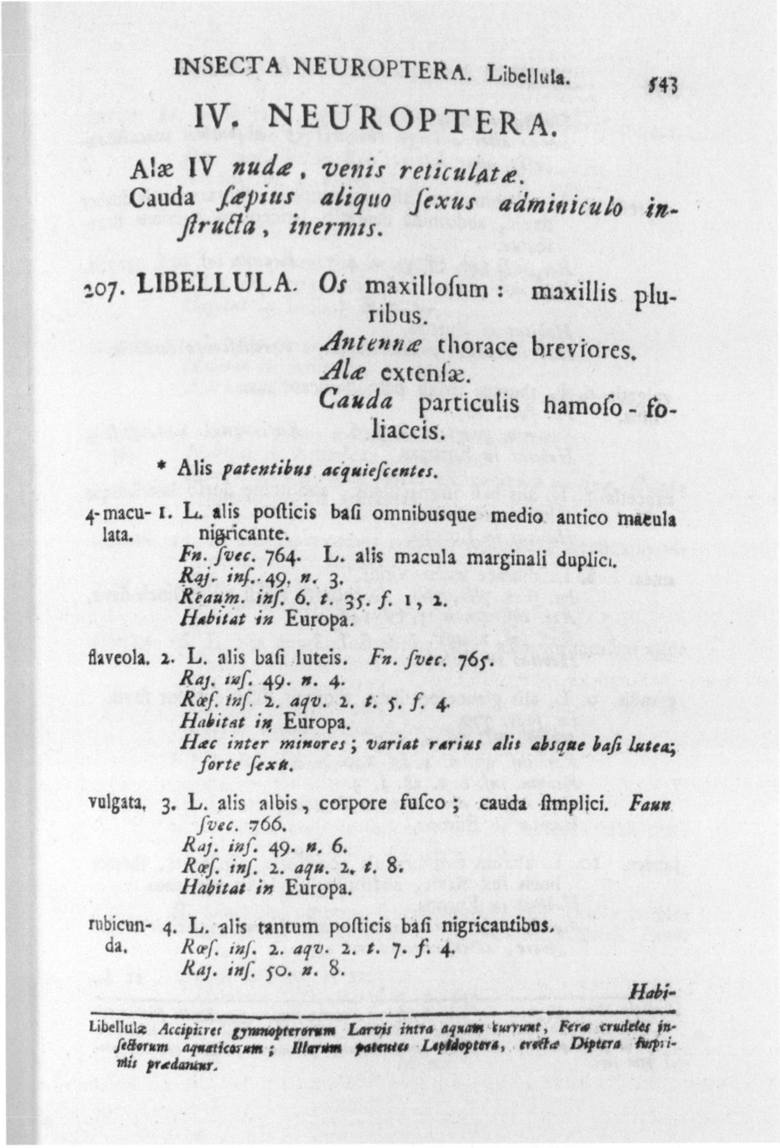

INSECTA NEUROPTERA. Libellula.   543

IV. NEUROPTERA.

Alæ IV *nudæ, venis reticulatæ.*
Cauda *fæpius aliquo fexus adminiculo in-*
ftructa, inermis.

207. LIBELLULA. *Os* maxillofum : maxillis plu-
            ribus.
        Antennæ thorace breviores.
        Alæ extenfæ.
        Cauda particulis hamofo - fo-
            liaceis.

* Alis *patentibus acquiefcentes.*

4-macu- 1. L. alis pofticis bafi omnibusque medio antico macula
lata.   nigricante.
        Fn. fvec. 764. L. alis macula marginali duplici.
        Raj. inf. 49. *n.* 3.
        Reaum. inf. 6. *t.* 35. *f.* 1, 2.
        Habitat in Europa.

flaveola. 2. L. alis bafi luteis. *Fn. fvec.* 765.
        Raj. inf. 49. *n.* 4.
        Ræf. inf. 2. *aqv.* 2. *t.* 5. *f.* 4.
        Habitat in Europa.
        Hæc inter minores ; variat rarius alis absque bafi lutea;
        forte fexu.

vulgata, 3. L. alis albis, corpore fufco ; cauda fimplici. *Faun.*
        fvec. 766.
        Raj. inf. 49. *n.* 6.
        Ræf. inf. 2. *aqu.* 2. *t.* 8.
        Habitat in Europa.

rubicun- 4. L. alis tantum pofticis bafi nigricantibus.
da.   *Ræf. inf.* 2. *aqv.* 2. *t.* 7. *f.* 4.
        Raj. inf. 50. *n.* 8.

                                Habi-

Libellulæ *Accipiter gymnopterorum Larvis intra aquam turvunt, Feræ crudeles in-*
fectorum aquaticorum ; Illarum patentes Lepidoptera, erectæ Diptera furpri-
mis prædantur.

FIG 123. The first page of descriptions of Odonata from Linnaeus's *Systema Naturae* (1758). Each species name is followed by Linnaeus's diagnostic description and references to mention of the species in previous publications. Species listed on this page are now placed in three genera, but Linnaeus placed all dragonflies in the genus *Libellula*.

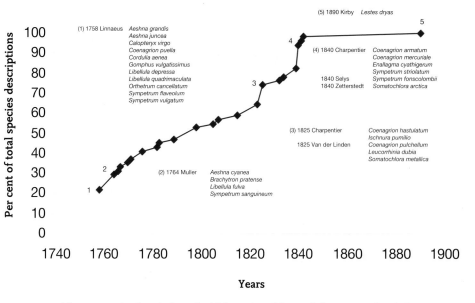

FIG 124. The progressive description of British species of dragonfly between 1758 and 1890, when William Kirby's description of *Lestes dryas* was published. Times of surges of descriptive activity before 1890 are annotated.

been named except one, *Lestes dryas*, which was described by the distinguished British entomologist William Kirby (1759–1850), like Ray a Cambridge graduate and a Fellow of the Royal Society of London, and regarded by some as 'the father of entomology'.[3]

The first species of dragonfly to be described by a British author was *Calopteryx splendens*, elegantly depicted in colour (Fig. 125) by Moses Harris (1730–88) (Fig. 126(a)), a Londoner and accomplished miniaturist painter and one of the leading entomologists of his time. He illustrated 16 species of dragonfly,[6] including *C. splendens*. Harris was followed by Edward Donovan (1768–1837), a wealthy Londoner who assembled a large collection of natural history objects and who published the first descriptions of *Cordulegaster boltonii* and *Sympetrum danae* (known then as *S. scoticum*).[7] Donovan published several books but died in poverty, a victim of the 'avaricious pre-Victorian literary trade'.[8]

The first formal classification of the British species was published by William Elford Leach (1790–1836), an entomologist working at the British Museum. Leach[9] described *Anax imperator* (see Box 1, p.5) and erected the genera *Anax*, *Calopteryx*, *Cordulegaster*, *Cordulia*, *Gomphus* and *Lestes*. Also working at this time

FIG 125. This plate in Moses Harris's *Exposition of English Insects* (1782) presents the first illustrations of adults of *Calopteryx splendens*, the species first described by this author and illustrator. He has also illustrated a *Calopteryx* larva.

was the printer and engraver John Curtis (1791–1862) (Fig. 126(b)) who published the 16-volume *British Entomology*.[10] Three dragonfly species were illustrated, including a new species, *Oxygastra curtisii*, which was first discovered in 1820 by

FIG 126. (a–d) (a) Moses Harris (1730–88). (b) John Curtis (1791–1862). (c) James Stephens (1792–1852). (d) Edward Newman (1801–76) (The Natural History Museum).

James Charles Dale (1792–1872) in Dorset. J.C. Dale, a country squire and High Sheriff of Dorset, well known for his broad interests in entomology and his meticulous records,[11] was a close associate of Curtis and provided him with many odonate specimens to illustrate. Dale also added *Aeshna isosceles* to the British fauna when he discovered it at Whittlesey Mere, Cambridgeshire, in 1818, before the site was drained in 1850.[12] Dale's collection also contained the first British specimen of *Leucorrhinia dubia*,[13] presented to him by William Beckitt who collected it at Thorne Moors, Yorkshire, in 1837. The species no longer occurs there following industrial-scale peat mining of the site in the last few decades.

The British list was increased to 48 species by James Stephens (1792–1852) (Fig. 126(c)), who worked with Leach at the British Museum after being seconded from the Admiralty. His list included the first record of *Lestes dryas* (as *L. nympha*) from the Thames Marshes but also 16 synonyms and vagrant species that cannot be considered as part of the British fauna.[14] Another important contribution to odonate *taxonomy* was made by Edward Newman (1801–76) (Fig. 126(d)), a Deptford ropemaker who later became a printer and published and edited *The Entomologist*. He was renowned for his 'strong constitution ... due to his regular and methodical habits'.[15] Newman recognised the genera *Sympetrum* and *Orthetrum* as being distinct from *Libellula*.[16]

Probably the most influential figure on the nineteenth-century dragonfly scene was the Paris-born Belgian, Baron Edmund de Sélys-Longchamps (1813–1900), who laid the foundations for modern odonate taxonomy. He authored many important publications containing descriptions and identification keys to the world Odonata which are still widely consulted today. During 1845 he toured Britain, examining all the important odonate collections in museums and in private hands and added *Coenagrion mercuriale, Somatochlora arctica* and *Sympetrum fonscolombii* to the British list.[17] A contemporary of de Sélys was the Scot, Robert McLachlan (1837–1904) (Fig. 127(a)), who made a large and important collection of the world Neuroptera, Trichoptera, Odonata, Ephemeroptera and Plecoptera which now forms the basis of the collections of these orders in the Natural History Museum, London. He established that *Aeshna caerulea, Somatochlora metallica* and *Coenagrion hastulatum* were resident in Britain[18] and his annotated list of British species included 40 that are still recognised as British.[19] Another Scottish entomologist having an interest in Odonata was Kenneth Morton (1858–1940) (Fig. 127(b)), a banker by profession. He discovered the first breeding colony in this country of *Lestes dryas* in 1893 and later of *Sympetrum fonscolombii* in 1922.[20]

Two nineteenth-century books were devoted to British Odonata. The first, by W.F. Evans, included colour paintings by the author of the males and females of 52 species.[21] The names of many of these will be unfamiliar to modern odonatologists because they have subsequently been recognised as synonyms. A few species are misidentified: for example, the Scottish species *Agrion* (= *Coenagrion*) *hastulatum* is said to be found near London and in Kent but the illustration appears to show a species of *Lestes*. It is clear that Evans knew little about the distribution of the species beyond southeast England and a few

(a)

(b)

(c)

(d)

FIG 127. (a–d) (a) Robert McLachlan (1837–1904). (b) Kenneth Morton (1858–1940). (c) Cynthia Longfield (1896–1991). (d) Cyril Hammond (1904–80) (The Natural History Museum).

well-known collecting localities such as the New Forest. The second book was published 45 years later by W. Harcourt Bath. Forty-five species are described and much of the synonymy has been clarified, although there is considerable emphasis on descriptions of varieties.[22] The distribution records are still patchy but do give a broader perspective. In contrast to the earlier book by Evans, few species are illustrated and those are in black and white, but the author does supply information on dragonfly biology as well as tips on collecting and rearing dragonflies.

The study of British Odonata took a great stride forward with the publication of a book by the schoolmaster William Lucas (1858–1932). As well as descriptions and handsome colour illustrations of the adults, he described and illustrated the eggs and larvae of some species that he had reared.[23] This book helped to popularise dragonflies and was still being widely referred to for many decades after its publication.[24] A subsequent volume by Lucas, describing the larvae of 32 British species, was later published by the Ray Society.[25] Professor Frank Balfour-Browne (1874–1967), famous for his work on water beetles, added *Coenagrion armatum* to the British list[26] after he discovered it at Stalham, northeast Norfolk, and he also described the egg and early larval stadia of *C. pulchellum* and *I. elegans*.[27]

Consolidation

From the 1930s the dragonfly collections at the British Museum (Natural History) were curated and developed by Cynthia Longfield (1896–1991) (Fig. 127(c)) and Douglas Kimmins (1905–85). Whereas both made significant contributions to world dragonfly taxonomy, it was Longfield who was the more influential of the two on the British scene, and from 1927 to 1957 she was at the centre of a network of British dragonfly workers. Longfield's treatment of the British Odonata, the first in a recognisably modern field-guide format (Warne's Wayside and Woodland series),[28] was highly influential in nurturing the next generation of British dragonfly enthusiasts. In the introduction to the second edition, Longfield described dragonflies as a 'neglected group of insects'.[29] Odonata never had the same appeal for most of the Victorian and Edwardian insect collectors as did butterflies, moths or beetles, probably because the body pigments of dragonflies fade after the animal has died. The specimens soon cease to look attractive in an insect cabinet. Longfield's work made a major contribution to the popularisation of dragonflies and provided a new stimulus to those wishing to study them seriously. Forty-four species were covered in her field guide, including a new addition to the British list, *Coenagrion scitulum*, which she herself had discovered in Essex.[30] Her book featured identification keys to adults accompanied by detailed line drawings of critical morphological features of adult damselflies and the caudal lamellae of damselfly larvae. The adult of each species was illustrated with a black-and-white photograph and a colour illustration from Evans's book.[21] Lucas's illustrations of the larvae of 32 species were also included.[25] As well as morphological descriptions of the adult and larva of each species, information on the distribution, flying season and habits was provided. Norman Moore described how, as a young man, this book inspired him to record the distribution of British Odonata and the excitement he felt when he was able to add a new vice-county record.[31] Philip Corbet was similarly inspired, both by Cynthia's book and by her enthusiasm and encouragement. Her book featured for the first time an attempt to introduce popular names for each species (based on a hybrid of the scientific generic name and an English descriptor). This was a decisive step forward in giving the group wider appeal. A full account of the life of Cynthia Longfield and her contribution to British odonatology has been given by her niece Jane Hayter-Hames.[32] Additional information is provided by Robert Gambles[33] and Philip Corbet.[34]

The British larvae were not comprehensively dealt with until the publication of Eric Gardner's outstanding work.[35] Gardner (1913–76), a Venetian-blind salesman whose work allowed him to travel widely in Britain and to sample promising dragonfly localities in the process,[36] reared almost all the British species from egg to adult. Because he kept each larva in a separate container he was able to record the characters of each stadium with confidence and also be sure of the total number and duration of stadia. His work still forms the cornerstone of British larval taxonomy. Another British dragonfly worker, who also contributed importantly to the taxonomy and systematics of world Odonata, was the energetic and forthright Lt-Colonel F.C. Fraser (1880–1963). He spent most of his career in the Indian Medical Service where he wrote numerous scientific papers and a three-volume identification manual, which remains the standard reference on the Indian Odonata.[37] On retirement he returned to England and published an identification handbook to British Odonata in the series produced by the Royal Entomological Society.[38]

The first chapter in the study of British dragonflies was drawing to a close. It had provided a taxonomic framework and established which species were resident in this country. The focus was now to change. Conservation concerns were being expressed as realisation grew of the damage inflicted on the British countryside by the postwar drive to improve the efficiency of farming. But conservation objectives could not be formulated effectively without information about the distribution, status, ecology and behaviour of the British species.

DEVELOPMENTS BETWEEN 1960 AND 1983

Volume 41 of Collins' New Naturalist series provided the first in-depth account of the biology of British Odonata and included for the first time maps showing the distribution, on a vice-county basis, of Odonata in Britain.[39] As an author of this book, Cynthia Longfield was joined by two younger dragonfly specialists: Norman Moore, who had completed his PhD thesis on adult behaviour, in particular male territorial behaviour, and Philip Corbet, who had studied the seasonal ecology of dragonflies, especially *Anax imperator*, also in the course of his PhD research. This volume in the New Naturalist series proved to be a seminal work. It inspired many people to take an interest in dragonflies by demonstrating how odonatology could be developed further than just collecting specimens for the cabinet, by asking questions about the distribution, behaviour and ecology of the British dragonfly fauna. This book was soon followed by Philip Corbet's *A Biology of Dragonflies* which dealt with the world fauna and placed the ecological and biological traits of the British species in a global context.[40] These two books synthesised, in a readable and popular format, what was then known about Odonata, much of it unpublished or in the specialist scientific literature and so unavailable to most British naturalists. Together these books provided an enormous stimulus to the study of dragonflies, both in Britain and across the world, and created many new dragonfly enthusiasts.

Systematic and organised study concerning the distribution of British dragonflies started to take shape after the establishment in 1964 of the Biological Records Centre (BRC) at Monks Wood in Cambridgeshire, and a project to record the distribution of Odonata pioneered in 1968 by John Heath, who was the BRC invertebrate specialist. By 1974, enough records had been received for the publication of the first dot maps showing the distribution of Odonata in Britain.[41] Each dot on the map represented one or more records within a 10-km square. Nevertheless, the study of dragonflies was still a minority interest nationally, and few regular recorders supported the scheme. In 1977 David Chelmick took over as organiser of the Odonata Mapping Scheme and produced a newsletter for contributors. For the first time there was a British forum for people with a mutual interest in dragonflies.

By the mid-1970s Longfield's guide[29] and the New Naturalist book[39] were long out of print and difficult to find in second-hand book shops; so there was little to stimulate or encourage the amateur enthusiast. This changed when a new identification guide appeared,[42] written by Cyril Hammond (1904–80) (Fig. 127(d)), a school teacher and leading amateur entomologist, formerly better known for his interest in Diptera.[43] The publication of his book was to prove a turning point in the recent history of odonatology in Britain. It provided, for the first time, attractive, full-colour, large-format illustrations of adults of all the British species, including males and females and the most common colour forms, together with brief ecological notes and the latest dot distribution maps. Gardner's key to larvae was also reproduced.[35] In addition, Hammond introduced fully anglicised names based on those first introduced by Longfield.[28] For many odonatologists, these names have stood the test of time and are widely used today, even though some present difficulties.

Although Hammond's book had shortcomings,[44] it did fulfil its author's hopes, expressed in the preface, to 'stimulate interest and study, especially among young students' and it undoubtedly increased the number of dragonfly enthusiasts in Britain. Hammond died in 1980 but such was the success of his book that in 1983 a second edition was published[45], having been extensively revised by Bob Merritt, who was by then organiser of the Odonata Recording Scheme (ORS). In the preface to the second edition Merritt confirmed that the publication of the first edition had given 'an enormous boost to the Odonata Recording Scheme'.[45] Indeed there had been an exponential rise in the number of records received by the ORS. For example, the annual number of records of the ubiquitous *Ischnura elegans* had risen from fewer than 50 per year before 1970 to 1,400 by 1983.[46] Consequently, the distribution maps for each species that appeared in the revised edition were all updated to include thousands of new records that had been received from the new cadre of dragonfly recorders. The revised maps now revealed something like the actual distribution of the British species rather than the distribution of dragonfly recorders.

This increase in recorder effort resulted in the discovery in 1981 of *Coenagrion lunulatum* in Co. Sligo, Ireland,[47] a species new to Britain, and the rediscovery of *Lestes dryas* in 1983 at two sites in Essex.[48] It had been feared that *L. dryas* had become extinct because it had not been seen since 1971. Within a few years *L. dryas* had been rediscovered at several other sites in the Thames Marshes and East Anglia. Probably the species had been overlooked because it was thought unlikely to have recolonised such a large area in so short a time. Recorders may have stopped close examination of *Lestes* specimens, assuming that all must be *L. sponsa*, because *L. dryas* was thought to be extinct. Once word was out that *L. dryas* was not after all extinct, recorders became more vigilant. The value of a large network of odonate enthusiasts had been amply demonstrated.

The significant increase in contributors to the ORS led to calls for the inception of a society for British odonatologists. It was felt that such a society would provide a forum for exchange of information, help co-ordinate the recording effort, focus ecological studies, improve and initiate conservation activities, and popularise dragonflies to the wider public. In 1983 the British Dragonfly Society (BDS) was launched[49] and so a new chapter in the study of British dragonflies began. The years ahead would see a consolidation of the recording effort, a focus on establishing which key sites held important breeding populations of the less common species, promotion of dragonfly conservation by provision of expert opinion to larger conservation organisations, and a rise in the profile of dragonflies in conservation and natural history circles.

DEVELOPMENTS FROM 1983

Formation and membership of the BDS

Formal organisation of the ORS, under first David Chelmick and then Bob Merritt, kept contributors in touch through the production of an annual newsletter. The ORS provided the kernel for the eventual establishment of the BDS. In 1978 a meeting of contributors to the ORS at the London headquarters of the Nature Conservancy Council (NCC) attracted 72 people. As the numbers of contributors to the ORS increased, discussion focused on the desirability of forming a society for people with an interest in dragonflies. Many expected that this would stimulate further study, recording and conservation of Odonata in Britain. However, fears were also expressed that it might also increase collection of rare species from vulnerable sites and impose intolerable administrative burdens on the officers of the new society. Nevertheless, in 1983 the BDS was formally established, Philip Corbet serving as the first President and Roderick Dunn as Secretary. Within two months of its inception nearly 220 people had joined.[49] As the society became established, membership continued to rise and by 1989 it had passed 500. On the tenth anniversary of the BDS there were over 1,100 members[50] and by 2004 over 1,600 had joined.[51] Since its inception the BDS has continued to grow and develop under the guidance of Presidents Andy McGeeney, Tim Beynon and Peter Mill, and Jill Silsby, Bill Wain and Henry Curry who have served as Secretaries. The present membership of the BDS has a broad base and includes many people who would describe themselves as 'non-expert' but with a general interest in dragonfly natural history.

The initial reluctance to establish a formal dragonfly society, centring on fears that it might encourage immoderate collecting of specimens, proved to be groundless.[49] Collection of specimens is a minority interest today. Odonatologists of earlier generations often took (and often needed for taxonomic purposes) long series of specimens, even of rare species, sometimes from many different localities, but this is no longer the practice today. Most dragonfly enthusiasts are content with photographic records of their dragonfly encounters. When it is necessary to take voucher specimens for scientific reasons only a few specimens are collected and this is very unlikely to damage the viability of populations (Appendix 2). The formation of the BDS has resulted in a huge increase in the number of dragonfly watchers in the field. Longfield acknowledged the contributions of distribution records from 112 people.[29] By 1990 over 2,000 people had contributed records to the recording scheme.[46] In 2002 the Dragonfly Recording Network held almost 100,000 records.[52] Practical measures to conserve dragonflies, knowledge about their ecology and habitat requirements, and general awareness of dragonflies have increased significantly in the last 20 years and it is difficult to see how this would have happened without the formation of a dedicated society.

Dragonfly Conservation Group

The primary objective of the BDS, as stated in its constitution, is 'to promote and encourage the study and conservation of Odonata'. The BDS has been active in promoting the conservation of British Odonata since the formation of the Society by supporting the activities of individual members and through initiatives promoted by the Society. The Dragonfly Conservation Group (DCG) was established in 1986 as a standing committee within the BDS to co-ordinate its conservation activities. The first convenor was Norman Moore, who was succeeded by Ian Johnson in 2000 and then Pam Taylor in 2001.

An early decision taken by the Trustees of the BDS was that there would not be active recruitment of members. Rather, membership would be allowed to grow gradually, as a natural outcome of the society's activities. Initially, the BDS did not have ambitions to employ staff or own nature reserves. For this reason the policy of the DCG was to influence the activities of larger conservation organisations, which owned land and had full-time staff, so that they were more likely to manage their reserves in a way that was beneficial to dragonfly conservation. This policy soon bore fruit when bodies such as the Royal Society for the Protection of Birds (RSPB) actively sought advice from the DCG when formulating management plans for their reserves.

BDS members were encouraged to work at a local level with other conservation organisations and to take opportunities to promote awareness of dragonflies through local media. The DCG would also make use of its contacts at senior management levels in organisations such as the RSPB, the Wildlife Trusts, the Farming and Wildlife Advisory Group (FWAG), the statutory nature conservation organisations (English Nature (EN); since 2006 Natural England (NE),

Scottish Natural Heritage, Countryside Council for Wales (ccw) and Joint Nature Conservation Committee (jncc) and, prior to its dismemberment, the Nature Conservancy Council), the National Trust, the Environment Agency (ea) and government departments, to influence conservation policy in favour of dragonflies. Awareness of dragonflies has also been promoted through the national media and through the publication of dragonfly identification charts. Two booklets have been published giving advice on pond design to attract dragonflies to breed in gardens, schools and nature reserves and on farms.[53] The bds has been actively involved in the Peat Campaign, together with several other conservation non-governmental organisations (NGOs), persuading gardeners to use peat-free composts and promoting awareness of the importance of peat bogs as a habitat for a unique mix of animals and plants. The bds has also been active in the Ponds in Partnership project, co-ordinated by the Ponds Conservation Trust. The intention is that production of a pond survey form, including a dragonfly recording sheet, will result in wider interest in ponds and dragonflies, and generate records for the national pond monitoring network.[54]

BRITISH DRAGONFLY SOCIETY INITIATIVES

During the course of its 25-year history, the bds has instigated many initiatives to promote the study of dragonflies, the most significant of which are reviewed below.

Periodicals

The membership of the bds is kept informed of Society business, field trips and meetings through the twice-annual *Dragonfly News*. The bds also produces, in two parts each year, the *Journal of the British Dragonfly Society*. This publication includes short papers and notes of a scientific nature on British dragonflies. The *Journal* has maintained a high standard, encouraging members to write up their observations on dragonflies and providing a stimulus for research. Many useful observations would probably have gone unrecorded were it not for the *Journal*.

Local groups

In order to build an active membership and encourage local conservation initiatives, the bds encouraged activists to form local bds branches by contacting members in their areas. The first local groups were formed in 1986, and by 1993, 26 groups had been formed. Activity peaked in 1997 when 34 local group contacts were listed in the bds Newsletter. Most groups held a few discussion meetings each year, organised field trips and mounted identification workshops. Some produced a newsletter and others were involved in conservation projects. For example, the North of London group investigated the ecology of *Cordulia aenea* in Epping Forest and Burnham Beeches in order to make management recommendations to the Corporation of London who owned these sites. In addition, over several years they monitored the dragonfly populations of Cornmill Meadows, in the Lea Valley on the fringes of north London, to assess the impact of habitat management at the site. This work helped towards the formal recognition by the Lea Valley Park Authority of the site as a 'Dragonfly Sanctuary'. Local groups now have less emphasis than formerly in BDS activities at the moment and only five were listed in the spring 2004 newsletter. This does not necessarily reflect a lack of local activity. For example, in Lancashire, Lincolnshire and Hertfordshire, dragonfly interest groups are co-ordinated through local natural history organisations.

Dragonfly recording

Following the inception of the BDS, the ORS remained independent of, but closely associated with, the BDS. Bob Merritt, the ORS organiser, served on the BDS Board of Trustees. The numbers of active recorders and records received remained high, boosted by new contributors who had been introduced through membership of the BDS. Although the ORS provided the BDS with much of its initial membership, many BDS members do not contribute to the ORS. In 1992 Brian Eversham noted that 60 per cent of people contributing records to the ORS were not members of the BDS, and that 70 per cent of BDS members were not on the ORS mailing list.[55] However, by 1987 the ORS had begun to run out of steam as the number of submitted records fell significantly. The scheme was reorganised to have central co-ordination from the Biological Records Centre (BRC) at Monks Wood, and a network was established of regional recorders who co-ordinated record collection and data validation within their own regions. The culmination of this effort was the publication of a definitive atlas that plotted over 160,000 records received up to 1990 from over 2,000 individual recorders.[46] The records covered about 87 per cent of all the 10-km squares in the British Isles and so the maps provided a realistic picture of the distribution of the British dragonfly fauna and can be used as a basis to detect future changes in odonate distribution and draw up and target conservation strategies and priorities.

The records as they stand are based on sightings of adult insects and do not take any account of breeding. Adult dragonflies are vagrants and are often seen near water bodies that do not support breeding populations (p.69), but it is the breeding sites that are of conservation importance. To address this issue the Key

Sites Project was launched.[56] A new recording card (RA70) was issued that required recorders to note estimated numbers of individuals of each species seen, and at what life stage they were recorded, and to record any evidence indicating reproductive activity (specifically F-o exuviae, copulating pairs or ovipositing females). This information, it was assumed, would identify those key sites of conservation importance that supported important breeding populations of dragonflies (i.e. 'stem habitats', Box 6, p.76). Although relatively few recorders submit details of breeding evidence (equating to about 15 per cent of total records), this information is extremely valuable and is used in the compilation of local atlases to plot maps indicating breeding and abundance data.[57] In 1992 a new card was issued that required recorders to focus specifically on non-resident migrant species.[46] This initiative has been developed by the BDS into the Migrants Recording Scheme, co-ordinated by Adrian Parr, who keeps members informed about trends in migrant species through a regular column in *Dragonfly News*. This scheme has been a great success and has led to the involvement of many new recorders, much activity and many records.

By 1996 the BRC no longer had the resources to manage the ORS, and responsibility for co-ordinating the scheme passed to the BDS. David Winsland took over as central co-ordinator. To reduce his workload, the scheme focused on a prescribed list of 16 nationally rare species and records of more widespread species from areas where they were locally uncommon. Nevertheless, records of all species were still entered into the national scheme. The scheme was known as the Rare Dragonfly Project (RDP). However, the RDP suffered from a paucity of submitted records.[58] A relatively low percentage of BDS members took part in the project and records were coming only from regional co-ordinators who were active members of the BDS. It was found difficult to obtain local recorders (often based at county museums and funded by local government) to submit records to the national scheme. Unfortunately, due to ill-health at the end of 1998, David Winsland was forced to retire as organiser of the RDP. The project was relaunched in 1999 as the Dragonfly Recording Network (DRN). Steve Cham took the helm, assisted by ten regional recorders, all affiliated to the BDS. Following the lukewarm reception given to the narrow focus of the RDP, the recording effort was restructured to cover all odonate species once more. The DRN is now receiving records from many active recorders and local record centres. The number of records received often depends on local initiatives, and recording effort is boosted when a county atlas is in preparation. The production of county and regional atlases has provided a focus for recording effort and many high-quality publications have resulted. Perhaps the most spectacular recent example is the published results of *Dragonfly Ireland*,[59] a recording initiative that galvanised odonate recording throughout the island of Ireland. In Britain, the publication of new field guides, increased migrant activity and the discovery of *Erythromma viridulum* have also attracted new people to Odonata recording, especially from among the bird-watching community.[57] The DRN is linked to the National Biodiversity Network (NBN), established in March 2000 to act as a conduit for all the biological recording schemes in Britain. The NBN provides internet access to records and maps via the NBN Gateway.[60] The maps we have reproduced in Appendix 4 are available online from the NBN Gateway. The BDS is working with the NBN and the JNCC to assemble all the dragonfly data into one database that will be accessible online. The data are also being used to compile a register of Key Sites and revised Key Sites criteria were available online in 2007.[63]

The DRN has revitalised dragonfly recording in Britain and a long-term objective is to produce an atlas in 2010, as part of a project known as *Dragonflies in focus* in conjunction with the NBN. The scheme has capitalised on purpose-designed recording software called DARTER, developed by Mike Thurner and made available at a subsidised rate to recorders submitting records to the DRN. The BDS secured funding in 2004 for a full-time post, filled by Graham French, to provide more resources for data management and provision. This requirement reflects one of the challenges facing the BDS and many other amateur-run entomological societies. UK Government commitments to biodiversity, following the Rio Convention on Biodiversity, mean that action plans must be drawn up to conserve the most threatened species. Before this can be done it is essential that the status and distribution of all species is fully documented. The great majority of non-microscopic organisms are insects, but most of the knowledge of these groups in the UK is held by a relatively few amateur enthusiasts. Huge numbers of distribution records are required and are being assembled, but few amateur enthusiasts have the time or inclination to undertake the necessary data management and this forms a major impediment to making this information available. Societies like the BDS are increasingly finding the need to take on full-time staff to achieve these goals but, compared to conservation organisations focusing on larger plants and animals, which nevertheless include fewer species, insect-focused groups are poorly resourced.

Appointment of Conservation Officer

In 2001, the BDS appointed Charlotte Murray as its first full-time Conservation Officer on a three-year contract with support from EN, the EA, Esmee Fairburn Foundation, RSPB and British Waterways. The support from these large organisations demonstrates how well established and respected the BDS had become. The support of these sponsoring organisations and the desirability of having a dedicated national expert to which organisations could turn for advice on dragonfly conservation is a further indication of how far dragonfly conservation has advanced in the last few decades: from a minority interest to an issue that is of concern to thousands of amateur enthusiasts and major conservation organisations, and a significant consideration in wetland conservation management.

One focus of the Conservation Officer's work has been to assemble information on the ecology and habitat requirements of each British species, the threats they face and how habitats can be managed to support them. By 2004, information had been compiled for ten species and was available on the BDS website[63] as Management Fact Files. Another important part of the Conservation Officer's job is to raise awareness about dragonflies through talks, guided walks and articles. Educational slide packs entitled *Learning about dragonflies* and *A dragonfly's world* have been produced. The former provides an introduction to dragonflies aimed at teachers of 7- to 11-year-old children, and the latter is aimed at conservation organisations and land managers. In 2003 Charlotte Murray moved to the EA and was replaced by Caroline Daguet. Resources were secured to fund the post for a further three years. In 2007 Katherine Parker became the new conservation officer.

Conservation grants

Since 1996 the BDS has provided small grants to fund research projects on odonate biology, monitoring or conservation. The Philip Corbet Award is available to researchers under the age of 25 and the Norman Moore Award is available to people over the age of 25. All the awards to date have been made to assist undergraduate students with their dissertation projects. Examples of projects include an investigation into the relationship between aquatic flora and the distribution of larval dragonflies, an investigation into predator-prey relationships between Anisoptera larvae and the Great Silver Diving Beetle, *Hydrophilus piceus*, the status of *Leucorrhinia dubia* at Abbots Moss, Cheshire and the distribution and territorial biology of *Orthetrum coerulescens*.

The late Dr Peter Miller[61] was one of the world's leading odonatologists and a great mentor to students. After his death in 1996 a memorial fund was set up that provided the means to create dragonfly ponds in schools. By the year 2000, nine ponds had been established and were providing a unique educational resource to promote the study of dragonflies and wetland wildlife.[62]

Website

In order to reach a wider audience, the BDS established a website in 1998.[63] This is kept up to date by George Mahoney. The website is attractive and informative and includes many high-quality images of Odonata. It has a page of answers to frequently asked questions and illustrations of all the British species, together with detailed management fact files for selected species and links to distribution maps on the NBN. There is a 'hot news' page featuring the most recent Odonata sightings, a page on recording Odonata which has downloadable versions of the recording cards and the recording network newsletter, and a page detailing forthcoming BDS field trips. A page on projects gives suggestions for studies that enthusiasts can carry out themselves. There are also details of the Migrant Dragonflies Project with a summary of highlights since 1995 and information about the Key Sites register. The website is rounded off with a shop, contact details and links to many other related sites.

STUDYING DRAGONFLIES

Odonata are an accessible group of insects for the amateur to study. The larvae can be maintained in aquaria with little difficulty and the adults of many species can be watched at the garden pond. Field studies are made more pleasant because the adults are best seen on warm sunny days during the summer.

Odonate larvae can be collected at any time of the year from a pond or river using a pond net. The pond net should have a sturdy rigid handle that is securely and inflexibly attached to a rigid, square or triangular, net frame. The handle should be about 1.5 metres in length, and it can be useful to have extension poles. The net-bag should be made of a strong material that is not easily torn, that dries quickly, and that has a 1-mm mesh. Odonate larvae can be collected from aquatic vegetation by sweeping the net through the plants. Two or three continuous passes of the net should be made. The contents of the net should be tipped into a shallow, pale plastic tray containing a little water where the catch can be examined. Larvae that live in the silt and leaf litter at the bottom of the pond can be collected with a net, but a metal sieve is also effective in these habitats.

Larvae that are claspers or sprawlers can be kept successfully in jars containing pond water, a few sprigs of submerged aquatic plants (such as *Elodea canadensis* (Canadian pond weed), obtainable from the aquarist) and most importantly a long stick which protrudes half a metre or so above the water.

The stick will be used as a perch and eventually an emergence support by the larva. Bottom-dwelling larvae (hiders and shallow burrowers, Table 2, p.119) should be provided with leaf litter and silt at the bottom of the jar. Odonate larvae must be provided with live food. Small larvae take water fleas and chironomid midge larvae, which can be purchased at the aquarist. Cultures of water fleas can be kept alive in small aquaria supplied periodically with fresh infusions of grass or cabbage leaves. Chironomid midges can easily be persuaded to lay their eggs in buckets of water left outside. Larger odonate larvae may need to be fed with small earthworms. It is advisable to keep each larva in a separate container so as to prevent large larvae eating smaller ones. The aquarium should not be placed in direct sunlight. A north-facing windowsill is ideal. Any dead, uneaten food should be removed within a few hours to prevent the water becoming deoxygenated due to decomposition. If the water begins to become cloudy and greyish, and smells unpleasant, it should be changed.

The behaviour of odonate larvae, which is usually out of sight beneath the surface of the pond, can now easily be observed. The most exciting event to witness is the emergence of the adult insect. This usually happens in the morning in damselflies, but aeshnids often emerge during the night (Fig. 85, p.158), and a nocturnal vigil may be necessary. It is well worth the wait. If the wing sheaths are swollen and the larva spends time with its head slightly protruding above the surface of the water, emergence is imminent (p.148). The shed larval exuvia, reliably identified by association with the adult insect, can form the basis of a reference collection.

A garden pond is a good place to study dragonflies, and if thoughtfully constructed will attract many different species (Box 23). F-0 exuviae collected from the leaves of plants emerging from a garden pond will confirm which species are completing development there. Over the years the numbers and species may change as the pond develops. The behaviour of adult Odonata can be observed over the pond. Mating, egg-laying and territorial behaviour are all easily seen. The places where adults roost and forage may be discovered around the garden.

Dragonflies are, of course, rewarding subjects to study away from the garden, and any observations may provide important information for the conservation of species. Little equipment is necessary apart from a notebook and pencil, a butterfly net to permit close examination of specimens to confirm identification or mark adults, and perhaps close-focus binoculars. Adult dragonflies can be handled without damage if they are gently held by all four wings closed over the body. Care should be taken when disentangling the legs from the net bag. On no

BOX 23

CREATING A DRAGONFLY POND

Many species of dragonflies can be encouraged to breed in a well-constructed garden pond (Fig. 128), even in the centre of the largest city. The requisites of a dragonfly pond are that:

1) it is open to the sun (trees create shade, which adult dragonflies avoid, and add leaves to the pond during autumn which may reduce the oxygen available to the larvae as the leaves decompose);
2) it has plenty of submerged, floating and emergent plants (to provide hiding places for the larvae, oviposition sites and emergence supports); and
3) it has some shelter from the wind (adult dragonflies will avoid windswept ponds).

The pond should be dug deep enough (over 1.5 metres) so that it does not freeze to the bottom in winter. Shallow sloping margins, preferably on the northern margin, should be incorporated which will allow the water to warm up where metamorphosing larvae can bask and will provide a place for pond plants to take root close to the water surface. A south-facing

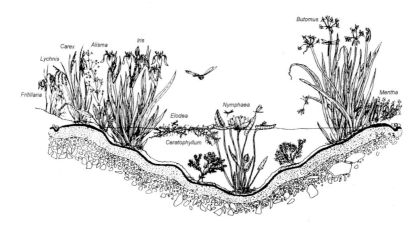

FIG 128. Profile of a dragonfly pond (after Kevin Caley).

bank with gravel or large stones will provide a basking site for adults. It is a good idea not to add fish (which may eat the dragonfly larvae) and it is best to avoid topping up the pond frequently with tap water because this will add nutrients (especially phosphates) that will encourage the growth of algae.

....

account should freshly emerged (teneral) adults (recognisable by shiny wings and pale pterostigmata) be handled because the wings are soft and could be irreparably damaged.

Long-term monitoring data from a local site can provide extremely valuable information on trends in abundance and diversity. Such data can give a warning of habitat deterioration, information about the response of species to habitat management or evidence of colonisation by new species. Long-term data are not available for most sites because they are so expensive to obtain, but this is an area to which local amateur enthusiasts can make an important contribution.

Adult Odonata can easily be monitored using the 'Pollard Walk' technique (Box 24). Monitoring data obtained in this way quickly reveal which parts of the site are important to particular species, which species are breeding at the site and which species are only visitors. Over time, fluctuations in numbers will be revealed. If habitat management is carried out at a site as a result of recommendations from a survey it is particularly important that monitoring continues for several years. All too frequently, follow-up surveys to assess the impact of new management programmes are lacking. A good example of the insights into dragonfly ecology, habitat management and the implications for dragonfly conservation that can be achieved from the long-term monitoring of a site is provided by Norman Moore's 40-year study of 20 small ponds at Woodwalton Fen, Cambridgeshire.[64]

Behaviour of adult dragonflies, for example dispersal and territorial activity, can be a rewarding and fascinating subject to study and also has relevance to habitat management. Such studies are much more informative if it is possible to recognise specimens as individuals. This can be achieved by marking each insect uniquely. The wings of mature adults are robust and can be marked with spots of quick-drying paint. By assigning the left-hand pair of wings as 'tens' and the right-hand pair as 'units', up to 99 individuals can be marked with a combination of spots (Fig. 129). By using different colours, hundreds of individuals can receive unique combinations of spots. For example, this technique was used by amateur dragonfly enthusiasts in a study of the behaviour of *Cordulia aenea* during which it was observed that several males 'time-shared' the same small territories.[65] It

BOX 24

A METHOD FOR MONITORING ADULT DRAGONFLY POPULATIONS

The most reliable way to monitor the size of a dragonfly population is to make a comprehensive collection of F-0 exuviae each year (Fig. 76, p.151). However, this can be time-consuming and may not be practical at a large site that has dense bankside vegetation. The size of a population of mature adults can be estimated using mark–recapture techniques[66] but this method is also time-consuming and may be impractical for someone who is able to visit the site only briefly and infrequently.

Norman Moore developed a way of monitoring the numbers of adult dragonflies active at water bodies. The method was subsequently modified and has been widely used to monitor adult butterfly populations and has become known as the Pollard Walk method.[67] The principle of the method[68] is that a surveyor visits a site during conditions that are optimal for adult dragonfly activity and counts adult Odonata visible within a defined area using a standardised recording routine. This method produces a measure of the relative size of the population of non-territorial dragonflies that can be compared throughout the year and from year to year, even if different surveyors have carried out the monitoring programme. The method is less effective for monitoring territorial dragonfly species because the density of males at a site is correlated with their size and the dimensions of the habitat. This governs the *highest steady density* (HSD)[69] of males that can be present at a site. This implies that whatever the actual size of a population of mature males, as long as it is above a certain level, counts of mature males at water will always be the same (i.e. the HSD). In this context, the method works least well for aeshnids, but is more useful for libellulids and corduliids because more individuals are required to reach HSD in these latter two families. Nevertheless, a crash in the numbers of mature males present at the water, even of territorial species, should act as a trigger for investigating changes in site quality. Despite these constraints, the results can reveal which parts of a site are preferred by particular species and whether these change from year to year. The results also provide useful information about which species are breeding at a site and where at the site they are breeding, and which species are frequent visitors and which visit the site only occasionally. Finally, the results provide information about changes in species diversity and the effects of habitat management on the distribution and diversity of the dragonfly assemblage.

The surveyor is required to walk slowly along the bank of the site to be monitored, following the same route on each visit. The route is divided into sections of about 50–100 metres. In each section every identifiable specimen is recorded (perched or flying) in front and to either side, but not behind, the surveyor. The surveyor should not stop and search vegetation for dragonflies but keep walking. However, in order to survey adequately species like *Erythromma najas* that use floating-leafed vegetation the surveyor must stop occasionally in each section and scan the floating leaves with one 180° sweep of the binoculars. In order to ensure that the survey coincides with maximum dragonfly activity the survey should take place between one hour before, and two hours after, solar noon, when the air temperature in the shade is above 17°C, when there is at least 50 per cent sunshine (as each new section of the survey route is entered the surveyor records whether or not a shadow is cast; provided that sunshine is recorded in at least half of the sections the survey is valid), and also when wind is light (leaves and branches moving is acceptable, but if trees are bending the wind is too strong). The site should be visited throughout the Odonata flying season (i.e. from May to October), ideally on a weekly basis, but fortnightly is adequate. Because the method is standardised, site visits can be shared among several people.

was also possible to establish that the resident male always successfully defended his territory from rivals. These observations would not have been possible if the observer had not been able to recognise each male individually. Marking can also be useful in 'capture–mark–recapture' studies to reveal the size of adult populations and longevity.[65]

Compiling distribution data on Odonata is a basic conservation requirement. Recording cards for the national recording scheme are readily available from the BDS website or the scheme organiser. Accurate identification of Odonata is essential of course, although all records are carefully vetted by the recording scheme organisers before incorporation into maps. Many county recording schemes are also in progress, often organised by local groups, and involvement in these projects is a good way to meet other dragonfly enthusiasts. County recording schemes are usually based on 2-km or 1-km grids, rather than the

FIG 129. This male *Cordulia aenea* has been marked as part of a study of territorial behaviour (Ann Brooks).

10-km grid used by the national scheme, and so are at the nub of dragonfly conservation at the local level.

Other examples of opportunities for investigation are given at the end of Chapters 2–9 in this book.

CONSERVATION OF BRITISH ODONATA AND THEIR HABITATS

Conservation – the need

Little is known about changes in the British dragonfly fauna before 1940. The study of Britain's dragonflies was then still in its pioneering stages as collectors established what constituted the resident fauna, which species were regular or irregular migrants and which species could properly be omitted from the British list as rare vagrants or erroneous records. However, we do know that at least three species, *Coenagrion armatum, C. scitulum* and *Oxygastra curtisii* (Fig. 130), which once bred in England, became extinct in this country between 1953 and 1963. It is likely that these species were never widespread. *Coenagrion armatum*, first discovered in 1902,[26] was known only from Stalham, Sutton and Hickling

FIG 130. *Oxygastra curtisii* became extinct in Britain in 1963 (Ann Brooks).

Broads, Norfolk.[70] The population declined in the 1950s as the breeding sites began to dry up and became overgrown with reed, sallow and alder carr. The species was last seen in 1957.[42] *Coenagrion scitulum* was known only briefly in Britain. It was first discovered in 1946 by E.B. Pinniger and Cynthia Longfield[30] when they visited the overgrown ditches that transect the marshes on the north bank of the Thames near Benfleet, Essex. The main population occupied one pond where Eric Gardner saw over 250 adults. This pond was inundated with sea water during the catastrophic floods that hit the east coast of England in early 1953, and *C. scitulum* was never seen again in this country.[46] In 1946 *O. curtisii* was known from The New Forest, Hampshire, and the River Tamar on the Devon–Cornwall border. This disjunct distribution suggests that it may once have been more widespread, at least in southwest England, on tree-lined rivers. However, by 1957 shading of the breeding sites by bankside trees had restricted the population to one short stretch of the West Moors River, in the New Forest.[71] The final cause of extinction, in 1963, is thought to have been accidental sewage discharge from a treatment works that had been built upstream of the colony to serve a new housing estate.[46]

These three species were vulnerable to extinction because each was restricted to one or two localities. Fortunately, none of the currently resident British species has quite such a limited distribution, although *Aeshna isosceles, Coenagrion hastulatum, C. mercuriale, Lestes dryas* and *Somatochlora arctica* are all restricted in Britain (occurring in less than 2 per cent of 10-km squares) and others, notably *Aeshna caerulea, Ceriagrion tenellum, Coenagrion lunulatum, Cordulia aenea, Gomphus vulgatissimus, Ischnura pumilio, Leucorrhinia dubia, Libellula fulva* and *Somatochlora metallica*, have patchy distributions featuring isolated local populations that could be vulnerable. Habitat loss through ecological succession, pollution and destruction gained momentum during the 1950s and 1960s and still threatens our odonate populations today. Distribution records reveal that the populations of many, if not most, species contracted between 1950 and 1975 but there are signs that this decline has slowed down[46] and there is now evidence that several species are actually expanding their range.[72] We now examine the main causes for these changes.

Agriculture

The fortunes of most of the British Odonata are closely tied to management practices in the farming industry. Farm ponds were once widespread and abundant throughout Britain and until relatively recently must have been an important habitat for our commonest and most widespread species. Unfortunately, most ponds in the farmed countryside have now disappeared. There has been a 75 per cent reduction in farm ponds over the last 100 years[73] as the need to provide watering holes for livestock has declined. Even those farm ponds that remain are often neglected and severely degraded, having become polluted by pesticides and nutrients washed in from intensively farmed fields, or overshaded by trees, or having gradually dried up as a result of ecological succession. Farm ditches and lowland rivers running through intensively farmed countryside have suffered a similar fate. This must have resulted in a massive, largely undocumented, reduction in the abundance of Odonata, especially the most common and widespread species. Populations appear to have been hardest hit in East Anglia, where formerly widespread species have become more local, notably *Brachytron pratense, Calopteryx virgo, Ceriagrion tenellum, Coenagrion pulchellum, Libellula depressa, Platycnemis pennipes, Pyrrhosoma nymphula* and *Sympetrum danae*,[74] but similar trends have probably occurred throughout lowland Britain. The fens of East Anglia have been seriously reduced over the last 300 years so that today few remain. They are now isolated among thousands of acres of intensively managed farmland and so suffer from the 'island effect'. Any dragonflies flying out of the fen are unlikely to find a breeding site and this represents a continual drain on established populations which in the long term may not prove viable. In Devon and Cornwall some populations of *Coenagrion mercuriale* were lost when the shallow, open streams in which they bred were deepened[75] or became overgrown when cattle-grazing ceased.[76]

If Odonata are to have any long-term future in Britain it is essential that they are conserved in the wider countryside. For this to come about, farmers will need to be encouraged to take positive steps to improve wetlands on their land. This is particularly important if global climate change continues as forecast because it may mean that nature reserves will be in the wrong place and will no longer support populations of rare species. It will be essential for species to be able to move across the countryside in order to track a favourable climate and find new, suitable breeding habitats, but this will not be possible if intensive farming has destroyed many natural habitats and the 'green corridors' along which Odonata (especially those poor at dispersing) move. Important progress has been made in this direction following the formation of FWAG in 1976. This umbrella organisation links farming, forestry and conservation groups with government departments to give farmers advice on good conservation practice. One positive outcome has been the creation and restoration of thousands of farm ponds.[77] Other developments having a positive influence on farming practices are

- the establishment of the Countryside Restoration Trust, an organisation that demonstrates through working practice on its own farms how a profit-making farm can also be a haven for wildlife;
- work by the Game and Wildlife Conservation Trust to encourage farmers to leave strips of land around field margins as reservoirs for wildlife and buffers against spray-drift;
- EU subsidies for environmentally friendly farming;
- the growth of organic farming.

Forestry

The postwar drive for home-produced timber led to the afforestation of many parts of Britain, often with a near monoculture of conifers. Drainage, to improve timber yields, and overshading by dense stands of conifers probably resulted in the destruction of many former breeding sites of *Aeshna caerulea* and *Somatochlora arctica* in the Scottish Highlands. Sites that once supported populations of *Aeshna juncea*, *Ceriagrion tenellum* and *Orthetrum coerulescens* on the lowland heaths of Dorset and the Brecklands of East Anglia have also probably been lost.[46] Similarly, populations of *Cordulegaster boltonii* have been adversely affected in Wales.[78] *Cordulia aenea* and *Somatochlora metallica* are mostly confined to woodland in England and these species may have been adversely affected by the fragmentation of woodlands and the loss of woodland ponds. The worst excesses of conifer afforestation are now past. Upland bogs are no longer seen as worthless. Conifer plantations and many conifer woods are being removed, or replanted as deciduous woodland in which the open canopy is more beneficial for odonates.

Extraction industries

In the last 50 years there has been a huge increase in demand for aggregate. Once exhausted, the resulting pits are often flooded to provide recreation amenities and, sometimes, nature reserves and country parks. These new wetlands can be valuable to dragonflies, especially when nature conservation is the principal motivation for restoration and a variety of features is included, especially long, shallow, gently shelving margins and a large area of water shallow enough to allow the establishment of a rich and diverse aquatic flora (Fig. 131). A single large lake is likely to support fewer dragonflies than several small lakes of the same total area because the combined length of marginal habitat will be greater in the small sites than in a single large lake. Dragonfly larvae are concentrated in shallow margins rather than deep, open expanses of water. Excellent examples of what can be achieved can be seen at the Cotswold Country Park,[79] Ouse Valley, Huntingdonshire,[80] and the Lea Valley, Essex,[81] which were once mineral extraction sites but now support many odonate species. Despite the initial

FIG 131. Restored gravel pits at Cotswold Country Park (Zoë Greenwell).

destruction when the pits were first dug, there has ultimately been a net gain in dragonfly breeding sites. However, such restoration does not necessarily favour all species. *Ischnura pumilio* is rare in Britain, but has successfully established populations in working quarries where it breeds in shallow seepages that are kept free of vegetation by mechanical disturbance (see p.43).

On peat bogs, traditional small-scale hand-cutting of peat for domestic fuel produces small pools and ditches. These pools harbour many Odonata that have a restricted distribution in Britain. However, industrial-scale mining of peat (Fig. 132) to supply the horticultural industry (and, in Ireland, to fuel power stations) threatens the bogs and the species they support. There has been a loss of 98 per cent of raised bogs and 90 per cent of blanket bogs in Britain and Ireland.[82] Removal of peat on an industrial scale destroys the hydrological integrity of a bog, allowing it to dry out and be colonised by trees. If peat extraction is total and the original bedrock is exposed, any pools are unlikely to retain their acidic character, even if the area is later restored as wetland; so the typical peatland dragonfly community is replaced by more widespread species able to colonise reclaimed gravel workings. As a result of peat extraction and drainage, *Ceriagrion tenellum* has been lost from the Somerset Levels and *Leucorrhinia dubia* from England's largest bog, Thorne Moors in Yorkshire.[83]

FIG 132. Peat mining near Clonfin Lough, Co. Offaly, Ireland (Robert Thompson).

Water pollution and river management

Many rivers are polluted with phosphates and nitrates, largely originating from detergents and sewage from sewage works, and fertilisers and slurry from farms. These nutrients encourage algal blooms that turn the water an opaque green, and encourage the growth of floating Duckweeds, *Lemna* spp., and filamentous algae (Fig. 133). This restricts the quantity of light that can penetrate the water and so suppresses submerged plants. Nutrients also promote bacterial growth which depletes dissolved oxygen. Toxic metals and dyes from industry and pesticides also find their way into rivers. Over-abstraction of water from the upper tributaries of rivers can lead to reduced flows causing pollutants to become more concentrated and oxygen levels to fall below acceptable concentrations in summer. All these pollutants reduce the quality of a river as a habitat for dragonflies. Other factors that reduce dragonfly diversity and abundance include clearance of aquatic plants and bankside trees, dredging, and construction of concrete banks to speed water flow and reduce the risk of floods. A study in South Carolina showed that streams that had been disturbed most recently featured the lowest species diversity of Odonata.[84] Fortunately, river water quality has been improving recently[85] and attitudes are now changing towards flood defence. So-called 'soft engineering' solutions, using the natural capacities of river catchments to absorb water, are being recognised and increasingly used in flood defence. As a result, meanders are being put back into rivers that were previously canalised, natural bank profiles are being restored, and buffer zones which periodically receive flood water are being introduced.[86] These measures improve the suitability of a river for dragonflies by introducing a mosaic of habitats.

Oxygastra curtisii became extinct as a result of sewage pollution in the Moors River, and *Gomphus vulgatissimus* and *Libellula fulva* are currently restricted to a few lowland rivers. However, following recent improvements in water quality and river management, there are signs that Odonata are responding by expanding into river systems in which they had not been recorded previously or from which they had disappeared decades before. These intra-range expansions differ from the response of other odonate species to climate change because they only affect species that breed in lowland rivers; expansion is not unidirectional, nor does it emanate from the edge of the species range. In particular, new populations have been established by *Brachytron pratense* (Fig. 134) in Cumbria,[87] Gloucestershire,[88] Lincolnshire,[89] Norfolk[90] and Warwickshire;[91] *Gomphus vulgatissimus* was first recorded in Warwickshire in 1997;[91] *Aeshna isosceles* is expanding westwards along the River Waveney in Norfolk;[90] and, since 1996, *Libellula fulva* has established colonies on the River Stour in Kent,[92] the River

FIG 133. Detergents in the water have caused this foam as the river falls over a weir. Detergents contain phosphates which are an important plant nutrient. Phosphates are difficult to remove at sewage treatment works (Ann Brooks).

FIG 134. Recently *Brachytron pratense* has been expanding its range throughout Britain, perhaps in response to improved habitat and water quality (Robert Thompson).

Wey in Surrey,[93] the River Nene in Northamptonshire and the River Stour in Suffolk,[94] *Platycnemis pennipes* is expanding into Warwickshire from the west and east.[91]

Disused canals, in which aquatic plants have been allowed to develop and the banks have reverted to their natural state, can also support rich dragonfly populations (Fig. 135). However, even relatively low-level boat traffic destroys submerged plants and leads to increased turbidity from algal blooms and suspended silt; and there is the more insidious threat of toxic anti-fouling paints. Emerging dragonflies may also be killed by the wash from boat traffic (p.53). Rich dragonfly populations are threatened or have already been damaged by canal restoration and the resumption of boating on the Montgomery Canal in the Welsh borders[95] and the Basingstoke Canal in Hampshire, southern England.[96] The Norfolk Broads have also suffered from the impacts of boat traffic, anti-fouling paints and eutrophication, and those few Broads that are hydrologically isolated are now a precious resource deserving careful protection.

FIG 135. The Grand Canal at Ballyshane is a haven for many species of Odonata (Robert Thompson).

Climate change

Since 1950, mean annual global temperatures have risen by about 0.5°C. There is good evidence that this is mainly a result of increased carbon dioxide in the atmosphere, derived mainly from combustion of fossil fuels.[97] Climate models predict that over the next 100 years global temperatures will increase further by anything from 2°–5°C, depending on future levels of carbon emissions. During the last two decades, Britain has experienced a series of unprecedentedly hot summers, and southeast England, in particular, has been subjected to summer droughts. These changes appear to have affected the odonate fauna. One way in which species can be expected to respond is through changes in phenology, but most noticeable has been the increase in the numbers and frequency of migrant species arriving in Britain. *Anax junius, Anax parthenope, Crocothemis erythraea, Lestes barbarus* and *Sympetrum pedemontanum* have all been recorded for the first time in Britain since 1992. *Anax parthenope* (Fig. 136) has been recorded in most years since 1995 and successful breeding was documented at two Cornish sites in 1999.[98] *Sympetrum flaveolum* and *S. fonscolombii* have been recorded as irregular migrants and occasional breeders in England for over a century, but in recent years both species have appeared more regularly and in higher numbers than before. *Sympetrum fonscolombii* is now recorded in most years and some breeding colonies have persisted in southern and northern England for several years.[99]

In 1999, *Erythromma viridulum* (Fig. 137) was first recorded in this country in Essex.[100] Since then it has expanded its range and is now locally common and breeding at many sites in southeast England. *Erythromma viridulum* appears to have successfully colonised England in just a few years and cannot be regarded as a migrant, but rather as a new resident species. The distribution map in Appendix 4 shows how the species has spread across eastern England since its arrival.

In addition to changes in the trends of migratory species, there have been well-documented northward range expansions of 37 resident species between 1960 and 1995.[101] More recent records show these trends continuing. In Scotland, *Aeshna cyanea* and *Sympetrum striolatum* have been recorded from several new localities, and between 2003 and 2006 *Aeshna grandis, A. mixta* (Fig. 138), *Anax imperator, Calopteryx splendens, Libellula depressa, Orthetrum cancellatum* and *Sympetrum sanguineum* were recorded there for the first time.[102] In Cumbria,

FIG 136. *Anax parthenope* is a recent migrant to Britain, but has been recorded in most years since it was first seen in 1995 (Steve Cham).

FIG 137. *Erythromma viridulum* first arrived in England in 1999 and since then has colonised many sites in south-east England (Steve Cham).

Anax imperator was recorded for the first time in 1995, *Aeshna mixta* for the first time in 1999[103] and *Brachytron pratense* for the first time in 2003.[104] *Libellula depressa* was reported as spreading north through Cumbria[87] and Lincolnshire.[88] In Cheshire, adults of *S. striolatum* have been emerging earlier each year; *A. imperator*, *O. cancellatum* and *Sympetrum sanguineum* have all recently established breeding colonies in the county and *A. mixta* has recently colonised uplands areas in the Peak District.[105] In Warwickshire, there has been a significant expansion in the range of *O. cancellatum* in the north and west of the county and *S. sanguineum* has expanded into northern parts of the county since 1997.[91] The first confirmed records of *Anax imperator* in Ireland were made in 2000 and successful breeding of the species was confirmed in 2002.[106] The species has now been recorded there from 24 sites.[59] Similarly, *Aeshna mixta* was first recorded in Ireland in 2000 and breeding was confirmed the following year.[106] The species is now widely distributed along southern and southeastern coastal localities.[59]

In addition to southern species expanding into the north of Britain, there has been a contraction in the range of *Leucorrhinia dubia* (Fig. 139), one of the few British species with a predominantly northern distribution in this country. The species became extinct on Thursley Common Nature Reserve in Surrey in 1999 (see p.61), and by 2003 only a few F-0 exuviae were found in the only

FIG 138. *Aeshna mixta* has expanded its range into northern England and southern Ireland in the last few years (Robert Thompson).

FIG 139. *Leucorrhinia dubia* is becoming increasingly rare in the southern part of its British range (Robert Thompson).

remaining colony in Cheshire.[105] None of these trends would have been apparent without the achievements of the dragonfly recording scheme that has been operating since 1970.

The recent increase in the use of standing-water breeding habitats by *P. pennipes*,[107] which is at the northern edge of its European range in Britain, may also be a response to climate change. The species breeds commonly in farm ponds in France. Formerly suboptimal habitats become acceptable as climatic conditions begin to approach the species' optimum. We may begin to see ecological changes in other species at the northwestern edge of their global range. For example, in Britain *Aeshna isosceles* is restricted to sites that support the aquatic plant *Stratiotes aloides* (Water Soldier). However, further south, in continental Europe, it is under no such constraint, and breeds in a wide variety of habitats. *Aeshna isosceles* is currently vulnerable to rising sea levels, induced by global climate warming, as many of its habitats in eastern England are at low altitude and close to the coast. These habitats will also be threatened if planning authorities decide that it is no longer technically or economically feasible to maintain coastal defences and adopt a retired line-of-defence strategy.

Conservation – the practice

Legislation

In response to the growing conservation crisis in Britain, legislation was introduced under the Wildlife and Countryside Act 1981 to protect individual species. Initially, *Aeshna isosceles* (Fig. 140) was the only extant odonate species to receive protection under this law, but in 1998 *Coenagrion mercuriale* was added. As a result it is illegal to kill, injure or handle specimens of either species without a licence. However, this legislation gives no protection to the sites in which the species breed. Protection of individuals from collection, while possibly essential for the conservation of mammals, birds and plants, is not appropriate for the conservation of most insect species because their populations, if stable, are so large that the removal of a few voucher specimens (being insignificant compared with the natural daily mortality) will not endanger the viability of a population (Appendix 2). Usually populations of even rare insects are large and robust enough to withstand the activities of responsible collectors. Indeed, strong

FIG 140. *Aeshna isosceles* is one of only two species of Odonata protected by law in Britain (Robert Thompson).

discouragement of insect collecting may be counterproductive since voucher specimens are often essential to confirm identification in some groups of insects and some people may thereby be deterred from beginning to study insects.

Far more important than protection of individuals is adequate protection of habitats. As a globally threatened species, *C. mercuriale* is the only extant British odonate species to be listed on Annex II of the EU Habitats Directive and Annex II of the Berne Convention. Under the Habitats Directive, Special Areas of Conservation (SAC) are designated for the species. This gives some protection to breeding sites. Rare species are also listed in the British Red Data List[108]. While this does not confer direct protection under law it does provide a hierarchical listing (extinct, endangered, vulnerable and rare, in descending order of status) against which conservation priorities and the conservation value of a site can be assessed. Nine species of Odonata are listed under one of the four Red Data Book categories.

The Biodiversity Convention was signed by the British Government in Rio de Janeiro in 1992. Under this treaty Britain was obliged to identify, notify, protect and enhance a suite of nationally threatened species and habitats, which include several categories of wetland. In 1994 the UK Biodiversity Action Plan (BAP) was published by Government.[109] Lists of organisms that had undergone significant range contraction over the previous 25 years were drawn up and species action plans (SAPs) were formulated for each of the 116 species on the shortlist. Each SAP includes a checklist of measurable targets set to improve the conservation prospects of that species. The Government is required to report on progress made towards achieving BAP targets and to report every six years on the condition of SAPs. *Coenagrion mercuriale* (Fig. 141), the distributional range of which is estimated to have declined in Britain by 30 per cent since 1960,[75] is currently the only odonate species to appear on the BAP shortlist. However, before any effective action can be taken to consolidate the British populations of *C. mercuriale*, basic ecological research on the species is needed to establish its biology and precise habitat requirements. A partnership of organisations has been assembled to form a national steering group involved in the SAP for *C. mercuriale*. The lead organisation is the Environment Agency. Ecological research is being conducted at Liverpool University under the guidance of David Thompson. Survey work, to establish the size and extent of populations, and to investigate dispersal and movement between populations, is being co-ordinated by the BDS, NE and the CCW. The BDS has established a rolling monitoring programme to survey at least ten of the sites that support *C. mercuriale* every year and to revisit each site every six years. A considerable input and commitment from amateur enthusiasts is required if this is to be

FIG 141A. The Biodiversity Action Plan process has prompted an ecological study of *Coenagrion mercuriale* covering the (A) larval and (B) adult stages of the life cycle and (C) habitat management implications (Robert Thompson).

FIG 141B.

FIG 141C.

achieved and Government is to meet its targets under the Biodiversity Convention. The BAP process has provided a focus and stimulus for conservation work on *C. mercuriale*, bringing together amateur Odonata enthusiasts and professional ecologists from universities, NGOs and statutory agencies. As a result, considerable progress has been made towards understanding the ecology of *C. mercuriale* and promoting good management practices which otherwise would probably never have been achieved.[110]

Dragonfly 'Theme Parks'

The Ashton Water Dragonfly Sanctuary and National Dragonfly BioMuseum (Fig. 142) was an initiative of Ruary Mackenzie Dodds and Kari de Koenigswarter. With advice from the BDS, in particular DCG convenor Norman Moore, support from Miriam Rothschild, the Patron of the BDS, and the WWF and the practical involvement of several volunteers, a large lake was managed specifically to attract Odonata. The number of dragonfly species recorded at the site rose from five to 16 within four years. An interpretation centre was set up and between 1991 and 1994 3,500 people were given guided walks around the Sanctuary. At the nearby

FIG 142. A school group viewing a libellulid larva tackling its prey under the microscope video link at the National Dragonfly BioMuseum at Ashton (Ruary Mackenzie Dodds).

National Dragonfly BioMuseum, established in 1995, there were displays about odonate biology, ecology and wetland conservation, as well as talks, guided walks on 'dragonfly trails', and courses on dragonfly identification. Unfortunately the BioMuseum was forced to close, when its lease expired, in late 2001. In the seven years during which it was open the BioMuseum received 22,000 visitors who learnt about dragonflies and the conservation issues affecting them. Despite the closure, the same team continues to run 'dragonfly days' at Woodwalton and Wicken Fen Nature Reserves under the auspices of the Dragonfly Project.[111]

A second dragonfly sanctuary was established in 1994 by the Lea Valley Park Authority at Cornmill Meadows, Waltham Abbey, Essex (Fig. 143). It includes a large area of water meadows crossed by several ditches and bounded on three sides by branches of the River Lea. Twenty-one species of Odonata have been recorded at the sanctuary, including a locally important population of *Platycnemis pennipes*. The site has recently been colonised by *Brachytron pratense*. A large interpretation centre provides multimedia displays on dragonfly ecology and biology, and there are guided dragonfly walks around the meadows. Members of the BDS had been monitoring the Odonata populations at the site for several years before its official designation and so were able to provide information on the species present and expertise, advice, images and written interpretative material. The sanctuary is open to visitors throughout the year.

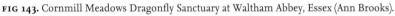

FIG 143. Cornmill Meadows Dragonfly Sanctuary at Waltham Abbey, Essex (Ann Brooks).

Conservation – the prospects

The prospects for British Odonata are probably better now than they have been at any time during the last 50 years. Fifty years ago Odonata in Britain were facing a crisis due to the destruction and degradation of wetlands following intensification of agriculture, forestry and building development. There were relatively few people interested in Odonata and there was inadequate knowledge of their distribution and ecology, so little was being done to conserve them. However, thanks to the pioneering work of a few enthusiasts, the publication of the first New Naturalist book on dragonflies[39] and later the production of an eye-catching field guide,[42] wider interest in the group has been generated. Now naturalists have access to a wide range of field guides (Box 2, p.14) and related publications on odonates to feed their interest. The BDS has a large and active membership and an influential voice in conservation circles. The contribution of thousands of records from hundreds of observers to the DRN means that odonatologists now have a realistic picture of the distribution of Odonata in Britain, enabling them to make informed judgements on conservation priorities and the changing status of species. Although wetlands are still being damaged and destroyed, many are now being sensitively managed by conservation organisations, and some private landowners and farmers are finding it possible actively to manage their land to promote biodiversity. The ravages of the 1960s and 1970s resulting from the scramble to press ever more acres of farmland into profitable production have slowed, mainly because relatively little marginal land remains. There does seem to be an increase in the number of farmers who have a genuine interest in increasing biodiversity on their land, a trend nurtured through the work of FWAG and the Countryside Restoration Trust (CRT) and subsidy structure. There are not enough nature reserves in Britain to conserve viable populations of all our species; so the wider countryside must still be made more favourable for wildlife. The recent improvement in the quality of British rivers appears to have resulted in the expansion of populations of riverine Odonata.

In order to build on the progress that has been made in odonate conservation the BDS must continue to be a significant player on the conservation stage. The appointment of a professional Conservation Officer has been an important development in maintaining this role. The strong membership base of the BDS must be retained. Members must be encouraged to make an active contribution to Odonata conservation at the local level by carefully monitoring sites that support important Odonata populations, by digging ponds in their gardens and as part of local school and community projects, and by eschewing the use of peat in their gardens. The DRN needs to maintain its high profile and continue to encourage dragonfly recorders, many of whom are not members of the BDS, to submit their records so that changes in odonate populations can continue to be closely monitored. The BDS also needs to continue to promote awareness of dragonflies and to reach new audiences.

The BAP process has acted as a focus for research on *Coenagrion mercuriale* and has resulted in many people from diverse backgrounds and organisations working together and making progress in understanding the ecology and habitat requirements of the species. This is a good example of how the legislative process can make a valuable contribution to odonate conservation. Species conservation must focus on protection and sympathetic management of habitats. Legislation to protect individual specimens from collection has little relevance and can often be counterproductive. There must also be a mutual understanding of the legitimate requirements of researchers to take voucher specimens when needed and the aspirations of enthusiasts to watch dragonflies unmolested in the field.

In future the greatest influence on populations of British Odonata, apart from habitat loss caused by the continuing expansion of the human population, will probably be climatic. The last decade has witnessed considerable changes in the distribution of many of the British species in response to unprecedentedly high annual temperatures. The predictions are that global warming will continue to increase. We are likely to see the arrival of new odonate colonists from continental Europe and an increasing frequency and abundance of migrant species. Many British Odonata are southern species at the northern edge of their range in Britain. We are already seeing many of them expanding north and westwards in this country. However, as global warming continues, southeast England is expected to become drier. This will inevitably result in lowering of water tables, increased water abstraction, reduced river flows and consequent increase in the impact of pollutants, and increased risk of wetlands drying up in this region, especially if demand for water by human populations continues undiminished or increases. An example of what is likely to occur with increasing frequency was reported by Tom Fort.[112] During the summer of 2003 the River Wylye, a species-rich chalk stream in Wiltshire, was greatly reduced in volume due to extraction of a quarter of a billion litres of water a week from underground aquifers by Wessex Water, with deleterious effects on the flora and fauna. This was done to avoid imposing hosepipe bans, a political rather than conservation-orientated motive. Plans to pump water from the lower Avon were also shelved to hold down water rates. Nature conservation will suffer if water companies and water industry regulating authorities are allowed to place short-term, consumer interests before wetland biodiversity.

Odonate species with exacting habitat requirements (stenotopic species) are unlikely to be able to track favourable climatic regimes, because habitats suitable for them are not widely available in the countryside at large. Nature reserves may soon appear to be in the wrong places for them. Species with distributions centred in northern and upland districts will have increasingly fewer climatically suitable habitats available to them.

During recent decades there have been positive, and encouraging, developments in the conservation of British Odonata. No species has become extinct in the last 40 years. Despite worrying trends during that period, declines appear to have slowed and, in several species, reversed. Warming climate is favouring many eurytopic species which are expanding northwards, although there are indications that boreal species are declining in the south of their ranges. Riverine species are benefiting from the improvement in water quality and management of British rivers, although increased water abstraction is likely to pose a threat in the future, especially in southern and eastern England where massive increases in housing are planned. Odonata now have a high profile in conservation circles and in the public perception. Dragonflies invariably feature in interpretative displays at country parks and nature reserves that include wetlands. Wetlands are being managed to enhance their suitability for odonates, and new wetlands suitable for dragonfly colonisation are being created on former mineral extraction sites, reservoirs and landfill sites. Ponds and lakes are often created to enhance country parks, schools and urban parks. Unlike butterflies, many species of which have suffered catastrophic declines in the last few decades as a result of changes in farming and forestry practices,[113] dragonflies are not so closely tied to the vagaries of the Common Agricultural Policy, grazing regimes, crop rotation and demands for timber. The worst damage to dragonfly populations (so far) was inflicted 40–50 years ago when farm ponds, ditches and lowland rivers were being drained and polluted wholesale. We now appear to be seeing a recovery of odonate populations from that low point. However, this is no excuse for complacency. The apparently unsustainable demands on Britain's wetlands remain. Nevertheless, many gains have resulted from amateur and professional dragonfly enthusiasts becoming actively involved in dragonfly and wetland conservation and demonstrating why everybody should want to see dragonflies from their doorstep and how that can be achieved.

Alongside all considerations of loss of biodiversity lie the imperatives of human numbers and economic development. Britain is a finite landmass, accommodating both humans and wildlife. As long as the human population of Britain, and its associated infrastructure, continue to demand more and more space, it is inevitable that the country's biodiversity will be placed under increasing pressure. With this in prospect, those who wish to maintain the viability of Britain's endowment of dragonflies cannot afford to relax. What will be needed, to an increasing extent, will be a clear recognition of priorities among habitats eligible for statutory protection. The most effective way that odonatologists can help to achieve this goal is to maintain recording effort, distinguishing where possible between stem and secondary habitats for each species, and supporting (and if necessary lobbying) those agencies, such as the wildlife trusts and appropriate statutory bodies, to ensure that the most valuable habitats are accorded official protection. To do this would be a fitting memorial to our predecessors, ancient and modern, who have helped to make the study of British dragonflies such a rewarding and inspiring pursuit.

Checklist of British Species

The English names in this list are those adopted by the British Dragonfly Society since 1991 or proposed in 2004 by Mill and others except the name for Anisoptera which has been changed to prevent the word 'dragonfly' having two meanings.

SUBORDER ZYGOPTERA — DAMSELFLIES

CALOPTERYGIDAE
Calopteryx splendens (Harris, 1782) — Banded Demoiselle
Calopteryx virgo (Linnaeus, 1758) — Beautiful Demoiselle

LESTIDAE
Chalcolestes viridis (Vander Linden, 1825) — Willow Emerald Damselfly
Lestes barbarus (Fabricius, 1798) — Southern Emerald Damselfly
Lestes dryas (Kirby, 1890) — Scarce Emerald Damselfly
Lestes sponsa (Hansemann, 1823) — Emerald Damselfly

PLATYCNEMIDIDAE
Platycnemis pennipes (Pallas, 1771) — White-legged Damselfly

COENAGRIONIDAE
Ceriagrion tenellum (de Villers, 1789) — Small Red Damselfly
Coenagrion armatum (Charpentier, 1840) — Norfolk Damselfly
Coenagrion hastulatum (Charpentier, 1825) — Northern Damselfly
Coenagrion lunulatum (Charpentier, 1840) — Irish Damselfly

Coenagrion mercuriale (Charpentier, 1840)	Southern Damselfly
Coenagrion puella (Linnaeus, 1758)	Azure Damselfly
Coenagrion pulchellum (Vander Linden, 1825)	Variable Damselfly
Coenagrion scitulum (Rambur, 1842)	Dainty Damselfly
Enallagma cyathigerum (Charpentier, 1840)	Common Blue Damselfly
Erythromma najas (Hansemann, 1823)	Red-eyed Damselfly
Erythromma viridulum (Charpentier, 1840)	Small Red-eyed Damselfly
Ischnura elegans (Vander Linden, 1823)	Blue-tailed Damselfly
Ischnura pumilio (Charpentier, 1825)	Scarce Blue-tailed Damselfly
Pyrrhosoma nymphula (Sulzer, 1776)	Large Red Damselfly

SUBORDER ANISOPTERA   WARRIORFLIES

AESHNIDAE

Aeshna caerulea (Ström, 1783)	Azure Hawker
Aeshna cyanea (Müller, 1764)	Southern Hawker
Aeshna grandis (Linnaeus, 1758)	Brown Hawker
Aeshna isosceles (Müller, 1767)	Norfolk Hawker
Aeshna juncea (Linnaeus, 1758)	Common Hawker
Aeshna mixta (Latreille, 1805)	Migrant Hawker
Anax imperator (Leach, 1815)	Emperor
Anax junius (Drury, 1770)	Green Darner
Anax parthenope (Selys, 1839)	Lesser Emperor
Brachytron pratense (Müller, 1764)	Hairy Hawker
Anax ephippiger (Burmeister, 1839)	Vagrant Emperor

GOMPHIDAE

Gomphus vulgatissimus (Linnaeus, 1758)	Common Club-tail

CORDULEGASTRIDAE

Cordulegaster boltonii (Donovan, 1807)	Golden-ringed Dragonfly

CORDULIIDAE

Cordulia aenea (Linnaeus, 1758)	Downy Emerald
Oxygastra curtisii (Dale, 1834)	Orange-spotted Emerald
Somatochlora arctica (Zetterstedt, 1840)	Northern Emerald
Somatochlora metallica (Vander Linden, 1825)	Brilliant Emerald

LIBELLULIDAE

Crocothemis erythraea (Brullé, 1832)	Scarlet Darter
Leucorrhinia dubia (Vander Linden, 1825)	White-faced Darter
Libellula depressa (Linnaeus, 1758)	Broad-bodied Chaser
Libellula fulva (Müller, 1764)	Scarce Chaser
Libellula quadrimaculata (Linnaeus, 1758)	Four-spotted Chaser
Orthetrum cancellatum (Linnaeus, 1758)	Black-tailed Skimmer
Orthetrum coerulescens (Fabricius, 1798)	Keeled Skimmer
Pantala flavescens (Fabricius, 1798)	Wandering Glider
Sympetrum danae (Sulzer, 1776)	Black Darter
Sympetrum flaveolum (Linnaeus, 1758)	Yellow-winged Darter
Sympetrum fonscolombii (Selys, 1840)	Red-veined Darter
Sympetrum meridionale (Selys, 1841)	Southern Darter
Sympetrum pedemontanum (Allioni, 1766)	Banded Darter
Sympetrum sanguineum (Müller, 1764)	Ruddy Darter
Sympetrum striolatum (Charpentier, 1840)	Common Darter
Sympetrum vulgatum (Linnaeus, 1758)	Vagrant Darter

Collecting and Photographing Dragonflies

We distinguish here between capturing a dragonfly (retaining the option of releasing it promptly) and collecting a dragonfly (with the intention of killing and preserving a specimen for future study). This distinction applies to adults and larvae.

CAPTURING

Adults

It may be necessary to capture a dragonfly in order to examine it closely (e.g. to identify it, or to estimate its degree of maturity) with the prospect of releasing it promptly. Unnecessary capture should always be avoided because sometimes an adult can be fatally injured during the process. This applies especially but not exclusively to large, swiftly flying species. To capture them a net may have to be swung with force and speed. If the rim of the net strikes the dragonfly's head the impact can damage the delicate head-arrester system (p.212) in the neck and so destroy the dragonfly's ability to manoeuvre in flight. Such damage will be fatal. Likewise marking should not be practised except for good cause because it sometimes reduces survivorship, especially if the marks are conspicuous, perhaps making the dragonfly more visible to predators.[1]

Existing books and manuals on Odonata contain ample guidelines for techniques and equipment, but in any case keen practitioners will soon learn from experience by noting the habits of fliers and perchers and by learning to avoid alerting a settled dragonfly by making a sudden movement or casting a shadow over it. It has recently been shown that adults of some stream-dwelling species (e.g. Cordulegastridae) are attracted visually to a rotating object such as a small electric fan.[2] It may not be necessary to kill a dragonfly if all that is needed is a sample for DNA analysis; a small part of a leg may suffice.

Larvae

To capture larvae one needs an inflexible, long-handled, sturdy net with a quick-drying bag (nylon is suitable), a mesh size of about 1 × 1 mm and a rigid triangular frame that allows the net to penetrate dense stands of aquatic plants. The contents of a sweep can be tipped into water in a shallow white tray for inspection. The mesh size of the net can be varied according to the bottom sediment and to the need to collect small larvae. Larvae that live in silt, leaf litter or peat can be collected effectively using a sieve. Larvae of all sizes usually reveal themselves by their movements and can be taken out of the sorting tray to be placed in holding containers, using a suction pipette (for small larvae) or fingers or forceps (for larger ones), and isolated to avoid predation. Some kinds of weed-dwelling larvae can be collected using a submerged trap (Fig. 71, p.142). After being isolated, each larva may have to be examined and measured individually in a small, translucent dish under a dissecting microscope.

Exuviae

It is encouraging to know that F-0 exuviae (left behind at the emergence site) (p.149) can, at least for Anisoptera, be determined reliably to species[3] and so can serve as voucher specimens. They have the added advantage that they provide unequivocal evidence of successful breeding. Also they are a reliable source of DNA for genetic analysis.[4]

COLLECTING

During an investigation it may be necessary to retain a specimen to be preserved for dissection or microscopic examination. Such a specimen is termed a voucher specimen or voucher. The consensus among odonatologists, at least those who are members of the Worldwide Dragonfly Association (WDA), is that collecting dragonflies should comply with four key principles. These form the basis of the Code of Practice for Collecting promulgated by the Association (see Box A.1).[5] This is the most comprehensive and practical code known to us and we recommend that it be adhered to by all odonatologists.

....

WDA CODE OF PRACTICE FOR COLLECTING DRAGONFLIES

Principle 1. To respect life, in the form of species, communities and habitats.

1.1. Unless needed for education or scientific research, no larval or adult dragonfly should be killed, either as a sequel to capture or through habitat destruction. Of these two types of intervention, the second is by far the more serious as a threat to the continuity of dragonfly populations.

1.2. Live dragonflies should only be held captive for good scientific reasons, under conditions that do not expose them to avoidable stress, and for no longer than necessary.

1.3. Specimens of dragonflies that have been collected should not be offered for sale.

1.4. Recognising that sometimes scientific study will require a series of specimens to be secured, no more specimens should be collected than are needed. The collector should always exercise discrimination and restraint and proceed in a spirit consistent with the principles espoused in the Code.

1.5. The habitat in which specimens are being collected should be damaged as little as possible.

1.6. Specimens of one species should not be collected in large numbers from the same locality in the same season.

Principle 2. To comply with existing regulations.

2.1. Before any dragonfly is collected, or collected material exported from its country of origin, all existing, relevant regulations, including the common law of the country, should have been complied with. Such regulations may include permission to enter land, to collect certain species, to collect biological material of any kind, and to export or retain it. It is recognised that an unexpected encounter may sometimes require an odonatologist to secure, and perhaps retain, a dragonfly without having obtained the requisite permission beforehand. In such an event, it is assumed that, if the specimen is collected in a place where restrictions are known to apply (e.g. a nature reserve), the appropriate authorities will be informed soon afterwards.

2.2. When the collecting site is a nature reserve or a site of known interest to conservationists, a list of species collected should be supplied in due course to the owner or managing authority, whether or not to do so is a requirement when permission is granted.

Principle 3. To respect the need for scientific rigour.
3.1 Sometimes larval or adult dragonflies have to be collected and preserved as voucher specimens in order to further odonatology through education and scientific research, including the validation of scientific identity. Sound taxonomy is central to odonatology and sound taxonomy almost invariably depends on the existence of properly annotated material. All voucher specimens should be adequately preserved and labelled, and thereafter properly curated. Where feasible, and in due course, they should be deposited in a suitable museum or institution or, if retained in a private working collection, their whereabouts should be made known to odonatologists generally.

Principle 4. To show, and expect to receive, tolerance of differing attitudes towards collecting biological material.
4.1. If a WDA member who is collecting in compliance with this Code encounters overt disapproval from anyone at the collecting site, that member should respond to that disapproval by explaining the need for voucher material and by citing the authority that legitimises the action of trying to obtain it.
4.2. It is recommended that WDA members conduct their activities in a manner consistent with this Code, and, at their discretion, report to the WDA Board any activity inconsistent with the Code. WDA unequivocally endorses the need to collect voucher specimens of dragonflies for the furtherance of odonatology through scientific research. WDA unequivocally deplores the behaviour of anyone who tries to obstruct, intimidate or slander anyone trying to collect dragonflies while complying with this WDA Code of Practice.

[Version of February 2002, revised October 2004.]

PHOTOGRAPHING

Settled dragonflies make rewarding subjects for colour photography. Guidelines for appropriate equipment and procedures are given by Robert Thompson and Dagmar Hilfert-Rüppell and Georg Rüppell.[6] An exciting, recent development has been the use of the auto-focus device which, coupled with a digital camera, makes it possible to take repeated images of a flying dragonfly at little cost, thus greatly increasing the likelihood of obtaining a crisp image of a dragonfly in flight.[7] Several of the plates in this book, taken by Steve Cham, are products of this innovative approach.

VOUCHER SPECIMENS

It is a fundamental tenet of the scientific method, including odonatology, that opportunity should exist for observations to be verified by an independent investigator. Sometimes this is possible only if vouchers are available for scrutiny, a need addressed by clause 3.1 in the WDA Code. Fortunately it is not always necessary that a voucher be retained in order to be confident of a diagnosis. Sometimes the use of close-focus binoculars or a photograph may suffice, or the close examination of an adult specimen in the hand, preferably using a magnifying glass and a modern field guide, for example when distinguishing species of *Erythromma*, *Lestes* and some species of Coenagrionidae. However, there are other instances when a voucher will need to be retained, as the following examples illustrate. *Anax ephippiger* and *A. parthenope*, two aeshnids that sometimes visit Britain, resemble each other in flight and are extremely difficult to photograph. In the absence of vouchers, we suspect that British records of *A. ephippiger*, which were fairly frequent before the 1990s, may represent *A. parthenope*. Since *A. parthenope* was first recorded in Britain (in 1996) there have been few (if any) substantiated records of *A. ephippiger* but regular (annual) records of *A. parthenope*. Another, confirmed example of the need for a voucher is the specimen of an adult *Sympetrum* from Dawlish, Devon, originally identified (by an experienced odonatologist) as *S. meridionale*, but much later found to be *S. striolatum*.[8] Sometimes exotic Odonata appear in Britain, probably having been imported as eggs on water weeds flown in to Britain for the aquarist trade.[9] One such species is the widespread Palaearctic and tropical libellulid *Crocothemis servilia*. We know of no way of reliably distinguishing this species from the Eurasian *C. erythraea* without recourse to a powerful magnifying glass or a microscope.[10] Yet *C. erythraea* is now being reported from Britain,[11] often without vouchers being retained to enable identifications to be checked. In 1998 the North American aeshnid, *Anax junius*, known as the Green Darner, an habitual migrant in the New World, was sighted several times in Cornwall and the Isles of Scilly, but no vouchers were retained.[12] So The Natural History Museum, London, was deprived of a specimen. This was especially unfortunate, partly because this was the first recorded case of a transatlantic passage by a North American dragonfly, and partly because the external diagnostic characters of this species are very variable, sometimes closely resembling those of *Anax imperator*.[13] Indeed it appears that *A. junius* may have reached Europe before the first recorded sighting in September 1998: in 1989 an undated observation was reported of a species of *Anax* (recorded as *A. imperator*) ovipositing in tandem near the Atlantic coast of France.[14] Such behaviour is rarely or never exhibited by *A. imperator*, but is commonplace in *A. junius*. Again no voucher was retained. In retrospect it seems highly likely that the tandem pair seen on that occasion was *A. junius*,[15] but of course we shall never know!

We recognise that opinions differ regarding the propriety of collecting dragonflies. However, there is no doubt that the interests of odonatology and nature conservation sometimes require that a voucher be secured and retained. Odonatology will suffer serious and lasting damage unless this fact is acknowledged, with a good grace, by people who prefer not to collect dragonflies. If and when conflicts arise there is a consensus among active odonatologists (and ornithologists) that the way forward must be through civilised dialogue based on mutual understanding and respect for differing points of view.[12] It would be tragic if unity of purpose among odonatologists and conservationists were to be jeopardised by a failure to acknowledge the imperatives of good science. We believe that the WDA Code offers sound guidelines for achieving the necessary compromise and understanding. In the few notorious cases when an odonatologist has been obstructed or abused for trying to secure a voucher[12] such behaviour has been denounced by some institutions that feel responsible for the conduct of their members.[16]

We are left with three conclusions:

1) sometimes a voucher must be secured;
2) in such a case the decision to secure a voucher must be made by an experienced odonatologist who should stand ready to explain on request why a voucher is needed; and

3) any attempt to obstruct or abuse an odonatologist trying to secure a voucher should be denounced publicly and promptly by institutions responsible for the integrity and conduct of the relevant branches of science.

Although we unreservedly endorse the principle that dragonflies (and other animals) should never be killed needlessly, we think it appropriate to emphasise (when the collection of vouchers is at issue) that, in general, populations of dragonflies are extremely unlikely to be endangered by the removal of one or two individuals. This is partly because populations are often deceptively large: David Thompson was surprised to discover that at two fen sites the annual population of adult *Coenagrion mercuriale* was close to 40,000 individuals, peaking at 5,000 to 6,000 a day;[17] also, as mentioned in the WDA Code (clause 1.1), the most severe and widespread threat to dragonfly populations results from habitat destruction caused by human activities. The latter is best constrained by habitat conservation for which a biological survey (which often requires vouchers) is a *sine qua non*.

One final point should be made. Anyone obtaining a voucher should be mindful of clause 3.1 of the WDA Code which stipulates that a voucher should be deposited in a place which is made known and where it can be available for scrutiny by other investigators. So collectors need to make appropriate arrangements. An obvious depository will always be an entomological museum, but this may not always be feasible in future as such museums reach their limits for further acquisitions. If the collector retains a voucher in a private working collection, the collection's contents and whereabouts should be made known through conventional channels.

When a faunistic or ecological survey is being undertaken and in other cases when an accurate identification of a dragonfly is essential, the retention of a voucher should be the rule and not (as now) the exception. Organisations dispensing grants for research and biodiversity surveys should be aware of this requirement. Under the auspices of the Biological Survey of Canada (Terrestrial Arthropods) comprehensive guidelines have been published for obtaining vouchers, and attention drawn to the pitfalls of failing to do so, when conducting systematic, faunistic and ecological research.[18]

SSSI Criteria Based on Odonata

The following guidelines have been reproduced with permission of the Joint Nature Conservation Committee. They are accessible via the JNCC website (http://www.jncc.gov.uk/page-2303). The guidelines were first drawn up in 1989 and are currently under revision in the light of changes in the known distribution and status of the British species. However, we reproduce them here to illustrate the method by which Sites of Special Scientific Interest (SSSIs) are selected on the basis of their dragonfly fauna. Although *Gomphus vulgatissimus* is listed as endangered in Europe, distributional evidence does not support this[1].

1. INTRODUCTION

A list of 15 resident species, ranging from the endangered to the scarce, has been selected as deserving individual representation in site selection. The remaining more widespread species are to be represented according to outstanding assemblages. Despite the fact that Scotland has a few species which are absent from England and Wales, dragonflies decrease in numbers of species with distance north in Britain, so allowance has to be made for this trend in site evaluation.

2. SSSI SELECTION REQUIREMENTS FOR INDIVIDUAL SPECIES OF DRAGONFLIES

2.1. Nationally rare and scarce species
Site selection should cover the following individual species

2.1.1. Believed extinct in Great Britain (Red Data Book category 1+).[2]

Oxygastra curtisii
Coenagrion armatum   } If rediscovered, all sites qualify for selection
C. scitulum

2.1.2. Endangered in Great Britain (Red Data Book category 1)
Aeshna isosceles   All sites qualify for selection
(listed in Schedule 5 of the Wildlife and Countryside Act 1981)

2.1.3. Vulnerable in Great Britain (Red Data Book category 2)
Coenagrion hastulatum
Lestes dryas   } Use guidelines under 2.2

2.1.4. Rare in Great Britain (Red Data Book category 3)
Somatochlora arctica
Libellula fulva   } Use guidelines under 2.2
Coenagrion mercuriale   Internationally endangered (see 2.1.6 and 2.2)

2.1.5. Nationally scarce (known or presumed to occur in 16–100 10-km squares in Great Britain, but not Red Data Book species)
Aeshna caerulea
Brachytron pratense
Coenagrion pulchellum
Cordulia aenea
Ischnura pumilio   } Use guidelines under 2.2
Leucorrhinia dubia
Somatochlora metallica
Ceriagrion tenellum
Gomphus vulgatissimus

2.1.6. Threatened in Europe and breeding in Britain.[3]
Coenagrion mercuriale
(endangered in Europe)
Gomphus vulgatissimus   } Use guidelines under 2.2
(endangered in Europe)

2.2. Guidelines for selection of sites for nationally rare and scarce species
2.2.1. The aim should be adequately to conserve strong populations of all nationally rare and scarce species present within each area of search (AOS). The

number of sites chosen for each species will vary, but sites containing combinations of species are especially valuable.

2.2.2. A single internationally threatened, Red Data Book category 2 or 3 or nationally scarce species qualifies a site for selection if it contains:

a) the largest or only population of this species in the AOS;
b) a strong population of the species on a site which, although a good example of a habitat type, has not already been selected;
c) a strong population of the species in an AOS supporting a substantial proportion of localities for the species; or
d) a strong population on the edge of the species' geographical range.

3. Outstanding assemblages

3.1. The map (Fig. A.1) shows total numbers of all dragonfly species regarded as outstanding assemblages in different parts of Britain. All sites which reach or exceed the relevant qualifying number should be considered for selection.

4. Further guidelines for site selection

4.1. All records should be within three years of the selection date. Only confirmed breeding records should be considered. Transient populations should not be considered.

4.2. If possible, every breeding species firmly established within the AOS should be present in at least one SSSI.

4.3. In the definition of site boundaries, semi-natural terrestrial habitats used for feeding and resting should be included, as well as the breeding sites themselves. It may also be necessary to include part of the catchment in order to protect water quality or quantity.

Crown Copyright reserved.

FIG A1. Total numbers of dragonfly species regarded as outstanding assemblages in different parts of Britain. (Note that the total number of species in Shetland is too small for this concept to be valid.)

APPENDIX 4

Distribution Maps for British Species

Notes

Red squares denote 1975–90 records and overlay all other records. Presence of red squares implies stable populations.

Orange squares denote 1700–1974 records and are overlain by any records from 1991–2005. Presence of orange squares implies range contraction, usually as a result of habitat degradation.

Yellow squares denote new locality records from 1991–2006. Presence of yellow squares implies range expansion. A response to climate change would typically be indicated by a preponderance of yellow squares at the northern or western edge of the range. A response to water quality improvements in riverine species is likely to be indicated by linear expansion of yellow squares or intra-range infilling.

Post-1990 records from Ireland are not available at the time of writing (except *A. mixta, A. cyanea, A. imperator* and *S. fonscolombii*).[1]

The maps are derived from the NBN Gateway and are reproduced with permission, and are arranged in alphabetical order of genus and species.

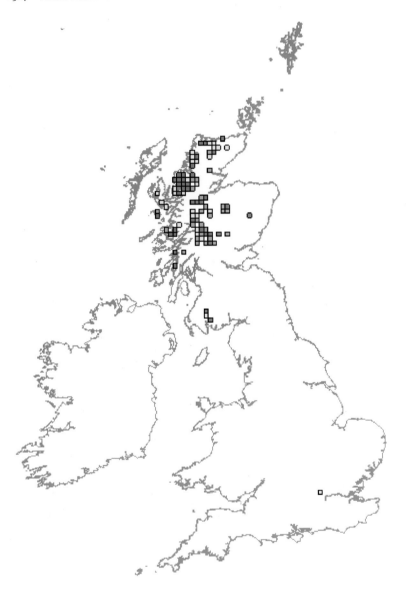

Aeshna caerulea. Records in England and Wales are dubious. Evidence of some range contraction in central Highlands and range expansion in western Highlands, but this could reflect differences in recorder effort.

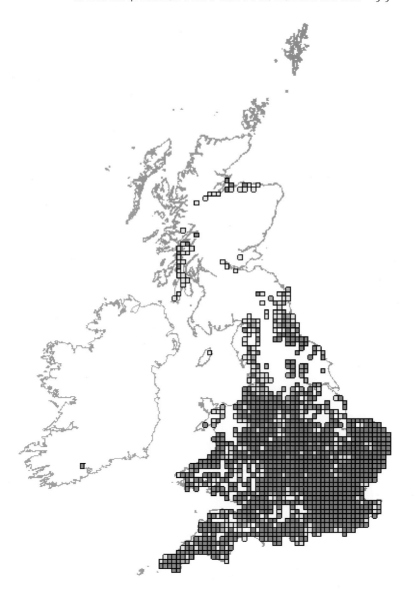

A. *cyanea*. Evidence for recent range expansion in northern England and Scotland which may be in response to climate change.

A. *grandis.* Possible range contraction in northern England. New Scottish records.

A. *isosceles*. Range contraction in eastern fens. Some evidence for recent expansion into Suffolk and Lincolnshire.

A. juncea. Population appears stable. New Scottish records may reflect increased recorder effort.

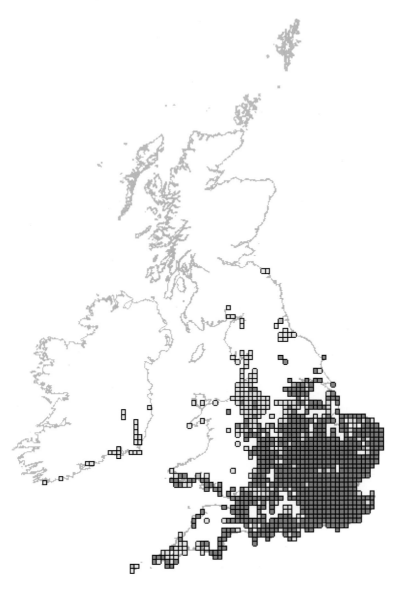

A. mixta. Evidence for recent westward and northward range expansion which may be in response to climate change.

Anax ephippiger. There are surprisingly few post-1991 records of this species considering the increase in the number of records of other migrant species over this period.

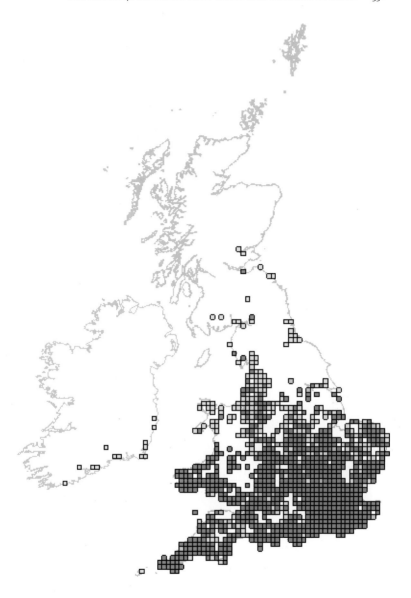

A. imperator. Evidence for recent northward range expansion which may be in response to climate change.

A. junius. Recent migrant.

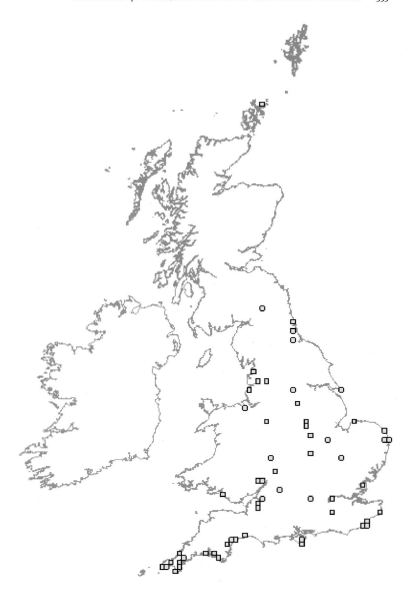

A. parthenope. Recent migrant.

Brachytron pratense. Evidence for pre-1974 range contraction in eastern English Midlands, but there is now an apparent reversal in this trend and recent records suggest the species is recolonising this area, possibly as a result of improvements in water quality.

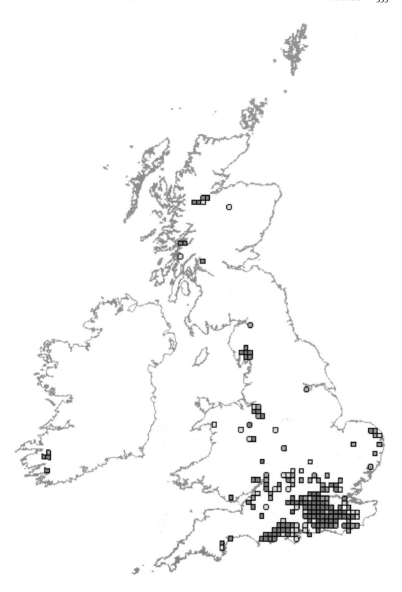

Cordulia aenea. The species appears to have been lost from several localities prior to 1974 but this trend appears to have been balanced to some extent by some recent records from new localities.

Coenagrion armatum. Extinct in Britain.

C. hastulatum. Population appears stable.

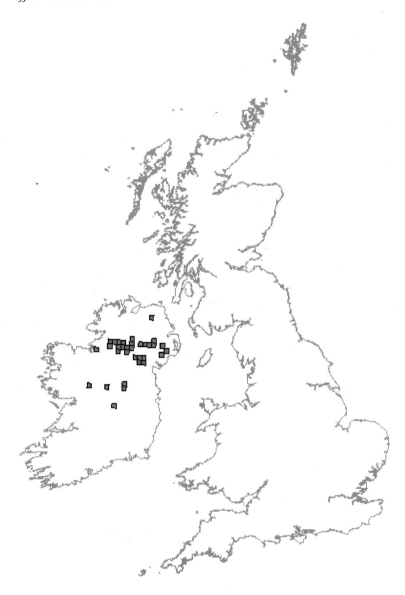

C. lunulatum. Recent records from Ireland are not included.

C. mercuriale. Some evidence for pre-1974 range contraction. Recent records from new localities in Devon. Recent survey work suggests the species has been lost from west Wales and from some sites in the New Forest, and is declining in the Gower Peninsula (see p.300).

C. puella. Possible recent range expansion in Scotland, although this may reflect changes in recorder effort.

C. pulchellum. Evidence for pre-1974 range contraction.

C. scitulum. Species extinct in Britain.

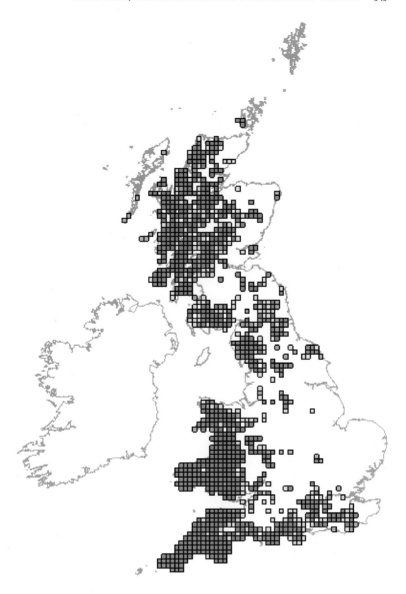

Cordulegaster boltonii. Population appears stable.

Crocothemis erythraea. Recent migrant.

Calopteryx splendens. Evidence for recent northward range expansion, which may be in response to climate change, but recent records from throughout its range may be in response to improvements in water quality.

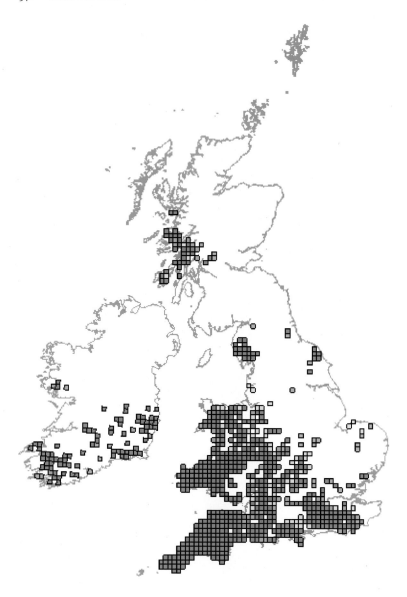

C. virgo. Evidence for pre-1974 range contraction especially in eastern England; some indication of expansion throughout range possibly in response to improvements in water quality and river management.

Ceriagrion tenellum. Evidence for pre-1974 range contraction especially in the eastern part of the species range.

Enallagma cyathigerum. Population appears stable. Recent records, especially those from Scotland, probably reflect changes in recorder effort.

Erythromma najas. There has been a recent increase in the number of records from eastern England.

E. viridulum. In this map red squares denote records from 1999–2001, orange squares are new locality records from 2002–3 and yellow squares denote new locality records from 2004–6. The species appears to be rapidly colonising England and spreading westwards from its original points of entry.

Gomphus vulgatissimus. Post-1991 records suggest a response to improvements in water quality.

Ischnura elegans. Population appears stable.

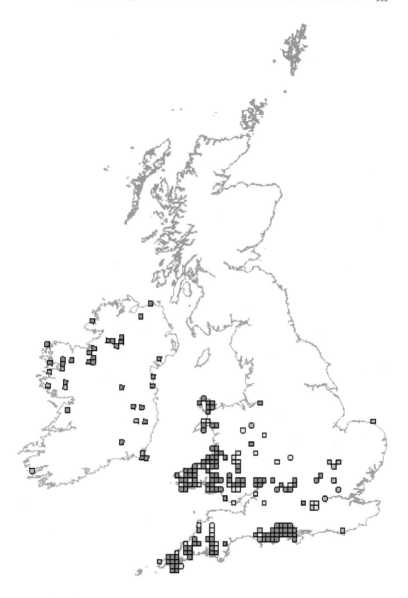

I. pumilio. The species appears to have suffered a pre-1974 range contraction in eastern England, but other sites appear to have been colonised more recently. This probably reflects the ruderal habits of this species.

Lestes barbarus. The species is a recent colonist.

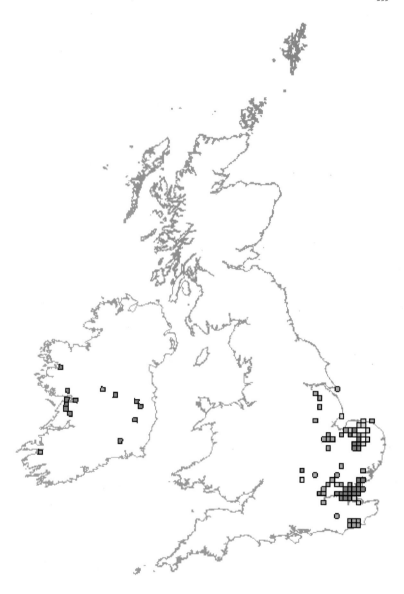

L. dryas. Evidence for a serious pre-1974 range contraction from which the population has not recovered except perhaps in northern Norfolk.

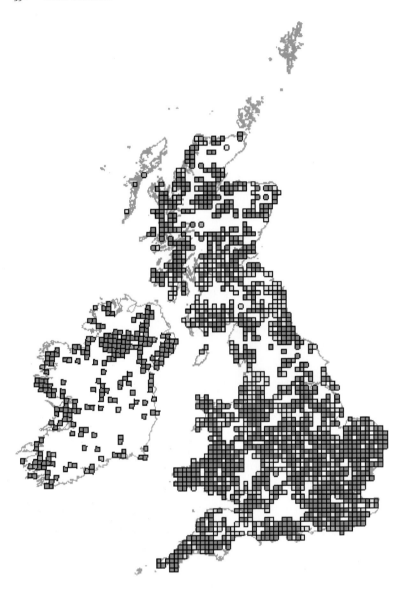

L. sponsa. Large increase in the number of localities that the species has been recorded in since 1991, especially in southern Scotland.

Libellula depressa. The species appears to have been expanding its range northwards in recent years which may be in response to climate change.

L. fulva. Increase in post-1991 records from new localities may be in response to improvements in water quality; however, the species has not recolonised sites in the Norfolk Broads from which it was recorded before 1974.

L. quadrimaculata. There seems to have been a considerable increase in the number of localities that this species has been recorded in since 1991, especially in Scotland and eastern and central England.

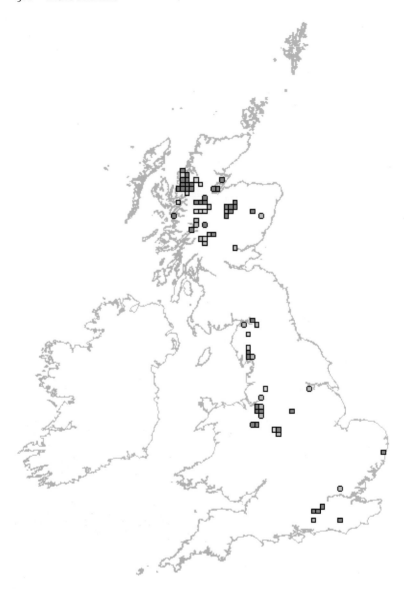

Leucorrhinia dubia. Southern edge of species range may be contracting northwards, possibly in response to climate change. New records from Scotland may reflect changes in recorder effort.

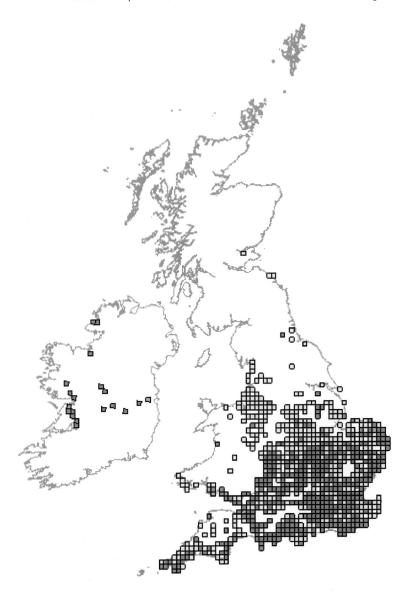

Orthetrum cancellatum. Evidence for a northwards and westwards range expansion consistent with a response to climate change.

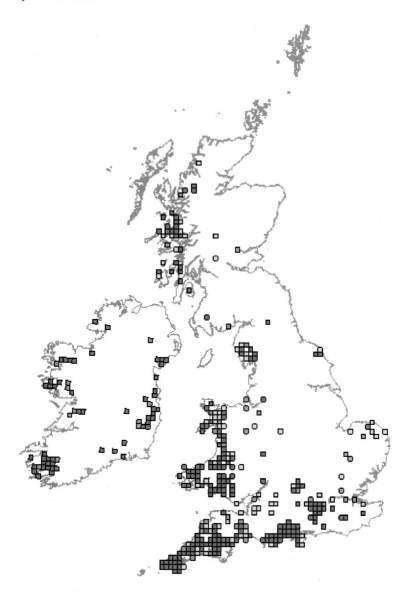

O. coerulescens. In most parts of its range the population appears stable, but there is evidence for expansion in the Somerset Levels and Norfolk Broads, possibly in response to improvements in habitat quality.

Oxygastra curtisii. Extinct in Britain.

Pyrrhosoma nymphula. Population apparently stable.

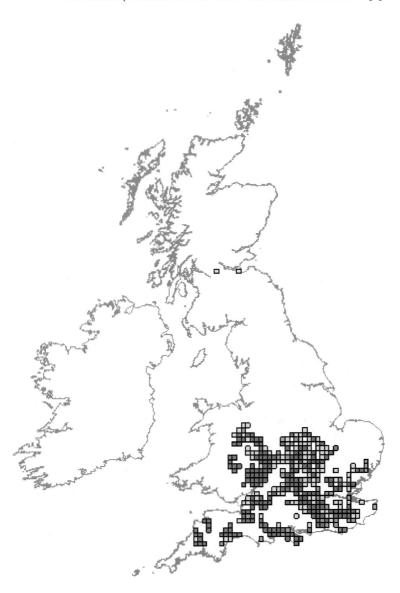

Platycnemis pennipes. Recent increase in localities, probably in response to improvements in water quality.

Somatochlora arctica. Apparent recent increase in localities may reflect changes in recorder effort.

S. metallica. Population apparently stable, except in southwest Scotland where local expansion apparent.

Sympetrum danae. Recent new records in coastal localities in southern and eastern England may be as a result of migrants arriving from continental Europe.

S. flaveolum. Large recent increase in sightings probably in response to climate change (migratory species).

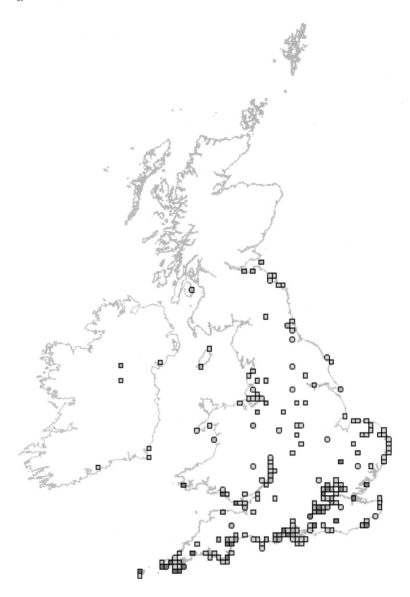

S. fonscolombii. Large recent increase in sightings probably in response to climate change (migratory species).

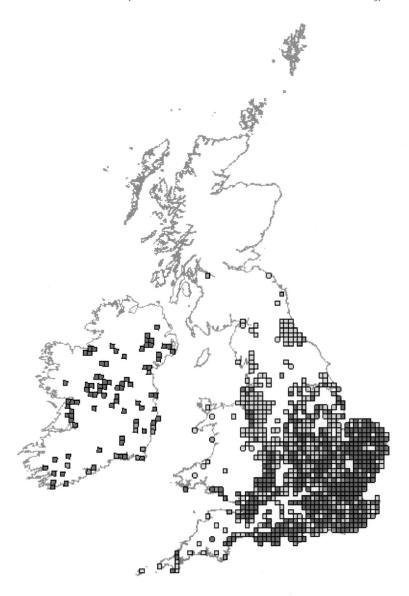

S. sanguineum. Recent increase in northern and western records probably reflects response to climate change.

S. striolatum. Recent increase in new locality records from southern and eastern Scotland probably reflects response to climate change. Populations in northwest Scotland are predominantly *S. striolatum* f. *nigrescens* which is cold adapted.

Glossary

Definitions refer to usage in this book. Terms included within a definition and that occur elsewhere in the glossary are italicised where to do so may assist comprehension.

accompanying behaviour A foraging strategy of adult dragonflies that entails accompanying large, slowly moving objects over grassland.

acute zone Area in *compound eye* having interommatidial angles less then 0.2 degrees; also termed a fovea.

aedeagus Tip of penis.

aestivation Summer *diapause*.

alpha male Territorial male who is dominant at the time of day when most receptive females arrive at the *rendezvous*.

anal pyramid The sharp, triangular projection at the posterior tip of the abdomen of anisopteran larvae made up of the *epiproct* and two *paraprocts*.

andromorph Colour form of female resembling the male

anterior pole The end of the egg that contains the *micropyles* (through which sperm enter), through which the *prolarva* issues and which faces the outside of the substrate enclosing eggs laid *endophytically*.

apolysis Separation of the new from the old *cuticle* before *ecdysis*; after apolysis but before ecdysis the developmental stage is termed *pharate*.

arthropod A jointed-limbed animal that possesses a hard exoskeleton.

assimilation efficiency (AE) Measure expressed (as a percentage) as 1 − (dry weight of faeces produced)/(dry weight of food consumed).

autotomy Voluntary severance by an animal of part of its own body.

bank lurker A non-territorial male who intercepts females as they fly near the water.

batch Pertaining to eggs. See *clutch*.

biochemical oxygen demand Measure of the deoxygenating ability of a sample of water.

biological control (biocontrol) Suppression of a pest organism or the reduction of the damage it causes (to a level considered acceptable to humans) by manipulating the pest's predators, parasites, *parasitoids* or pathogens.

biological productivity Total mass of organic material manufactured by organism or ecosystem during a specified time.

biomass Weight of living material, usually expressed as dry weight, carbon, nitrogen or calorific content, in all or part of an organism, population or community.

biota A characteristic association of animals and plants.

biotope Local area containing a *biota*.

blastokinesis Revolution of the embryo within the egg during embryogenesis; equivalent to katatrepsis.

BOD *Biochemical oxygen demand.*

bout Applied to oviposition, a spell of uninterrupted egg laying during an *episode* that may include several bouts, each separated by perching.

branchial basket Complex of gills lining the inner wall of the rectum of Anisoptera.

burrower Dragonfly larva that normally rests with all or almost all of the body hidden within sediment.

bursa copulatrix Part of the female *genitalia* that receives and stores sperm after insemination.

carrying capacity Maximum number of organisms (of a given species) that a habitat can sustain.

caudal appendages *Epiproct* and *paraprocts* arising from abdominal segment 11 or its vestiges.

caudal lamellae Flattened, leaf-like *caudal appendages* of Zygoptera that are used for respiration and swimming.

chitin The tough, horny, nitrogenous polysaccharide that makes up the bulk of the insect cuticle.

circadian rhythm Periodically repeated fluctuation (with a period close to 24 hours) maintained by an innate time-measuring sense; sometimes termed the 'biological clock'.

clasper Dragonfly larva that at rest uses the legs to hold the body tightly against a support, usually a stem or a branch.

clutch Complement of *oocytes* that mature together to produce a *batch* of eggs which are typically laid during an *episode*.

cohort Members of a generation that share a time (usually a year) of hatching or emergence.

commensal An organism that benefits from its association with its host but does not impose a cost on it.

compound eye The typical eye of insects (very well developed in dragonflies) comprising many, separate, hexagonal units (*facets*), each with its own lens and efferent nerve, which together contribute to a composite image.

congeneric Belonging to the same genus.

conspecific Belonging to the same species.

courtship Behavioural interaction between a male and a female that facilitates copulation; refers especially to displays by males.

crepuscular Active during twilight.

crypsis Aspect of the appearance (usually coloration, pattern or posture) of an organism that renders it inconspicuous.

cuticle Non-cellular outer layer of the body wall of an insect covering the epidermis.

damselfly Dragonfly of the suborder Zygoptera.

definitive host Pertaining to a parasite, the *host* in which reproduction takes place.

diapause State of suspended or retarded development that may supervene at some stage or stages in the life cycle and that typically constitutes an anticipatory response to conditions unfavourable for uninterrupted development. See *dormancy*.

diel Pertaining to the 24-hour period; the 24-hour period.

dispersal Spatial displacement by individuals (usually adults) that, being centrifugal, causes them to become farther apart. See *migration*.

diurnal Pertaining to the light period during the *diel*.

divided emergence Separation of a *diel* emergence cohort into two instalments by the advent of low temperature during stage 1 of emergence.

dormancy Reduction in activity or metabolism in direct response to conditions unfavourable for uninterrupted development.

dorsal Pertaining to the back or upperside of an animal.

dragonfly Member of the order Odonata.

ecdysis (plural **ecdyses**) Moulting; the shedding of the outer skin.

eclosion Moulting or issuing from the egg.

ecological energetics The study of the energy transformations that occur within *ecosystems*.

ecosystem Natural unit consisting of living and nonliving parts that interact to form a stable system.

ectotherm Animal that regulates its body temperature by gaining (or losing) heat from its environment.

embryogenesis The development of the embryo.

emergence *Ecdysis* from larva to adult; the final moult.

emergence curve Curve describing the seasonal pattern of *emergence*, usually on a cumulative basis. The notation EM_{50} denotes the time at which 50 per cent of the annual population has emerged.

endemic Restricted to a particular geographic region.

endocuticle Thick, colourless, elastic, innermost layer of *cuticle*. See *epi-* and *exocuticle*.

endophytic Pertaining to *oviposition* into a substrate, usually plant tissue. See *epiphytic* and *exophytic*.

endotherm Animal that regulates its body temperature by generating heat within the body by its own activity.

energy budget An inventory for an individual or population showing the balance between energy acquisition and expenditure.

epibiont Organism attached to the outside of the body of a carrier organism.

epicuticle Very thin, refractile membrane, at most a few micrometres thick, forming the outer layer of the *cuticle*. See *endo-* and *exocuticle*.

epiphytic Pertaining to oviposition when eggs are placed on, and usually adhere to, the surface of a substrate, typically a plant. See *endophytic* and *exophytic*.

epiproct Middle, dorsal, backwardly pointing, appendage thought to be a vestige of the 11th abdominal segment; it is sharp and robust in anisopteran larvae.

episode Applied to *oviposition*, a single visit to the oviposition site during which egg laying may occur in several *bouts*, each separated by perching.

eurytopic Able to tolerate a wide range of environmental conditions.

eutrophic Possessing abundant, sometimes excessive, nutrients; usually applied to aquatic habitats. See *mesotrophic* and *oligotrophic*.

evolution Cumulative, heritable change in the organisms in a population.

exocuticle Rigid layer, usually amber-coloured, between the *endocuticle* and *epicuticle*.

exophytic Pertaining to *oviposition* when eggs are dropped, or washed, from the abdomen without being placed into or directly onto a substrate. See *endophytic* and *epiphytic*.

Exopterygota Insects (including dragonflies) in which the wings develop externally during the later larval *stadia* and which lack a pupal stage.

exploitation competition Competition between coexisting individuals (of the same or different species) that entails use of the same resource.

exuvia (plural **exuviae**) Outer skin(s) shed at the end of each *stadium*.

F-0 Last larval *stadium*. Compare **F-1, F-2** etc., denoting the penultimate and antepenultimate larval stadia.

facet See *ommatidium*.

facultative Optional; contingent on external stimuli. See *obligate*.

fecundity Number of fertilised eggs laid by a female during her lifetime.

feeding Behaviour that follows prey capture; handling and ingestion (the predatory sequence). See *foraging*.

fitness The relative ability of an organism to transmit its genes to the next generation.

flier Dragonfly that, when active at the *rendezvous*, typically remains on the wing except for brief interludes of perching. See *percher*.

flying season Period of the year during which reproductively mature adults are active.

foraging Behaviour that increases the likelihood of prey capture. See *feeding*.

frons Anterior-facing plate on the upper surface of the head between the *compound eyes*.

gamont Immature sexual form of gregarine Protozoa.

genitalia External reproductive organs.

gonad Organ in which gametes are produced; a *testis* or *ovary*.

growing-degree day Day when the ambient temperature has exceeded the lower threshold permitting growth.

growth ratio Proportionate change in size of a specified part of the body between one *stadium* and the next.

guarding Behaviour of male adult when escorting a female, usually his recent copulation partner, and usually while she is *ovipositing*. He may be attached to her (in contact guarding) or unattached, flying close to her (in non-contact guarding).

habitat Place where a given species or community lives.

habitat selection The process by which an organism exercises a preference for one type of *habitat*.

haemolymph Internal circulatory fluid conveying nutrients and hormones around the body.

handling time Interval, beginning with prey pursuit, during which a predator is sufficiently preoccupied with its current prey that it cannot resume searching.

hanging type A type of emergence in which, during the resting stage, the angle between the anterior part of the body and the horizontal is 90–180°.

head-arrester system Fields of hair-like structures on the back of the head and on the neck which help to stabilise the dragonfly in flight.

heterothermy A type of thermoregulation that combines methods used by an *ectotherm* and an *endotherm*.

hibernation Suspension of development during winter.

hider Dragonfly larva that rests beneath a thin layer of detritus or leaf litter.

highest steady density (**HSD**) Equilibrium number of sexually active males in a given area of the *rendezvous* resulting from intramale interaction.

host An organism attacked by a *parasite, parasitoid* or *pathogen.*

hyperparasite *Parasite* that parasitises another parasite.

hyperparasitoid *Parasitoid* that lives at the expense of another parasitoid.

imago (plural **imagines**) The adult stage of an insect.

in copula In the wheel, or mating, position.

inclusive fitness The extent to which (all factors considered) an animal contributes genetical material to its descendants.

insect An arthropod in which the body is typically divided into three regions: head, thorax and abdomen.

insolation Exposure to the sun's rays.

instar Interval between two *apolyses.* See *stadium.*

interference competition Competition between coexisting individuals (of the same or different species) that entails direct interaction, including predation.

interspecific Between species.

intramale sperm translocation (IST) Transfer by a male of sperm from his primary gonopore to his secondary genitalia.

intra-odonate predation Predation by one species of dragonfly on the same or another species of dragonfly; when the predation is intraspecific it is termed 'cannibalism'.

intraspecific Within a species.

invertebrate Animal lacking a vertebral column; a non-chordate metazoan.

Joule Unit of work performed or energy consumed.

K strategist Organism that produces few offspring and contributes to a population that stays close to the species' *carrying capacity.*

katatrepsis Revolution of the embryo during *embryogenesis.*

labial suture Hinged joint of the larval *labium* situated between the *pre-* and *postmentum.*

labium Fused second maxillae, specialised in the dragonfly larva to form a prehensile organ that can be extended during prey capture.

larva Developmental stage between egg and adult. The term 'nymph' has sometimes been used instead of *larva.* It is ambiguous, having been used at different times to denote (1) the larva of an *exopterygote* insect; (2) the last larval stadium of such an insect when the wing sheaths are prominent; and (3) the pupa of an *endopterygote* insect. The term 'nymph' is not needed in reference to the Odonata.

latency habitat For a *metapopulation* of a given species, the suboptimal *habitat* type serving as a habitat reserve where mainly larvae, rarely F-0 *exuviae,* and almost no adults are found, and where a population cannot normally survive for more than one generation without immigration. See *secondary habitat* and *stem habitat.*

lentic Pertaining to standing water.

lifetime reproductive success (LRS) The survival of progeny of an individual.

littoral Pertaining to the marginal strip of relatively shallow water in which rooted *macrophytes* can grow.

localisation Behavioural sequence of the adult by which *site attachment* develops.

lotic Pertaining to flowing water.

macrophyte Macroscopic, multicellular, water plant at least part of which is submerged.

maiden flight Flight or succession of flights that take a *teneral* adult from the emergence site to the place of first protracted rest or the place from which flight is no longer oriented away from the emergence site.

mating success Number of copulations achieved by an individual during a lifetime.

mating system General behavioural strategy employed when obtaining mates.

maturation period See *prereproductive period*.

melanic Darkened by black cuticular pigments.

mesotrophic Pertaining to an aquatic habitat having an intermediate nutrient content. See *eutrophic* and *oligotrophic*.

metamorphosis Irreversible changes in morphology, physiology and behaviour that take place during the transition from the F-0 *stadium* to the adult.

metapopulation Population of a species that has components coexisting in, and exchanging individuals among, *habitat* types offering different opportunities for reproduction and larval survival. See *latency habitat*, *secondary habitat* and *stem habitat*.

microhabitat Particular part of a *habitat* in which an individual is normally found during a specified stage of its life cycle or when performing a specified activity.

micropyle Conical or nipple-like projection at the anterior pole of the egg through which sperm travels when entering the egg.

microtrichia Minute hair-like *setae* on an external body surface, e.g. the wing.

migration Spatial displacement that entails part or all of a population leaving the *habitat* where emergence took place and moving to a different habitat where reproduction ensues; migration may be *obligate* or *facultative*, and migrating adults may or may not travel in aggregations. See *dispersal*.

moult Process of shedding the cuticle; *ecdysis*.

natural selection Elimination of an inferior genetic trait from a population through differential survival and reproduction of individuals bearing that trait. Widely regarded as the main mechanism giving rise to evolution. See *sexual selection*.

niche Functional role and position of an organism in an *ecosystem*.

non-trivial flight Type of spatial displacement which, in contrast to *trivial flight*, is characterised by relatively protracted, long-range, persistent, non-appetitive movement (e.g. migration).

nymphochrysalis An aquatic developmental stage of a hydracarine mite immediately after it has dropped off the dragonfly *host*.

obelisk posture Position adopted by a *percher*, usually when the sun is at the zenith, such that the abdomen points towards the sun and the body's shadow is minimised.

obligate Invariable. See *facultative*.

oligotrophic Pertaining to a body of extremely clear water having a low nutrient content and low productivity. See *eutrophic* and *mesotrophic*.

ommatidium (plural **ommatidia**) A single optical unit of the *compound eye*; each ommatidium is a cone-shaped structure comprising a lens, a crystalline cone and light-sensitive retinulae; also called a facet.

ontogeny Development of the individual from the fertilised egg to adulthood.

operational sex ratio The proportion of males and females active at the *rendezvous*.

optimal foraging theory Proposition that fitness is likely to be enhanced by foraging strategies that increase the net rate of energy or nutrient intake.

oviposition Act of laying eggs.
ovipositor The egg-laying apparatus of the female.

paraprocts Three robust, backwardly directed appendages, on *larva* and adult, arising from abdominal segment 10.
parasitism Interaction between members of two species in which one (typically small) species, the *parasite*, lives in or on the other species, the *host*, from which it obtains benefit (e.g. food or shelter) at the host's expense; the host is not necessarily killed by the interaction. See *parasitoid*.
parasitoid Parasite that invariably kills its *host* and so in this respect resembles a predator.
parthenogenesis Development of an egg without fertilisation.
partivoltine Completing a generation in more than two years.
percher Dragonfly that, when active at the *rendezvous*, typically remains on a perch from which it makes brief flights.
pharate Condition in which, before *ecdysis*, the outer and inner layers of the *cuticle* have become separated. See *apolysis*.
phenology The study of life cycles and seasonal distribution.
philopatry Tendency of an adult, after maturation, to return to the water body whence it emerged.
phoresy (is) Interaction during which one species is carried on the outside of the body of another species without being parasitic on it.
postmentum Unpaired part of the larval *labium* proximal to the *labial suture*.
prementum Unpaired part of the larval *labium* distal to the *labial suture*; it bears the paired palpal setae.
prereproductive period Phase of adult life, including the *teneral* stage, that precedes the attainment of reproductive maturity and therefore the *flying season*.
prolarva First, often very abbreviated, larval *stadium*.
prothorax The most anterior thoracic segment; the one lacking wings.
proximate cues Attributes of their external environment to which individuals respond positively when behaving in a specific way.
pruinescence Bloom on body surface of adults, more often males, caused by supracuticular pigment that typically strongly reflects ultraviolet light.
pseudopterostigma Counterpart of *pterostigma*, though less robust or well defined, as found in Calopterygidae.
pterostigma Pigmented 'cell' near the distal end of the leading edge of the fore and hind wings of almost all species.
pursuer A non-territorial male who pursues females for up to 50 metres.

reflex immobilisation Antipredation behaviour, of larva or adult, characterised by persistent immobility; also termed 'death feigning' or '*thanatosis*'.
rendezvous Venue where males and females meet as a direct prelude to copulation; if there are several such venues, typically one – the primary rendezvous – is sought preferentially by the most competitive males.
resting stage The phase during stage 2 of *emergence* when the head, thorax and legs are out of the *exuvia* and attached to it by the posterior part of the abdomen, which remains inside.
roosting site attacker A non-territorial male who grasps females at the roosting site.

satellite Male who stations himself near a dominant male in a dominant–

subordinate relationship and tries to intercept approaching females or steal copulations when the dominant male is preoccupied.

secondary habitat For a *metapopulation* of a given species, suboptimal *habitat* type serving as a population reserve with a near-normal population structure but in which the small population cannot normally survive for more than one generation without immigration. See *latency habitat* and *stem habitat.*

semivoltine Completing a generation in two years.

sentinel position Upright position of a male when in tandem during guarded *oviposition.*

seta (plural **setae**) Hollow, hair-like structure which is an extension of the *cuticle.*

sexual selection Selection by one sex for specific traits in adults of the opposite sex, often exercised through *courtship* behaviour. See *natural selection.*

siccatation Suspension of development during the hot, dry season.

sink population Typical occupant of a *latency* or *secondary habitat.*

site attachment Association over time between an individual adult and a particular site.

site fidelity Duration of *site attachment.*

sneaker A non-territorial male who patrols along the edge of an occupied *territory* trying to intercept females.

speciation *Evolution* of a new species.

sperm competition Competition between the sperm of two or more males, within a single female, for fertilisation of her eggs.

sperm displacement The process by which the male repositions the sperm of previous rivals during copulation.

sperm precedence Measure of proportion of eggs laid that are fertilised by sperm received during the most recent insemination.

spermatheca Small, sac-like branch of the female reproductive tract (of *insects* and other *arthropods*) in which sperm may be stored.

spermatodesm Specialised *spermatophore* from which sperm are not released promptly after insemination.

spermatophore Packet of sperm transferred to the female during copulation.

sprawler Larva that uses the long, laterally extended legs to support the body on or within a matrix, usually of detritus or *macrophytes.*

spring species Species that spends the last winter before *emergence* as a *stadium F-0 larva* and consequentially typically emerges synchronously and early. Also called a Type 1 species. See *summer species.*

stadium Stage of morphological development between two successive moults; not, strictly speaking, equivalent to an *instar.* In almost every case when the word 'instar' has been used, 'stadium' correctly conveys the intended meaning.

stealer A non-territorial male who attacks and splits tandem pairs.

stem habitat For a *metapopulation* of a given species, optimal *habitat* type that persistently produces large populations, emigrants from which supply suboptimal *latency* and *secondary habitats.*

stenotopic Unable to tolerate a wide range of environmental conditions.

subordinate male Displaced or submissive male in a male–male encounter.

succession Progressive changes in a community of organisms from initial colonisation to the establishment of a stable (climax) state.

summer species Species that spends that last winter before *emergence* in a *stadium* before *F-0* and consequentially typically emerges later and with less synchronisation than *spring species*. Also called a Type 2 species.

tandem linkage Physical connection, as a prerequisite for copulation, formed by the male grasping the female's head or *prothorax* with his anal appendages.

taxonomy Study of the classification and naming of organisms.

temperature coefficient Rate of increase of an activity or process resulting from an increase in temperature of 10°C; sometimes referred to as the Q_{10}.

teneral Condition of a larva or adult, soon after moulting, when the *cuticle* is almost colourless and still unhardened.

territory Area occupied by an individual (or occasionally more than one individual of the same species) and defended against intruders.

testis (plural **testes**) Primary reproductive organ of males, producing spermatozoa.

thanatosis Reflex immobilisation, sometimes termed death feigning.

thermal conformer Individual whose body temperature equates to ambient temperature.

thermoregulation Process by which an individual maintains its body temperature within a particular range and largely independent of ambient temperature.

thorax Body section of an insect between the head and abdomen, comprising three segments, often fused together, and bearing the legs and wings.

tracheae Breathing tubes of insects, opening to spiracles on the outside of the body.

trivial flight Type of spatial displacement which, in contrast to *non-trivial flight*, is associated with an obvious immediate goal, such as thermoregulation or escape.

ultimate factors Environmental factors that exert *selection* pressure that maintains a specific trait.

ultraviolet light Wavelengths between 40 and 400 µm of the electromagnetic spectrum.

univoltine Completing a generation in one year.

upright type A type of emergence in which, during the resting stage, the angle between the anterior part of the body and the horizontal is 0–120°.

ventral Pertaining to the underside of an animal.

vitelline membrane Structureless, colourless investment of the yolk within the egg.

voltinism Number of generations completed within a year.

voucher specimen Specimen collected and preserved for future investigatory need.

vulvar scale Small flap, an extension of the ventral surface of abdominal segment 8, used during exophytic oviposition to regulate the flow of eggs.

wanderer A non-localised, non-territorial male who travels through or near many territories when searching for females.

warriorfly Dragonfly of the suborder Anisoptera.

water lurker A non-territorial male who searches *oviposition* sites and forms *tandems* with females that are submerging or surfacing and may even pursue them beneath the water.

wheel position Copulatory position in dragonflies.

wing sheaths Transparent cuticular envelopes that contain the developing wings during the last few larval *stadia*.

Endnotes

Authors' Foreword

1 Corbet 1991.

Chapter 1: Introduction

1 Brauckmann & Zessin 1989; Carpenter 1992*a*.
2 Lane 2002.
3 Wootton 1981.
4 Clausnitzer & Jödicke 2004.
5 Carpenter 1992*a, b*.
6 Nel *et al.* 1993; Bechly 1995.
7 Rüppell 1989*a*; Pfau 1991.
8 Linnaeus 1758.
9 Longfield 1937, p.213.
10 Gabb 1988.
11 Hammond 1977.
12 Nelson & Thompson 2004, pp.48–9.
13 DSA 1996.
14 d'Aguilar *et al.* 1986; Mill *et al.* 2004.
15 Réaumur 1742, pp.387, 438.
16 Fabricius 1792–9.
17 Sélys-Longchamps 1853.
18 Needham & Heywood 1929, p.11.
19 Longfield 1937, p.6.
20 Silsby 1993.
21 Cham 2004*a*, p.1.
22 Moore 1957.
23 Corbet 2000.
24 Greenwood 2000.
25 Corbet *et al.* 1960.
26 Corbet 1962*a*, 1980, 1999.
27 Waage 1979.
28 Corbet 2003*b*.
29 Robert 1958.
30 Sternberg & Buchwald 1999, 2000; Wildermuth *et al.* 2005.
31 Hammond 1977, 1983.
32 Brooks 2004.
33 Lucas 1900.
34 Longfield 1937, 1949.
35 Lucas 1930.
36 Gardner 1954*a*.
37 Hammond & Merritt 1983; McGeeney 1986; Miller 1995*a*; Brooks 1999.
38 Askew 2004.
39 Merritt *et al.* 1996.
40 Silsby 2001.
41 Brooks 2002.
42 Dunbar 1937; Evans 1963; Corbet 2003*c*.
43 Tillyard 1917.
44 http://www.jcu.edu.au/school/tbiol/ zoology.auxillry/odonata/htm which links with http://www.jcu.edu.au/ school/tbiol.zoology.auxillry/odonata/ tillyar1.htm

Chapter 2: The British Species

1 Merritt *et al.* 1996.
2 Nelson & Thompson 2004.
3 Cham 2004*a*.
4 Brooks *et al.* 1997.
5 Siva-Jothy 1997*b*.
6 Ward & Mill 2005.
7 Prendergast 1988.
8 Corbet 1957*c*.
9 Stoks *et al.* 1997.
10 Thompson 1997*b*.
11 Corbet *et al.* 2006.
12 Gladwin 1997.
13 Brook & Brook 2003.
14 d'Aguilar *et al.* 1986; Dijkstra 2006.
15 Jurzitza 1969; Dreyer 1978.
16 Nobes 2003.
17 Parr, A.J. 2004.
18 Parr 2005*a*.
19 Donath 1981.
20 Drake 1990, 1991.
21 Perrin 1995.
22 Cham 2003*a*.
23 Cham 1997*a*.
24 Corbet 1957*b*.
25 Hammond 1977.
26 Smith & Smith 1997*a*.
27 Cotton 1982.
28 Nelson 1999.
29 Jenkins 2001.
30 Purse & Hopkins 2003.
31 Jenkins 1998.
32 Winsland 1997*a*.
33 Parr 1970.
34 Moore 1995.
35 Parr 1997.
36 Kemp 1997*a*.
37 Parr 1976; Corbet & Chowdhury 2002.
38 Dewick & Gerussi 2000.
39 Cham 2003*b*, 2004*c*.
40 Parr 1969*b*; Thompson 1978*b*.
41 Pickup & Thompson 1990.
42 Cham 1997*b*; Taylor 2005.
43 Cham 1993.
44 Pennington 2005.
45 Corbet 1957*c*; Macan 1964; Lawton 1970*b*; Corbet & Harvey 1989; Bennett & Mill 1993.
46 Corbet & Harvey 1989.
47 Meurgey 2005.
48 Kaiser 1974*a*.
49 Clarke 1997.
50 Corbet 1999, p.663.
51 Clarke *et al.* 1990.
52 Clarke 1994; Smith *et al.* 2000.
53 S.A. Corbet 1959.
54 Leyshon & Moore 1993.
55 Macan 1964.
56 Longfield 1937.
57 Corbet 1957*a*.
58 Pellow 1999.
59 Corbet 2000, 2007.
60 Phillips 1997.
61 Jones 2000.
62 Holmes 1984.
63 Corbet 1999, pp.412–13.
64 Moore 1991*c*.
65 Kemp 1988.
66 Vick 1997*a*.
67 Kaiser 1982.
68 Ormerod *et al.* 1990.
69 Brooks 1997*b*; Smith & Smith 1997*b*;.Vick 1997*b*.
70 Smith 1984; Fox 1991.
71 Cham 2004*g*.
72 Moore 1991*d*.
73 Smith & Smith 1997*b*.
74 Vick 1997*b*.
75 Merritt *et al.* 1996; Miller 1997*a*.
76 Siva-Jothy 1987; Merritt *et al.* 1996; Winsland 1997*b*.
77 Michiels & Dhondt 1989*a*; Kemp 1997*b*.
78 Brooks 1988.
79 Ott 2001, 2005*a*.
80 Kemp 1997*b*; Merritt *et al.* 1996.
81 Winsland 1991; Holmes & Randolph 1994.
82 Follett 1996; Brook & Brook 2004.

83 Merritt *et al.* 1996; Miller 1997*a*.
84 Kumar 1984; Wissinger 1988*b*; Hawking & Ingram 1994; Suhling *et al.* 2004.
85 Parr 1996; Silsby & Ward-Smith 1997; Parr 2006.
86 Parr 1996, 2001.
87 Parr 1996.
88 Parr, A.J. 1999*b*.
89 Radford 1995.
90 Lucas 1912.
91 Merritt & Vick 1983.
92 Corbet 1956*b*.
93 Longfield 1948.

Chapter 3: Habitat Selection and Oviposition

1 Utzeri *et al.* 1976, 1984.
2 Lempert 1995*b*.
3 Thompson & Purse 1999.
4 Gibbons & Pain 1992.
5 Corbet 1999, p.11.
6 Wildermuth 1994*a*.
7 Schwind 1991.
8 Horváth 1995*a*.
9 Horváth 1995*b*.
10 Wildermuth 1998*a*.
11 Schwind 1991; Schwind & Horváth 1993.
12 Schwind 1995.
13 Bernáth *et al.* 2004.
14 Mokrushov & Frantsevich 1976.
15 Martens 1993.
16 Horváth *et al.* 1998.
17 Wildermuth & Horváth 2005.
18 Mizera *et al.* 2001.
19 Bernáth *et al.* 2001.
20 Frost 2000.
21 Wildermuth 2000*c*.
22 Weihrauch 1998; Burbach & Weihrauch 2000.
23 Smith *et al.* 1998.
24 Long 1991.
25 Sternberg & Sternberg 2004.
26 Martens 1996.
27 Leyshon & Moore 1993.

28 Higler 1976.
29 Merritt *et al.* 1996.
30 De Knif 2001; Haacks & Peschel 2007.
31 Poosch 1973.
32 Belyshev 1973.
33 Corbet 1999, p.591.
34 Barnard & Wildermuth 2005.
35 Brooks 1997*a*.
36 Rouquette & Thompson 2005.
37 Buchwald 1989; Corbet 1999, p.14.
38 Buchwald 1989; Buchwald 1995; Clausnitzer *et al.* 2007.
39 Wildermuth 2005*b*.
40 Cham 2004*a*.
41 Ward & Mill 2005.
42 Waage 1981.
43 McPeek 1990.
44 McPeek 1995.
45 McPeek 1989.
46 Zahner 1959.
47 Schiel 1998*a*.
48 Wildermuth 2005*b*.
49 Schiel 1998*b*.
50 Hunger 1998.
51 Kuhn 2000.
52 Müller 2002.
53 Schütte 2002.
54 Levins 1968; Hanski & Gilpin 1997.
55 Sternberg 1995*b*.
56 Pulliam 1988.
57 De Block *et al.* 2005.
58 Corbet 1957*a*.
59 Matushkina & Gorb 2002*b*.
60 Müller 1991.
61 Askew 1988.
62 Martens 1992*a*.
63 Dunn 1985.
64 S.A. Corbet 1991.
65 Wildermuth 2005*b*.
66 Parr, M.J. 1999*a*.
67 Schmidt 2005.
68 Walker 2005.
69 Wesenberg-Lund 1913; Robert 1958, plate 10, p.44.

70   Gorb 1994a; Matushkina & Gorb 2002, 2007.
71   Hellmund & Hellmund 2002.
72   Miller 1994.
73   Stoks et al. 1997.
74   Wildermuth 1984.
75   Uéda 1979; McMillan 1991.
76   Siva-Jothy & Tsubaki 1989.
77   Miller & Miller 1989.
78   Rehfeldt 1990.
79   Rüppell & Hilfert 1995.
80   Uéda 1979.
81   Convey 1989a.
82   Matsubara & Hironaka 2005.
83   Miller 1987.
84   Miller et al. 1984.
85   Balança & Visscher 1989.
86   Meurgey 2004.
87   Corbet 2000; Meurgey 2004.
88   Corbet 1999, p.29.
89   Nagasu 1999.
90   Cham 2004c.
91   Tyrrell 2004.
92   Martens 1992b.
93   Martens 2000.
94   Martens 1994.
95   Rehfeldt 1990.
96   Rehfeldt 1992.
97   Ott 2005b.
98   Svihla 1984.
99   Miller 1994.
100 Macan 1964.
101 Hawking et al. 2004.
102 Kurata 1974.
103 Zeiss et al. 1999.
104 Dijkstra et al. 2001.
105 Siva-Jothy 1997a.
106 Kaiser 1985.
107 Kaiser 1975.
108 Brooks et al. 1997.
109 Hilfert & Rüppell 1997.
110 Moore 1960; Jödicke 1997a.
111 Thompson 2004.
112 Wildermuth 2005b.

113 Kaiser 1974a; Bennett & Mill 1995a; Martens 1996; Matushkina & Gorb 2002b.
114 Martens 1996.
115 McVey 1984; Martens 1996.
116 Wesenberg-Lund 1913.
117 Bechly et al. 2001.
118 Michiels & Dhondt 1991.
119 Kaiser 1974a.
120 Lambert 1994.
121 Banks & Thompson 1987.
122 Thompson 1990a.
123 Stoks 2000.
124 Reinhardt & Gerighausen 2001.
125 Proctor & Pritchard 1989.
126 Legris & Pilon 1985.

Chapter 4: The Egg and the First Two Larval Stadia

1   Corbet 1956a.
2   Sternberg 1995a.
3   Robert 1958, p.281.
4   Corbet 1960a, pp.61–3.
5   Corbet 1999, pp.601–2.
6   Corbet 1960a, pp.61–3, 1999, pp.601–2.
7   Sternberg & Buchwald 1999, 2000.
8   Sahlén 1994.
9   Cham 1992.
10   Gardner 1955.
11   Gardner & MacNeill 1950.
12   Gardner 1951.
13   Gardner 1953.
14   Corbet 1955a.
15   Suhling & Müller 1996.
16   Kato et al. 1997.
17   Cordero-Rivera et al. 2001, 2005a.
18   Belle & van Tol 1990.
19   Cordero et al. 2005b.
20   Thipsakorn et al. 2003.
21   Donnelly 1990.
22   Ando 1962.
23   Boehms 1971.
24   Tagg 2003.
25   Schütte 1997.

26 Huggert 1982.
27 Proctor & Pritchard 1989.
28 Reinhardt & Gerighausen 2001.
29 Corbet 1999, p.603.
30 Clausen 1972.
31 Askew 1971.
32 Corbet 1999, pp.63–4.
33 Ganin 1869.
34 Clausen 1976, p.343.
35 Carlow 1992.
36 Davis 1962.
37 Degrange 1974.
38 Thompson 1993.
39 Corbet 1999, p.69.
40 Tillyard 1916.
41 Corbet 2002.
42 Crumpton 1976, 1979.
43 Inoue et al. 1981.
44 Asahina 1950.
45 Arai 1988.
46 Pierre 1904.
47 Corbet 1955b.
48 Corbet 1950.
49 Sternberg 1993.

Chapter 5: The Larva: Survival Under Water

1 Calvert 1929.
2 Robinson et al. 1991.
3 Corbet 1955b.
4 Rüppell et al. 2005, p.31.
5 Corbet 2004.
6 Zottoli et al. 2001.
7 Lawton 1973.
8 Wissinger 1989b.
9 Corbet 1953a.
10 Tanaka & Hisada 1980; Mill 1982; Pritchard 1986.
11 Pritchard 1965.
12 Rowe 1994.
13 Corbet 1999, p.104; Sell 2007.
14 Weber 1933.
15 Johansson 1992a.
16 Tagg 2003.
17 Padeffke & Suhling 2003.

18 Blois 1985.
19 Rowe 1985, p.122.
20 Rowe 1994.
21 Sherk 1977.
22 Corbet 1999, p.149.
23 Wildermuth 1998b.
24 Wildermuth 2001a.
25 Johansson 1991.
26 Smith et al. 1998.
27 Sternberg 1994a.
28 Krishnaraj & Pritchard 1995.
29 Corbet 1957a.
30 Van Buskirk 1992.
31 Corbet 1955a.
32 Münchberg 1930; Wildermuth 2005a.
33 Corbet 1956b.
34 Wildermuth 1998b.
35 Corbet et al. 2006.
36 Suhling & Müller 1996.
37 Prodon 1976.
38 Corbet 1962a, p.71.
39 Prodon 1976; Lloyd & Ormerod 1992; Lang 1999.
40 Dombrowski 1989.
41 Griffiths 1970.
42 Lawton 1970a.
43 Johansson 1992b.
44 Johansson & Johansson 1992.
45 Phillipson 1966.
46 Lawton 1971.
47 Corbet 1999, p.114.
48 Glass 1971; Heinrich 1972.
49 Lawton 1973.
50 Evans 1987.
51 Benke 1976.
52 Woodward & Hildrew 1998.
53 Corbet 1999, p.121.
54 Fincke et al. 1997.
55 Sebastian et al. 1990.
56 Corbet 1999, pp.124–39.
57 Weihrauch 1999; Postler & Postler 2000; Weihrauch & Borcherding 2002.
58 Wildermuth 2001b.
59 Wildermuth 2001c.

60 Corbet 1961*b*.
61 Desportes 1963; Pavlyuk 1971.
62 Åbro 1974.
63 Córdoba-Aguilar *et al.* 2003*a*.
64 Canales-Lazcano *et al.* 2005.
65 Siva-Jothy & Plaistow 1999.
66 Pavlyuk 1998; Corbet 1999, pp.124–34.
67 Snyder & Janovy 1996.
68 Krull 1931; Goodchild 1943; Macy 1964.
69 Timon-David 1965.
70 Street 1976.
71 Manning 1971.
72 Dumont & Hinnekint 1973.
73 Wright 1946; Corbet 1961*a*; Pushkin *et al.* 1979.
74 Kennedy 1950.
75 Davies & Everett 1975.
76 P.S. Corbet 1959.
77 McPeek & Peckarsky 1998.
78 Johansson & Brodin 2003.
79 Thompson 1978*b*.
80 Wissinger 1989*a*.
81 Wissinger 1988*a*.
82 McPeek 1989, 1998.
83 McPeek 1999.
84 Rowe 1995.
85 Macan 1964.
86 Steiner *et al.* 2000.
87 Schultz 1995, p.91.
88 Stoks *et al.* 2005; Turgeon *et al.* 2005.
89 Macan 1966; Corbet & Chowdhury 2002.
90 Richardson & Anholt 1995.
91 Rowe & Harvey 1985.
92 Rowe 2002.
93 Crowley *et al.* 1988.
94 Ross 1971.
95 Heymer 1970.
96 Münchberg 1930; Batty 1998.
97 Henrikson 1988.
98 Arai 1987.
99 Wildermuth 2000*b*.
100 Stoks *et al.* 1999.
101 Brown *et al.* 1996.
102 Chivers *et al.* 1996; McBean *et al.* 2005.
103 Johansson 1993; McBean *et al.* 2005; Gyssel & Stoks 2006; McGuffin *et al.* 2006.
104 Legrand 1974.
105 Stoks *et al.* 1999.
106 Ubukata 1981.
107 Wissinger 1988*b*.
108 Lawton 1970*b*.
109 Wissinger 1988*b*.
110 Schütte *et al.* 1998.
111 Kurata 1974.
112 Johnson & Crowley 1989.
113 MacArthur & Wilson 1972.
114 Merritt *et al.* 1996.
115 Gentry *et al.* 1975.
116 Arai 1983; Corbet 1999, p.626.
117 Dommanget 1998.
118 Williamson & Meurgey 2001.
119 Knapp *et al.* 1983.
120 Arai 1983.
121 Willey & Eiler 1972.
122 Askew 1988.
123 Sühling & Muller 1996, p.79.
124 Strommer *et al.* 1989.
125 Mylecreest 1978.
126 Tittizer *et al.* 1989; Tittizer 1994.
127 Leipelt 2005.
128 Hart & Fuller 1974.
129 Raven 1987.
130 Hammond & Merritt 1983.
131 Zahner 1959.
132 Schmidt 1984.
133 Jones 1985.
134 Meyer *et al.* 1986.
135 Corbet 1999, p.202.
136 Corbet 1993*a*.
137 Corbet 1999, p.605.
138 Masseau & Pilon 1982.
139 Norling & Sahlén 1997.
140 Zloty *et al.* 1993*a, b*.
141 Sukhacheva *et al.* 2003.
142 Soeffing 1987.
143 Krüner 1990.

Chapter 6: Larval Development and Emergence

1 Corbet 2002.
2 Pritchard *et al.* 2000.
3 Stoks & Johansson 2000.
4 Stoks 2001.
5 Corbet & Harvey 1989.
6 Corbet 1957*a*.
7 Ferreras-Romero & Corbet 1999.
8 Corbet & Prosser 1986.
9 Mill 1981.
10 Corbet 1952.
11 Brooks 1996*a*.
12 Meurgey 1999.
13 Weihrauch 2003.
14 Jacobs 1955; Busse & Jödicke 1996.
15 Wildermuth 2000*a*.
16 Dodds 1992; Meurgey 1999.
17 Gerken & Sternberg 1999.
18 Corbet & Hoess 1998.
19 Corbet 1999, p.666; Johansson *et al.* 2005.
20 Thompson 1989.
21 Suhling & Müller 1996.
22 Hammond 1928.
23 Kurata 1974.
24 Testard 1975.
25 Corbet 1999, p.242.
26 May 1995*a*.
27 Trottier 1973*b*.
28 Jödicke & Jödicke 1996.
29 Smith 1997.
30 Schorr 2000; Reder & Vogel 2000.
31 Torralba Burrial & Ocharan 2005.
32 Corbet 1962*a*, p.166, 1999, pp.637–8.
33 Purse & Thompson 2003.
34 Pajunen 1962*a*.
35 Bennett & Mill 1993.
33 Gribbin & Thompson 1990.
37 Treacher 1996.
38 Westermann 2006.
39 Wesenberg-Lund 1913.
40 Münchberg 1930, 1931, 1932.
41 Corbet 1954.
42 Corbet & Corbet 1958.
43 Taketo 1960.
44 Westermann 2002.
45 Corbet 1957*a*; Corbet & Harvey 1989; Johansson *et al.* 2005.
46 Corbet 1960*c*.
47 Corbet 1957*b*.
48 Lutz 1968.
49 Danks 1987; Saunders 2002.
50 Corbet 1955*c*; Johansson & Rowe 1999.
51 Corbet 2003*a*.
52 Corbet 1960*b*.
53 Norling 1984*a*.
54 Sternberg 1995*a*.
55 Corbet 1957*b*; Lutz 1968.
56 Corbet 1956*b*.
57 Smith *et al.* 2000.
58 Sternberg & Sternberg 2000.
59 Sternberg & Buchwald 1999, 2000.
60 Norling 1984*b*.
61 Norling 1984*a*, *b*, *c*.
62 Clarke 2002.
63 Van Doorslaer & Stoks 2005.
64 Johansson & Stoks 2005.
65 Pritchard 1982.
66 Rota & Carchini 1988.
67 Thomas 2002.
68 Ott 2001.
69 Sternberg 1998.
70 Paulson 2001.
71 Hughes 1981.

Chapter 7: Adult Life

1 Uéda 1989.
2 Pajunen 1962*a*.
3 Schmidt 1964.
4 Parr 1969*b*, pp.141–2.
5 M.J. Parr 1973*a*, 1999*b*.
6 M.J. Parr 1973*a*, 1999*b*.
7 Wesenberg-Lund 1913.
8 Buchholtz 1951; Mayhew 1994.
9 Langenbach 1993.
10 Parr 1973*b*.
11 Parr 1965.

12 Parr 1976.
13 Ubukata 1973.
14 Inden-Lohmar 1997.
15 Wildermuth 1994*b*.
16 Corbet 1999, p.259.
17 Samraoui *et al*. 1998.
18 McGeeney 1997.
19 Merritt *et al*. 1996.
20 Parr 1992.
21 Robert 1958, p.281.
22 Uéda 1978.
23 Jödicke 1997*b*, p.189.
24 Jödicke 1997*b*, p.69.
25 Samraoui & Corbet 2000*a*.
26 Samraoui & Corbet 2000*b*.
27 Heinrich 1993.
28 Rüppell *et al*. 2005, p.46.
29 May 1991.
30 May 1995*a*.
31 Corbet 1984*a*; Corbet & May 2008.
32 Sternberg 1994*b*.
33 Corbet 1962*a*, p.131.
34 Tiefenbrunner 1990.
35 Fliedner 2004.
36 Veron 1973.
37 Hilfert-Rüppell 1998.
38 Dumont 1971.
39 Askew 1982.
40 Utzeri *et al*. 1983.
41 Tsubuki 1987.
42 Hilfert & Rüppell 1997.
43 Rüppell 1989*b*.
44 Polcyn 1994.
45 Corbet 1957*a*; Jödicke 1997*a*.
46 Kiauta 1965; Parr 1969*b*.
47 Waringer 1982.
48 Hilfert 1994.
49 Corbet 1999, pp.312–13.
50 Lutz & Pittman 1970.
51 Hanel 2000; Houghton 2004.
52 Dommanget & Williamson 1999; Kiauta & Kiauta 1999.
53 Bick & Bick 1961.
54 Wildermuth 1980.

55 Thompson 1989.
56 Corbet 1952.
57 Corbet & Corbet 1958.
58 Degrange & Seasseau 1968.
59 Corbet 1999, pp.302–3.
60 Banks & Thompson 1985*a*.
61 Michiels & Dhondt 1991.
62 Corbet 1962*a*.
63 Anholt 1991.
64 Purse & Hopkins 2003.
65 Kirkton & Schultz 2001.
66 Beukema 2004.
67 Maslin 2002.
68 Ubukata 1997.
69 Eversham & Cooper 1988.
70 Hickling *et al*. 2005.
71 Termaat *et al*. 2005.
72 Ott 2001, 2005*a*.
73 Sternberg 1993.
74 Siva-Jothy & Plaistow 1999.
75 Gledhill 1985; Cassagne-Méjean 1966.
76 Smith & Oliver 1986.
77 Mitchell 1961.
78 Stechmann 1978.
79 Rolff & Martens 1997.
80 Rolff 1997.
81 Rehfeldt 1994.
82 Åbro 1990; Mitchell 1969.
83 Münchberg 1952.
84 Åbro 1990.
85 Corbet 1962*b*.
86 Corbet & Harvey 1989.
87 Corbet 1953*b*.
88 Rolff 2000*a*.
89 Rolff *et al*. 2000; Rolff 2001.
90 Rolff *et al*. 2000.
91 Conrad *et al*. 2002.
92 Rolff 2000*b*.
93 Downes 1958.
94 Dell'Anna *et al*. 1995.
95 Clastrier *et al*. 1994.
96 Rehfeldt 1995; Rüppell *et al*. 2005, p.99.
97 Martin 1910, 1911.
98 Brownett 1998.

99   Clarke *et al.* 1996.
100 Tinbergen 1968.
101 Wildermuth 2006.
102 Kalko 2001.
103 Cham 2004*b*.
104 Mauersberger & Mauersberger 2001.
105 Garbutt 1998.
106 Truscott 1999.
107 Cross 1998.
108 Fliedner & Fliedner 2000.
109 Parr 1969*b*, p.131.
110 Johnson 1806.
111 Parr 1965.
112 Rüppell *et al.* 2005, p.45.
113 Erickson 1989.
114 Rüppell *et al.* 2005, p.99.
115 Moore 1991*a*.
116 Lempert 1995*a*.
117 Sternberg 1999*b*.
118 Bennett & Mill 1995*b*.
119 Thompson 2005.
120 Rouquette & Thompson 2005.
121 Watts *et al.* 2004.
122 Parr 1969*b*, p.153.
123 Johnson 1969.
124 Corbet 1999, p.384.
125 Smith 1995.
126 Norling 1967.
127 Pellow 1999; Corbet 2000.
128 Meurgey 2004.
129 Russell *et al.* 1998; Corbet 1999, pp.414–17.
130 Woodford 1967.
131 Rubenstein & Hobson 2004.
132 Dockx *et al.* 2004.
133 Wikelski *et al.* 2006.
134 McGeeney 1997.
135 Jenkins 2001.
136 Conrad *et al.* 1999.
137 Moore 1964.
138 Parr & Parr 1974.
139 Utzeri 1988.

Chapter 8: Foraging in Flight
1   Wootton & Kukalova-Peck 2000.
2   Wootton 2001.
3   Gorb 1999*a*, Frese 2000.
4   Norberg 1975.
5   Norberg 1972.
6   D'Andrea & Carfi 1994.
7   Grabow & Rüppell 1995.
8   Land 1989.
9   Land 1997.
10   Gorb 1998*a*, 1999*b*, 2000.
11   Mittelstaedt 1950.
12   Gorb 1999*b*.
13   Gorb 1998*a*, *c*, 2000; Gorb & Popov 2002.
14   McClanahan 1971.
15   Johnson 1966; Van Gossum *et al.* 2003.
16   Corbet 1999, p.355.
17   Parr & Parr 1996.
18   Cordero 2004.
19   Veltman 1991.
20   Weihrauch 2002.
21   Tennessen 2004.
22   Rüppell *et al.* 2005, p.91.
23   Worthington & Olberg 1999.
24   Rüppell *et al.* 2005, p.94.
25   Campion 1914; Hobby 1933, 1936.
26   Montgomery 1925; Ubukata 1979; Utzeri *et al.* 1987.
27   Goodyear 1970.
28   Hobby 1933.
29   Hinnekint 1987.
30   MacArthur & Pianka 1966.
31   Corbet 1999, p.361.
32   Cham & Banks 1986.
33   Dunkle 1984.
34   Corbet & Miller 1991.
35   Corbet 1962*a*, p.154.
36   St Quentin 1934.
37   Corbet 1999, p.369.
38   Moore 1991*b*.
39   Higashi *et al.* 1979, 1982.
40   Mayhew 1994.
41   Lambert 1994.

42 Wesenberg-Lund 1913.
43 Corbet 1999, p.370.
44 Corbet 1999, p.377.
45 Parr 1980.
46 Inden-Lohmar 1997; Kaiser 1974a, 1981.
47 Brooks et al. 1997b.
48 Ottolenghi 1987.
49 Moore 1960.
50 Kaiser 1981.
51 Kaiser 1974a.
52 Fried & May 1983.
53 Lamborn 1890.
54 Wright 1945, 1946.
55 Knight et al. 2005.
56 Wright 1944.
57 Fry 1983.
58 Corbet 1999, p.380.
59 Sebastian et al. 1990.
60 Corbet 1962a, p.148.
61 May 1984.
62 Corbet 1999, p.356.
63 Oehme 1999.
64 Parr 1983b.
65 Baird & May 2003.

Chapter 9: Reproductive Behaviour
1 Michiels & Dhondt 1989a.
2 Watanabe & Matsunami 1990; Stoks et al. 1997.
3 Parr 1976.
4 Miller 1987.
5 Kaiser 1985.
6 Convey 1989b.
7 Poethke & Kaiser 1987; Ubukata 1987.
8 Kaiser 1974b.
9 Heymer 1972; Krüner 1977.
10 Hilfert-Rüppell 1999.
11 Ubukata 1980b.
12 Utzeri & Dell'Anna 1989.
13 Pajunen 1962a.
14 Parr 1983b.
15 Klötzli 1971.
16 Corbet 1999, p.435.
17 Kaiser 1974a.

18 Krüner 1977.
19 Zahner 1960.
20 Plaistow & Siva-Jothy 1996.
21 Brooks et al. 1997.
22 Miller 1995b.
23 Sonehara 1964.
24 Sternberg 1989.
25 Kotarac 1993.
26 Lambert 1994.
27 Heymer 1964.
28 Ubukata 1975.
29 Miller 1982.
30 Heymer 1964; Ubukata 1975.
31 Johnson 1962.
32 Parr 1983a, b.
33 Ottolenghi 1987.
34 Börzsöny 1993.
35 Pajunen 1964.
36 Moore 1964.
37 Miller 1987.
38 Gorb 1994.
39 Moore 1995.
40 Pajunen 1964; Campanella 1975.
41 Corbet 1999, p.661.
42 Pajunen 1964, 1966b.
43 Corbet 1999, p.444.
44 Pajunen 1966b.
45 Rüppell 1985.
46 Heymer 1966; Ubukata 1975, 1979.
47 Gribbin & Thompson 1991.
48 Pajunen 1962b.
49 Rüppell 1989a.
50 Miller 1995b.
51 Jacobs 1955.
52 Campanella 1975.
53 Clement & Meyer 1980; Fraser & Herman 1993.
54 Thompson 1990b.
55 Waltz & Wolf 1988.
56 Waage 1983, 1988.
57 Hilton 1983.
58 Marden 1989.
59 Poethke 1988; Ubukata 1975.
60 Kaiser 1974c.

61 Buchholtz 1951; Zahner 1960.
62 Mokrushov 1982; Heymer 1969; Krüner 1977.
63 Moore 1987.
64 Brooks *et al.* 1997; Ubukata 1975.
65 Kaiser 1974*c*; Kaiser & Poethke 1984.
66 Miller 1994.
67 Michiels 1989*a*; Michiels & Dhondt 1991.
68 Higashi 1969.
69 Rehfeldt 1995.
70 Uéda 1980.
71 Pajunen 1966*b*.
72 Jacobs 1955; Neville 1959.
73 Waltz & Wolf 1984.
74 Moore 1989.
75 Campanella & Wolf 1974.
76 Parr 1983*b*; Convey 1989*b*.
77 Corbet 1999, p.458.
78 Rüppell & Hilfert 1996.
79 Beukema 2002; Siva-Jothy 1999.
80 Corbet 1962*a*, p.168.
81 Gardner 1953.
82 Gorb 1996.
83 Frantsevich & Mokrushov 1984.
84 Moore 2000.
85 Boano & Rolando 2003.
86 Sawkiewicz 1989.
87 Moore 1952.
88 Calvert 1920.
89 Robertson & Paterson 1982.
90 Jacobs 1955.
91 Moore 1960.
92 Ubukata 1975.
93 Gorb 1998*b*.
94 Clausnitzer 2000.
95 Parr 1999*b*.
96 Van Gossum *et al.* 1999.
97 Cordero *et al.* 1998.
98 Gorb 1999*c*.
99 Ishizawa & Arai 2003.
100 Ishizawa 2005*a*, 2005*b*.
101 Corbet 1999, p.470.
102 Thompson 2004.
103 Alcock 1983.
104 Cordero 1999.
105 Pajunen 1966*b*.
106 Buchholtz 1956.
107 Lempert 1995*b*.
108 Heymer 1967.
109 Corbet 1999, p.661.
110 Logan 1971.
111 Utzeri 1986.
112 Siva-Jothy & Tsubaki 1989.
113 Waage 1986.
114 Corbet 2003*b*.
115 Waage 1979.
116 Parker 1970.
117 Miller 1991.
118 Siva-Jothy 1988.
119 Miller & Miller 1981.
120 Miller 1987.
121 Corbet 1999, p.663.
122 Corbet 1999, p.664.
123 Michiels 1992; Michiels & Dhondt 1988.
124 Langenbach 1995.
125 Cordero 1990.
126 Perry & Miller 1991.
127 Siva-Jothy 1987.
128 Waage 1979; Lindeboom 1995.
129 Siva-Jothy 1988.
130 Miller 1987, 1990*b*; McVey & Smittle 1984; Michiels 1989*b*.
131 Córdoba-Aguilar *et al.* 2003*b*.
132 Córdoba-Aguilar 1999.
133 Lindeboom 1998.
134 Åbro 2004.
135 Hilfert 1997.
136 Utzeri & Dell'Anna 1989.
137 Corbet 1999, plate L.5.
138 Paine 1998.
139 Gibson 2003.
140 Cordero & Andrés 2002.
141 Pajunen 1966*b*; Waage 1973.
142 Cordero 1999.
143 Stoks *et al.* 1997; Utzeri & Ercoli 2004.

144   Miller & Miller 1989.
145   Tembhare & Thakare 1982.
146   Hadrys & Siva-Jothy 1994.
147   Siva-Jothy 1995.
148   Åbro 2000.
149   Åbro 1999.
150   Robert 1958; Walker 1958.
151   Conrad & Pritchard 1992.
152   Emlen & Oring 1977.
153   Corbet 1999, p.550–4.
154   Cham 1993.
155   Fincke & Hadrys 2001.

Chapter 10: Odonatology in Britain

  1   Mouffet 1634.
  2   Ray 1710.
  3   Salmon *et al.* 2000.
  4   Raven 1942.
  5   Linnaeus 1758.
  6   Harris 1782.
  7   Donovan 1792–1813.
  8   Lisney 1960.
  9   Leach 1815.
 10   Curtis 1823–40.
 11   Anon. 1872.
 12   Dale 1901.
 13   Lucas 1908.
 14   Stephens 1835–7.
 15   Anon. 1876.
 16   Newman 1833.
 17   Sélys-Longchamps 1846.
 18   McLachlan 1865, 1870, 1900.
 19   McLachlan 1884.
 20   Longfield 1960.
 21   Evans 1845.
 22   Bath 1890.
 23   Lucas 1900.
 24   Gambles 1976.
 25   Lucas 1930.
 26   Balfour-Browne 1904.
 27   Balfour-Browne 1909.
 28   Longfield 1937.
 29   Longfield 1949.
 30   Pinniger 1947.
 31   Moore 2004.
 32   Hayter-Hames 1991.
 33   Gambles 1975.
 34   Corbet 1991*a*, *b*.
 35   Gardner 1954*a*.
 36   Corbet 1976.
 37   Fraser 1933–6.
 38   Fraser 1949, 1956.
 39   Corbet *et al.* 1960.
 40   Corbet 1962*a*.
 41   Skelton 1974.
 42   Hammond 1977.
 43   Colyer & Hammond 1951.
 44   Parr 1978.
 45   Hammond & Merritt 1983; Merritt 1983.
 46   Merritt *et al.* 1996.
 47   Cotton 1982.
 48   Benton & Payne 1983.
 49   Merritt 1987.
 50   Corbet 1993*b*.
 51   Wain 2004.
 52   NBN Gateway http:/www.nbn.org.uk
 53   BDS 1992, 1993.
 54   Taylor 2004*a*; Weatherby 2004.
 55   Eversham 1992.
 56   Merritt 1988.
 57   Cham 2004*h*.
 58   Winsland 1998.
 59   Nelson & Thompson 2004.
 60   www.searchnbn.net
 61   Corbet 1996*a*, *b*.
 62   Miller *et al.* 2001.
 63   http://www.dragonflysoc.org.uk
 64   Moore 1991*e*; 2001.
 65   Brooks *et al.* 1997.
 66   Corbet 1952; Jolly 1965; Manly & Parr 1968.
 67   Pollard 1979; Pollard *et al.* 1975.
 68   Moore & Corbet 1990; Brooks 1993.
 69   Moore 1953, 1964.
 70   Porritt 1912; Merritt *et al.* 1996.
 71   Moore 1991*c*.
 72   Brooks 2001.
 73   Pond Conservation Group 1993.

74 Moore 1986.
75 Thompson & Purse 1999.
76 Evans 1989; Merritt *et al.* 1996.
77 Moore 1991*d*.
78 Ormerod *et al.* 1990.
79 Fox *et al.* 1992.
80 Milne 1984.
81 Brooks 1989.
82 Foss 1997.
83 Brooks 1997*c*; Merritt *et al.* 1996.
84 Worthen 2002.
85 http://www.environment-agency.gov.uk
86 http://www.therrc.co.uk
87 Clarke 2004.
88 Twissell 2004.
89 Chadd & Hiley 2004.
90 Taylor 2004*b*.
91 Reeve & Reeve 2004.
92 Brook & Brook 2004.
93 Follett 1996.
94 Cham 2000.
95 Wistow 1989.
96 Taverner *et al.* 2004.
97 IPCC 2001.
98 Jones 2000.
99 Parr, A.J. 1999*a*.
100 Dewick & Gerussi 2000.
101 Hickling *et al.* 2005.
102 Smith 2004; Perrin 2005; Batty 2007.
103 Clarke 2001.
104 Jones 2003.
105 Kitching 2004.
106 Nelson *et al.* 2003.
107 Cham 2003*a*.
108 Shirt 1987.
109 HMSO 1994.
110 Hopkins & Day 1997; Thompson & Purse 1999; Jenkins 2001; Kerry 2001; Purse & Thompson 2005.
111 http://www.dragonflyproject.org.uk; Dodds 2001, 2002.
112 Fort 2004.
113 Fox 2001.

Appendix 2

1 Utzeri 1988.
2 Ishizawa & Arai 2003.
3 Gerken & Sternberg 1999.
4 Watts *et al.* 2005.
5 WDA 2002, 2005.
6 Thompson 2002; Hilfert-Rüppell & Rüppell 2007.
7 Cham 2006.
8 Merritt *et al.* 1996, p.110.
9 Brooks 1988.
10 Lohmann 1981; Schneider 1985.
11 Parr 2003.
12 Corbet 2000, 2007.
13 Meurgey 2005.
14 Balança & Visscher 1989.
15 Meurgey 2004.
16 Greenwood 2000; Mill 2005.
17 Thompson 2005.
18 Wheeler 2003.

Appendix 3

1 Sutiling & Müller 1996, p.134; Askew 2004, p.125; Dijkstra 2006, p.182.

Appendix 4

1 Nelson & Thompson 2004.
2 Shirt 1987.
3 van Tol & Verdonk 1988.

Bibliography

Åbro, A. (1974). The gregarine infection in different species of Odonata from the same habitat. *Zoologica Scripta* **3**: 111–20.

Åbro, A. (1990). The impact of parasites in adult populations of Zygoptera. *Odonatologica* **19**: 223–33.

Åbro, A. (1999). The size range of sperm bundles in aeshnid dragonflies (Anisoptera: Aeshnidae). *Odonatologica* **28**: 273–7.

Åbro, A. (2000). Sperm clusters in Zygoptera (Coenagrionidae, Lestidae, Calopterygidae). *Odonatologica* **29**: 51–6.

Åbro, A. (2004). The female seminal receptacle and accessory glands in *Pyrrhosoma nymphula* (Sulzer) (Zygoptera: Coenagrionidae). *Odonatologica* **33**: 237–44.

Alcock, J. (1983). Mate guarding and the acquisition of new mates in *Calopteryx maculata* (P. de Beauvois) (Zygoptera: Calopterygidae). *Odonatologica* **12**: 153–9.

Anders, N. & Nilsson, N. (Eds) (1997). *Aquatic Insects of North Europe*. Volume 2. Apollo Books: Stenstrup, Denmark.

Ando, H. (1962). *The comparative embryology of Odonata with special reference to a relic dragonfly* Epiophlebia superstes. Japanese Society for Promotion of Science: Tokyo.

Anholt, B.R. (1991). Measuring selection on a population of damselflies with a manipulated phenotype. *Evolution* **45**: 1091–1106.

Anon. (1872). Obituary: James Charles Dale (1792–1872). *Entomologist's Monthly Magazine* **8**: 255–6.

Anon. (1876). Obituary: Edward Newman (1801–1876). *Entomologist's Monthly Magazine* **13**: 45–6.

Anon. (1999). From individual behaviour to population dynamics – dragonflies as models. *Proceedings of the First European Dragonfly Workshop*, Gut Sunder, Meissendorf, Germany.

Arai, Y. (1983). [Hibernation ecology of odonate larvae in a dried-up swamp.] [In Japanese.] *Gekkan-Mushi* **146**: 15–17.

Arai, Y. (1987). [Dragonfly nymphs feigning death.] [In Japanese.] *Insectarium (Tokyo)* **24**: 358–61.

Arai, Y. (1988). [Observations on the larval life of *Planaeschna milnei* (Selys).] [In Japanese. English summary.] *Tombo* **31**: 53–6.

Asahina, S. (1950). On the life-history of *Epiophlebia superstes* (Odonata, Anisozygoptera). *Proceedings of the 8th*

International Congress of Entomology, Stockholm, 337–41.

Askew, R.R. (1971). Parasitic insects. Heinemann: London.

Askew, R.R. (1982). Roosting and resting site selection by coenagrionid dragonflies. Advances in Odonatology 1: 1–8.

Askew, R.R. (1988). The Dragonflies of Europe. First Edition. Harley Books: Colchester.

Askew, R.R. (2004). The Dragonflies of Europe. Revised Edition. Harley Books: Colchester.

Baird, J.M. & May, M.L. (1997). Foraging behavior of Pachydiplax longipennis (Odonata: Libellulidae). Journal of Insect Behavior 10: 655–78.

Baird, J.M. & May, M.L. (2003). Fights at the dinner table. Agonistic behavior in Pachydiplax longipennis (Odonata: Libellulidae) at feeding sites. Journal of Insect Behavior 8: 189–216.

Balança, G. & Visscher, M.-N. de (1989). Observation de la ponte en tandem d'Anax imperator Leach, 1815 dans l'Herault (34) (Odonata, Anisoptera, Aeshnidae). Martinia 5: 90.

Balfour-Browne, F. (1904). A bionomical investigation of the Norfolk Broads. Transactions of the Norfolk and Norwich Naturalists' Society 7: 661–73.

Balfour-Browne, F. (1909). The life-history of the agrionid dragonfly. Proceedings of the Zoological Society of London 18: 253–85.

Banks, M.J. & Thompson, D.J. (1985a). Emergence, longevity and breeding area fidelity in Coenagrion puella (L.) (Zygoptera: Coenagrionidae). Odonatologica 14: 279–86.

Banks, M.J. & Thompson, D.J. (1985b). Lifetime mating success in the damselfly Coenagrion puella. Animal Behaviour 33: 1175–83.

Banks, M.J. & Thompson, D.J. (1987). Lifetime reproductive success of females of the damselfly Coenagrion puella. Journal of Animal Ecology 56: 815–32.

Barnard, R. & Wildermuth, H. (2005). Nehalennia speciosa (Charpentier, 1840) in Europe: a case of a vanishing relict (Zygoptera: Coenagrionidae). Odonatologica 34: 335–78.

Bath, W.H. (1890). An illustrated handbook of British dragonflies. E.W. Allen: London.

Batty, P. (1998). Brachytron pratense in mid-Argyll. Journal of the British Dragonfly Society 14: 21–8.

Batty, P. (2007) Scottish dragonfly news. Darter. Newsletter of the Dragonfly Recording Network 24: 5

BDS (British Dragonfly Society) (c. 1992). (Undated). Dig a pond for dragonflies. British Dragonfly Society.

BDS (British Dragonfly Society) (c. 1993). (Undated). Managing habitats for dragonflies. British Dragonfly Society.

BDS (British Dragonfly Society) (1998). Members' code of practice on collecting dragonflies. British Dragonfly Society.

Bechly, G.H.P. (1995). Morphologische Untersuchungen am Flügelgeäder der rezenten Libellen und deren Stammgruppen vertreter (Insecta; Pterygota; Odonata) unter besonderer Berücksichtigung der Phylogenetischen Systematik und des Grundplanes der Odonata. Petalura, Special Volume 1: 1–341.

Bechly, G., Brauckmann, C., Zessin, W. & Gröning, E. (2001). New results concerning the morphology of the most ancient dragonflies (Insecta: Odonatoptera) from the Namurian of Hagen-Vorhalle (Germany). Journal of Zoological Systematics and Evolutionary Research 39: 209–26.

Belle, J. & Van Tol, J. (1990). Anomalagrion hastatum (Say), an American damselfly indigenous to the Azores (Odonata, Coenagrionidae). Tijschrift voor Entomologie 133: 143–7.

Belyshev, B.F. (1973). [*The Dragonflies of Siberia (Odonata)*. Volume 2, part 3.] [In Russian.] Nauka, Siberian Branch, Novosibirsk.

Benjamin, B., Cox, P.R & Peel, J. (Eds) (1973). *Resources and population*. Academic Press: London.

Benke, A.C. (1976). Dragonfly production and prey turnover. *Ecology* **57**: 915–27.

Bennett, S. & Mill, P.J. (1993). Larval development and emergence in *Pyrrhosoma nymphula* (Sulzer) (Zygoptera: Coenagrionidae). *Odonatologica* **22**: 133–45.

Bennett, S. & Mill, P.J. (1995a). Lifetime egg production and egg mortality in the damselfly *Pyrrhosoma nymphula* (Sulzer) (Zygoptera: Coenagrionidae). *Hydrobiologia* **310**: 71–8.

Bennett, S. & Mill, P.J. (1995b). Pre- and post-maturation survival in adults of the damselfly *Pyrrhosoma nymphula* (Zygoptera: Coenagrionidae). *Journal of the Zoological Society of London* **235**: 559–75.

Benton, E. & Payne, R.G. (1983). On the rediscovery of *Lestes dryas* Kirby in Britain. *Journal of the British Dragonfly Society* **1**: 28–30.

Bernáth, B., Szedenics, G., Molnár, G., Kriska, G. & Horváth, G. (2001). Visual ecological impact of "shiny black anthropogenic products" on aquatic insects: oil reservoirs and plastic sheets as polarized traps for insects associated with water. *Archiv für Naturschutz und Landskreisforschung* **40**: 89–109.

Bernáth, B., Gal, J. & Horváth, G. (2004). Why is it worth flying at dusk for aquatic insects? Polarotactic water detection is easiest at low solar elevations. *Journal of Experimental Biology* **207**: 755–65.

Bernauer, D., Grabow, K. & Martens, A. (2006). Der Nachweis der Larven von *Cordulegaster boltonii* mit Hilfe von elektrofischereilichen Methoden

(Odonata: Cordulegastridae). *Libellula* **26**: 165–9.

Beukema, J.J. (2002). Changing distribution patterns along a stream in adults of *Calopteryx haemorrhoidalis* (Odonata: Calopterygidae): a case of larval-drift compensation? *International Journal of Odonatology* **5**: 1–14.

Beukema, J.J. (2004). Recognition of conspecific females by males of *Calopteryx haemorrhoidalis* (Vander Linden) (Zygoptera: Calopterygidae). *Odonatologica* **33**: 147–56.

Bick, G.H. & Bick, J.C. (1961). An adult population of *Lestes disjunctus australis* Walker (Odonata: Lestidae). *Southwestern Naturalist* **6**: 111–37.

Blois, C. (1985). Variations of predatory behaviour in *Anax imperator* larvae in relation to different prey types. *Biology of Behaviour* **10**: 183–214.

Boano, G. & Rolando, A. (2003). Aggressive interactions and demographic parameters in *Libellula fulva* (Odonata, Libellulidae). *Italian Journal of Zoology* **70**: 159–66.

Boehms, C. (1971). The influence of temperature upon embryonic diapause and seasonal regulation in *Sympetrum vicinum* (Hagen) (Odonata: Libellulidae). PhD thesis, University of North Carolina, Chapel Hill.

Börzsöny, L. (1993). Some notes on the territorial behaviour of *Somatochlora flavomaculata* (Vander Linden). Unpublished manuscript.

Brauckmann, C. & Zessin, W. (1989). Neue Meganeuridae aus dem Namurium von Hagen-Vorhalle (BRD) und die Phylogenie der Meganisoptera (Insecta, Odonata). *Deutsches Entomologische Zeitung (Neue Folge)* **36**: 177–215.

Brewster, D. (1830). *The Edinburgh Encyclopaedia*. 20 volumes. John Murray: London.

Brook, J. & Brook, G. (2003). The Willow Emerald Damselfly *Chalcolestes viridis* (Vander Linden) in Kent: a case of mistaken identity. *Journal of the British Dragonfly Society* **19**: 51–4.

Brook, J. & Brook, G. (2004). Addendum to the southeast report: history of *Libellula fulva* in Kent. *Newsletter of the Dragonfly Recording Network* **21**: 15.

Brooks, S.J. (1988). Exotic dragonflies in north London. *Journal of the British Dragonfly Society* **4**: 9–12.

Brooks, S.J. (1989). The dragonflies (Odonata) of London: the current status. *London Naturalist* **68**: 109–31.

Brooks, S.J. (1993). Review of a method to monitor adult dragonfly populations. *Journal of the British Dragonfly Society* **9**: 1–4.

Brooks, S.J. (1995). The dragonflies (Odonata) of woodland ponds. *In:* Hine (1995), pp.22–6.

Brooks, S.J. (1996). Miscellaneous. *In:* Paine (1996), p.63.

Brooks, S.J. (Ed.) (1997a). *Field Guide to the Dragonflies and Damselflies of Great Britain and Ireland.* 1st Edition. British Wildlife Publishing: Rotherwick.

Brooks, S.J. (1997b). *Cordulia aenea. In:* Brooks (1997a), pp.123–5.

Brooks, S.J. (1997c). Peatland dragonflies (Odonata) in Britain: a review of their distribution, status and ecology. *In:* Parkyn *et al.* (1997), pp.112–16.

Brooks, S.J. (2001). Dragonflies and damselflies. *In:* Hawksworth (2001), pp.340–54.

Brooks, S. (2002). *Dragonflies.* The Natural History Museum: London.

Brooks, S.J. (Ed.) (2004). *Field Guide to the Dragonflies and Damselflies of Great Britain and Ireland.* 4th Edition. British Wildlife Publishing: Rotherwick.

Brooks, S. & Askew, R. (2004). A guide to the dragonflies and damselflies of Britain. (Identification chart with accompanying text.) 2nd Edition. Field Studies Council Publications: Preston Montford, Shrewsbury.

Brooks, S.J., McGeeney, A. & Cham, S.A. (1997). "Time-sharing" in the male Downy Emerald, *Cordulia aenea* (L.) (Corduliidae). *Journal of the British Dragonfly Society* **13**: 10–15.

Brown, G.E., Chivers, D.P. & Smith, R.J.F. (1996). Localized defecation by pike: a response to labeling by cyprinid alarm pheromone? *Behavioral Ecology and Sociobiology* **36**: 105–10.

Brownett, A. (1998). Predation of adult *Anax imperator* Leach by the Hobby (*Falco subbuteo* L.) – how frequently does this occur? *Journal of the British Dragonfly Society* **14**: 45–52.

Buchholtz, C. (1951). Untersuchungen an der Libellen-Gattung *Calopteryx*-Leach unter besonderer Berücksichtigung ethologischer Fragen. *Zeitschrift für Tierpsychologie* **8**: 273–93.

Buchholtz, C. (1956). Eine Analyse des Paarungsverhaltens und der dabei wirkenden Auslöser bei den Libellen *Platycnemis pennipes* Pall. und *P. dealbata* Klug. *Zeitschrift für Tierpsychologie* **13**: 13–25.

Buchwald, R. (1989). Die Bedeutung der Vegetation für die Habitatbindung einiger Libellenarten der Quellmoore und Fliegenwässer. *Phytocoenologia* **17**: 307–448.

Buchwald, R. (1995). Structure and floristic composition of vegetation: what is their significance for the occurrence of dragonfly species? *Proceedings of the 13th International Symposium of Odonatology, Essen,* p.15.

Buchwald, R., Höppner, B. & Röske, W. (1989). Gefährdung und Schutzmöglichkeiten grundwasserbeeinflusster Wiesenbache und –gräben in der

Oberrheinebene. Naturschutzorientierte Untersuchungen an Habitaten der HelmAzurjungfer (*Coenagrion mercuriale*, Odonata). *Natur und Landschaft* **64**: 398–403.

Burbach, K. & Weihrauch, F. (2000). Entwicklung von drei Gomphiden-Arten in einem Baggersee bei München (Odonata: Gomphidae). *Libellula* **19**: 237–40.

Buskirk, V. (1992). Competition, cannibalism, and size-class dominance in a dragonfly. *Oikos* **65**: 455–64.

Busse, R. & Jödicke, R. (1996). Langstrecken marsch bei der Emergenz von *Sympetrum fonscolombii* (Selys) in der marokkanischen Sahara (Anisoptera: Libellulidae). *Libellula* **15**: 89–92.

Calvert, P.P. (1920). The Costa Rican species of *Epigomphus* and their mutual mating adaptations. *Transactions of the American Entomological Society* **46**: 323–54.

Calvert, P.P. (1929). The significance of odonate larvae for insect phylogeny. *Transactions of the 4th International Congress of Entomology, Ithaca, New York*, 919–25.

Campanella, P.J. (1975). The evolution of mating systems in temperate zone dragonflies (Odonata: Anisoptera). II. *Libellula luctuosa* (Burmeister). *Behaviour* **54**: 278–310.

Campanella, P.J. & Wolf, L.L. (1974). Temporal leks as a mating system in a temperate zone dragonfly (Odonata: Anisoptera) I: *Plathemis lydia* (Drury). *Behaviour* **51**: 49–87.

Campion, H. (1914). Some dragonflies and their prey. *Annals & Magazine of Natural History*, Series 8 **13**: 495–504.

Canales-Lazcano, J., Contrereas-Garduño, J. & Córdoba-Aguilar, A. (2005). Fitness-related attributes and gregarine burden in a non-territorial damselfly *Enallagma*

praevarum Hagen (Zygoptera: Coenagrionidae). *Odonatologica* **34**: 123–30.

Carlow, T. (1992). *Thoronella* sp. (Hymenoptera: Scelionidae) discovered on the thorax of an Aeshnidae (Anisoptera). *Notulae Odonatologicae* **3**: 149–50.

Carpenter, F.M. (1992a). *Treatise on Invertebrate Palaeontology. Part R. Arthropoda 4. Volume 3: Superclass Hexapoda.* Geological Survey of America: Boulder, Colorado, and University of Kansas: Lawrence.

Carpenter, F.M. (1992b). *Treatise on Invertebrate Palaeontology. Part R. Arthropoda 4. Volume 4: Superclass Hexapoda.* Geological Survey of America: Boulder, Colorado, and University of Kansas: Lawrence.

Cassagne-Méjean, F. (1966). Contribution a l'étude des Arrenuridae (Acari, Hydrachnellae) de France. Dr thesis, Université de Montpellier, France.

Chadd, R. & Hiley, A. (2004). News from Lincolnshire. *Newsletter of the Dragonfly Recording Network* **21**: 8.

Cham, S. (1991). The Scarce Blue-tailed Damselfly, *Ischnura pumilio* (Charpentier): its habitat preferences in south-east England. *Journal of the British Dragonfly Society* **7**: 18–25.

Cham, S. (1992). Ovipositing behaviour and observations on the eggs and prolarvae of *Ischnura pumilio* (Charpentier). *Journal of the British Dragonfly Society* **8**: 6–10.

Cham, S. (1993). Further observations on generation time and maturation of *Ischnura pumilio* with notes on the use of a mark-recapture programme. *Journal of the British Dragonfly Society* **9**: 40–46.

Cham, S. (1997a). *Platycnemis pennipes. In:* Brooks (1997a), pp.68–9.

Cham, S. (1997b). *Ischnura pumilio. In:* Brooks (1997a), pp.90–91.

Cham, S. (2000). Discovery of a 'new' population of the Scarce Chaser *Libellula fulva* Müller on the River Stour in the Dedham Vale. *Journal of the British Dragonfly Society* **16**: 17–19.

Cham, S. (2002). Mate guarding behaviour during intense competition for females in the Common Blue Damselfly *Enallagma cyathigerum* (Charpentier). *Journal of the British Dragonfly Society* **18**: 46–8.

Cham, S. (2003*a*). Factors influencing the distribution of the White-legged Damselfly *Platycnemis pennipes* (Pallas) in Great Britain. *Journal of the British Dragonfly Society* **19**: 15–23.

Cham, S. (2003*b*). Small Red-eyed Damselfly *Erythromma viridulum* (Charpentier) records in 2002. *Atropos* **19**: 19–24.

Cham, S. (2004*a*). *Dragonflies of Bedfordshire*. Bedfordshire Natural History Society: Bedford.

Cham, S. (2004*b*). Dragonfly predation by European Hornets *Vespa crabro* (L.) (Hymenoptera, Vespidae). *Journal of the British Dragonfly Society* **20**: 1–3.

Cham, S. (2004*c*). Oviposition behaviour of the two British species of Red-eyed Damselflies *Erythromma najas* (Hansemann) and *E. viridulum* (Charpentier). *Journal of the British Dragonfly Society* **20**: 37–41.

Cham, S. (2004*d*). Observations on an inland population of the Small Red-eyed Damselfly *Erythromma viridulum* (Charpentier) with notes on the first discovery of larvae in Britain. *Journal of the British Dragonfly Society* **20**: 31–4.

Cham, S. (2004*e*). Personal communication to S.J.B.

Cham, S. (2004*f*). *Erythromma viridulum*. *In:* Brooks (2004), p.96.

Cham, S. (2004*g*). The Downy Emerald – an enigmatic dragonfly? *British Wildlife* **16**: 108–19.

Cham, S. (2004*h*). Letter of 14 February to S.J.B.

Cham, S. (2006). Aspects of dragonfly flight behaviour revealed by digital still photography. *Journal of the British Dragonfly Society* **22**: 41–53.

Cham, S. (2007). *Field guide to the larvae and exuviae of British dragonflies*. Volume 1: Dragonflies (Anisoptera). British Dragonfly Society.

Cham, S. (2008). *Field Guide to the larvae and exuviae of British dragonflies*. Volume 2: Damselflies (Zygoptera). British Dragonfly Society.

Cham, S.A. & Banks, C. (1986). Unusual feeding behaviour by *Aeshna grandis* (L.). *Journal of the British Dragonfly Society* **2**: 43–4.

Chivers, D.P., Wisenden, R. & Smith, J. (1996). Damselfly larvae learn to recognize predators from chemical cues in the predators' diet. *Animal Behaviour* **52**: 315–20.

Clarke, A., Prince, P. A. & Clarke, R. (1996). The energy content of dragonflies (Odonata) in relation to predation by falcons. *Bird Study* **43**: 300–304.

Clarke, D. (1994). Notes on the larva and generation time of *Aeshna caerulea* (Ström) in Scotland, with particular reference to the south-west. *Journal of the British Dragonfly Society* **10**: 29–36.

Clarke, D. (1997). *Aeshna caerulea*. *In:* Brooks (1997*a*), pp.100–101.

Clarke, D.J. (2001). First occurrence of the Migrant Hawker Dragonfly (*Aeshna mixta* Latreille) in Cumbria. *Carlisle Naturalist* **9**: 40–41.

Clarke, D. (2002). Growth and autumnal decline of feeding in captive-reared first-year larvae of the Azure Hawker *Aeshna caerulea* (Ström). *Journal of the British Dragonfly Society* **18**: 9–12.

Clarke, D. (2004). 'Southern' dragonflies

make headway in Cumbria in 2003. *Newsletter of the Dragonfly Recording Network* **21**: 6–7.

Clarke, D.J., Hewitt, S.M., Smith, E.M. & Smith, R.W.J. (1990). Observations on the breeding habits and habitat of *Aeshna caerulea* (Ström) in Scotland. *Journal of the British Dragonfly Society* **6**: 24–9.

Clastrier, J., Grand, D. & Legrand, J. (1994). Observations exceptionelles en France de *Forcipomyia* (*Pterobosca*) *paludis* (Macfie), parasite des ailes de libellules (Diptera, Ceratopogonidae et Odonata). *Bulletin de Société d'Entomologie Française* **99**: 127–30.

Clausen, C.P. (1972). *Entomophagous insects.* Hafner: New York.

Clausen, C.P. (1976). Phoresy among entomophagous insects. *Annual Review of Entomology* **21**: 343–68.

Clausen, W. (1984). The exuviae of *Aeshna juncea* (L.) and *Aeshna subarctica* (Wlk.). *Journal of the British Dragonfly Society* **1**: 59–67.

Clausen, W. (1986). More characters to separate *Aeshna subarctica* (Walker) from *Aeshna juncea* (L.) in the field. *Journal of the British Dragonfly Society* **2**: 8–10.

Clausnitzer, H.-J., Clausnitzer, C. & Hengst, R. (2007). Zur Ökologie von *Ceriagrion tenellum* im Bereich der nordöstlichen Verbreitungsgrenze in Niedersachsen (Odonata: Coenagrionidae). *Libellula* **26**: 19–34.

Clausnitzer, V. (2000). Interspecific competition in rainforest dragonflies (Tetratheminae, Libellulidae). Oral communication to 13 Jahrestagung der Deutschen Gesellschaft für Tropenökologie, Wurzburg, 1–3 March.

Clausnitzer, V. & Jödicke, R. (Eds) (2004). Guardians of the watershed. Global status of dragonflies: critical species, threat and conservation. *International Journal of Odonatology* **7**: 111–430.

Clement, S.L. & Meyer, R.P. (1980). Adult biology and behavior of the dragonfly *Tanypteryx hageni* (Odonata: Petaluridae). *Journal of the Kansas Entomological Society* **53**: 711–19.

Colyer, C.N. & Hammond, C.O. (1951). *Flies of the British Isles.* Warne: London.

Conrad, K.F. & Pritchard, G. (1992). An ecological classification of odonate mating systems: the relative influence of natural, inter- and intra-sexual selection on males. *Biological Journal of the Linnean Society of London* **45**: 255–69.

Conrad, K.F., Willson, K.H., Harvey, I.F., Thomas, C.J. & Sherratt, T. N. (1999). Dispersal characteristics of seven odonate species in an agricultural landscape. *Ecography* **22**: 524–31.

Conrad, K.F, Willson, K.H., Whitfield, K., Harvey, I.F., Thomas, C.J. & Sherratt, T.N. (2002). Characteristics of dispersing *Ischnura elegans* and *Coenagrion puella* (Odonata): age, sex, size, morph and ectoparasitism. *Ecography* **25**: 439–45.

Convey, P. (1989*a*). Post-copulatory guarding strategies in the non-territorial dragonfly *Sympetrum sanguineum* (Odonata: Libellulidae). *Animal Behaviour* **37**: 56–63.

Convey, P. (1989*b*). Influences of the choice between territorial and satellite behaviour in male *Libellula quadrimaculata* Linn. (Odonata: Libellulidae). *Behaviour* **109**: 125–41.

Corbet, P.S. (1950). Observations on the development and ecology of *Sympetrum striolatum* (Charpentier) (Odonata). BSc thesis, University of Reading, UK.

Corbet, P.S. (1952). An adult population study of *Pyrrhosoma nymphula* (Sulzer) (Odonata: Coenagrionidae). *Journal of Animal Ecology* **21**: 206–22.

Corbet, P.S. (1953*a*). A terminology for the labium of larval Odonata. *Entomologist* **86**: 191–6.

Corbet, P.S. (1953b). The seasonal ecology of dragonflies. PhD thesis, University of Cambridge, UK.

Corbet, P.S. (1954). Seasonal regulation in British dragonflies. *Nature, London* **174**: 655; 777.

Corbet, P.S. (1955a). The immature stages of the Emperor Dragonfly, *Anax imperator* Leach (Odonata: Aeshnidae). *Entomologist's Gazette* **6**: 189–204.

Corbet, P.S. (1955b). The larval stages of *Coenagrion mercuriale* (Charp.) (Odonata: Coenagriidae). *Proceedings of the Royal Entomological Society of London (A)* **30**: 115–26.

Corbet, P.S. (1955c). A critical response to changing length of day in an insect. *Nature, London* **175**: 338.

Corbet, P.S. (1956a). The influence of temperature on diapause development in the dragonfly *Lestes sponsa* (Hansemann) (Odonata: Lestidae). *Proceedings of the Royal Entomological Society of London (A)* **31**: 45–8.

Corbet, P.S. (1956b). The life-histories of *Lestes sponsa* (Hansemann) and *Sympetrum striolatum* (Charpentier) (Odonata). *Tijdschrift voor Entomologie* **99**: 217–29.

Corbet, P.S. (1957a). The life-history of the Emperor Dragonfly, *Anax imperator* Leach (Odonata: Aeshnidae). *Journal of Animal Ecology* **26**: 1–69.

Corbet, P.S. (1957b). The life-histories of two summer species of dragonfly (Odonata: Coenagriidae). *Proceedings of the Zoological Society of London* **128**: 403–18.

Corbet, P.S. (1957c). The life-histories of two spring species of dragonfly (Odonata: Zygoptera). *Entomologist's Gazette* **8**: 79–89.

Corbet, P.S. (1959). Notes on the insect food of the Nile crocodile in Uganda. *Proceedings of the Royal Entomological Society of London (A)* **34**: 17–22.

Corbet, P.S. (1960a). The egg and egg-laying. *In:* Corbet *et al.* (1960), pp.55–65.

Corbet, P.S. (1960b). The larva. *In:* Corbet *et al.* (1960), pp.66–86.

Corbet, P.S. (1960c). Seasonal regulation. *In:* Corbet *et al.* (1960), pp.138–48.

Corbet, P.S. (1961a). The food of non-cichlid fishes in the Lake Victoria basin, with remarks on their adaptation to lacustrine conditions. *Proceedings of the Zoological Society of London* **136**: 1–101.

Corbet, P.S. (1961b). The biological significance of the attachment of immature stages of *Simulium* to mayflies and crabs. *Bulletin of Entomological Research* **52**: 695–99.

Corbet, P.S. (1962a). *A Biology of Dragonflies.* Witherby: London.

Corbet, P.S. (1962b). Age-determination of adult dragonflies. *Proceedings of the 11th International Congress of Entomology, Vienna* **3**: 287–9.

Corbet, P.S. (1962c). Observations on the attachment of *Simulium* pupae to larvae of Odonata. *Annals of Tropical Medicine and Parasitology* **56**: 136–40.

Corbet, P.S. (1976). Obituary: A.E. Gardner (1913–1976). *Odonatologica* **5**: 387–90.

Corbet, P.S. (1980). Biology of Odonata. *Annual Review of Entomology* **25**: 189–217.

Corbet, P.S. (1984a). Orientation and reproductive condition of migrating dragonflies. *Odonatologica* **13**: 81–8.

Corbet, P.S. (Ed.) (1984b). Current topics in dragonfly biology. *Rapid Communications, Societas Internationalis Odonatologica (Supplement)* **2**: x+46.

Corbet, P.S. (1991a). Obituary: Cynthia Longfield. *The Independent,* 5 July, p.27.

Corbet, P.S. (1991b). Obituary: Cynthia Longfield (1896–1991). *Journal of the British Dragonfly Society* **7**: 29–32.

Corbet, P.S. (1993a). Are Odonata useful as bioindicators? *Libellula* **12**: 91–102.

Corbet, P.S. (1993b). The first ten years of the British Dragonfly Society. *Journal of the British Dragonfly Society* 9: 25–39.

Corbet, P.S. (1996a). Obituary: Peter Miller. *The Independent*, 6 May, p.16.

Corbet, P.S. (1996b). Peter Miller – a tribute. *Selysia* 24: 1.

Corbet, P.S. (1999). *Dragonflies. Behaviour and Ecology of Odonata*. Harley Books: Colchester.

Corbet, P.S. (2000). The first recorded arrival of *Anax junius* Drury (Anisoptera: Aeshnidae) in Europe: a scientist's perspective. *International Journal of Odonatology* 3: 153–62.

Corbet, P.S. (2002). Stadia and growth ratios of Odonata: a review. *International Journal of Odonatology* 5: 45–73.

Corbet, P.S. (2003a). A positive correlation between photoperiod and development rate in summer species of Odonata could help to make emergence date appropriate to latitude: a testable hypothesis. *Journal of the Entomological Society of British Columbia* 100: 3–17.

Corbet, P.S. (2003b). Reproductive behaviour of Odonata: the history of a mystery. *International Journal of Odonatology* 6: 185–93.

Corbet, P.S. (2003c). R.J. Tillyard FRS (1881–1937): a giant among odonatologists. *Agrion* 7: 21–4.

Corbet, P.S. (2004). Ballistic defaecation by Anisoptera larvae (Odonata): a way to increase foraging success? *International Journal of Odonatology* 7: 25–32.

Corbet, P.S. (2006). Forests as habitats for dragonflies. *In:* Cordero (2006), pp.13–36.

Corbet, P.S. (2007). Two current threats to the future of entomology in Britain. *Antenna* 31: 208–13.

Corbet, S.A. (1959). The larval development and emergence of *Aeshna cyanea* (Müll.)

(Odon., Aeshnidae). *Entomologist's Monthly Magazine* 95: 241–245.

Corbet, S.A. (1991). Personal communication to P.S.C.

Corbet, P.S. & Chowdhury, S.H. (2002). Voltinism of the Common Blue Damselfly, *Enallagma cyathigerum* (Charpentier) in a Scottish loch: a preliminary study. *Journal of the British Dragonfly Society* 18: 23–39.

Corbet, P.S. & Corbet, S.A. (1958). Emergence of a summer species of dragonfly. *Nature, London* 182: 194.

Corbet, P.S. & Harvey, I.F. (1989). Seasonal regulation in *Pyrrhosoma nymphula* (Sulzer) (Zygoptera: Coenagrionidae). 1. Seasonal development in nature. *Odonatologica* 18: 133–45.

Corbet, P.S. & Hoess, R. (1998). Sex ratio of Odonata at emergence. *International Journal of Odonatology* 1: 99–118.

Corbet, P.S. & May, M.L. (2008). Fliers and perchers among Odonata: dichotomy or multidimensional continuum? A reappraisal. *International Journal of Odonatology* 11: (in press).

Corbet, P.S. & Miller, P.L. (1991). "Accompanying" behaviour as a means of prey acquisition by *Brachythemis leucosticta* (Burmeister) and other Anisoptera. *Odonatologica* 20: 29–36.

Corbet, P.S. & Prentice, R.M. (Eds) (1971). *Biological Control Programmes against Insects and Weeds in Canada 1959–1968*. Technical Communication No. 4, Commonwealth Institute of Biological Control, Slough, U.K.

Corbet, P.S. & Prosser, R.J.S. (1986). Diagnosis of interecdysial development in final-instar larvae of *Pyrrhosoma nymphula* (Sulzer) (Zygoptera: Coenagrionidae). *Odonatologica* 15: 23–8.

Corbet, P.S., Longfield, C. & Moore, N.W. (1960). *Dragonflies*. Collins: London.

Corbet, P.S., Harvey, I.F., Abisgold, J. & Morris, F. (1989). Seasonal regulation in *Pyrrhosoma nymphula* (Sulzer) (Zygoptera: Coenagrionidae). 2. Effect of photoperiod on larval development in spring and summer. *Odonatologica* 18: 333–48.

Corbet, P.S., Suhling, F. & Soendgerath, D. (2006). Voltinism of Odonata: a review. *International Journal of Odonatology* 9: 1–44.

Cordero, A. (1990). The adaptive significance of the prolonged copulations of the damselfly, *Ischnura graellsii* (Odonata: Coenagrionidae). *Animal Behaviour* 40: 43–48.

Cordero, A. (1999). Forced copulations and female contact guarding at a high male density in a calopterygid damselfly. *Journal of Insect Behavior* 12: 27–37.

Cordero, A. & Córdoba-Aguilar, A. (1999). Sperm competition in the Odonata: current state and possible trends. *In*: Anon. (1999), p.8.

Cordero-Rivera, A. (2004). Personal communication to P.S.C., 1 July.

Cordero-Rivera, A. (Ed.) (2006). *Forests and Dragonflies*. Pensoft: Sofia-Moscow.

Cordero, A. & Abad, J.A.A. (1999). Lifetime mating success, survivorship and synchronized reproduction in the damselfly *Ischnura pumilio* (Odonata: Coenagrionidae). *International Journal of Odonatology* 2: 105–14.

Cordero, A. & Andrés, J.A. (2002). Male coercion and convenience polyandry in a calopterygid damselfly. *Journal of Insect Science* 2: 14, 7 pp.

Cordero, A., Carbone, S.S. & Utzeri, C. (1998). Mating opportunities and mating costs are reduced in androchrome female damselflies, *Ischnura elegans* (Odonata). *Animal Behaviour* 33: 185–97.

Cordero-Rivera, A., Lorenzo Carballa, M.O. & Utzeri, C. (2001). Evidence for parthenogenetic reproduction in populations of *Ischnura hastata* from the Azores. *Abstracts of the 2nd WDA International Symposium of Odonatology, Gallivåre*, 11.

Cordero-Rivera, A., Lorenzo Carballa, M.O., Utzeri, C. & Vieira, V. (2005a). Parthenogenetic *Ischnura hastata* (Say, 1839), widespread in the Azores Islands (Zygoptera: Coenagrionidae). *Odonatologica* 34: 1–9.

Cordero-Rivera, A., Lorenzo, O. & Andrés, J. (2005b). Endosymbiont-induced parthenogenesis in a diplo-diploid damselfly? *Tagungsband der 24 Jahrestagung der Gesellschaft duetschsprachiger Odonatologen, Freisung, Germany*, 25.

Córdoba-Aguilar, A. (1999). Male copulatory sensory stimulation induces female ejection of rival sperm in a damselfly. *Proceedings of the Royal Society of London (B)* 266: 779–84.

Córdoba-Aguilar, A., Salamanca-Ocanat, J. C. & Lopezaraiza, M. (2003a). Female reproductive decisions and parasite burden in a calopterygid damselfly (Insecta: Odonata). *Animal Behaviour* 66: 81–7.

Córdoba-Aguilar, A., Uhia, E. & Cordero Rivera, A. (2003b). Sperm competition in Odonata (Insecta): the evolution of female sperm storage and rival's sperm. displacement. *Journal of Zoology, London* 261: 381–98.

Cotton, D.C.F. (1982). *Coenagrion lunulatum* (Charpentier) (Odonata: Coenagrionidae) new to the British Isles. *Entomologist's Gazette* 33: 213–14.

Cross, I. (1998). Mistaken identity? In Paine (1998), p.31.

Crowley, P.H., Gillett, S. & Lawton, J.H. (1988). Contests between larval damselflies: empirical steps towards a better ESS model. *Animal Behaviour* 36: 1496–1510.

Crumpton, W.J. (1976). Letter to P.S.C., 29 January.

Crumpton, W.J. (1979). Aspects of the biology of *Xanthocnemis zealandica* and *Austrolestes colensonis* (Odonata: Zygoptera) at three ponds in the South Island, New Zealand. *New Zealand Journal of Zoology* **6**: 285–97.

Curtis, J. (1823–1840). *British Entomology: being illustrations and descriptions of the genera of insects found in Great Britain and Ireland,&c.* 8 Volumes. Privately published.

D'Aguilar, J., Dommanget, J.-L. & Préchac, R. (1986). *A Field Guide to the Dragonflies of Britain, Europe and North Africa.* (Ed. S. Brooks) Collins: London.

Dale, C.W. (1901). Notes on British dragonflies. *Entomologist* **34**: 53.

D'Andrea, M. & Carfi, S. (1994). Spines on the wing veins in Odonata. 3. The vein edge. *Advances in Odonatology* **6**: 21–43.

Danks, H.V. (1987). *Insect Dormancy: an Ecological Perspective.* Biological Survey of Canada (Terrestrial Arthropods): Ottawa.

Davies, R.W. & Everett, R.P. (1975). The feeding of four species of freshwater Hirudinea in southern Alberta. *Verhandlungen der Internationalen Verein Limnologie* **19**: 2816–27.

Davis, C.C. (1962). Ecological and morphological notes on *Hydrophylita aquivalens* (Math. and Crosby). *Limnology and Oceanography* **7**: 390–92.

De Block, M., Geenen, S., Jordaens, K., Backeljau, T. & Stoks, R. (2005). Spatiotemporal allozyme variation in the damselfly, *Lestes viridis* (Odonata: Zygoptera): gene flow among permanent and temporary ponds. *Genetica* **124**: 137–44.

Degrange, C. (1974). L'oeuf et l'éclosion de *Calopteryx virgo* L. (Odonata, Zygoptera, Calopterygidae). Considérations générales sur l'éclosion des larves des odonates.

Travaux du Laboratoire d'Hydrobiologie et de Pisciculture de l'Université de Grenoble **64–65**: 269–86.

Degrange, C. & Seassau, M.-D. (1968). Longévité des odonates anisoptères adults en captivité. *Travaux de Laboratoire de Hydrobiologie et Hygrographie (Grenoble)* **59–60**: 83–6.

De Knif, G. (2001). Personal communication to P.S.C.

Dell'Anna, L., Utzeri, C., Sabatini, A. & Coluzzi, M. (1995). *Forcipomyia* (*Pterobosca*) *paludis* (Macfie, 1936) (Diptera, Ceratopogonidae) on adult dragonflies (Odonata) in Sardinia, Italy. *Parasitologia* **37**: 79–82.

Desportes, I. (1963). Quelques grégarines parasites d'insectes aquatiques de France. *Annales de Parasitologie Humaine et Comparée* **38**: 341–77.

Dewick, S. & Gerussi, R. (2000). Small Red-eyed Damselfly *Erythromma viridulum* (Charpentier) found breeding in Essex – the first British records. *Atropos* **9**: 3–4.

Dijkstra, K.-D. & Kalkman, V.J. (2001). Early spring records of Odonata from southern Turkey, with special reference to the sympatric occurrence of *Crocothemis erythraea* (Brullé) and *C. servilia* (Drury) (Anisoptera: Libellulidae). *Notulae Odonatologicae* **5**: 85–96.

Dijkstra, K.-D.B., Cordero-Rivera, A. & Andrés, J.A. (2001). Repeated predation of Odonata by the hornet *Vespa crabro* (Hymenoptera: Vespidae). *International Journal of Odonatology* **4**: 17–21.

Dijkstra, K.-D.B. (Ed.) (2006). *Field Guide to the Dragonflies of Britain and Europe.* British Wildlife Publishing: Gillingham.

Dockx, C., Brower, L.P., Wassenaar, L.I. & Hobson, K.A. (2004). Do North American Monarch Butterflies travel to Cuba? Stable isotope and chemical tracer techniques. *Ecological Applications* **14**: 1106–14.

Dodds, R.M. (1992). Inverted emergence by *Ischnura elegans* (Vander Linden) at Ashton Water Dragonfly Sanctuary. *Journal of the British Dragonfly Society* **8**: 13–15.

Dodds, R.M. (2001). How a dream came true: ten years of dragonflies and the public at Ashton Water. *Dragonfly News* **39**: 19–22.

Dodds, R.M. (2002). Goodbye National Dragonfly Museum. *Dragonfly News* **41**: 22.

Dombrowski, A. (1989). Ökologische Untersuchungen an *Cordulegaster bidentatus* Selys, 1843. Diploma thesis, Georg-August-Universität, Göttingen, Germany.

Dommanget, J.-L. (1998). Microhabitats refuges pour les larves d'*Aeshna cyanea* (Müller, 1764) lors de l'asséchement du milieu (Odonata, Anisoptera, Aeshnidae). *Martinia* **14**: 56.

Dommanget, J.-L. & Williamson, T. (1999). Réactions de quelques Odonates en forêt de Rambouillet lors de l'éclipse de soleil du 11 août 1999 (Departement des Yvelines). *Martinia* **15**: 79–82.

Domoto, A. & Iwatsuki, K. (Eds) (1997). [*Threats of Global Warming to Biological Diversity.*] Takijishokan, Tokyo. [In Japanese.]

Donath, H. (1981). Verbreitung und Ökologie von *Lestes barbarus* (F.) in der nordwestlichen Niederlausitz (Odonata, Lestidae). *Novius* **3**: 33–6.

Donnelly, T.W. (1990). The Fijian genus *Nesobasis* Part 1: species of Viti Levu, Ovalau, and Kadavu (Odonata: Coenagrionidae). *New Zealand Journal of Zoology* **17**: 87–117.

Donovan, E. (1792–1813). *Natural history of British insects: with the history of such minute insects as require investigation by the microscope.* 16 volumes. London.

Downes, J.A. (1958). The feeding habits of biting flies and their significance in classification. *Annual Review of Entomology* **3**: 249–66.

Drake, C.M. (1990). Records of larval *Lestes dryas* Kirby in Essex during 1987. *Journal of the British Dragonfly Society* **6**: 34–41.

Drake, C.M. (1991). The condition of *Lestes dryas* Kirby larval populations in some Essex grazing marshes in May 1990. *Journal of the British Dragonfly Society* **7**: 10–17.

Dreyer, W. (1978). Etho-ökologische untersuchungen an *Lestes viridis* (v.d. Linden) (Zygoptera: Lestidae). *Odonatologica* **7**: 309–22.

DSA (Dragonfly Society of the Americas) (1996). Common names of North American dragonflies and damselflies, adopted by the Dragonfly Society of the Americas. *Argia (Supplement)* **8**: 4 pp.

Dumont, H.J. (1971). A contribution to the ecology of some Odonata. The Odonata of a "trap" area around Denderleeuw (eastern Flanders: Belgium). *Bulletin et Annales de la Société Royale Entomologique de Belge* **107**: 211–35.

Dumont, H.J. & Hinnekint, B.O.N. (1973). Mass migration in dragonflies, especially in *Libellula quadrimaculata* L.: a review; a new ecological approach and a new hypothesis. *Odonatologica* **2**: 1–20.

Dunbar, C.O. (1937). Obituary. Robin John Tillyard. 1881–1937. *American Journal of Science* **33**: 217–18.

Dunkle, S.W. (1984). Contribution to discussion. *In:* Corbet (1984b), p.22.

Dunn, R.H. (1985). Some observations of *Aeshna cyanea* (Müller) ovipositing in unusual substrates. *Journal of the British Dragonfly Society* **1**: 99–100.

Emlen, S.T. & Oring, L.W. (1977). Ecology, sexual selection, and the evolution of mating systems. *Science* **197**: 215–33.

Erickson, C.J. (1989). Interactions between the dragonfly *Hagenius brevistylus* Selys, and the damselfly *Calopteryx maculata* (P. de Beauv.) (Anisoptera: Gomphidae; Zygoptera: Calopterygidae). *Notulae Odonatologicae* **3**: 59–60.

Evans, F. (1989). A review of the management of lowland wet heath in Dyfed, west Wales. Nature Conservancy Council: Peterborough.

Evans, J.W. (1963). *The life and work of Robin John Tillyard 1881–1937*. University of Queensland Press: St Lucia, Australia.

Evans, R. (1987). Singing in the acid rain: *Leucorrhinia* dominates benthos of acidified, fishless lakes. *Bulletin of the North American Benthological Society* **4**: 96.

Evans, W.F. (1845). *British Libellulinae or Dragonflies*. J.C. Bridgewater: London.

Eversham, B.C. (1992). Introductions: their place in British wildlife. *In*: Harding (1992), pp.44–59.

Eversham, B.C. & Cooper, J.M. (1998). Dragonfly species-richness and temperature: national patterns and latitude trends in Britain. *Odonatologica* **27**: 307–16.

Fabricius, J.C. (1792–99). *Entomologia Systematica Emedata et Aucta. Secundum Classes, Ordines, Genera, Species, Adjectis Synonymis, Locis, Observationibus, Descriptionibus*. C.G. Proft: Copenhagen.

Fellowes, M.D.E., Holloway, G.J. & Rolff, J. (Eds) (2005). Insect evolutionary ecology. Royal Entomological Society. Blackwells: Oxford.

Ferreras-Romero, M. & Corbet, P.S. (1999). The life cycle of *Cordulegaster boltonii* (Donovan, 1807) in the Sierra Morena Mountains (southern Spain). *Hydrobiologia* **405**: 39–48.

Fincke, O.M. & Hadrys, H. (2001). Unpredictable offspring survivorship in the damselfly *Megaloprepus coerulatus*

shapes parental behavior, constrains sexual selection, and challenges traditional fitness estimates. *Evolution* **55**: 762–72.

Fincke, O.M., Yanoviak, S.P. & Hanschu, R.D. (1997). Predation by odonates depresses mosquito abundance in water-filled tree holes in Panama. *Oecologia* **112**: 244–53.

Fliedner, H. (2004). Flügel als Sonnenreflektoren bei *Lestes viridis*? (Odonata: Lestidae). *Libellula* **23**: 179–82.

Fliedner, T. & Fliedner, H. (2000). *Aeshna cyanea* als Beute von *Vespa vulgaris*: ergänzende Beobachtungen zu Angriffen sozialer Faltenwespen auf schlüpfende Libellen (Odonata: Aeshnidae; Hymenoptera: Vespidae). *Libellula* **19**: 71–7.

Follett, P. (1996). *Dragonflies of Surrey*. Surrey Wildlife Trust: Woking, Surrey.

Forman, R.T.T. (1966). *Land Mosaics. The Ecology of Landscapes and Regions*. Cambridge University Press: Cambridge.

Fort, T. (2004). Down the drain. *The Times*, 26 June, p.30.

Foss, P. (1997). Ten years of Save the Bogs Campaign. *In*: Parkyn *et al.* (1997), pp.391–7.

Fox, A.D. (1991). How common is terrestrial oviposition in *Somatochlora metallica* Vander Linden? *Journal of the British Dragonfly Society* **7**: 38–9.

Fox, A.D., Jones, T. & Holland, S.C. (1992). Habitat preferences of dragonflies in the Cotswold Water Park. *Journal of the British Dragonfly Society* **8**: 4–9.

Fox, R. (2001). Butterflies and moths. *In*: Hawksworth (2001), pp.300–17.

Frantsevich, L.L. & Mokrushov, P.A. (1984). Visual stimuli releasing attack of a territorial male in *Sympetrum* (Anisoptera: Libellulidae). *Odonatologica* **13**: 335–50.

Fraser, A.M. & Herman, T.B. (1993). Territorial and reproductive behaviour in a sympatric species complex of the Neotropical damselfly *Cora Selys* (Zygoptera: Polythoridae). *Odonatologica* **22**: 411–29.

Fraser, F.C. (1933–36). *The Fauna of British India, including Ceylon and Burma*. Volumes 1–3. Taylor & Francis: London.

Fraser, F.C. (1949). *Odonata*. Handbooks for the identification of British insects. Volume 1, part 10. 1st Edition. Royal Entomological Society of London: London.

Fraser, F.C. (1956). *Odonata*. Handbooks for the indentification of British insects. Volume 1, part 10. 2nd Edition. Royal Entomological Society of London: London.

Frese, W. (2000). "Rubber protein" enables the dragonfly to perform aerobatic stunts. *Max Planck Research* **2000/2**: 26–7.

Fried, C.S. & May, M.L. (1983). Energy expenditure and food intake of territorial male *Pachydiplax longipennis* (Odonata: Libellulidae). *Ecological Entomology* **8**: 283–92.

Frost, R.A. (2000). Strange behaviour of Golden-ringed Dragonfly. *Journal of the Derbyshire and Nottinghamshire Entomological Society* **140**: 2.

Fry, C.H. (1983). Honeybee predation by bee-eaters, with economic considerations. *Bee World* **64**: 65–78.

Gabb, R. (1988). English names for dragonflies. *Journal of the British Dragonfly Society* **4**: 19–21.

Gambles, R.M. (1975). To Miss Cynthia Longfield FRES. *Odonatologica* **4**: 55–6.

Gambles, R.M. (1976). A history of odonatology in the British Isles. *Odonatologica* **5**: 1–10.

Ganin, M. (1869). Beiträge zur Erkenntnis der Entwickelungsgeschichte bei den Insekten. *Zeitschrift für Wissenschaftliche Zoologie* **19**: 253–60.

Garbutt, A. (1998). Hornet predation on a dragonfly. *Journal of the British Dragonfly Society* **14**: 30–31.

Gardner, A.E. (1951). The life history of *Sympetrum danae* (Sulzer) = *S. scoticum* (Donovan) (Odonata). *Entomologist's Gazette* **2**: 109–28.

Gardner, A.E. (1953). The life-history of *Libellula depressa* Linn. (Odonata). *Entomologist's Gazette* **4**: 175–201.

Gardner, A.E. (1954a). A key to the larvae of the British Odonata. Introduction and Part I, Zygoptera; Part II, Anisoptera. *Entomologist's Gazette* **5**: 157–71; 193–213.

Gardner, A.E. (1954b). The life-history of *Coenagrion hastulatum* (Charp.) (Odonata: Coenagriidae). *Entomologist's Gazette* **5**: 17–40.

Gardner, A.E. (1955). The egg and mature larva of *Aeshna isosceles* (Müller) (Odonata: Aeshnidae). *Entomologist's Gazette* **6**: 13–20.

Gardner, A.E. & MacNeill, N. (1950). The life history of *Pyrrhosoma nymphula* (Sulzer) (Odonata). *Entomologist's Gazette* **1**: 163–82.

Garner, P. (2005). *The Dragonflies of Herefordshire*. Herefordshire Biological Records Centre: Hereford.

Gentry, J.B., Garten, C.T., Howell, F.G. & Smith, M.H. (1975). Thermal ecology of dragonflies in habitats receiving reactor effluent. *International Atomic Energy Agency (Vienna)* **187**: 563–74.

Gerken, B. & Sternberg, K. (1999). *Die Exuvien Europäischer Libellen (Insecta, Odonata)*. Arnica & Eisvogel: Höxter & Jena.

Gewecke, M. & Wendler, G. (1985). *Insect Locomotion*. Verlag Paul Parey: Berlin.

Gibbons, D.W. & Pain, D. (1992). The influence of river flow rate on the breeding of *Calopteryx* damselflies. *Journal of Animal Ecology* **61**: 283–9.

Gibson, V. (2003). Communication between the sexes at the end of copulation: a study of three species of Anisoptera. *Journal of the British Dragonfly Society* **19**: 44–6.

Gilbert, P. (1977). *A Compendium of the Biographical Literature on Deceased Entomologists*. British Museum (Natural History): London.

Gladwin, T.W. (1997). The error in treating the Green Emerald Damselfly *Lestes viridis* as a British species. *Journal of the British Dragonfly Society* **13**: 50–51.

Glass, N.R. (1971). Computer analysis of predation energetics in the large-mouth bass. *In:* Patten (1971), pp.325–63.

Gledhill, T. (1985). Water mites – predators and parasites. *Freshwater Biological Association Annual Report* **53**: 45–59.

Goodchild, C.G. (1943). The life-history of *Phyllodistomum solidum* Rankin 1937, with observations on the morphology, development and taxonomy of the Gorgoderinae (Trematoda). *Biological Bulletin* **84**: 59–86.

Goodyear, K.G. (1970). *Lestes sponsa* (Hansemann) (Odonata: Lestidae) as a predator of *Tipula melanoceros* Schummel (Diptera: Tipulidae). *Entomologist* **103**: 215–16.

Gorb, S.N. (1994a). Central projections of ovipositor sense organs in the damselfly, *Sympecma annulata* (Zygoptera, Lestidae). *Journal of Morphology* **220**: 139–46.

Gorb, S.N. (1994b). Female perching behaviour in *Sympetrum sanguineum* (Müller) at feeding places (Anisoptera: Libellulidae). *Odonatologica* **23**: 341–53.

Gorb, S.N. (1996). Initial stage of tandem contact in *Platycnemis pennipes* (Pallas) (Zygoptera: Platycnemididae). *Odonatologica* **25**: 371–6.

Gorb, S.N. (1998a). Origin and pathway of the epidermal secretion in the damselfly head-arresting system (Insecta: Odonata). *Journal of Insect Physiology* **44**: 1053–61.

Gorb, S.N. (1998b). Visual cues in mate recognition by males of the damselfly, *Coenagrion puella* (L.) (Odonata: Coenagrionidae). *Journal of Insect Behavior* **11**: 73–92.

Gorb, S. (1998c). Functional morphology of the head-arrester system in Odonata. *Zoologica, Stuttgart* **148**: 1–132.

Gorb, S. (1999a). Serial elastic elements in the damselfly wing: mobile vein joints contain resilin. *Naturwissenschaften* **86**: 552–5.

Gorb, S.N. (1999b). Evolution of the dragonfly head-arresting system. *Proceedings of the Royal Society of London (B)* **266**: 1–11.

Gorb, S.N. (1999c). Visual cues in mate recognition in the damselfly *Ischnura elegans* Vander Linden (Zygoptera: Coenagrionidae). *International Journal of Odonatology* **2**: 83–93.

Gorb, S.N. (2000). Ultrastructure of the neck membrane in dragonflies (Insecta, Odonata). *Journal of Zoology* **250**: 479–94.

Gorb, S.N. & Popov, V.L. (2002). Probabilistic fasteners with parabolic elements: biological system, artificial model and theoretical considerations. *Philosophical Transactions of the Royal Society of London (A)* **360**: 211–25.

Grabow, K. & Rüppell, G. (1995). Wing loading in relation to size and flight characteristics of European Odonata. *Odonatologica* **24**: 175–86.

Greenwood, J.J.D. (2000). Through the Director's binoculars. *British Trust for Ornithology News* **229** (July/August): 3.

Gribbin, S.D. (1989). Ecology and reproductive behaviour of damselflies. PhD thesis, University of Liverpool, UK.

Gribbin, S.D. & Thompson, D.J. (1990). A quantitative study of mortality at emergence in the damselfly *Pyrrhosoma nymphula* (Sulzer) from two adjacent ponds in northern England. *Freshwater Biology* **24**: 295–302.

Gribbin, S.D. & Thompson, D.J. (1991). The effects of size and residency on territorial disputes and short-term mating success in the damselfly *Pyrrhosoma nymphula* (Sulzer) (Zygoptera: Coenagrionidae). *Animal Behaviour* **41**: 689–95.

Griffiths, D. (1970). Observations on the food of dragonfly nymphs from a bog water in north Norway. *Entomologist's Monthly Magazine* **106**: 41–7.

Gyssel, F. & Stoks, R. (2006). Behavioral responses to fish kairomones and autotomy in a damselfly. *Journal of Ethology* **24**: 79–83.

Haacks, M. & Peschel, R. (2007). Die rezente Verbreitung von *Aeshna viridis* und *Leucorrhinia pectoralis* in Schleswig-Holstein – Ergebnisse einer vierjährigen Untersuctiungen (Odonata: Aeshnidae, Libellulidae). *Libellula* **26**: 41–57.

Hadrys, H. & Siva-Jothy, M. (1994). Unravelling the components that underlie insect reproductive traits using a simple molecular approach. *In:* Schierwater *et al.* (1994), pp.75–90.

Hammond, C.O. (1928). The emergence of *Erythromma najas*, Hans. (Paraneuroptera). *The Entomologist* **61**: 54–5.

Hammond, C.O. (1977). *The Dragonflies of Great Britain and Ireland.* 1st Edition. Curwen: London.

Hammond, C.O. & Merritt, R. (1983). *The Dragonflies of Great Britain and Ireland.* 2nd Edition. Harley Books: Colchester.

Hanel, L. (2000). The influence of the solar eclipse on dragonfly activities. *In: Vazky 2000. Sbornik referátu III. Celostátniho semináre odonatologu, ktery se konai v Chránene krajinné oblasti Trebonsko 15–18.6.2000* (Ed. Hanel, L.). Vlasim,

Czechoslovakia. [In Czech; English summary.]

Hanski, I. & Gilpin, M.E. (1997). *Metapopulation Biology: Ecology, Genetics, and Evolution.* Academic Press: San Diego.

Harding, P.T. (Ed.) (1992). *Biological Recording of Changes in British Wildlife.* Her Majesty's Stationery Office: London.

Harris, M. (1782). *Exposition of English Insects.* White: London.

Hart, C.W. & Fuller, S.L.H. (1974). *Pollution Ecology of Freshwater Invertebrates.* Academic Press: London.

Harvey, I.F. (1985). Larval spacing behaviour of two species of damselfly (Odonata: Zygoptera). PhD thesis. University of Dundee, UK.

Hawking, J.H. & Ingram, B.A. (1994). Rate of larval development of *Pantala flavescens* (Fabricius) at its southern limit of range in Australia (Anisoptera: Libellulidae). *Odonatologica* **23**: 63–8.

Hawking, J., Suhling, F., Wilson, K., Theischinger, G. & Reels, G. (2004). Underwater and epilithic oviposition by Australian Aeshnidae (Odonata). *International Journal of Odonatology* **7**: 33–6.

Hawksworth, D.L. (Ed.) (2001). *The Changing Wildlife of Great Britain and Ireland.* Systematics Association, Taylor & Francis: London.

Hayter-Hames, J. (1991). *Madam Dragonfly. The Life and Times of Cynthia Longfield.* Pentland Press: Soham.

Heinrich, B. (1972). Temperature regulation in the bumblebee *Bombus vagans*: a field study. *Science* **175**: 185–7.

Heinrich, B. (1993). *The Hot-blooded Insects: Strategies and Mechanisms of Thermoregulation.* Springer-Verlag: Berlin.

Hellmund, M. & Hellmund, W. (2002). Eigelege fossiler Zygopteren auf Dikotylenblättern aus dem Mittelmiozän von Salzhausen (Vogelsberg, Hessen, Deutschland). *Odonatologica* **31**: 253–72.

Henrikson, B.-I. (1988). The absence of antipredator behaviour in the larvae of *Leucorrhinia dubia* (Odonata) and the consequences of their distribution. *Oikos* **51**: 179–83.

Heymer, A. (1964). Ein Beitrag zur Kenntnis der Libelle *Oxygastra curtisi* (Dale, 1834) (Odonata: Anisoptera). *Beiträge zur Entomologie* **14**: 31–44.

Heymer, A. (1966). Études comparées du comportement inné de *Platycnemis acutipennis* Selys 1841 et de *Platycnemis latipes* Rambur 1842 (Odon. Zygoptera). *Annales de la Société Entomologique de France (N.S.)* **2**: 39–73.

Heymer, A. (1967). Contribution a l'étude du comportement de ponte du genre *Platycnemis* Burmeister, 1839 (Odonata; Zygoptera). *Zeitschrift für Tierpsychologie* **24**: 645–50.

Heymer, A. (1969). Fortpflanzungsverhalten und Territorialität bei *Orthetrum coerulescens* (Fabr., 1798) und *O. brunneum* (Fonsc., 1837) (Odonata; Anisoptera). *Revue de Comportement Animal, Paris* **3**: 1–24.

Heymer, A. (1970). Die Funktion der Kaudalstacheln bei *Aeschna*-Larven beim Beutefang und Aggressionsverhalten (Odon. Anisoptera). *Annales de la Société Entomologique de France (N.S.)* **6**: 637–45.

Heymer, A. (1972). Comportements social et territorial des Calopterygidae (Odon. Zygoptera). *Annales de la Société Entomologique de France (N.S.)* **8**: 3–53.

Hickling, R., Roy, D.B., Hill, J.K. & Thomas, C.D. (2005). A northward shift of range margins in British Odonata. *Global Change Biology* **11**: 502–6.

Higashi, K. (1969). Territoriality and dispersal in the population of dragonfly, *Crocothemis servilia* Drury (Odonata: Anisoptera). *Memoirs of the Faculty of Science, Kyushu University, Series E (Biology)* **5**: 95–113.

Higashi, K., Nomakuchi, S., Maeda, M. & Yasuda, T. (1979). Daily food consumption of *Mnais pruinosa* Selys (Zygoptera: Calopterygidae). *Odonatologica* **8**: 159–69.

Higashi, K., Nomakuchi, S., Okame, Y. & Harada, M. (1982). Length of maturation period and daily food consumption of immature damselfly, *Mnais pruinosa* Selys (Zygoptera: Calopterygidae), *Tombo* **25**: 23–6.

Higler, L.W.G. (1976). Analysis of the macrofauna community on *Stratiotes* vegetations. *Verhandlungen der Internationalen Verein Limnologie* **19**: 2773–77.

Hilfert, D. (1994). Flugactivität von Libellen am Fortpflanzungsgewässer in Abhängigkeit von verschiedenen klimatischen Faktoren und unterschiedlichen geographischen Lagen. Diploma thesis, Technische Universität, Braunschweig, Germany.

Hilfert, D. (1997). Motivation as a mechanism to optimize mating success in *Calopteryx* (Odonata: Calopterygidae). [Abstract only.] *Advances in Ethology* **32**: 235.

Hilfert, D. & Rüppell, G. (1997). Early morning oviposition of dragonflies with low temperatures for male-avoidance (Odonata: Aeshnidae, Libellulidae). *Entomologia Generalis* **21**: 177–88.

Hilfert-Rüppell, D. (1998). Temperature dependence of flight activity of Odonata by ponds. *Odonatologica* **27**: 45–59.

Hilfert-Rüppell, D. (1999). To stay or not to stay: decision-making during territorial behaviour of *Calopteryx haemorrhoidalis* and *Calopteryx splendens splendens* (Zygoptera: Calopterygidae). *International Journal of Odonatology* **2**: 167–75.

Hilfert-Rüppell, D. & Rüppell, G. (2007).

Juwelenschwingen – Geheimnisvolle Libellen. Gossamer Wings – Mysterious Dragonflies. Splendens-Verlag: Cremlingen.

Hilton, D.F.J. (1983). Reproductive behaviour of *Cordulia shurtleffi* Scudder (Anisoptera: Corduliidae). *Odonatologica* **12**: 115–24.

Hine, A. (Ed.) (1995). *Woodland Pond Management.* Richmond Publishing Co.: London.

Hinnekint, B.O.N. (1987). Odonata hoarding food. *Notulae Odonatologicae* **2**: 154.

HMSO (Her Majesty's Stationery Office). (1994). *Biodiversity. The UK Action Plan.* HMSO: London.

Hobby, B.M. (1933). The prey of British dragonflies. *Transactions of the Entomological Society of the South of England* **8**: 65–76.

Hobby, B.M. (1936). Dragonflies and their prey. *Proceedings of the Royal Entomological Society of London (A)* **11**: 101–3.

Holmes, J.D. (1984). Rapid larval development in *Brachytron pratense* (Müller). *Journal of the British Dragonfly Society* **1**: 38.

Holmes, J.D. & Randolph, S. (1994). An early emergence (one year life cycle) of *Libellula depressa* Linnaeus and *Anax imperator* Leach. *Journal of the British Dragonfly Society* **10**: 25–8.

Hopkins, G.W. & Day, K.J. (1997). *The Southern Damselfly, Coenagrion mercuriale: Dispersal and Adult Behaviour.* Countryside Council for Wales: Bangor.

Horváth, G. (1995a). How do aquatic insects find their aquatic habitat? *World of Nature* **1995**: 45–9.

Horváth, G. (1995b). Reflection-polarization patterns at flat water surfaces and their relevance for insect polarization vision. *Journal of Theoretical Biology* **175**: 27–37.

Horváth, G., Bernáth, B. & Molnár, G. (1998). Dragonflies find crude oil more attractive then water: multiple-choice experiments on dragonfly polarotaxis. *Naturwissenschaften* **85**: 292–7.

Houghton, J. (2004). *Global Warming.* Cambridge University Press: Cambridge.

Houghton, J.T. & Ding, Y. (2001). *Climate Change 2001: the Scientific Basis. Contribution of Working Group I to the Third Assessment Report of the Intergovernmental Panel on Climate Change.* Intergovernmental Panel on Climate Change: Cambridge.

Huggert, L. (1982). Descriptions and redescriptions of *Trichopria* species from Africa and the Oriental and Australian regions (Hymenoptera, Proctotrupoidea: Diapridae). *Entomologica Scandinavica* **13**: 109–22.

Hughes, J.P. (1981). The attainment of metamorphosis-readiness in the dragonfly, *Pyrrhosoma nymphula* in eastern Scotland (Odonata: Zygoptera). (Supplement, 1982: continuing report of *Pyrrhosoma nymphula*; unpubl.). BSc thesis, University of Dundee, UK.

Hunger, H. (1998). Biozönologische Untersuchungen zum Habitatschema des Kleinen Granatauges (*Erythromma viridulum* Charpentier 1840) in der südlichen Oberrheinebene. *Naturschutz am südlichen Oberrhein* **2**: 149–58.

Inden-Lohmar, C. (1995). Population structure and reproductive behaviour of *Aeshna cyanea* Müller (Aeshnidae). *Abstracts of the 13th International Symposium of Odonatology, Essen*, p.25.

Inden-Lohmar, C. (1997). Suksession, Struktur und Dynamik von Libellenpopulationen an Kleingewässern unter besonderer Berücksichtigung von *Aeshna cyanea* (Odonata: Aeshnidae). Doctor thesis, University of Bonn, Germany.

Inoue, K. & Shimizu, N. (1976). Moniliform egg-strings laid by *Davidius moiwanus taruii* Asahina and Inoue, a case of "non-contact sitting oviposition". (Anisoptera: Gomphidae). *Odonatologica* **5**: 265–72.

Inoue, K., Obana, S. & Fujiwara, Y. (1981). [Life history of *Aeschnophlebia longistigma*.] [In Japanese; English summary.] *Tombo* **23**: 23–7.

IPCC (Intergovernmental Panel on Climate Change) (2001). [Houghton J.T., Ding, Y., Griggs, D.J., Noguer, M., Van der Linden, P.J., Dai, X., Maskell, K. & Johnson, C.A. (Eds). Cambridge University Press: Cambridge.]

Ishizawa, N. (2005a). The response to rotating objects by *Anotogaster sieboldii* (Selys) males, pt 2 (Anisoptera: Cordulegastridae. *Odonatologica* **34**: 211–18.

Ishizawa, N. (2005b). Letter to P.S.C., 21 August.

Ishizawa, N. & Arai, Y. (2003). The response to rotating objects by *Anotogaster sieboldii* (Selys) males (Anisoptera: Cordulegastridae). *Odonatologica* **32**: 19–28.

Ito, Y., Brown, J.L. & Kikkawa, J. (Eds) (1987). *Animal Societies: Theories and Facts.* Japan Scientific Societies Press: Tokyo.

Jacobs, M.E. (1955). Studies on territorialism and sexual selection in dragonflies. *Ecology* **36**: 566–86.

Jacquemin, G. (2005). A propos de l'identification à distance des odonates adultes. *Martinia* **21**: 47–50.

Jenkins, D.K. (1998). A population study of *Coenagrion mercuriale* (Charpentier) in the New Forest. Part 7. Mark/recapture used to determine the extent of local movement. *Journal of the British Dragonfly Society* **14**: 1–4.

Jenkins, D.K. (2001). Population studies of the Southern Damselfly *Coenagrion mercuriale* (Charpentier) in the New Forest. *Journal of the British Dragonfly Society* **17**: 13–19.

Jödicke, R. (1997a). Tagesperiodik der Flugaktivität von *Anax imperator* Leach (Anisoptera: Aeshnidae). *Libellula* **16**: 111–29.

Jödicke, R. (1997b). *Die Binsenjungfern und Winterlibellen Europas.* Westarp Wissenschaften: Magdeburg.

Jödicke, M. & Jödicke, R. (1996). Changes in diel emergence rhythm of *Orthetrum cancellatum* (L.) at a Mediterranean irrigation tank (Odonata: Libellulidae). *Opuscula Zoologica Fluminensia* **140**: 1–11.

Johansson, A. & Johansson, F. (1992). Effects of two different caddisfly case structures on predation by a dragonfly larva. *Aquatic Insects* **14**: 73–84.

Johansson, F. (1991). Foraging modes in an assemblage of odonate larvae: effects of prey and interference. *Hydrobiologia* **209**: 79–87.

Johansson, F. (1992a). Effects of zooplankton availability and foraging mode on cannibalism in three dragonfly larvae. *Oecologia* **91**: 179–83.

Johansson, F. (1992b). Predator life style and prey mobility: a comparison of two predatory odonate larvae. *Archiv für Hydrobiologie* **126**: 163–73.

Johansson, F. (1993). Effects of prey type, prey density and predator presence on behaviour and predation risk in a larval damselfly. *Oikos* **63**: 481–9.

Johansson, F. (2000). The slow-fast life style characteristics in a suite of six species of odonate larvae. *Freshwater Biology* **43**: 149–59.

Johansson, F. & Brodin, T. (2003). Effects of fish predators and abiotic factors on dragonfly community structure. *Journal of Freshwater Ecology* **18**: 415–23.

Johansson, F. & Norling, U. (1994). A five-year study of the larval life history of *Coenagrion hastulatum* (Charpentier) and *C. armatum* (Charpentier) in northern

Sweden (Zygoptera: Coenagrionidae). *Odonatologica* **23**: 355–64.

Johansson, F. & Rowe, L. (1999). Life history and behavioural responses to time constraints in a damselfly. *Ecology* **80**: 1242–52.

Johansson, F. & Stoks, R. (2005). Adaptive plasticity in response to predators in dragonfly larvae and other aquatic insects. *In:* Fellowes *et al.* (Eds) (2005), pp.347–70.

Johansson, F., Crowley, P.H. & Brodin, T. (2005). Sexual size dimorphism and sex ratios in dragonflies (Odonata). *Biological Journal of the Linnean Society of London* **86**: 507–13.

Johnson, C. (1962). Breeding behaviour and oviposition in *Calopteryx maculatum* (Beauvois) (Odonata: Calopterygidae). *American Midland Naturalist* **68**: 242–7.

Johnson, C. (1966). Improvements for colonizing damselflies in the laboratory. *Texas Journal of Science* **18**: 179–83.

Johnson, C.G. (1969). *Migration and Dispersal of Insects by Flight*. Methuen: London.

Johnson, D.M. & Crowley, P.H. (1989). A ten-year study of the odonate assemblage of Bays Mountain Lake, Tennessee. *Advances in Odonatology* **4**: 27–43.

Johnson, D.M., Martin, T.H., Mahato, M., Crowder, L.B. & Crowley, P.H. (1995). Predation, density dependence, and life histories of dragonflies: a field experiment in a freshwater community. *Journal of the North American Benthological Society* **14**: 547–62.

Johnson, S. (1806). *Dictionary of the English Language*. 9th Edition. Volume 1. Privately printed: London.

Jolly, G.M. (1965). Explicit estimates from capture-recapture data with both death and immigration – a stochastic model. *Biometrika* **52**: 225–47.

Jones, G. (2003). The Hairy Dragonfly (*Brachytron pratense* (Müller)) – an Odonata species new to Cumbria. *Carlisle Naturalist* **11**: 39–40.

Jones, R.A. & Jones, K. (1997). *In:* Jones (1997*b*), p.17.

Jones, S.P. (1985). A note on the survival of dragonflies in adverse conditions in Cornwall. *Journal of the British Dragonfly Society* **1**: 83–4.

Jones, S.P. (1997*a*). The summer of 1996. *In:* Jones (1997*b*), pp.14–18.

Jones, S.P. (Ed.) (1997*b*). *Cornwall Dragonfly Group Newsletter* **7**: 37 pp.

Jones, S.P. (2000). First proof of successful breeding by the Lesser Emperor *Anax parthenope* (Selys) in Britain. *Journal of the British Dragonfly Society* **16**: 20–23.

Jurzitza, G. (1969). Eiablage von *Chalcolestes viridis* (Van der Linden) in postcopula und ohne Begleitung durch das Mannchen sowie Gedanken zur Evolution des Fortpflanzungsverhaltens bei den Odonaten. *Tombo* **12**: 25–7.

Kaiser, H. (1974*a*). Verhaltensgefüge und Temporalverhalten der Libelle *Aeschna cyanea* (Odonata). *Zeitschrift für Tierpsychologie* **34**: 398–429.

Kaiser, H. (1974*b*). Intraspezifische Aggression und räumliche Verteilung bei der Libelle *Onychogomphus forcipatus* (Odonata). *Oecologia* **15**: 223–34.

Kaiser, H. (1974*c*). Die Regelung der Individuendichte bei Libellenmännchen (*Aeschna cyanea*, Odonata). Eine Analyse mit systemtheoretischem Ansatz. *Oecologia* **14**: 53–74.

Kaiser, H. (1975). Räumliche und zeitliche Aufteilung des Paarungsplatzes bei Grosslibellen (Odonata, Anisoptera). *Verhandlungen Gesellschaft der Ökologie (Vienna)* **1975**: 115–20.

Kaiser, H. (1981). Intraspecific aggression, territorial behaviour and "territorial" behaviour in dragonflies. *Abstracts of the 6th International Symposium of Odonatology,* Chur, 21–2.

Kaiser, H. (1982). Do *Cordulegaster* males defend territories? A preliminary investigation of mating strategies in *Cordulegaster boltonii* (Donovan) (Anisoptera: Cordulegastridae). *Odonatologica* 11: 139–52.

Kaiser, H. (1985). Availability of receptive females at the mating place and mating chances of males in the dragonfly *Aeschna cyanea. Behavioral Ecology and Sociobiology* 18: 1–7.

Kaiser, H. & Poethke, H.-J. (1984). Analyse und Simulation eines Paarungssystems von Libellen. I. Beobachtungsdaten und Simulationmodell. *In:* Moller (1984), pp.59–64.

Kalko, E. (2001). Bats gleaning dragonflies. *Argia* 13: 27.

Kato, K., Watanabe, Y. & Yokota, H. (1997). [Preliminary note on artificial parthenogenesis in *Stylurus oculatus* (Odonata, Gomphidae).] [In Japanese; English summary.]. *New Entomologist* 46: 16–19.

Kemp, R.G. (1997a). *Coenagrion scitulum. In:* Brooks (1997a), pp.85–6.

Kemp, R.G. (1997b). *Leucorrhinia dubia. In:* Brooks (1997a), pp.156–7.

Kemp, R.G. (1988). Is *Gomphus vulgatissimus* exclusively a riverine species in the British Isles? *Journal of the British Dragonfly Society* 4: 8–9.

Kennedy, C.H. (1950). The relation of American dragonfly-eating birds to their prey. *Ecological Monographs* 20: 103–43.

Kerry, L. (2001). Habitat management for the Southern Damselfly *Coenagrion mercuriale* (Charpentier) on Aylesbeare Common, Devon. *Journal of the British Dragonfly Society* 17: 45–8.

Ketelaar, R. (2002). The recent expansion of the Small Red-eyed Damselfly *Erythromma viridulum* (Charpentier) in the Netherlands. *Journal of the British Dragonfly Society* 18: 1–8.

Kiauta, B. (1965). Notes on the odonate fauna of some brackish waters of Walcheren Island. *Entomologische Berichten (Amsterdam)* 25: 54–8.

Kiauta, B. & Kiauta, M. (1995). Odonatological periodicals in print. *Notulae Odonatologicae* 4: 77–80.

Kiauta, B. & Kiauta, M. (1999). A note on dragonfly response during the 93.8% solar eclipse of 11 August 1999 in the Netherlands (Odonata). *Opuscula Zoologica Fluminensia* 172: 1–6.

Kirby, W.F. (1890). *A Synonymic Catalogue of Neuroptera Odonata, or Dragonflies. With an Appendix of Fossil Species.* Gurney & Jackson: London.

Kirkton, S.D. & Schultz, T.D. (2001). Age-specific behavior and habitat selection of adult male damselflies, *Calopteryx maculata* (Odonata: Calopterygidae). *Journal of Insect Behavior* 14: 545–56.

Kitching, D. (2004). News from Cheshire. *Newsletter of the Dragonfly Recording Network* 21: 8–9.

Klötzli, A.M. (1971). Zur Revierstetigkeit von *Calopteryx virgo* (L.) (Odonata). *Mitteilungen der Schweizerischen Entomologische Gesellschaft* 43: 240–48.

Knapp, E., Krebs, A. & Wildermuth, H. (1983). Libellen. *Neujahrsblatt der Naturforschenden. Gesellschaft Schaffhausen* 35: 1–90.

Knight, T.M., McCoy, M.W., Chase, J.M., McCoy, K.A. & Holt, R.D. (2005). Trophic cascades across ecosystems. *Nature, London* 437: 880–83.

Kotarac, M. (1993). Dragonfly observations in the Raka area, Lower Carniola, eastern Slovenia, with a note on the behaviour of *Somatochlora meridionalis* Nielsen

(Anisoptera: Corduliidae). *Notulae Odonatologicae* **4**: 1–4.

Krishnaraj, R. & Pritchard, G. (1995). The influence of larval size, temperature and components of the functional response to prey density, on growth rates of the dragonflies *Lestes disjunctus* and *Coenagrion resolutum* (Insecta, Odonata). *Canadian Journal of Zoology* **73**: 1672–80.

Krull, W.H. (1931). Life history studies on two frog lung flukes, *Pneumonoeces medioplexus* and *Pneumonobites parviplexus*. *Transactions of the American Microscopical Society* **50**: 215–77.

Krüner, U. (1977). Revier- und Fortpflanzungsverhalten von *Orthetrum cancellatum* (Linnaeus) (Anisoptera: Libellulidae). *Odonatologica* **6**: 263–70.

Krüner, U. (1990). Eine Wasserfalle für Kleinlibellenlarven. *Libellula* **9**: 145–9.

Kuhn, K. (2000). Untersuchungen zum Vorkommen der Heim-Azurjungfer (*Coenagrion mercuriale* Charpentier, 1840) im mittleren Mindeltal (Insecta, Odonata). *Berichte Naturforschung Gesellschaft Augsberg* **59**: 39–50.

Kumar, A. (1984). On the life history of *Pantala flavescens* (Fabricius) (Libellulidae: Odonata). *Annals of Entomology* **2**: 43–50.

Kurata, M. (1974). [*Alpine dragonflies. A Survey and an Account of a Pursuit of Aeshna juncea.*] [In Japanese.] Seibundo–shinkosha: Tokyo.

Lambert, C.L. (1994). The influence of larval density on larval growth, and the consequences for adult survival and reproductive success in the damselfly *Calopteryx virgo* (Odonata). PhD thesis, University of Plymouth, UK.

Lamborn, R.H. (1890). *Dragonflies versus Mosquitoes. Can the Mosquito Pest be Mitigated?* Appleton: New York.

Land, M.F. (1989). Variations in the structure and design of compound eyes. *In:* Stavenga & Hardie (1989), pp.90–111.

Land, M.F. (1997). Visual acuity in insects. *Annual Review of Entomology* **42**: 147–77.

Lane, N. (2002). The big O. *New Scientist* **2002**: 41–3.

Lang, C. (1999). Zur Biologie und Mikrohabitatwahl der Larven von *Cordulegaster heros* Theischinger, 1979 und *Cordulegaster bidentata* Selys, 1843 (Insecta: Odonata) im Weidlingbach (Nieder Österreich). Doctor thesis, Universität Wien, Austria.

Langenbach, A. (1993). Time of colour change in female *Ischnura pumilio* (Charpentier) (Zygoptera: Coenagrionidae). *Odonatologica* **22**: 469–77.

Langenbach, A. (1995). Female colour polymorphism and reproductive behaviour in *Ischnura pumilio* (Charpentier) (Odonata: Coenagrionidae). Unpublished manuscript.

Lawton, J.H. (1970a). Feeding and food energy assimilation in larvae of the damselfly *Pyrrhosoma nymphula* (Sulz.) (Odonata: Zygoptera). *Journal of Animal Ecology* **39**: 669–89.

Lawton, J.H. (1970b). A population study on larvae of the damselfly *Pyrrhosoma nymphula* (Sulzer) (Odonata: Zygoptera). *Hydrobiologia* **36**: 33–52.

Lawton, J.H. (1971). Ecological energetics studies on larvae of the damselfly *Pyrrhosoma nymphula* (Sulzer) (Odonata: Zygoptera). *Journal of Animal Ecology* **40**: 385–423.

Lawton, J.H. (1973). The energy cost of "food gathering". *In:* Benjamin *et al.* (1973), pp.59–76.

Leach, W. (1815). Entomology. *In:* Brewster (1830) **9**: 150–76.

Legrand, J. (1974). Étude comparative de l'autotomie chez les larves de zygoptères

(Odon.). *Annales de Société Entomologique Française, N.S.,* **10**: 635–646.

Legris, M. & Pilon, J.-G. (1985). Ponte et action de la température sur le développement embryonnaire d'*Argia moesta* (Hagen) (Zygoptera: Coenagrionidae). *Odonatologica* **14**: 357–62.

Leipelt, K.G. (2005). Behavioural differences in response to current: implications for the longitudinal distribution of stream odonates. *Archiv für Hydrobiologie* **163**: 81–100.

Lempert, J. (1988). Untersuchungen zur Fauna, Ökologie und zum Fortpflanzungsverhalten von Libellen (Odonata) an Gewässern des tropischen Regenwaldes in Liberia, Westafrika. Diploma thesis, Universität Instelling, Bonn, Germany.

Lempert, J. (1995a). Personal communication to P.S.C., 21 August.

Lempert, J. (1995b). On the habitat and reproductive behaviour of *Indocnemis orang* (Foerster) in West Malaysia (Zygoptera: Platycnemididae). *Unpublished* M S.

Levins, R. (1968). *Evolution in Changing Environments. Some Theoretical Explorations.* Princeton University Press: Princeton.

Leyshon, O.J. & Moore, N.W. (1993). A note on the British Dragonfly Society's survey of *Anaciaeschna isosceles* at Castle Marshes, Barnby, Suffolk. *Journal of the British Dragonfly Society* **9**: 5–9.

Lindeboom, M. (1995). Copulation behaviour of *Calopterx splendens*. *Abstracts of the 13th International Symposium of Odonatology, Essen,* p.32.

Lindeboom, M. (1998). Post-copulatory behaviour in *Calopteryx* females (Insecta, Odonata, Calopterygidae). *International Journal of Odonatology* **1**: 175–84.

Linnaeus, C. (1758). *Systema Naturae: Regnum Animale.* 10th Edition, revised. Laurentius Salvius: Holmiae, Sweden.

Lisney, A.A. (1960). *A Bibliography of British Lepidoptera.* Chiswick Press: London.

Lloyd, E.C. & Ormerod, S.J. (1992). Further studies on the larvae of the Golden-Ringed Dragonfly, *Cordulegaster boltonii* (Donovan) (Odonata: Cordulegastridae), in upland streams. *Entomologist's Gazette* **43**: 275–81.

Logan, E.R. (1971). A comparative ecological and behavioral study of two species of damselflies, *Enallagma boreale* (Selys) and *Enallagma carunculatum* Morse (Odonata: Coenagrionidae). PhD thesis, Washington State University, Pulman, USA.

Lohmann, H. (1981). Taxonomie einiger *Crocothemis*-Arten, nebst Beschreibung einer neuen Art von Madagascar (Anisoptera: Libellulidae). *Odonatologica* **10**: 109–16.

Long, R. (1991). An observation of an apparently water-divining dragonfly. *Journal of the British Dragonfly Society* **7**: 34.

Longfield, C. (1937). *The Dragonflies of the British Isles.* 1st Edition. Warne: London.

Longfield, C. (1948). A vast immigration of dragonflies into the south coast of Co. Cork. *Irish Naturalists' Journal* **9**: 133–41.

Longfield, C. (1949). *The Dragonflies of the British Isles.* 2nd Edition. Warne: London.

Longfield, C. (1960). History of the British dragonflies. *In:* Corbet *et al.* (1960), pp.25–32.

Lovelock, J. (2006). *The Revenge of Gaia.* Allen Lane: London.

Lucas, W.J. (1900). *British Dragonflies (Odonata).* Upcott Gill: London.

Lucas, W.J. (1908). Notes on the British dragonflies of the 'Dale collection'. *Entomologist's Monthly Magazine* **45**: 79–83.

Lucas, W.J. (1912). British Odonata in 1911. *Entomologist* **45**: 171–3.

Lucas, W.J. (1930). *The Aquatic (Naiad) Stage of the British Dragonflies (Paraneuroptera).* Ray Society: London.

Lutz, P.E. (1968). Effects of temperature and photoperiod on larval development in *Lestes eurinus* (Odonata: Lestidae). *Ecology* **49**: 637–44.

Lutz, P.E. & Pittman, A.R. (1970). Some ecological factors influencing a community of adult Odonata. *Ecology* **51**: 279–84.

Macan, T.T. (1964). The Odonata of a moorland fish pond. *Internationale Revue der gesamten Hydrobiologie und Hydrographie* **49**: 325–60.

Macan, T.T. (1966). The influence of predation on the fauna of a moorland fishpond. *Archiv für Hydrobiologie* **61**: 432–52.

Macarthur, R. & Pianka, E. (1966). On optimal use of a patchy environment. *American Naturalist* **100**: 603–9.

Macarthur, R.H. & Wilson, E.O. (1972). *The Theory of Island Biogeography.* Princeton University Press: Princeton.

Macy, R.W. (1964). Life cycle of the digenetic trematode *Pleurogenoides tener* (Looss, 1898) (Lecithodendriidae). *Journal of Parasitology* **50**: 564–8.

Manly, B.F.J. & Parr, M.J. (1968). A new method of estimating population size, survivorship and birth-rate from capture-recapture data. *Transactions of the Society for British Entomology* **18**: 81–9.

Manning, G.S. (1971). Study of novel intestinal parasites in Thailand. *Proceedings of the 1st International Seminar, SEATO Medical Research Laboratory, Bangkok*, pp.43–6.

Marden, J.H. (1989). Bodybuilding dragonflies: costs and benefits of maximizing flight muscle. *Physiological Zoology* **62**: 505–21.

Marden, J.H. & Waage, J.K. (1990). Escalated damselfly territorial contests are energetic wars of attrition. *Animal Behaviour* **398**: 954–9.

Marren, P. (2005). Obituary: Miriam Rothschild (1908–2005). *Natural World* **73**: 11.

Martens, A. (1992a). Egg deposition rates and duration of oviposition in *Platycnemis pennipes* (Pallas) (Insecta: Odonata). *Hydrobiologia* **230**: 63–70.

Martens, A. (1992b). Aggregationen von *Platycnemis pennipes* (Pallas) während der Eiablage (Odonata: Platycnemidae), Braunschweig, Germany. Doctor thesis, Universität Carolo-Wilhelmina, Braunschweig, Germany.

Martens, A. (1993). Influence of conspecifics and plant structures on oviposition site selection in *Pyrrhosoma nymphula* (Sulzer) (Zygoptera: Coenagrionidae). *Odonatologica* **22**: 487–94.

Martens, A. (1994). Field experiments on aggregation behaviour and oviposition in *Coenagrion puella* (L.) (Zygoptera: Coenagrionidae). *Advances in Odonatology* **6**: 49–58.

Martens, A. (1996). *Die Federlibellen Europas [Platycnemididae].* Westarp Wissenschaften: Magdeburg.

Martens, A. (2000). Group oviposition in *Coenagrion mercuriale* (Charpentier) (Zygoptera: Coenagrionidae). *Odonatologica* **29**: 329–32.

Martin, R. (1910). Sur les oiseaux de France qui se nourissent de libellules. *Revue Française d'Ornithologie* **12**: 178–80.

Martin, R. (1911). Sur les oiseaux qui se mourissent de libellules (3e note). *Revue Française d'Ornithologie* **26**: 97–9.

Maslin, M. (2002). *Global Warming.* Colin Baxter Photography: Grantown-on-Spey, Scotland.

Masseau, M.J. & Pilon, J.-G. (1982). Clef de determination des stades larvaires de *Enallagma boreale* Selys, *E. ebrium* (Hagen), *E. hageni* (Walsh) et *E. vernale* Gloyd (Zygoptera: Coenagrionidae). *Odonatologica* **11**: 189–99.

Matsubara, K. & Hironaka, M. (2005). Postcopulatory guarding behaviour in a territorial damselfly, *Pseudagrion p. pilidorsum* (Brauer), for submerged ovipositing females (Zygoptera: Coenagrionidae). *Odonatologica* **34**: 387–96.

Matushkina, N.A. & Gorb, S.N. (2002a). Patterns of endophytic egg-sets in damselflies (Odonata, Zygoptera). *Vestnik Zoologii (Supplement)* **14**: 152–59.

Matushkina, N.A. & Gorb, S.N. (2002b). Stylus of the odonate endophytic ovipositor: a mechanosensory organ controlling egg positioning. *Journal of Insect Physiology* **48**: 213–19.

Matushkina, N.A. & Gorb, S.N. (2007). Mechanical properties of the endophytic ovipositor in damselflies (Zygoptera, Odonata) and their oviposition substrates. *Zoology* **2007**: doi:10.1016/j.zool.2006.11.003.

Mauersberger, H. & Mauersberger, R. (2001). Hornisse *Vespa crabro* als Prädator von *Aeshna cyanea* (Hymenoptera: Vespidae; Odonata: Aeshnidae). *Libellula* **20**: 87–9.

May, M.L. (1984). Energetics of adult Anisoptera, with special reference to feeding and reproductive behavior. *Advances in Odonatology* **2**: 95–116.

May, M.L. (1991). Thermal adaptations of dragonflies revisited. *Advances in Odonatology* **5**: 71–88.

May, M.L. (1995a). Simultaneous control of head and thoracic temperature by the Green Darner Dragonfly *Anax junius* (Odonata: Aeshnidae). *Journal of Experimental Biology* **198**: 2373–84.

May, M.L. (1995b). Dependence of flight behavior and heat production on air temperature in the Green Darner Dragonfly *Anax junius* (Odonata: Aeshnidae). *Journal of Experimental Biology* **198**: 2385–92.

Mayhew, P.J. (1994). Food intake and adult feeding behaviour in *Calopteryx splendens* (Harris) and *Erythromma najas* (Hansemann) (Zygoptera: Calopterygidae, Coenagrionidae). *Odonatologica* **23**: 115–24.

McBean, M.C., White, S.A. & MacGregor, J.A. (2005). Foraging behaviour of the damselfly larva *Pyrrhosoma nymphula* (Sulzer) in response to predator presence (Zygoptera: Coenagrionidae). *Odonatologica* **34**: 155–64.

McGeeney, A. (1986). *A Complete Guide to British Dragonflies*. Jonathan Cape: London.

McGeeney, A. (1997). Migrant Hawker *Aeshna mixta* Latreille. In: Brooks (1997a), pp.104–5.

McLachlan, R. (1865). Note on the occurrence of *Aeshna borealis* and other dragonflies at Rannoch. *Entomologist's Monthly Magazine* **2**: 117–18.

McLachlan, R. (1870). Occurrence of *Cordulia metallica*, Van der Lind.: a dragonfly new to Britain. *Entomologist's Monthly Magazine* **7**: 38.

McLachlan, R. (1884). The British dragonflies annotated. *Entomologist's Monthly Magazine* **20**: 251–6.

McLachlan, R. (1900). *Agrion hastulatum* Charp., a new British dragonfly. *Entomologist's Monthly Magazine* **11**: 226.

McClanahan, R.J. (1971). 25. *Trialeurodes vaporariorum* (Westwood), Greenhouse Whitefly (Homoptera: Aleyrodidae). In: Corbet & Prentice (1971), pp.57–9.

McGuffin, M.A., Baker, R.L. & Forbes, M.R. (2006). Detection and avoidance of fish predators by adult *Enallagma* damselflies. *Journal of Insect Behavior* **19**: 77–91.

McMillan, V.E. (1991). Variable mate-guarding in the dragonfly *Plathemis lydia* (Odonata: Libellulidae). *Animal Behaviour* **41**: 979–87.

McPeek, M.A. (1989). Differential dispersal tendencies among *Enallagma* damselflies

(Odonata) inhabiting different habitats. *Oikos* **56**: 187–95.

McPeek, M.A. (1990). Determination of species composition in the *Enallagma* damselfly assemblages of permanent lakes. *Ecology* **71**: 83–98.

McPeek, M.A. (1995). Morphological evolution mediated by behavior in the damselflies of two communities. *Evolution* **49**: 749–69.

McPeek, M.A. (1998). The consequences of changing the top predator in a food web: a comparative experimental approach. *Ecological Monographs* **68**: 1–23.

McPeek, M.A. (1999). Biochemical evolution associated with antipredator adaptation in damselflies. *Evolution* **53**: 1835–45.

McPeek, M.A. & Peckarsky, B.L. (1998). Life histories and the strengths of species interactions combining mortality, growth and fecundity effects. *Ecology* **79**: 867–79.

McVey, M.E. (1984). Egg release rates with temperature and body size in libellulid dragonflies (Anisoptera). *Odonatologica* **13**: 377–85.

McVey, M.E. & Smittle (1984). Sperm precedence in the dragonfly *Erythemis simplicicollis*. *Journal of Insect Physiology* **30**: 619–628.

Merritt, R. (1983). Preface to Second Edition. *In:* Hammond & Merritt (1983), pp.9–10.

Merritt, R. (1987). The origins and early history of the British Dragonfly Society: a personal account. *Journal of the British Dragonfly Society* **3**: 21–7.

Merritt, R. (1988). Key Sites Project. *Odonata Recording Scheme Newsletter* **10**: 1–12.

Merritt, R. & Vick, G.S. (1983). Is *Sympetrum nigrescens* Lucas a good species? *Journal of the British Dragonfly Society* **3**: 21–7.

Merritt, R., Moore, N.W. & Eversham, B.C. (1996). *Atlas of the Dragonflies of Britain and Ireland*. Her Majesty's Stationery Office: London.

Meurgey, F. (1999). Quelques observations sur les émergences d'Odonates sur les ponts d'une rivière (Département de Charente-Maritime). *Martinia* **15**: 23–9.

Meurgey, F. (2004). Première observation d'*Anax junius* (Drury, 1773) en France (Odonata, Anisoptera, Aeshnidae). *Martinia* **20**: 13–15.

Meurgey, F. (2005). Complément à l'identification d'*Anax junius* (Drury, 1773) après sa récente observation en France métropolitaine. *Martinia* **21**: 31–4.

Meyer, W., Harisch, G. & Sagredost, A.N. (1986). Biochemical aspects of lead exposure in dragonfly larvae (Odonata: Anisoptera). *Ecotoxicology and Environmental Safety* **11**: 308–19.

Michiels, N.K. (1989a). Populatie- und gedragsecologie van de Zwarte Heidelibel *Sympetrum danae* (Sulzer) (Odonata: Libellulidae) [Section VII]. Doctor thesis, Universitet Instelling, Antwerp, Belgium.

Michiels, N.K. (1989b). Morphology of male and female genitalia in *Sympetrum danae* (Sulzer), with special reference to the mechanism of sperm removal during copulation (Anisoptera: Libellulidae). *Odonatologica* **18**: 21–31.

Michiels, N. (1992). Consequences and adaptive significance of variation in copulation duration in the dragonfly *Sympetrum danae*. *Behavioral Ecology and Sociobiology* **29**: 429–33.

Michiels, N. & Dhondt, A.A. (1988). Direct and indirect estimates of sperm precedence and displacement in the dragonfly *Sympetrum danae* (Odonata: Libellulidae). *Behavioral Ecology and Sociobiology* **23**: 257–63.

Michiels, N. & Dhondt A.A. (1989a). Differences in male and female activity patterns in the dragonfly *Sympetrum danae* (Sulzer) and their relation to mate-finding

(Anisoptera: Libellulidae). *Odonatologica* **18**: 349–64.

Michiels, N. & Dhondt, A.A. (1989b). Effects of emergence characteristics on longevity and maturation in the dragonfly *Sympetrum danae* (Anisoptera: Libellulidae). *Hydrobiologia* **171**: 149–58.

Michiels, N. & Dhondt, A.A. (1991). Sources of variation in male mating success and female oviposition rate in a nonterritorial dragonfly. *Behavioral Ecology and Sociobiology* **29**: 17–25.

Mill, P.J. (1981). Metamorphosis and neuromuscular changes in Aeshnidae. *Abstracts of the 6th International Symposium of Odonatology, Chur*, p.31.

Mill, P.J. (1982). A decade of dragonfly neurobiology. *Advances in Odonatology* **1**: 151–73.

Mill, P. (2005). The 'Penlee Incident'. *Dragonfly News* **47**: 33.

Mill, P.J., Taylor, P. & Parr, A.J. (2004). Vernacular names for the dragonflies of northwestern Europe. *Journal of the British Dragonfly Society* **20**: 73–6.

Miller, A.K., Miller, P.L. & Siva-Jothy, M.T. (1984). Pre-copulatory guarding and other aspects of reproductive behaviour in *Sympetrum depressiusculum* (Selys) at rice fields in southern France (Anisoptera: Libellulidae). *Odonatologica* **13**: 407–414.

Miller, K., Miller, C. & Miller, F. (2001). Peter Miller's ponds. *Dragonfly News* **40**: 12.

Miller, P.L. (1982). Temporal partitioning and other aspects of reproductive behaviour in two African libellulid dragonflies. *Entomologist's Monthly Magazine* **118**: 177–88.

Miller, P.L. (1987). An examination of the prolonged copulations of *Ischnura elegans* (Vander Linden) (Zygoptera: Coenagrionidae). *Odonatologica* **16**: 37–56.

Miller, P.L. (1990a). The rescue service provided by male *Enallagma cyathigerum* (Charpentier) for females after oviposition. *Journal of the British Dragonfly Society* **6**: 8–14.

Miller, P.L. (1990b). Mechanisms of sperm removal and sperm transfer in *Orthetrum coerulescens* (Fabricius) (Odonata: Libellulidae). *Physiological Entomology* **15**: 199–209.

Miller, P.L. (1991). The structure and function of the genitalia in the Libellulidae (Odonata). *Zoological Journal of the Linnean Society of London* **102**: 43–73.

Miller, P.L. (1994). Submerged oviposition and responses to oxygen lack in *Enallagma cyathigerum* (Charpentier) (Zygoptera: Coenagrionidae). *Advances in Odonatology* **6**: 79–88.

Miller, P.L. (1995a). *Dragonflies*. Richmond Press: Slough.

Miller, P.L. (1995b). Personal communication to P.S.C., including letter of 4 January.

Miller, P.L. (1997a). *Orthetrum cancellatum, Orthetrum coerulescens*. In: Brooks (1997a), pp.138–41.

Miller, P.L. (1997b). *Sympetrum striolatum*. In: Brooks (1997a), pp.143–4.

Miller, P.L. (1999). *Enallagma cyathigerum*. In: Brooks (1999), pp.87–8.

Miller, P.L. & Miller, A.K. (1989). Post-copulatory "resting" in *Orthetrum coerulescens* (Fabricius) and some other Libellulidae: time for "sperm handling"? *Odonatologica* **18**: 33–41.

Miller, P.L. & Miller, C.A. (1981). Field observations on copulatory behaviour in Zygoptera, with an examination of the structure and activity of the male genitalia. *Odonatologica* **10**: 201–18.

Milne, B.S. (1984). The dragonfly fauna of the Ouse Valley gravel pits. *Journal of the British Dragonfly Society* **1**: 55–9.

Mitchell, R. (1961). Behaviour of the larvae

of *Arrenurus fissicornis* Marshall, a water mite parasitic on dragonflies. *Animal Behaviour* **9**: 220–4.

Mitchell, R. (1963). Parasite-host relations of a water mite. *Year Book of the American Philosophical Society* **1963**: 342–4.

Mitchell, R. (1969). The use of parasitic mites to age dragonflies. *American Midland Naturalist* **82**: 359–66.

Mittelstaedt, H. (1950). Physiologie des Gleichgewichtssinnes bei fliegenden Libellen. *Zeitschrift für vergleichende Physiologie* **32**: 422–63.

Mizera, F., Bernáth, B., Kriska, G. & Horváth, G. (2001). Stereo videopolarimetry: measuring and visualising polarization patterns in three dimensions. *Journal of Imaging Science and Technology* **45**: 393–9.

Mokrushov, P.A. (1982). [Territorial behaviour of the Four-spotted Dragonfly, *Libellula quadrimaculata* (Odonata, Anisoptera)] [In Russian; English summary.] *Vestnik Zoologii, Kiev* **1982**: 58–62.

Mokrushov, P.A. & Frantsevich, L.I. (1976). [Visual stimuli in behaviour of dragonflies. II. Choice of settling place in *Erythromma najas*.] [In Russian; English summary.] *Vestnik Zoologii, Kiev* **1976**: 20–24.

Moller, D.P.F. (Ed.) (1984). *Systemanalyse Biologischer Prozesse.* Springer: Berlin.

Montgomery, B.E. (1925). Records of Indiana dragonflies, I. *Proceedings of the Indiana Academy of Science* **34**: 383–9.

Moore, A.J. (1987). The behavioral ecology of *Libellula luctuosa* (Burmeister) (Anisoptera: Libellulidae): I. Temporal changes in the population density and the effects on male territorial behavior. *Ethology* **75**: 246–54.

Moore, A.J. (1989). The behavioral ecology of *Libellula luctuosa* (Burmeister) (Anisoptera: Libellulidae): III. Male density, OSR, and male and female mating behavior. *Ethology* **80**: 120–36.

Moore, N.W. (1952). On the so-called "territories" of dragonflies (Odonata – Anisoptera). *Behaviour* **4**: 85–100.

Moore, N.W. (1953). Population density in adult dragonflies. *Journal of Animal Ecology* **22**: 344–59.

Moore, N.W. (1957). Territory in dragonflies and birds. *Bird Study, Oxford* **4**: 125–30.

Moore, N.W. (1960). The behaviour of the adult dragonfly. In: Corbet *et al.* (1960), pp.106–26.

Moore, N.W. (1964). Intra- and interspecific competition among dragonflies (Odonata): an account of observations and field experiments on population density control in Dorset, 1954–60. *Journal of Animal Ecology* **33**: 49–71.

Moore, N.W. (1986). Acid water dragonflies in eastern England – their decline, isolation and conservation. *Odonatologica* **15**: 377–85.

Moore, N.W. (1991a). The development of dragonfly communities and the consequences of territorial behaviour: a 27-year study on small ponds at Woodwalton Fen, Cambridgeshire, United Kingdom. *Odonatologica* **20**: 203–31.

Moore, N.W. (1991b). Male *Sympetrum striolatum* (Charp.) "defends" a basking spot rather than a particular locality (Anisoptera: Libellulidae). *Notulae Odonatologicae* **3**: 112.

Moore, N.W. (1991c). Where do adult *Gomphus vulgatissimus* (L.) go during the middle of the day? *Journal of the British Dragonfly Society* **7**: 40–3.

Moore, N.W. (1991d). The last of *Oxygastra curtisii* (Dale) in England? *Journal of the British Dragonfly Society* **7**: 6–10.

Moore, N.W. (1991e). Recent developments in the conservation of Odonata in Great Britain. *Advances in Odonatology* **5**: 103–8.

Moore, N.W. (1995). Experiments on population density of male *Coenagrion puella* (L.) by water (Zygoptera: Coenagrionidae). *Odonatologica* **24**: 123–8.

Moore, N.W. (2000). Interspecific encounters between male aeshnids. Do they have a function? *International Journal of Odonatology* **3**: 141–51.

Moore, N.W. (2001). Changes in the dragonfly communities at the twenty ponds at Wood Walton Fen, Cambridgeshire, United Kingdom, since the study of 1962–1988. *Odonatologica* **30**: 289–98.

Moore, N.W. (2004). The early days of recording. *Darter. Newsletter of the Dragonfly Recording Network* **21**: 3.

Moore, N.W. & Corbet, P.S. (1990). Guidelines for monitoring dragonfly populations. *Journal of the British Dragonfly Society* **6**: 21–3.

Mouffet, T. (1634). *Insectorum sive Minimorum Animalium Theatrum.* Cotes: London.

Müller, L. (1991). Oviposition in *Libellula depressa* L. (Anisoptera: Libellulidae). *Abstracts of the 11th International Symposium of Odonatology, Trevi,* p.20.

Müller, O. (2002). Die Habitate von Libellenlarven in der Oder (Insecta, Odonata). *Naturschutz und Landschaftspflege in Brandenburg* **11**: 205–12.

Münchberg, P. (1930). Zur Biologie der Odonatengenera *Brachytron* Evans und *Aeschna* Fbr. *Zeitschrift für Morphologie und Ökologie der Tiere* **20**: 172–232.

Münchberg, P. (1931). Beiträge zur Kenntnis der Biologie der Odonatengenera *Libellula* L., *Orthetrum* Newm. und *Leucorrhinia* Britt. in NO-Deutschland. *Abhandlungen und Berichte der Naturwissenschaftlichen Abteilung der Grenzmärkischen Gesellschaft zur Erforschung und Pflege der Heimat, Schneidemuhl Abteilung* **6**: 128–44.

Münchberg, P. (1932). Zur Biologie des Odonatengenus *Anax. Sitzungsberichte der Gesellschaft naturforschender Freunde zu Berlin* **1932**: 66–86.

Münchberg, P. (1952). Über Fortpflanzung, Lebensweise und Korperbau von *Arrenurus planus* Marsh, zugleich ein weiterer Beitrag zur Ökologie und Morphologie der im arctogäischen Raum eine libellenparasitische Larvenphase aufweisenden Arrenuri (Acari, Hydrachnellae). *Zoologische Jahrbucher (Abteilung Systematik, Ökologie und Geografie)* **81**: 27–46.

Mylecreest, P.H.W. (1978). Some effects of a unique hydroelectric development on the littoral benthic community and ecology of trout in a large New Zealand lake. MSc thesis, University of British Columbia, Vancouver.

Nagasu, F. (1999). [Mass oviposition in *Lestes sponsa*.] [In Japanese.]. *Nature & Insects* **34**: 36.

Needham, J.G. & Betten, C. (1901). Aquatic insects in the Adirondacks. *Bulletin of the New York State Museum* **47**: 383–612.

Needham, J.G. & Heywood, H.B. (1929). *A Handbook of the Dragonflies of North America.* Charles C. Thomas: Springfield.

Nel, A., Martinez-Delclos, X., Paicheler, J.C. & Henrotay, M. (1993). Les 'Anisozygoptera' fossils. Phylogenie et classification (Odonata). *Martinia Hors-série* **3**: 1–311.

Nelson, B. (1997). *Lestes dryas.* In: Brooks (1997a), pp.64–6.

Nelson, B. (1999). The status and habitat of the Irish damselfly *Coenagrion lunulatum* (Charpentier) (Odonata) in Northern Ireland. *Entomologist's Monthly Magazine* **135**: 59–68.

Nelson, B. & Thompson, R. (2004). *The Natural History of Ireland's Dragonflies.* National Museums and Galleries of Northern Ireland: Belfast.

Nelson, B., Ronayne, C. & Thompson, R. (2003). Colonization and changing status of four Odonata species, *Anax imperator, Anax parthenope, Aeshna mixta* and *Sympetrum fonscolombii*, in Ireland 2000–2002. *Irish Naturalists' Journal* **27**: 266–72.

Neville, A.C. (1959). Mating swarm in *Enallagma cyathigerum* (Charp.) (Odon., Coenagriidae). *Entomologist's Monthly Magazine* **95**: 181.

Newman, E. (1833). Entomological notes. *The Entomological Magazine* **1**: 505–14.

Nobes, G. (2003). Southern Emerald Damselfly *Lestes barbarus* (Fabr.) – the first British record. *Atropos* **18**: 3–6.

Norberg, R.A. (1972). The pterostigma of insect wings, an inertial regulator of pitch. *Journal of Comparative Physiology* **81**: 9–22.

Norberg, R.A. (1975). Hovering flight of the dragonfly *Aeshna juncea* L., kinematics and aerodynamics. *In:* Wu *et al.* (1975), pp.763–81.

Norling, U. (1967). *Hemianax ephippiger* (Burm.) found in Iceland. *Opuscula Entomologica* **32**: 99–100.

Norling, U. (1976). Seasonal regulation in *Leucorrhinia dubia* (Vander Linden) (Anisoptera: Libellulidae). *Odonatologica* **5**: 245–63.

Norling, U. (1984a). Life history patterns in the northern expansion of dragonflies. *Advances in Odonatology* **2**: 127–56.

Norling, U. (1984b). Photoperiodic control of larval development in *Leucorrhinia dubia* (Vander Linden): a comparison between populations from northern and southern Sweden (Anisoptera: Libellulidae). *Odonatologica* **13**: 529–50.

Norling, U. (1984c). The life cycle and larval photoperiodic responses of *Coenagrion hastulatum* (Charpentier) in two climatically different areas (Zygoptera: Coenagrionidae). *Odonatologica* **13**: 429–49.

Norling, U. & Sahlén, G. (1997). Odonata, Dragonflies and Damselflies. *In:* Anders & Nilsson (1997), pp.13–65.

Oehme, H. (1999). Jagderfolg und Jagdtaktik bei *Sympetrum striolatum* (Charpentier) (Anisoptera: Libellulidae). *Libellula* **18**: 79–87.

Ormerod, S.J., Weatherley, N.S. & Merrett, W.J. (1990). The influence of coniferous plantations on the distribution of the Golden-Ringed Dragonfly *Cordulegaster boltonii* in the upper catchment of the River Tywi. *Biological Conservation* **53**: 241–51.

Ott, J. (2001). Expansion of Mediterranean Odonata in Germany and Europe – consequences of climatic changes. *In:* Walther *et al.* (2001), pp.89–111.

Ott, J. (2005a). The effects of climatic changes for the distribution of dragonflies in Europe and their possible effects on the biocoenosis of the waters. *Abstracts of the 4th International Symposium of the Worldwide Dragonfly Association, Pontevedra*, p.49.

Ott, J. (2005b). Larve des Gauklers *Cybister lateralimarginalis* erbeutet Weibchen von *Aeshna grandis* bei der Eiablage (Coleoptera: Dytiscidae; Odonata: Aeshnidae). *Libellula* **24**: 233–6.

Ottolenghi, C. (1987). Reproductive behaviour of *Sympetrum striolatum* (Charp.) at an artificial pond in northern Italy. *Odonatologica* **16**: 297–306.

Padeffke, T. & Suhling, F. (2003). Temporal priority and intraguild predation in temporary waters: an experimental study using Namibian desert dragonflies. *Ecological Entomology* **28**: 340–47.

Paine, A. (Ed.) (1996). Notes and observations. *Journal of the British Dragonfly Society* **12**: 62–4.

Paine, A. (Ed.) (1998). Notes and observations. *Journal of the British Dragonfly Society* **14**: 31–2.

Pajunen, V.I. (1962a). Studies on the population ecology of *Leucorrhinia dubia* V. d. Lind. *Annales Zoologici Societatis Zoologicae Botanicae Fennicae 'Vanamo'* **24**: 1–79.

Pajunen, V.I. (1962b). A description of aggressive behaviour between males of *Leucorrhinia dubia* V. d. Lind. (Odon., Libellulidae). *Annales Entomologici Fennici* **28**: 108–18.

Pajunen, V.I. (1964). Aggressive behaviour in *Leucorrhinia caudalis* Charp. (Odon., Libellulidae). *Annales Zoologici Fennici* **1**: 357–69.

Pajunen, V.I. (1966a). The influence of population density on the territorial behaviour of *Leucorrhinia rubicunda* L. (Odon., Libellulidae). *Annales Zoologici Fennici* **3**: 40–52.

Pajunen, V.I. (1966b). Aggressive behaviour and territoriality in a population of *Calopteryx virgo* L. (Odon., Calopterygidae). *Annales Zoologici Fennici* **3**: 201–14.

Parker, G.A. (1970). Sperm competition and its evolutionary consequences in the insects. *Biological Reviews* **45**: 525–67.

Parkyn, L., Stoneman, R.E. & Ingram, H.E.P. (Eds) (1997). *Conserving Peatlands.* CAB International: Wallingford.

Parr, A.J. (1996). Dragonfly movement and migration in Britain and Ireland. *Journal of the British Dragonfly Society* **12**: 33–50.

Parr, A.J. (1999a). Migrant and dispersive dragonflies in Britain and Ireland during 1998. *Journal of the British Dragonfly Society* **15**: 51–7.

Parr, A.J. (1999b). Potential new Odonata for the British list. 2. The possibility of vagrant or colonist damselflies. *Atropos* **8**: 21–5.

Parr, A.J. (2001). Migrant and dispersive dragonflies in Britain during 2000. *Journal of the British Dragonfly Society* **17**: 49–54.

Parr, A.J. (2003). Migrant and dispersive dragonflies in Britain during 2002. *Journal of the British Dragonfly Society* **19**: 8–14.

Parr, A.J. (2004). Migrant and dispersive dragonflies in Britain during 2003. *Journal of the British Dragonfly Society* **20**: 42–50.

Parr, A.J. (2005a). Dragonflies. *British Wildlife* **17**: 124–5.

Parr, A.J. (2005b). Scarlet Darters *Crocothemis* spp. in Britain. *Atropos* **25**: 43–6.

Parr, A.J. (2006). Dragonflies. *British Wildlife* **18**: 51–52.

Parr, M.J. (1965). A population study of a colony of imaginal *Ischnura elegans* (Vander Linden) (Odonata: Coenagriidae) at Dale, Pembrokeshire. *Field Studies* **2**: 237–82.

Parr, M.J. (1969a). Comparative notes on the distribution, ecology and behaviour of some damselflies (Odonata: Coenagriidae). *Entomologist* **102**: 151–61.

Parr, M.J. (1969b). Population studies of some zygopteran dragonflies (Odonata). PhD thesis, University of Salford, UK.

Parr, M.J. (1970). The life histories of *Ischnura elegans* (Van der Linden) and *Coenagrion puella* (L.) in south Lancashire. *Proceedings of the Royal Entomological Society of London (A)* **45**: 172–81.

Parr, M.J. (1973a). Ecological studies of *Ischnura elegans* (Vander Linden) (Zygoptera: Coenagrionidae). I. Age groups, emergence patterns and numbers. *Odonatologica* **2**: 139–57.

Parr, M.J. (1973b). Ecological studies of *Ischnura elegans* (Vander Linden) (Zygoptera: Coenagrionidae). II. Survivorship, local movements and dispersal. *Odonatologica* **2**: 159–74.

Parr, M.J. (1976). Some aspects of the population ecology of the damselfly *Enallagma cyathigerum* (Charpentier) (Zygoptera: Coenagrionidae). *Odonatologica* **5**: 45–57.

Parr, M.J. (1978). Book review. *Notulae Odonatologicae* **1**: 14–16.

Parr, M.J. (1980). Territorial behaviour of the African libellulid *Orthetrum julia* Kirby (Anisoptera). *Odonatologica* **9**: 75–99.

Parr, M.J. (1983*a*). An analysis of territoriality in libellulid dragonflies (Anisoptera: Libellulidae). *Odonatologica* **12**: 39–57.

Parr, M.J. (1983*b*). Some aspects of territoriality in *Orthetrum coerulescens* (Fabricius) (Anisoptera: Libellulidae). *Odonatologica* **12**: 239–57.

Parr, M.J. (1992). Contribution to discussion: "Survival during the hot, dry season". *In:* Pritchard, G. (Ed.) (1992), p.16.

Parr, M. (1997). *Coenagrion pulchellum*. *In:* Brooks (1997*a*), pp.82–3.

Parr, M.J. (1999*a*). Personal communication to P.S.C.

Parr, M.J. (1999*b*). The terminology of female polymorphs of *Ischnura elegans* Vander Linden (Zygoptera: Coenagrionidae). *International Journal of Odonatology* **2**: 95–9.

Parr, M.J. & Parr, M. (1974). Studies on the behaviour and ecology of *Nesciothemis nigeriensis* Gambles (Anisoptera: Libellulidae). *Odonatologica* **3**: 21–47.

Parr, M.J. & Parr, M. (1996). Risky gleaning behaviour by *Ischnura elegans* (Vander L.) (Zygoptera: Coenagrionidae). *Notulae Odonatologicae* **4**: 124.

Patten, B.C. (Ed.) (1971). *Systems Analysis and Simulation in Ecology*. Academic Press: London.

Paulson, D.R. (2001). Recent Odonata records from southern Florida – effects of global warming? *International Journal of Odonatology* **4**: 57–69.

Pavlyuk, R.S. (1971). [Dragonfly-invading gregarines of the western provinces of the Ukrainian SSR.] [In Russian.]. *Abstracts of the 1st All-Union Congress of the Protozoological Society, Elm, Baku*, pp.294–5.

Pavlyuk, R. (1998). Eine Beständsaufnahme der Parasitenfauna der Odonaten in der Ukraine (Odonata; – Sporozoa, Trematoda, Cestoda, Nematoda, Acari). *Opuscula Zoologica Fluminensia* **164**: 1–23.

Pellow, K. (1999). Common Green Darner *Anax junius* (Drury) in Cornwall and Isles of Scilly. The first British and European records. *Journal of the British Dragonfly Society* **15**: 21–2.

Pennington, M.G. (2005). First record of *Pyrrhosoma nymphula* (Odon.: Coenagrionidae) in Shetland. *Entomologist's Record* **117**: 84.

Perrin, V.L. (1995). Observations on *Lestes dryas* Kirby habitat in Norfolk: is there a typical inland site for this species? *Journal of the British Dragonfly Society* **11**: 25–6.

Perrin, V.L. (2005). Dragonflies. *British Wildlife* **16**: 356.

Perry, S. & J. Miller, P.L. (1991). The duration of the stages of copulation in *Enallagma cyathigerum* (Charpentier) (Zygoptera: Coenagrionidae). *Odonatologica* **20**: 349–55.

Pfau, H.-K. (1991). Contributions of functional morphology to the phylogenetic systematics of Odonata. *Advances in Odonatology* **5**: 109–41.

Phillips, J. (1997). Lesser Emperor Dragonfly *Anax parthenope* (Selys) in Gloucestershire; the first British record. *Journal of the British Dragonfly Society* **13**: 22–4.

Phillipson, J. (1966). *Ecological Energetics*. Edward Arnold: London.

Pickup, J. & Thompson, D.J. (1990). The effects of temperature and prey density on the development rates and growth of damselfly larvae (Odonata: Zygoptera). *Ecological Entomology* **15**: 187–200.

Pierre, Abbé (1904). L'éclosion des oeufs

de *Lestes viridis* Van der Lind. (Nevr.). *Annales de la Société Entomologique Française* **73**: 477–84.

Pinniger, E.B. (1947). *Coenagrion scitulum*, Rambur, a dragonfly new to Britain. *London Naturalist* **26**: 80.

Plaistow, S. & Siva-Jothy, M.T. (1996). Energetic constraints and male mate-securing tactics in the damselfly *Calopteryx splendens xanthostoma* (Charpentier). *Proceedings of the Royal Society of London (B)* **263**: 1233–8.

Poethke, H.-J. (1988). Density-dependent behaviour in *Aeshna cyanea* (Müller) males at the mating place (Anisoptera: Aeshnidae). *Odonatologica* **17**: 205–12.

Poethke, H.-J. & Kaiser, H. (1987). The territoriality threshold: a model for mutual avoidance in dragonfly mating systems. *Behavioural Ecology and Sociobiology* **20**: 11–19

Polcyn, D.M. (1994). Thermoregulation during summer activity in Mojave dragonflies (Odonata: Anisoptera). *Functional Ecology* **8**: 441–9.

Pollard, E. (1977). A method for assessing changes in the abundance of butterflies. *Biological Conservation* **12**: 115–34.

Pollard, E. (1979). A national scheme for monitoring the abundance of butterflies: the first three years. *Proceedings and Transactions of the British Entomological and Natural History Society* **12**: 77–90.

Pollard, E., Elias, D.O., Skelton, M.J. & Thomas, J.A. (1975). A method of assessing the abundance of butterflies in Monks Wood National Nature Reserve in 1973. *Entomologist's Monthly Magazine* **26**: 79–88.

Pond Conservation Group (1993). *A future for Britain's ponds. An agenda for action.* Pond Conservation Group: Oxford.

Poosch, H. (1973). Zum Vorkommen und zur Populationsdynamik von Libellen an zwei Kleingewässern in Mittelmecklenburg. *Natur und Naturschutz Mecklenburg* **11**: 5–14.

Porritt, G.T. (1912). *Agrion armatum*, Charp. in the Norfolk Broads. *Entomologist's Monthly Magazine* **48**: 163.

Postler, E. & Postler, W. (2000). Entwicklung von *Gomphus vulgatissimus* im Datteln-Hamm-Kanal (Odonata: Gomphidae). *Libellula* **19**: 233–5.

Prendergast, N.H.D. (1988). The distribution and abundance of *Calopteryx splendens* (Harris), *C. virgo* (L.) and *Platycnemis pennipes* (Pallas) on the Wey river system (Hampshire and Surrey). *Journal of the British Dragonfly Society* **4**: 37–44.

Pritchard, G. (1965). Prey capture by dragonfly larvae (Odonata; Anisoptera). *Canadian Journal of Zoology.* **43**: 271–89.

Pritchard, G. (1982). Life-history strategies in dragonflies and the colonization of North America by the genus *Argia* (Odonata: Coenagrionidae). *Advances in Odonatology* **1**: 227–41.

Pritchard, G. (1986). The operation of the labium in larval dragonflies. *Odonatologica* **15**: 451–6.

Pritchard, G. (Ed.) (1992). *Current Topics in Dragonfly Biology.* Volume 5. *Societas Internationalis Odonatologica Rapid Communications (Supplements)* **15**: viii+29.

Pritchard, G., Harder, L.D., Kortello, A. & Krishnaraj, R. (2000). The response of larval growth rate to temperature in three species of coenagrionid dragonflies with some comments on *Lestes disjunctus* (Odonata: Coenagrionidae, Lestidae). *International Journal of Odonatology* **3**: 105–10.

Proctor, H. & Pritchard, G. (1989). Neglected predators: water mites (Acari: Parasitengona: Hydrachnellae) in freshwater communities. *Journal of the*

North American Benthological Society
8: 100–111.

Prodon, R. (1976). Le substrat, facteur écologique et ethologique de la vie aquatique: observations et expériences sur les larves de *Micropterna testacea* et *Cordulegaster annulatus*. Doctor thesis, Université Claude Bernard, Lyon, France.

Pulliam, H.R. (1988). Sources, sinks, and population regulation. *American Naturalist* **132:** 652–61.

Purse, B.V. & Hopkins, G.W. (2003). Dispersal characteristics and management of a rare damselfly. *Journal of Applied Ecology* **40:** 716–28.

Purse, B.V. & Thompson, D.J. (2003). Emergence of the damselflies, *Coenagrion mercuriale* and *Ceriagrion tenellum* (Odonata: Coenagrionidae) at their northern range margin in Britain. *European Journal of Entomology* **100:** 93–9.

Purse, B.V. & Thompson, D.J. (2005). Lifetime mating success in a marginal population of a damselfly, *Coenagrion mercuriale*. *Animal Behaviour* **69:** 1303–15.

Pushkin, Y.A., Morozov, A.E., Antonova, E.L. & Kortunova, T.A. (1979). [Aquatic fauna of the cooling effluent of the Yaiva Power Station, Perm District.] [In Russian.]. *Sbornik nauchnykh trudov Gosudarstvennyi nauchno-issledovatelskii institut ozernogo I rechnogo rybnogo khoziaistva (Leningrad)* **1979:** 61–8.

Radford, A.P. (1995). *Sympetrum sanguineum* (Müller) ovipositing on dry land. *Journal of the British Dragonfly Society* **11:** 30.

Raven, C.E. (1942). *John Ray, Naturalist. His Life and Works.* Cambridge University Press: Cambridge.

Raven, P.J. (1987). Odonate recovery following a major pesticide insecticide pollution of the River Roding, Essex. *Journal of the British Dragonfly Society* **3:** 37–44.

Ray, J. (1710). *Historia Insectorum.* Churchill: London.

Réaumur, R.-A.F. de (1742). Mémoires pour servir à l'histoire naturelle et à l'anatomie des insectes. Volume 6. L'Imprimerie Royale: Paris.

Reder, G. & Vogel, W. (2000). Wellenschlag als limitierender Faktor bei der Emergenz von Libellen? Beobachtungen beim Schlupf von *Gomphus flavipes* (Charpentier) (Anisoptera: Gomphidae). *Fauna und Flora Rheinland-Pfalz* **9:** 681–5.

Reeve, K. & Reeve, P. (2004). Recent changes in dragonfly distribution in Warwickshire. *Newsletter of the Dragonfly Recording Network* **21:** 10–11.

Rehfeldt, G.E. (1990). Anti-predator strategies in oviposition site selection of *Pyrrhosoma nymphula* (Zygoptera: Odonata). *Oecologia* **85:** 233–7.

Rehfeldt, G.E. (1992). Aggregation during oviposition and predation risk in *Sympetrum vulgatum* L. (Odonata: Libellulidae). *Behavioral Ecology and Sociobiology* **30:** 317–22.

Rehfeldt, G. (1994). Natural predators of imaginal dragonflies and their influence on reproductive systems and population dynamic. *Unpublished* MS.

Rehfeldt, G. (1995). *Natürliche Feinde, Parasiten und Fortpflanzen von Libellen.* Wolfram Schmidt: Braunschweig.

Reinhardt, K. & Gerighausen, U. (2001). Oviposition site preference and egg parasitism in *Sympecma paedisca* (Odonata: Lestidae). *International Journal of Odonatology* **4:** 221–30.

Richardson, J.M.L. & Anholt, B.R. (1995). Ontogenetic behaviour changes in larvae of the damselfly *Ischnura verticalis* (Odonata: Coenagrionidae). *Ethology* **101:** 308–34.

Robert, P.-A. (1958). *Les Libellules (odonates).* Delachaux & Niestlé: Neuchâtel.

Robertson, H.M. & Paterson, H.E.H. (1982). Mate recognition and mechanical isolation in *Enallagma* damselflies (Odonata: Coenagrionidae). *Evolution* **36**: 243–50.

Robinson, J.V., Hayworth, D.A. & Harvey, M.B. (1991). The effect of caudal lamellae loss on swimming speed of the damselfly *Argia moesta* (Hagen) (Odonata: Coenagrionidae). *American Midland Naturalist* **125**: 240–44.

Rolff, J. (1997). Better hosts dive: detachment of ectoparasitic water mites (Hydrachnellae: Arrenuridae) from damselflies (Odonata: Coenagrionidae). *Journal of Insect Behavior* **10**: 819–27.

Rolff, J. (2000a). Intime Interaktionen: ektoparasitische Wassermilben an Libellen (Hydrachnida; Odonata). *Libellula* **19**: 41–52.

Rolff, J. (2000b). Water mite parasitism in damselflies during emergence: two hosts, one pattern. *Ecography* **23**: 273–82.

Rolff, J. (2001). Evolutionary ecology of watermite-insect interactions: a critical appraisal. *Archiv für Hydrobiologie* **152**: 353–68.

Rolff, J. & Martens, A. (1997). Completing the life cycle: detachment of an aquatic parasite (*Arrenurus cuspidator*, Hydrachnellae) from an aerial host (*Coenagrion puella*, Odonata). *Canadian Journal of Zoology* **75**: 655–9.

Rolff, J., Antvogel, H. & Schrimpf, H. (2000). No correlation between ectoparasitism and male mating success in a damselfly: why parasite behavior matters. *Journal of Insect Behavior* **13**: 563–71.

Rolff, J., Braune, P. & Siva-Jothy, M.T. (2001). Ectoparasites do not affect ejaculate volume in the dragonfly *Coenagrion puella*. *Physiological Entomology* **26**: 315–19.

Ross, Q.E. (1971). The effect of interspecific interactions on growth and feeding behavior of *Anax junius* (Drury) naiads. PhD thesis, Michigan State University, Ann Arbor, USA.

Rota, E. & Carchini, G. (1988). Considerations on an autumn record of *Lestes* larvae in Italy. *Notulae Odonatologicae* **3**: 9–13.

Rouquette, J.R. & Thompson, D.J. (2005). Habitat associations of the endangered damselfly, *Coenagrion mercuriale*, in a water meadow ditch system in southern England. *Biological Conservation* **123**: 225–35.

Rowe, G.W. & Harvey, I.F. (1985). Information content in finite sequences: communication between dragonfly larvae. *Journal of Theoretical Biology*. **116**: 275–90.

Rowe, R.J. (1985). A taxonomic revision of the genus *Xanthocnemis* (Zygoptera: Coenagrionidae) and an investigation of the larval behaviour of *Xanthocnemis zealandica*. PhD thesis, University of Canterbury, Christchurch, New Zealand.

Rowe, R.J. (1994). Predatory behaviour and predatory versatility in young larvae of the dragonfly *Xanthocnemis zealandica* (Odonata, Coenagrionidae). *New Zealand Journal of Zoology* **21**: 151–66.

Rowe, R.J. (1995). Letter to P.S.C.

Rowe, R.J. (2002). Agonistic behaviour in final-instar larvae of *Agriocnemis pygmaea* (Odonata: Coenagrionidae). *Australian Journal of Zoology* **50**: 215–24.

Rubenstein, D.R. & Hobson, K.A. (2004). From birds to butterflies: animal movement patterns and stable isotopes. *Trends in Ecology and Evolution* **19**: 256–63.

Rüppell, G. (1985). Kinematic and behavioural aspects of flight of the male Banded Agrion, *Calopteryx (Agrion) splendens* L. *In:* Gewecke & Wendler (1985), pp.195–204.

Rüppell, G. (1989a). Fore legs of dragonflies

used to repel males. *Odonatologica*
18: 391–6.

Rüppell, G. (1989*b*). Kinematic analysis of symmetrical flight manoeuvres of Odonata. *Journal of Experimental Biology* **144**: 13–42.

Rüppell, G. (1992). Cinefilm and oral commentary. Annual Meeting of British Dragonfly Society, Oxford, UK.

Rüppell, G. (1999). Prey capture flight of *Calopteryx haemorrhoidalis* (Vander Linden) (Zygoptera: Calopterygidae). *International Journal of Odonatology* **2**: 123–31.

Rüppell, G. & Hilfert, D. (1994). Cinefilm and oral commentary. Annual Meeting of British Dragonfly Society, Cambridge, UK.

Rüppell, G. & Hilfert, D. (1995). Oviposition in triple connection of *Sympetrum frequens* (Selys). *Tombo* **38**: 33–5.

Rüppell, G., & Hilfert, D. (1996). Personal communications to P.S.C., 25 August, 25 September and 2 October.

Rüppell, G., Hilfert-Rüppell, D., Rehfeldt, G. & Schütte, C. (2005). *Die Prachtlibellen Europas*. Westarp Wissenschaften: Magdeburg.

Russell, R.W., May, M.L., Soltesz, K.L. & Fitzpatrick, J.W. (1998). Massive swarm migrations of dragonflies (Odonata) in Eastern North America. *American Midland Naturalist* **140**: 325–42.

Sahlén, G. (1994). Ultrastructure of the eggshell of *Aeshna juncea* (L.) (Odonata: Aeshnidae). *International Journal of Insect Morphology and Embryology* **23**: 345–54.

Salmon, M.A., Marren, P. & Harley, B. (2000). *The Aurelian Legacy*. Harley Books: Colchester.

Samraoui, B. & Corbet, P.S. (2000*a*). The Odonata of Numidia, northeastern Algeria. Part I. Status and distribution. *International Journal of Odonatology* **3**: 11–25.

Samraoui, B. & Corbet, P.S. (2000*b*). The Odonata of Numidia, northeastern Algeria. Part II. Seasonal ecology. *International Journal of Odonatology* **3**: 27–39.

Samraoui, B., Bouzid, S., Boulabahl, R. & Corbet, P.S. (1998). Postponed reproductive maturation in upland refuges maintains life-cycle continuity during the hot dry season in Algerian dragonflies (Anisoptera). *International Journal of Odonatology* **1**: 119–35.

Saunders, D.S. (2002). *Insect Clocks*. 3rd Edition. Elsevier: London.

Sawkiewicz, L. (1989). An interesting method of collecting dragonflies. *Notulae Odonatologicae* **3**: 45–6.

Schiel, F.-J. (1998*a*). Zur Habitatbindung der Becher-Azurjungfer (*Enallagma cyathigerum* Charpentier 1840) (Odonata: Zygoptera) am südlichen Oberrhein. *Naturschutz südlichen Oberrhein* **2**: 139–47.

Schiel, F.-J. (1998*b*). Zur Habitatbindung des Grossen Granatauges (*Erythromma najas* Hansemann 1823) (Zygoptera: Coenagrionidae) am südlichen Oberrhein. *Naturschutz südlichen Oberrhein* **2**: 129–38.

Schierwater, B., Streit, B., Wagner, G.P. & DeSalle, R. (Eds) (1994). *Molecular Ecology and Evolution: Approaches and Applications*. Birkhäuser Verlag, Basel.

Schmidt, B. (2005). Gartenfreuden mit Blauen Drachen. *Mercuriale* **5**: 41–2.

Schmidt, E. (1964). Biologische-ökologische Untersuchungen an Hochmoorlibellen (Odonata). *Zeitschrift für wissenschaftliche Zoologie (A)* **169**: 313–86.

Schmidt, E. (1984). *Gomphus vulgatissimus* L. an einem belasteten Havelsee, dem Tegeler See (Insel Scharfenberg) in Berlin (West). *Libellula* **3**: 35–51.

Schneider, W. (1985). Die Gattung *Crocothemis* Brauer 1868 im Nahen Osten (Insecta: Odonata: Libellulidae). *Senckenbergiana biologica* **66**: 79–88.

Schorr, M. (2000). Störungsökologische

Wirkungen von Bootsportaktivitäten auf Fliessgewässer-Libellen dargestelt am Beispiel der Wieslauter (Pfalzwald, Pheinland-Pfalz. *Fauna und Flora Rheinland-Pfalz* 9: 663–79.

Schulz, S. (1995). Eiablage und Entwicklungserfolg der Larven von *Enallagma cyathigerum* (Charpentier, 1840) (Odonata: Coenagrionidae). Diploma thesis, Technische Universität, Braunschweig, Germany.

Schütte, C. (1997). Egg development and early instars in *Cordulegaster boltonii immaculifrons* Selys: a field study (Anisoptera: Cordulegastridae). *Odonatologica* 26: 83–7.

Schütte, C. (2002). Personal communication to P.S.C.

Schütte, C., Schridde, P. & Suhling, F. (1998). Life history patterns of *Onychogomphus uncatus* (Charpentier) (Anisoptera: Gomphidae). *Odonatologica* 27: 71–86.

Schwind, R. (1991). Polarization vision in water insects and insects living on a moist substrate. *Journal of Comparative Physiology (A)* 169: 531–40.

Schwind, R. (1995). Spectral regions in which aquatic insects see polarized light. *Journal of Comparative Physiology (A)* 177: 439–48.

Schwind, R. & Horváth, G. (1993). Reflection-polarization pattern at water surfaces and correction of a common representation of the polarization pattern on the sky. *Naturwissenschaften* 80: 82–3.

Sebastian, A., Sein, M.M., Thu, M.M. & Corbet, P.S. (1990). Suppression of *Aedes aegypti* (Diptera: Culicidae) using augmentative release of dragonfly larvae (Odonata: Libellulidae) with community participation in Yangon, Myanmar. *Bulletin of Entomological Research* 80: 223–32.

Sell, S. (2007). Personal communication to P.S.C., 17 June.

Sélys-Longchamps, E. de (1846). Revision of the British Libellulidae. *Annals and Magazine of Natural History* 18: 217–27.

Sélys-Longchamps, M.E. de (1853). Synopsis des caloptérygines. *Bulletin de l'Académie Royale de Belgique* 20 (Annexe), 1–73.

Sherk, T.E. (1977). Development of the compound eyes of dragonflies (Odonata). 1. Larval compound eyes. *Journal of Experimental Zoology* 201: 391–416.

Shirt, D.B. (1987). *British Red Data Books: 2. Insects*. Nature Conservancy Council: Peterborough.

Silsby, J. (1992). Thoughts on distinguishing between Odonata and Anisoptera when using the English word "dragonfly". *Journal of the British Dragonfly Society* 8: 1–2.

Silsby, J. (1993). A final thought on distinguishing between Odonata and Anisoptera when using "Dragonfly". *Journal of the British Dragonfly Society* 9: 17.

Silsby, J. (Ed.) (2001). *Dragonflies of the World.* The Natural History Museum: London, and CSIRO: Collingwood, Australia.

Silsby, J. & Ward-Smith, J. (1997). The influx of *Sympetrum flaveolum* (L.) during the summer of 1995. *Journal of the British Dragonfly Society* 13: 14–22.

Siva-Jothy, M.T. (1987). Variation in copulation duration and the resultant degree of sperm removal in *Orthetrum cancellatum* (L.) (Libellulidae: Odonata). *Behavioral Ecology and Sociobiology* 20: 147–51.

Siva-Jothy, M.T. (1988). Sperm "repositioning" in *Crocothemis erythraea*, a libellulid dragonfly with a brief copulation. *Journal of Insect Behavior* 1: 235–45.

Siva-Jothy, M.T. (1989). Spermatodesm structure and function. *Abstracts of the 10th*

International Symposium of Odonatology, Johnson City, Tennessee, 33.

Siva-Jothy, M.T. (1995). Letter to P.S.C., 3 January.

Siva-Jothy, M.T. (1997a). Odonate ejaculate structure and mating systems. Odonatologica 26: 415–37.

Siva-Jothy, M.T. (1997b). Calopteryx splendens, Calopteryx virgo. In: Brooks (1997a), pp.59–62.

Siva-Jothy, M.T. (1999). Male wing pigmentation may affect reproductive success via female choice in a calopterygid damselfly (Zygoptera). Behaviour 136: 1365–77.

Siva-Jothy, M.T. & Hooper, R.E. (1995a). Differential use of stored sperm during oviposition in the damselfly Calopteryx splendens xanthostoma (Charpentier). Behavioral Ecology and Sociobiology 39: 389–93.

Siva-Jothy, M.T. & Hooper, R.E. (1995b). The disposition and genetic diversity of stored sperm in females of the damselfly Calopteryx splendens xanthostoma (Charpentier). Proceedings of the Royal Society of London (B) 259: 313–18.

Siva-Jothy, M.T. & Plaistow, S.J. (1999). A fitness cost of eugregarine parasitism in a damselfly. Ecological Entomology 24: 465–70.

Siva-Jothy, M.T. & Tsubaki, Y. (1989). Variation in copulation duration in Mnais pruinosa pruinosa Selys (Odonata: Calopterygidae). 1. Alternative mate-securing tactics and sperm precedence. Behavioral Ecology and Sociobiology 24: 39–45.

Skelton, M.J.L. (1974). Insect distribution maps scheme: Orthoptera, Dictyoptera and Odonata preliminary distribution maps. Biological Records Centre: Huntingdon.

Smith, B. (2004). Report from Scotland 2002/2003. Newsletter of the Dragonfly Recording Network 21: 5–6.

Smith, E.M. (1984). Some observations at breeding sites of Emeralds (Corduliidae) in Scotland. Journal of the British Dragonfly Society 1: 37–8.

Smith, E.M. (1997). Personal communication to P.S.C., 8 November.

Smith, E.M. & Smith, R.W.J. (1997a). Coenagrion hastulatum. In: Brooks (1997), pp.76–7.

Smith, E.M. & Smith, R.W.J. (1997b). Somatochlora arctica. In: Brooks (1997), pp.128–9.

Smith, E.M., Smith, R.W. & Batty, P.M. (1998). Breeding of the Southern Hawker Aeshna cyanea (Müller) in rock pools. Journal of the British Dragonfly Society 14: 58–9.

Smith, I.M. & Oliver, D.R. (1986). Review of parasitic associations of larval water mites (Acari: Parsitengona: Hydrachnida) with insect hosts. Canadian Entomologist 118: 407–72.

Smith, R.W.J., Smith, E.M. & Richards, M.A. (2000). Habitat and development of larvae of the Azure Hawker Aeshna caerulea (Ström) in northern Scotland. Journal of the British Dragonfly Society 16: 1–16.

Smith, R.W.J. (1995). Personal communication to P.S.C.

Snyder, S.D. & Janovy, J. (1996). Behavioral basis of second intermediate host specificity among four species of Haematoloechus (Digenea: Haematoloechidae). Journal of Parasitology 82: 94–9.

Soeffing, K. (1987). Eine Wasserfalle für Libellenlarven. Libellula 6: 102–104.

Sonehara, I. (1964). [Discovery of the larva and ecological observations on the adult behaviour of Aeshna mixta Latreille in Komoro-city, Nagano Prefecture.] [In Japanese; English summary.]. Tombo 7: 2–12.

St Quentin, D. (1934). Beobachtungen und

Versuche an Libellen in ihren Jagdrevieren. *Konowia* **13**: 275–82.

Stavenga, D.G.H. & Hardie, R.C. (Eds) (1989). *Facets of Vision*. Springer-Verlag: Berlin.

Stechmann, D.-H. (1978). Eiablage, Parasitismus und postparasitische Entwicklung von *Arrenurus*-Arten (Hydrachnellae, Acari). *Zeitschrift für Parasitenkunde* **57**: 169–88.

Steiner, C, Siegert, B. Schulz, S. & Suhling, F. (2000). Habitat selection in the larvae of two species of Zygoptera (Odonata): biotic interactions and abiotic limitation. *Hydrobiologia* **427**: 167–76.

Stephens, J.F. (1835–37). *Illustrations of British Entomology: A Synopsis of Indigenous Insects: containing their Generic and Specific Distinctions: with an Account of their Metamorphoses, Times of Appearance, Localities, Food, and Economy*. 11 Volumes. Baldwin and Craddock: London.

Sternberg, K. (1989). Beobachtungen an der Feuerlibelle (*Crocothemis erythraea*) bei Freiburg im Breslau (Odonata: Libellulidae). *Veröffentlichungender Naturschutz Landschaftspflege Bad-Württemberg* **64/65**: 237–54.

Sternberg, K. (1993). First record of commensal flies, *Desmetopa* sp., on a dragonfly, *Cordulegaster boltonii* (Donovan) (Diptera: Milichidae; – Anisoptera: Cordulegastridae). *Notulae Odonatologicae* **4**: 9–12.

Sternberg, K. (1994a). Eine Güllegrube und eine wassergefüllte Fahrspur als zwei extreme Sekundärbiotope für Libellen. *Libellula* **13**: 59–72.

Sternberg, K. (1994b). Niche specialization in dragonflies. *Advances in Odonatology* **6**: 177–98.

Sternberg, K. (1995a). Influence of oviposition date and temperature upon embryonic development in *Somatochlora*

alpestris and *S. arctica* (Odonata: Corduliidae). *Journal of Zoology, London* **235**: 163–74.

Sternberg, K. (1995b). Regulierung uns Stabilisierung von Metapopulationen bei Libellen, am Beispiel von *Aeshna subarctica elisabethae* Djakonov im Schwarzwald (Anisoptera: Aeshnidae). *Libellula* **14**: 1–39.

Sternberg, K. (1995c). Populationsökologische Untersuchungen einer Metapopulation der Hochmoor-Mosaikjungfer (*Aeshna subarctica elisabethae* Djakonov, 1922) (Odonata, Aeshnidae) im Schwarzwald. *Zeitschrift für Ökologie Naturforschung* **4**: 53–60.

Sternberg, K. (1998). The postglacial colonization of Central Europe by dragonflies, with special reference to southwestern Germany (Insecta, Odonata). *Journal of Biogeography* **25**: 319–37.

Sternberg, K. (1999a). *Ischnura pumilio* (Charpentier, 1825). *In:* Sternberg & Buchwald (Eds) (1999), pp.348–58.

Sternberg, K. (1999b). Die Bedeutung von Fliessgewässern. *In:* Sternberg & Buchwald (Eds) (1999), p.127.

Sternberg, K. (2000). *Somatochlora arctica* (Zetterstedt, 1840). *In:* Sternberg & Buchwald (Eds) (2000), pp.251–64.

Sternberg, K. & Buchwald, R. (Eds) (1999). *Die Libellen Baden-Württembergs: Band 1. Kleinlibellen (Zygoptera)*. Verlag Eugen Ulmer: Stuttgart.

Sternberg, K. & Buchwald, R. (Eds) (2000). *Die Libellen Baden-Württembergs. Band 2: Grosslibellen (Anisoptera)*. Verlag Eugen Ulmer: Stuttgart.

Sternberg, K. & Schmidt, B. (2000). *Somatochlora metallica* (Vander Linden 1825). *In:* Sternberg & Buchwald (Eds) (2000), pp.275–84.

Sternberg, K. & Sternberg, M. (2004). Veränderungen der Artzusammensetzung und erhöhte Abwanderrate bei Libellen durch die Mahd der Uferwiesen zweier Fliessgewässer (Odonata). *Libellula* **23**: 1–43.

Sternberg, K. & Sternberg, S. (2000). *Aeshna caerulea* (Ström, 1783). *In:* Sternberg & Buchwald (Eds) (2000), pp.23–38.

Sternberg, K., Hoppner, B. & Buchwald, R. (2000). *Libellula fulva* Müller, 1764. *In:* Sternberg & Buchwald (Eds) (2000), pp.448–58.

Stoks, R. (2000). Components of lifetime mating success and body size in males of a scrambling damselfly. *Animal Behaviour* **59**: 339–48.

Stoks, R. (2001). Food stress and predator-induced stress shape developmental performance in a damselfly. *Oecologia* **127**: 222–9.

Stoks, R. & Johansson, F. (2000). Trading off mortality risk against foraging effort in damselflies that differ in life cycle length. *Oikos* **91**: 559–67.

Stoks, R., De Bruyn, L. & Matthysen, E. (1997). The adaptiveness of intense contact mate guarding by males of the Emerald Damselfly *Lestes sponsa* (Odonata: Lestidae): the male's perspective. *Journal of Insect Behavior* **10**: 289–98.

Stoks, R., De Block, M., Van Gossum, H., Valck, F., Lauwers, K., Verhagen, R., Matthysen, E. & De Bruyn, L. (1999). Lethal and sublethal costs of autotomy and predator presence in damselfly larvae. *Oecologia* **120**: 87–91.

Stoks, R., Nystrom, J.L., May, M.L. & McPeek, M.A. (2005). Parallel evolution in ecological and reproductive traits to produce cryptic damselfly species across the Holarctic. *Evolution* **59**: 1976–88.

Street, P. (1976). *Animal Migration and Navigation*. David & Charles: Newton Abbot, UK.

Strommer, J.L. & Smock, L.A. (1989). Vertical distribution and abundance of invertebrates within the sandy substrate of a low-gradient headwater stream. *Freshwater Biology* **22**: 263–74.

Sukhacheva, G.A., Kryukova, N.A. & Glupov, V.V. (2003). On the roles of morphological and biochemical criteria in species identification: an example of dragonfly of the genus *Aeshna*. *Biology Bulletin* **30**: 63–8.

Suhling, F. & Lepkojus, S. (2001). Different growth and behaviour influences asymmetric predation among early instar dragonfly larvae. *Canadian Journal of Zoology* **79**: 854–60.

Suhling, F. & Müller, O. (1996). *Die Flussjungfern Europas*. Westarp Wissenschaften: Magdeburg.

Suhling, F., Schenk, K., Padeffke, T. & Martens, A. (2004). Larval development of some dragonflies from experimental temporary ponds in the Pro-Namib desert. *Hydrobiologia* **526**: 75–85.

Svihla, A. (1984). Notes on the habits of *Tanypteryx hageni* Selys in the Olympic Mountains, Washington, U.S.A. *Tombo* **27**: 23–5.

Tagg, D. (2003). Raising *Brachytron* larvae. *Dragonfly News* **43**: 34.

Taketo, A. (1960). [On the ecology of several species of dragonflies.] [In Japanese.] *Tokkuribachi* **9**: 7–21. [Cited by Inoue & Shimizu (1976).]

Tanaka, Y. & Hisada, M. (1980). The hydraulic mechanism of the predatory strike in dragonfly larvae. *Journal of Experimental Biology* **88**: 301–7.

Taverner, J. Cham, S. & Hold, A. (2004). *The Dragonflies of Hampshire*. Pisces Publications: Newbury.

Taylor, P. (2004a). Report of the Dragonfly Conservation Group. *Dragonfly News* **46**: 21–3.

Taylor, P. (2004b). News from Norfolk. *Newsletter of the Dragonfly Recording Network* **21**: 12–13.

Taylor, P. (2005). Report of the Dragonfly

Conservation Group. Scarce Blue-tailed Damselfly. *Dragonfly News* **48**: 15.

Tembhare, D.B. & Thakare, V.K. (1982). Some histophysiological studies on the male reproductive system of the dragonfly, *Ictinogomphus rapax* (Rambur) (Odonata: Gomphidae). *Journal of Advances in Zoology* **3**: 95–100.

Tennessen, K. (2004). *Enallagma exsulans* gleaning at the water surface. *Argia* **15**: 13.

Termaat, T., Ketelaar, R., De Vries, H. & Mensing, V. (2005). Temperature mediated changes in dragonfly phenology. Flight peak trends for dragonflies from the Netherlands. *Poster presentation. 4th WDA International Symposium of Odonatology, Pontevedra, Spain.*

Testard, P. (1972). Observations sur l'activité reproductrice d'une population tardive de *Sympetrum striolatum* Charpentier dans le sud de l'Espagne (Odon. Libellulidae). *Bulletin de la Société Entomologique de France* **77**: 118–22.

Testard, P. (1975). Note sur l'émergence, le sex ratio et l'activité des adultes de *Mesogomphus genei* Selys dans le sud de l'Espagne (Anisoptera: Gomphidae). *Odonatologica* **4**: 11–26.

Thipsakorn, A., Jamnongluk, W. & Kittayapong, P. (2003). Molecular evidence of *Wohlbachia* infection in natural populations of tropical odonates. *Current Microbiology* **47**: 314–18.

Thomas, B. (2002). Temperaturrekorde in den 1990er Jahren und früher Beginn von Flugzeit und Fortpflanzen dei häufigen Libellenarten in Nordwestdeutschland (Odonata). *Libellula* **21**: 25–35.

Thompson, D.J. (1978a). Towards a realistic predator-prey model: the effect of temperature on the functional response and life history of larvae of the damselfly *Ischnura elegans*. *Journal of Animal Ecology* **47**: 409–23.

Thompson, D.J. (1978b). The natural prey of larvae of the damselfly, *Ischnura elegans* (Odonata: Zygoptera). *Freshwater Biology* **8**: 377–84.

Thompson, D.J. (1989). A population study of the Azure Damselfly *Coenagrion puella* (L.) in northern England. *Journal of the British Dragonfly Society* **5**: 17–22.

Thompson, D.J. (1990a). The effects of survival and weather on lifetime egg production in a model damselfly. *Ecological Entomology* **15**: 455–62.

Thompson, D.J. (1990b). On the biology of the damselfly *Nososticta kalumburu* Watson & Theischinger (Zygoptera: Protoneuridae). *Biological Journal of the Linnean Society of London* **40**: 347–56.

Thompson, D.J. (1991). Size-based dispersal prior to breeding in a damselfly: conflicting evidence from a natural population. *Oecologia* **87**: 600–601.

Thompson, D.J. (1993). Lifetime reproductive success and fitness in dragonflies. *Abstracts of the 12th International Symposium of Odonatology, Osaka*, p.42.

Thompson, D.J. (1997a). Lifetime reproductive success, weather and fitness in dragonflies. *Odonatologica* **26**: 89–94.

Thompson, D.J. (1997b). *Lestes sponsa. In:* Brooks (1997a), pp.63–4.

Thompson, D.J. (2004). Honest signals and female damselflies. *Journal of the British Dragonfly Society* **20**: 35–6.

Thompson, D.J. (2005). The genetic structure of the UK population of *Coenagrion mercuriale. Oral presentation to the 18th Annual Meeting of the British Dragonfly Society, Lincoln, 26 November.*

Thompson, D.J. & Harvey, I.F. (1994). On describing members of the insect order Odonata. *Journal of the British Dragonfly Society* **10**: 37.

Thompson, D.J. & Purse, B.V. (1999). A

search for long-distance dispersal in the Southern Damselfly *Coenagrion mercuriale* (Charpentier). *Journal of the British Dragonfly Society* **15**: 46–50.

Thompson, R. (2002). *Close-up on Insects. A Photographer's Guide.* Guild of Master Craftsman Publications: Lewes, UK.

Tiefenbrunner, W. (1990). *Sympecma fusca* (Vander Linden, 1820): Korrelation zwischen Flügelstellung und Lichteinfallswinkel in Abhängigkeit von der Temperatur (Zygoptera: Lestidae). *Libellula* **9**: 121–32.

Tillyard, R.J. (1916). Further observations on the emergence of dragonfly larvae from the egg, with special reference to the problem of respiration. *Proceedings of the Linnean Society of New South Wales* **41**: 388–416.

Tillyard, R.J. (1917). *The Biology of Dragonflies.* Cambridge University Press: Cambridge.

Timon-David, J. (1965). Trématodes parasites des odonates. *Annales de la Faculté des Sciences (Marseilles)* **38**: 15–41.

Tinbergen, N. (1968). *Curious Naturalists.* Anchor Doubleday: New York.

Tittizer, T. (1994). Letter to P.S.C., 23 March.

Tittizer, T., Scholl, F., Schleuter, M. & Leuchs, H. (1989). Beitrag zur Kenntnis der Libellenfauna der Bundeswasserstrassen und angrenzender limnischer Bereiche. *Verhandlungen Westdeutscher Entomologische Tag (Dusseldorf)* **1988**: 89–102.

Torralba Burrial, A. & Ocharan, F.J. (2005). Comportamiento de búsqueda de hembras inmaduras como estrategia reproductive en machos de *Aeshna juncea* (Linnaeus, 1758) (Odonata: Aeshnidae). *Boletin Sociedad Entomológica Aragonesa* **36**: 123–6.

Treacher, P. (1996). Mortality of emerging *Pyrrhosoma nymphula* (Sulzer) at a garden pond. *Journal of the British Dragonfly Society* **12**: 61–2.

Trottier, R. (1973a). Influence of temperature and humidity on the emergence behaviour of *Anax junius* Drury (Odonata: Aeshnidae). PhD thesis, University of Toronto, Canada.

Trottier, R. (1973b). Influence of temperature and humidity on the emergence behaviour of *Anax junius* (Odonata: Aeshnidae) in Canada. *Canadian Entomologist* **105**: 975–84.

Truscott, L. (1999). The Hornet Robberfly *Asilus crabroniformis* L. (Diptera, Asilidae): Odonata as prey. *Journal of the British Dragonfly Society* **15**: 50.

Turgeon, I., Stoks, R., Thum, R.A., Brown, J.M. & McPeek, M.A. (2005). Simultaneous Quaternary radiation of three damselfly clades across the Holarctic. *American Naturalist* **165**: E78–E107.

Tsubuki, T. (1987). [The flight activity of the libellulid dragonfly *Sympetrum frequens* (Odonata) in relation to the environmental factors.] [In Japanese; English summary.] *New Entomologist* **36**: 12–20.

Twissell, I. (2004). News in brief from Gloucestershire. *Newsletter of the Dragonfly Recording Network* **21**: 18.

Tyrrell, M. (2004). Group oviposition behaviour in the Brown Hawker *Aeshna grandis* (L.). *Journal of the British Dragonfly Society* **20**: 79.

Tyrrell, M. (2006). *The Dragonflies of Northamptonshire.* Northants Dragonfly Group: Northampton.

Ubukata, H. (1973). Life history and behavior of a corduliid dragonfly, *Cordulia aenea amurensis* Selys. I. Emergence and pre-reproductive periods. *Journal of the Faculty of Science, Hokkaido University Series 6, Zoology* **19**: 251–69.

Ubukata, H. (1975). Life history and behavior of a corduliid dragonfly, *Cordulia aenea amurensis* Selys. II. Reproductive period with special reference to territoriality. *Journal of the Faculty of Science, Hokkaido University, Series 6, Zoology* **19**: 812–33.

Ubukata, H. (1979). Behaviour of *Somatochlora viridiaenea viridiaenea* Uhler in Kushiro District (Odonata, Corduliidae). *New Entomologist* **28**: 1–7.

Ubukata, H. (1980a). Life history and behavior of a corduliid dragonfly, *Cordulia aenea amurensis* Selys. III. Aquatic period with special reference to larval growth. *Kontyu* **48**: 414–27.

Ubukata, H. (1980b). Territoriality as a density-dependent mating strategy in *Cordulia*. *Abstracts of the 16th International Congress of Entomology, Kyoto, Japan*, p.234.

Ubukata, H. (1981). Survivorship curve and annual fluctuation in the size of emerging population of *Cordulia aenea amurensis* Selys (Odonata: Corduliidae). *Japanese Journal of Ecology* **31**: 335–46.

Ubukata, H. (1987). Mating system of the dragonfly *Cordulia aenea amurensis* Selys and a model of mate searching and territorial behaviour in Odonata. *In:* Ito *et al.* (1987), pp.213–28.

Ubukata, H. (1997). [Impact of global warming on insects.] *In:* Domoto, A. & Iwatsuki, K. (1997), pp.273–307. [In Japanese.]

Uéda, T. (1978). Geographic variation in the life cycle of *Lestes sponsa*. *Tombo* **21**: 27–34.

Uéda, T. (1979). Plasticity of the reproductive behaviour in a dragonfly, *Sympetrum parvulum* Barteneff, with reference to the social relationship of males and the density of territories. *Research in Population Ecology* **21**: 135–52.

Uéda, T. (1980). Males' site selection process and mating success in a damselfly, *Cercion calamorum*. *Abstracts of the 16th International Congress of Entomology, Kyoto, Japan*, p.140.

Uéda, T. (1989). Sexual maturation, body colour changes and increase of body weight in a summer diapause population of the damselfly *Lestes sponsa* (Hansemann) (Zygoptera: Lestidae). *Odonatologica* **18**: 75–87.

Utzeri, C. (1986). Field observations on sperm translocation behaviour in the males of *Crocothemis erythraea* (Brullé) and *Orthetrum cancellatum* (L.) (Libellulidae), with a review of the same in Anisoptera. *Odonatologica* **14**: 227–37.

Utzeri, C. (1988). Effetti della marcatura sulla longevità di odonati. *Riassunti 52 Congresso Nazionale Unione zoological italiana, Camerino* (Abstract), p.21.

Utzeri, C. & Dell'Anna, L. (1989). Wandering and territoriality in *Libellula depressa* L. (Anisoptera: Libellulidae). *Advances in Odonatology* **4**: 133–47.

Utzeri, C. & Ercoli, C. (2004). Distribution by unpaired males prolongs postcopulatory guarding duration in the damselfly *Lestes virens* (Charpentier) (Zygoptera: Lestidae). *Odonatologica* **33**: 291–301.

Utzeri, C., Falchetti, E. & Carchini, G. (1976). Alcuni aspetti etologici della ovideposizione di *Lestes barbarus* (Fabricius) presso pozze temporanee (Zygoptera: Lestidae). *Odonatologica* **5**: 175–9.

Utzeri, C., Falchetti, E. & Carchini, G. (1983). The reproductive behaviour in *Coenagrion lindeni* (Selys) in central Italy (Odonata: Coenagrionidae). *Odonatologica* **12**: 259–78.

Utzeri, C., Carchini, G., Falchetti, E. & Belfiore, C. (1984). Philopatry, homing and dispersal in *Lestes barbarus* (Fabricius) (Zygoptera: Lestidae). *Odonatologica* **13**: 573–84.

Utzeri, C., Falchetti, E. & Raffi, R. (1987). Adult behaviour of *Lestes barbarus* (Fabricius) and *L. virens* (Charpentier)

(Zygoptera, Lestidae). *Fragmenta Entomologica* **20**: 1–22.

Van Buskirk, J. (1992). Competition, cannibalism, and size-class dominance in a dragonfly. *Oikos* **65**: 455–64.

Van Doorslaer, W. & Stoks, R. (2005). Thermal reaction norms in two *Coenagrion* damselfly species: contrasting embryonic and larval life-history traits. *Freshwater Biology* **50**: 1982–90.

Van Emden, H., Thomas, J. & Claridge, M. (2005). Obituary: Dame Miriam Rothschild FRS, Hon FRES, 1908–2005. *Antenna* **29**: 96–101.

Van Gossum, H., Stoks, R., Matthysen, E., Valck, F. & De Bruyn, L. (1999). Male choice for female colour morphs in *Ischnura elegans* (Odonata, Coenagrionidae): testing the hypotheses. *Animal Behaviour* **57**: 1229–32.

Van Gossum, H., Sanchez, R. & Cordero Rivera, A. (2003). Observations on rearing damselflies under laboratory conditions. *Animal Biology* **53**: 37–45.

Van Gossum, H., De Bruyn, L. & Stoks, R. (2005). Male harassment on female colour morphs in *Ischnura elegans* (Vander Linden): testing two frequency-dependent hypotheses (Zygoptera: Coenagrionidae). *Odonatologica* **34**: 407–14.

Van Tol, J. & Verdonk, M.J. (1988). *The Protection of Dragonflies (Odonata) and their Biotopes*. Council of Europe (Nature and Environment Series, No. 38): Strasbourg.

Veltman, A. (1991). Aas-etende libellen. *Entomologische Berichten (Amsterdam)* **51**: 98–9.

Veron, J.E.N. (1973). Physiological control of the chromatophores of *Austrolestes annulosus* (Odonata). *Journal of Insect Physiology* **19**: 1689–1703.

Vick, G.S. (1997a). *Gomphus vulgatissimus*. *In*: Brooks (1997a), pp.119–20.

Vick, G.S. (1997b). *Somatochlora metallica*. *In*: Brooks (1997a), pp.126–7.

Waage, J.K. (1973). Reproductive behavior and its relation to territoriality in *Calopteryx maculata* (Beauvois) (Odonata: Calopterygidae). *Behaviour* **47**: 240–56.

Waage, J.K. (1979). Dual function of the damselfly penis: sperm removal and transfer. *Science* **203**: 916–18.

Waage, J.K. (1981). Oral contribution to plenary discussion. *6th International Symposium of Odonatology, Chur, Switzerland.*

Waage, J.K. (1983). Sexual selection, ESS theory and insect behaviour: some examples from damselflies (Odonata). *Florida Entomologist* **66**: 19–31.

Waage, J.K. (1986). Evidence for widespread sperm displacement ability among Zygoptera (Odonata) and the means for predicting its presence. *Biological Journal of the Linnean Society of London* **28**: 285–300.

Waage, J.K. (1988). Confusion over residency and the escalation of damselfly territorial disputes. *Animal Behaviour* **36**: 586–95.

Wain, W. (2004). Personal communication to S.J.B.

Walker, A. (2005). Untitled photograph. *Natural World* **75**: 13.

Walker, E.M. (1958). *The Odonata of Canada and Alaska. Volume 1. Part I. General. Part II. Zygoptera – Damselflies.* University of Toronto Press: Toronto.

Walther, G.R., Burga, C.A. & Edwards, P.J. (Eds) (2001). *"Fingerprints" of climate change.* Kluwer Academic/Plenum: New York.

Waltz, E.C. & Wolf, L.L. (1984). By Jove! Why do alternative mating tactics assume so many different forms? *American Zoologist* **24**: 333–43.

Waltz, E.C. & Wolf, L.L. (1988). Alternative mating tactics in male White-faced

Dragonflies (*Leucorrhinia intacta*). *Evolutionary Ecology* **2**: 205–31.

Ward, L. & Mill, P.J. (2005). Habitat factors influencing the presence of adult *Calopteryx splendens* (Odonata: Zygoptera). *European Journal of Entomology* **102**: 47–51.

Waringer, J. (1982). Notes on the effect of meteorological parameters on flight activity and reproductive behaviour of *Coenagrion puella* (L.) (Zygoptera: Coenagrionidae). *Odonatologica* **11**: 239–43.

Warren, A. (1915). A study of the food habits of the Hawaiian dragonflies. *Bulletin of the College of Hawaii Publications* **3**: 4–45.

Watanabe, M. & Matsunami, E. (1990). A lek-like system in *Lestes sponsa* (Hansemann), with special reference to the diurnal changes in flight activity and mate-finding tactics (Zygoptera: Lestidae). *Odonatologica* **19**: 47–59.

Watts, P.C., Rouquette, J.R., Saccheri, J., Kemp, S.J. & Thompson, D.J. (2004). Molecular and ecological evidence for small-scale isolation by distance in an endangered damselfly, *Coenagrion mercuriale*. *Molecular Ecology* **13**: 2931–45.

Watts, P.C., Thompson, D.J., Daguet, C. & Kemp, S.J. (2005). Exuviae as a reliable source of DNA for population-genetic analysis of odonates. *Odonatologica* **34**: 183–7.

WDA (Worldwide Dragonfly Association) (2002, 2005). *WDA Code of Practice for Collecting Dragonflies. Agrion* **6**: 22–3; **9**: 2.

Weber, H. (1933). *Lehrbuch der Entomologie.* Fischer: Jena.

Weatherby, A. (2004). The national pond monitoring network. *Dragonfly News* **45**: 22–3.

Weihrauch, F. (1998). Die Entwicklung von *Gomphus vulgatissimus* (L.) in Kiesgruben-wässern: seltene Ausnahme oder lediglich übersehen? (Anisoptera: Gomphidae). *Libellula* **17**: 149–61.

Weihrauch, F. (1999). Larven von *Gomphus vulgatissimus* (L.) als Substrat der Wandermuschel *Dreissena polymorpha* (Pallas) (Anisoptera: Gomphidae; Bivalvia: Dreissenidae). *Libellula* **18**: 97–102.

Weihrauch, F. (2002). Ein Weibchen von *Enallagma cyathigerum* als Unterwasser-Prädator der Grossen Weidenrindenlaus (Odonata: Coenagrionidae; Homoptera: Lachnidae). *Libellula* **21**: 175–80.

Weihrauch, F. (2003). Emergenzstudien an *Cordulegaster b. boltonii* von einem niederbayerischen Waldbach (Odonata: Cordulegastridae). *Libellula Supplement* **4**: 3–18.

Weihrauch, F. & Borcherding, J. (2002). The zebra mussel, *Dreissena polymorpha* (Pallas), as an epizoon on anisopteran larvae (Anisoptera: Gomphidae, Corduliidae, Libellulidae). *Odonatologica* **31**: 85–94.

Wesenberg-Lund, C. (1913). Odonaten-Studien. *Internationale Revue der gesamten Hydrobiologie und Hydrographie* **6**: 155–228; 373–422.

Westermann, K. (2002). Phänologie der Emergenz bei der Gemeinen Weidenjungfer (*Chalcolestes viridis*) an südbadischen Altrheinen. *Naturschutz südlichen Oberrhein* **3**: 201–14.

Westermann, K. (2006). Strategien frisch geschlüpfter *Lestes viridis* zur Vermeidung von Regenschäden (Odonata: Lestidae). *Libellula* **26**: 47–60.

Wheeler, T.A. (2003). *The Role of Voucher Specimens in Validating Faunistic and Ecological Research.* Biological Survey of Canada (Terrestrial Arthropods): Ottawa, 22 pp.

Wikelski, M., Moskowitz, D., Adelman, J.S., Cochran, J., Wilcove, D.S. & May, M.L. (2006). Simple rules guide dragonfly migration. *Biology Letters*, 1–5.

Wildermuth, H. (1980). Die Libellen der Drumlinlandschaft für die

Naturschutzpraxis in der Gemeinde. *Vierteljahrsschrift der Naturforschenden Gesellschaft in Zürich* **125**: 201–37.

Wildermuth, H. (1984). Drei aussergewöhnliche Beobachtungen zum Fortpflanzenverhalten der Libellen. *Mitteilungen Entomologische Gesellschaft Basel* **34**: 121–9.

Wildermuth, H. (1994a). Habitatselektion bei Libellen. *Advances in Odonatology* **6**: 223–57.

Wildermuth, H. (1994b). Populationsdynamik der Grossen Mossjungfer, *Leucorrhinia pectoralis* Charpentier, 1825 (Odonata, Libellulidae). *Zeitschrift für Ökologie und Naturschutz* **3**: 25–39.

Wildermuth, H. (1994c). Personal communication: letter to P.S.C., 19 March.

Wildermuth, H. (1998a). Dragonflies recognize the water of rendezvous and oviposition sites by horizontally polarized light: a behavioural field test. *Naturwissenschaften* **85**: 297–302.

Wildermuth, H. (1998b). Ethologische und ökologische Beobachtungen an Larven von *Cordulia aenea* (Linnaeus) (Anisoptera: Corduliidae). *Libellula* **17**: 1–24.

Wildermuth, H. (2000a). Larvae of the Downy Emerald *Cordulia aenea* (L.) examine the space for eclosion with their hind legs. *Journal of the British Dragonfly Society* **16**: 59–62.

Wildermuth, H. (2000b). Totstellreflex bei Grosslibellenlarven. *Libellula* **19**: 17–39.

Wildermuth, H. (2000c). Alternative Taktiken beider Weibensuche von *Boyeria irene* (Odonata: Aeshnidae). *Libellula* **19**: 143–55.

Wildermuth, H. (2001a). Concealment in European *Somatochlora* larvae (Anisoptera: Corduliidae). *Exuviae* **8**: 1–12.

Wildermuth, H. (2001b). Moostierchen und Zuckmücken als Epizoen von *Macromia amphigena* (Bryozoa: Plumatellidae; Diptera: Chironomidae; Odonata: Macromiidae). *Libellula* **20**: 97–102.

Wildermuth, H. (2001c). Zuckmückenlarven als Epizoen von *Somatochlora metallica* (Diptera: Chironomidae; Odonata: Corduliidae). *Libellula* **20**: 171–4.

Wildermuth, H. (2005a). Beitrag zur Larvalbiologie von *Boyeria irene* (Odonata: Aeshnidae). *Libellula* **24**: 1–30.

Wildermuth, H. (2005b). Letter to P.S.C., 7 December.

Wildermuth, H. (2006). Reciprocal predation involving Odonata, Asilidae and Saltatoria. *International Journal of Odonatology* **9**: 225–34.

Wildermuth, H. & Horváth, G. (2005). Visual deception of a male *Libellula depressa* by the shiny surface of a parked car (Odonata: Libellulidae). *International Journal of Odonatology* **8**: 97–105.

Wildermuth, H., Gonseth, Y. & Maibach, A. (Eds) (2005). *Odonata – Les Libellules de Suisse. Fauna Helvetica 11*. Schweizerische Entomologische Gesellschaft SEG & Centre Suisse de la Cartographie de la Faune CSCF: Neuchâtel, Switzerland.

Willey, R.L. & Eiler, H.O. (1972). Drought resistance in subalpine nymphs of *Somatochlora semicircularis* Selys (Odonata: Corduliidae). *American Midland Naturalist* **87**: 215–21.

Williamson, T. & Meurgey, F. (2001). Microhabitats refuges pour les larves d'*Ischnura elegans* (Vander Linden, 1820) et *Platycnemis pennipes* (Pallas, 1771) (Odonata, Zygoptera, Platycnemididae et Coenagrionidae). *Martinia* **17**: 110.

Winsland, D. (1997a). *Coenagrion mercuriale*. In: Brooks (1997), pp.74–5.

Winsland, D. (1997b). *Libellula fulva*. In: Brooks (1997), pp.134–5.

Winsland, D. (1991). Field meetings: Drove

House Farm, Bursledon, Hants. *British Dragonfly Society Newsletter* 20: 4.

Winsland, D. (1998). A message from the National Recorder. *Newsletter of the Dragonfly Recording Scheme* 18: 2.

Wissinger, S.A. (1988a). Effects of food availability on larval development and inter-instar predation among larvae of *Libellula luctuosa* (Odonata: Anisoptera). *Canadian Journal of Zoology* 66: 543–9.

Wissinger, S.A. (1988b). Spatial distribution, life history and estimate of survivorship in a fourteen-species assemblage of larval dragonflies (Odonata: Anisoptera). *Freshwater Biology* 20: 329–40.

Wissinger, S.A. (1989a). Seasonal variation in the intensity of competition and predation among dragonfly larvae. *Ecology* 70: 1017–27.

Wissinger, S.A. (1989b). Comparative population ecology of the dragonflies *Libellula lydia* and *Libellula luctuosa* (Odonata: Libellulidae). *Canadian Journal of Zoology* 67: 931–6.

Wistow, R.J. (1989). Dragonflies of the Mongomery Canal. *Journal of the British Dragonfly Society* 5: 28–35.

Wolwood, I. & Reynolds, D.R. (Eds) (2001). *Insect Movement: Mechanisms and Consequences.* CABI Publishing: Wallingford.

Woodford, J. (1967). The dragonfly project. *Ontario Naturalist* 5 (June), 14–16.

Woodward, G. & Hildrew, A.G. (1998). Invasion of a stream food web by a new top predator. *Bulletin of the North American Benthological Society* 15: 141 (Abstract only.)

Wootton, R. (1981). Palaeozoic insects. *Annual Review of Entomology* 26: 319–44.

Wootton, R.J. (2001). How insect wings evolved. *In:* Wolwood & Reynolds (2001), pp.43–64.

Wootton, R.J. & Kukalova-Peck, J. (2000). Flight adaptations in Palaeozoic

Palaeoptera (Insecta). *Biological Reviews* 75: 129–67.

Worthen, W.B. (2002). The structure of larval odonate assemblages in the Enoree River Basin of South Carolina. *Southeastern Naturalist* 1: 205–16.

Worthington, A.M. & Olberg, R. (1999). Visual tracking and prey pursuit in dragonflies. *Abstracts of the 1st Symposium of the Worldwide Dragonfly Association, Hamilton, New York,* 22.

Wright, M. (1944). Some random observations on dragonfly habits with notes on their predaceousness on bees. *Journal of the Tennessee Academy of Science* 19: 295–301.

Wright, M. (1945). Dragonflies predaceous on the Stablefly, *Stomoxys calcitrans* (L.). *Florida Entomologist* 28: 11–13.

Wright, M. (1946). The economic importance of dragonflies (Odonata). *Journal of the Tennessee Academy of Science* 21: 60–71.

Wu, T.Y., Brokaw, C.J. & Brennan, C. (Eds). (1975). *Swimming and Flying in Nature.* Plenum Press: New York.

Zahner, R. (1959). Über die Bindung der mitteleuropäischen *Calopteryx*-Arten (Odonata, Zygoptera) an den Lebensraum des strömenden Wassers. I. Der Anteil der Larven an der Biotopbindung. *Internationale Revue der gesamten Hydrobiologie* 44: 51–130.

Zahner, R. (1960). Über die Bindung der mitteleuropäischen *Calopteryx*-Arten (Odonata, Zygoptera) an den Lebensraum des strömenden Wassers. II. Der Anteil der Imagines an der Biotopbindung. *Internationale Revue der gesamten Hydrobiologie* 45: 101–23.

Zeiss, C., Martens, A. & Rolff, J. (1999). Male mate guarding increases females' predation risk? A case study on tandem oviposition in the damselfly *Coenagrion*

puella (Insecta: Odonata). *Canadian Journal of Zoology* **77**: 1013–16.

Zloty, J., Pritchard, G. & Esquivel, C. (1993*a*). Larvae of the Costa Rican *Hetaerina* (Odonata: Calopterygidae) with comments on distribution. *Systematic Entomology* **18**: 253–65.

Zloty, J., Pritchard, G. & Krishnaraj, R. (1993*b*). Larval insect identification by cellulose acetate gel electrophoresis and its application to life history evaluation and cohort analysis. *Journal of the North American Benthological Society* **12**: 270–78.

Zottoli, S.J., Walfish, D.T.O., Westbrooks, D.A. & Smith, D.C. (2001). Small tadpoles do not initiate a startle response before being struck by the labium of dragonfly larvae. *Society for Neuroscience* **27**: 1984.

Index

Each species is listed under its English and scientific name; no distinction is made between entries for eggs, larvae or adults. A page reference may encompass more than one appearance of an item on a single page. Any entry qualified by a sex designation refers to the adult insect. Where a term is abbreviated in the text, the abbreviation follows the index entry for that term.

Prefixes to page numbers indicate the location of (B) boxes, (F) figures, (M) distribution maps, and T (tables).

The New Naturalist Library